Performing Opera

Performing Opera: A Practical Guide for Singers and Directors

Michael Ewans

Bloomsbury Methuen Drama
An imprint of Bloomsbury Publishing Plc

B L O O M S B U R Y
LONDON · OXFORD · NEW YORK · NEW DELHI · SYDNEY

Bloomsbury Methuen Drama

An imprint of Bloomsbury Publishing Plc

Imprint previously known as Methuen Drama

50 Bedford Square	1385 Broadway
London	New York
WC1B 3DP	NY 10018
UK	USA

www.bloomsbury.com

BLOOMSBURY, METHUEN DRAMA and the Diana logo are trademarks of Bloomsbury Publishing Plc

First published 2016

© Michael Ewans, 2016
Foreword © Stefan Janski, 2016

British Library Cataloguing-in-Publication Data
A catalogue record for this book is available from the British Library.

ISBN: HB: 978-1-4742-3908-0
PB: 978-1-4742-3907-3
ePDF: 978-1-4742-3910-3
ePub: 978-1-4742-3909-7

Library of Congress Cataloging-in-Publication Data
A catalog record for this book is available from the Library of Congress.

Typeset by Fakenham Prepress Solutions, Fakenham, Norfolk NR21 8NN
Printed and bound in India

CONTENTS

Operas Studied viii
Foreword xi
Preface xiii
How to use this book xv
Acknowledgements xviii
About the Author xix

1   Introduction 1

PART ONE: FORMS

2   Arias and Monologues 15
   2.1 'Great work, boss!' (Mozart) 15
   2.2 Wotan confides in his 'will' (Wagner) 21
   2.3 *I believe in a cruel God* (Verdi) 33
   2.4 'One fine day …' (Puccini) 41
   2.5 Kát'a's ecstasy (Janáček) 47
   2.6 *Now the great Bear* … (Britten) 56
   2.7 Conclusion 59

3   Duets 61
   3.1 *The Art of Seduction* (Mozart) 61
   3.2 'On Such a Night …' (Berlioz) 69
   3.3 Love in a garret (Puccini) 74
   3.4 Jenůfa and Laca alone (Janáček) 84
   3.5 Conclusion 90

4   Confrontations 93
   4.1 Elektra and Klytämnestra (Strauss) 93
   4.2 Kát'a and Tichon (Janáček) 108

4.3 Lulu masters Dr Schön (Berg) 115
    4.4 Not going to church (Britten) 128
    4.5 Conclusion 137

5   Ensembles 139
    5.1 A cruel departure (Mozart) 140
    5.2 Lust and treachery (Verdi) 147
    5.3 Death in the cards (Bizet) 152
    5.4 Siegfried must die! (Wagner) 162
    5.5 'Stone her!' (Janáček) 168
    5.6 Conclusion 178

PART TWO: ENCOUNTERS

6   Noises Off 183
    6.1 Cassandre and the Trojan Horse (Berlioz) 183
    6.2 The death of Carmen (Bizet) 192
    6.3 *Hoé! Hisse hoé!* (Debussy) 199
    6.4 Treasure, garden and domain (Bartók) 210
    6.5 'Peter Grimes!' (Britten) 218
    6.6 Conclusion 226

7   Interactions with the Numinous 229
    7.1 The trial by fire and water (Mozart) 231
    7.2 Parsifal and the Grail (Wagner) 235
    7.3 Kát'a and the river voices (Janáček) 245
    7.4 Wozzeck in the open field (Berg) 248
    7.5 'Fire! Fire! St John's Fire.' (Tippett) 253
    7.6 Conclusion 263

PART THREE: SHAPING THE OPERA

8   Characterization 267
    8.1 Véronique Gens as Iphigénie, directed by Pierre Audi 268
    8.2 Rodney Gilfrey as Don Giovanni, directed by Jürgen Flimm 278
    8.3 Teresa Stratas as Salome, directed by Götz Friedrich 283
    8.4 Conclusion 292

9 The Sense of Inevitability 293

    9.1 *Carmen:* Meilhac and Halévy/Bizet/Zambello 295

    9.2 *Elektra:* Hofmannsthal/Strauss/Friedrich 301

    9.3 Conclusion 311

10 Conclusion 313

Bibliography 315

Select Discography 319

Scores 323

Index 325

OPERAS STUDIED

	Music	Libretto/source text	First performance
Iphigénie en Aulide *Directed by Pierre Audi*	*Gluck*	*Du Roullet*	1774[1]
Le nozze di Figaro *Directed by Peter Sellars* *and Olivier Mille*	*Mozart*	*Da Ponte*	1786
Don Giovanni *Directed by Jürgen Flimm*	*Mozart*	*Da Ponte*	1787
Così fan tutte *Directed by Jürgen Flimm*	*Mozart*	*Da Ponte*	1790
Die Zauberflöte *Directed by* *Ingmar Bergman*	*Mozart*	*Schikaneder*	1791
Les Troyens *Directed by* *Yannis Kokkos*	*Berlioz*	*Berlioz* after *Virgil*	1890[2]
Rigoletto *Directed by* *Jonathan Miller*	*Verdi*	*Piave*	1851
Die Walküre *Directed by* *Patrice Chéreau*	*Wagner*	*Wagner*	1870
Carmen *Directed by Adrian Noble* *and Francesca Zambello*	*Bizet*	*Meilhac/Halévy*	1875

---

[1] Revised version 1775.
[2] First performance of all five Acts.

Götterdämmerung *Directed by Harry Kupfer*	*Wagner*	*Wagner*	1876
Parsifal *Directed by* *Nikolaus Lehnhoff*	*Wagner*	*Wagner*	1882
Otello *Directed by* *Elijah Moshinsky*	*Verdi*	*Boito*	1887
La Bohème *Directed by* *Franco Zeffirelli and* *Baz Luhrmann*	*Puccini*	*Giacosa/Illica*	1896
Pelléas et Mélisande *Directed by Peter Stein*	*Debussy*	*Maeterlinck*	1902
Madama Butterfly *Directed by* *Moffatt Oxenbould*	*Puccini*	*Giacosa/Illica*	1904
Jenůfa *Directed by* *Stéphane Braunschweig* *and Orpha Phelan*	*Janáček*	*Preissová*	1904
Salome *Directed by* *Götz Friedrich*	*Strauss*	*Wilde*	1905
Elektra *Directed by* *Götz Friedrich*	*Strauss*	*Hofmannsthal*	1909
Duke Bluebeard's Castle *Directed by* *Leslie Megahey*	*Bartók*	*Balázs*	1918
Kát'a Kabanová *Directed by* *Nikolaus Lehnhoff*	*Janáček*	*Ostrovsky*	1921
Wozzeck *Directed by* *Patrice Chéreau*	*Berg*	*Büchner*	1925

Lulu *Directed by Graham* *Vick and Olivier Py*	*Berg*	*Wedekind*	1979[3]
Peter Grimes *Directed by* *Elijah Moshinsky and* *Tim Albery*	*Britten*	*Slater*	1945
The Midsummer Marriage *Directed by* *Elijah Moshinsky*	*Tippett*	*Tippett*	1955

---

[3]First complete performance. First two Acts, and fragments from Act III, 1937.

FOREWORD

In my career spanning over forty years as a teacher, a freelance director of plays, musicals and opera, and currently as Head of Opera at the Royal Northern College of Music in Manchester, I have read countless books on my principal study discipline and allied subjects of interest. When, in May 2014, Michael first sent me his ideas and requested my opinion of his draft manuscript, I was immediately enthused by this highly original guide and its detailed structure. Here was a practical handbook specifically written for prospective opera singers, teachers of stagecraft and acting in opera, and for stage directors learning their craft to direct opera. I was privileged to discover Michael's unique style and his enthusiastic individual approach to opera studies.

Michael's expert insight, knowledge, experience and passion is evident on every page. His depth of detailed research, lists of examples and links to multimedia recordings and resources are a stimulus for all interested parties now and for generations to come, be they students of music and drama, amateur and professional artists, or those who simply wish to know, enjoy and learn about the magical world of opera.

A student's opera education involves acquiring numerous practical skills in voice, speech, language, movement, dance and stagecraft. They learn repertory and communication skills in performance and presentation requiring dramatic intensity, emotional depth and truth. They rely on their professors, directors, coaches and choreographers to teach, guide and share their considerable knowledge and experience.

The professional commercial world of opera requires that aspiring directors and singers learn the allied arts of networking, communicating with opera company managements, casting directors, agents and critics. It entails knowing how to work with demanding maestri, stage directors, assistants, stage set and costume designers, production managers, wardrobe mistresses, stage managers, lighting designers, fight directors, surtitle operators and technicians, besides financial advisors and accountants.

This book is most welcome because it returns to the essential work: the score, the original text. It also generously provides text translations and available stage directions. Students should conscientiously prepare their own word-for-word translation of all texts to be performed.

Maestri and directors are leaders, some more dictatorial than others. Opera productions and interpretation of individual characters can easily be

swallowed up in idealized concepts. It is essential to be creatively collabo-
rative and to be open to exploration and interpretation of both music
and text. All students are taught and encouraged to formulate their own
interpretation of music, text and character based on supportive evidence
and reasoning. This teaching aid most certainly provides the required infor-
mation and launch pad for interactive scholarly discussion.

Opera singers focus on their own voice type and the specific repertory
of opera roles composed for them. This book investigates a broad span
of opera characters, not only as soloists in arias and monologues but the
important interaction between characters in duets and their inevitable
points of conflict and confrontation in opera ensembles.

The cleverly structured sections guide the students, stage by stage, in
their journey of practical analysis using opera repertory that spans three
centuries, from 1774 C. W. Gluck to 1955 M. Tippett. Singers and directors
will surely be enthralled by the characterizations of opera roles portrayed in
iconic performances, together with the provision of detailed analysis of two
specific productions that portray the sense of inevitability in tragic operas.

I am immensely proud to read the inclusion of professional friends and
colleagues, including RNCM alumni: Graham Vick – international opera
director, and international artists Amanda Roocroft, Ashley Holland and
Ryland Davies.

This is an excellent, insightful and most valuable educational tool that
does not fail to stimulate creative thought and provocative response. We
all have opinions and I particularly like and welcome the discussion points,
questions and practical activities provided throughout. I sincerely wish that
this most rare and valuable study had been available to me for purchase
from my favourite bookshop when I was a young opera staff director at
Glyndebourne and English National Opera.

Stefan Janski,
Head of Opera, Royal Northern College of Music, UK

PREFACE

This book is, as far as I know, the first scholarly treatment of opera which fully recognizes the centrality of performance, by analysing how scenes have been directed in productions recorded on VHS and DVD. It is designed primarily to be a text for students and teachers of operatic acting and directing, and also to be helpful to established directors and singers; but I hope that lovers of opera and musicologists will also be attracted by my detailed analyses of the interactions between words, music and action in thirty scenes and five complete operas.

I begin with Gluck because his 'reform' operas turned away from the by then clichéd features of *opera seria* – conflicts between love and duty, love triangles and static, over-ornamented arias – and focused single-mindedly on character and situation; in and after them the orchestra begins to become a significant vehicle for the illumination of action. I end with Britten and Tippett, since I think that more time will need to pass before we can be certain which of the operas of the last sixty years are truly great *dramma per musica*.[1] Though, if I may be allowed a prophecy, the great success throughout America and Europe, after its première at Covent Garden, of Thomas Adès' *The Tempest* (now recorded superlatively by DGG from Robert Lepage's Metropolitan Opera production) suggests that it may be such an opera, and if space had permitted I would have analysed an ensemble from it in Chapter 5.[2]

If parts of this book seem to you to be subjective, then you are quite right! Subjectivity is a necessary part of any analysis of performance, especially when dealing with opera. The majority of the operas which have gained a firm place in the international repertory have as their subject-matter sex, violence, or both – highly emotional content, especially when illuminated by passionate music.[3] Detached objectivity is neither possible nor desirable. And I have deliberately made this a pragmatic treatment of a practical subject – how music illuminates words, and in turn how stage action can interact with music and text to create the meanings of opera in performance.

---

[1] Also only a limited (and not very representative) selection of late twentieth- and early twenty-first century operas is available on DVD.
[2] Adès' opera is studied in Ewans 2016 (forthcoming).
[3] Clément 1988 is a remarkable study of how women die and are killed in opera.

I have had an academic career, first in Classics, and since 1981 in Drama, and from 1995 also in Music, so I have never had the privilege of directing a professional production; but from 1996 to 2005 the then Faculty of Music at the University of Newcastle gave me the opportunity to direct a series of chamber operas, including *Dido and Aeneas, Riders to the Sea* and *The Medium,* casting Honours, Masters' and PhD voice students in the lead roles, and senior undergraduates in minor roles and as chorus. I have also taught workshops in operatic acting for voice students. So I have been able to experience for myself, not just as a spectator, the kinds of decision which directors need to make, and the ways in which it is possible (and indeed necessary) for them to guide the singers so as to illuminate in stage action both the text and the music of an opera.

This book was my first major work after I retired from the Chair of Drama late in 2011. I am grateful to the University of Newcastle for appointing me on retirement to a Conjoint Professorship, which gives me among other things access to library and IT resources. Many thanks also to Matthew Hopcroft, who painstakingly drew the music examples in Finale for me.

My special thanks are due to my daughter Hanna, who has been an excellent companion, growing through her teenage years while I developed the argument of this book. Her musical tastes are different from mine, but she is a remarkable young woman; it is a great pleasure to have her living with me as I write.

Michael Ewans
The University of Newcastle, Australia

HOW TO USE THIS BOOK

Preliminaries

I have not provided synopses of opera plots; it is assumed that readers either know them already, or have access to resources such as Grove Music Online.

I do however provide new translations of the texts for the scenes under study. I expect singing translations, printed in vocal scores, to be free versions because of the need to match English words to the notes of a vocal line conceived for another language; it is much less forgivable that translations accompanying CDs and in the ENO/Covent Garden Opera Guides, which do not have to meet that requirement, often stray from the librettist's original meaning, and are sometimes seriously misleading.

For consistency, names are spelt as in the original language of all the operas. So in *Duke Bluebeard's Castle* I write Judit not Judith, and in *Les Troyens* Didon and Énée not Dido and Aeneas. And of course therefore I write Jago not Iago, even though in *Otello* English is the language of the source text from which the libretto is drawn.

Stage directions from the libretti are printed in *italics*.

Essentials

All students should read Chapters 1–5, 8 and 9. Chapters 6 and 7 are primarily for potential directors, although singers will also learn much from them.

I have provided clips of almost all the scenes which I discuss; they are on YouTube. I recommend that you play through each clip before turning to my discussion of the performance, and then play it again, section by section, as you read my analysis.[1]

I have provided discussion points for students and teachers at the end of each section. You can either consider these on your own or incorporate discussion of them into your classes.

---

[1]To follow the argument of Chapters 8 and 9 you need access to the complete DVDs of *Iphigénie en Aulide*, *Don Giovanni*, *Salome*, *Carmen* and *Elektra*.

But these discussion points should be only part of your engagement with the book; the whole book should be seen as an invitation to you to react, discuss and agree or disagree. You could begin by working with the text of each scene drawn from a French, German or Italian text; does my translation adequately reflect all the nuances of the original language; and what steps would be needed to make a good modern *singing* translation of each extract?

Then you should proceed to read, absorb and critically analyse the section of the book which is devoted to the scene that you are studying. The interpretation of an opera's text and music is a subjective discourse, for me as a writer as much as for you as singers and directors; you must form your own opinions on every point – down to small details of blocking, posture, gesture and facial expression. You can do this by yourself, but it is greatly preferable to work with a group of fellow-students who have all studied the scene in question, worked through my commentary, and thought through their answers to the discussion points in advance.

If you use the book in this way, you will be prepared for the complex processes which are involved when you yourself take part in an opera production. Whether you are a singer or a director, you should be able to offer your own creative and constructive ideas at all stages of the discussion when planning and preparing to work on a production – or even just on a workshop of a single scene.

It is not of course expected that young singers will be capable of singing for themselves, at an early stage in their development, all the excerpts studied in this book. For example Wotan (**2.2**), Jago (**2.3**) and Salome (**1.1** and **8.3**) demand mature voices. But it would have been extremely limiting to confine my examples only to those which relatively light voices can tackle. And studying operas, such as those of Wagner, Strauss and Berg, where the singer needs to be aware of a complex system of recurrent musical motifs is an essential asset for demands which singers will encounter later in their careers.

If you are a student of directing, you should use this book to learn from examples how to steer between the two undesirable extremes of excessive traditionalism and *Regietheater* (see below, Chapter 1). If you hope to gain the complete co-operation of your singers, your production must make sense in its relationship to both text and music. And it must do so *in detail*; my analysis shows just how closely the great directors have studied both text and music before venturing to direct their singers. These examples also give plenty of food for thought about some other aspects of opera production which are not my prime concern in this book – costume and set design.

This book does not go into the questions of time management, rehearsal organization and other aspects of production planning. A whole separate book would be needed to deal adequately with these topics, and I hope that someone who is involved with the professional scene of opera training and/ or production will write it.

Referencing

Referencing is by Act, scene, number (if applicable), rehearsal figure (or letter), and bar numbers within the figure, e.g. I.1.8.6 = Act I scene 1 number 8 bar 6. Exceptions are Berg's two operas, in which there is continuous numbering of bars throughout each Act (so I.3.957 = bar 957 of Act I, in scene 3), and *Rigoletto* and *The Nibelung's Ring* where – since the editions provide neither rehearsal figures nor bar numbers – I have given page references to study scores. The Bibliography includes not only books and articles cited but also complete lists of the recorded performances which I discuss, and of the scores which I have consulted.

I divide each scene into musico-dramatic sections for the purposes of analysis, equivalent to the 'beats' of straight plays. In the texts given at the start of each discussion I number these in bold in square brackets, e.g. [1], and I refer to these sections by number in the analyses. And also in those texts, places where motifs which I print as music examples are heard are marked thus **1.1.1**, etc. Here is a sample passage of text; the first music example for this section (Chapter 2 section one) comes at the start of the text, and the first section of the aria begins where the [1] is marked at the beginning of the *allegretto*.

2.1.1 Bravo, signor padrone!	Great work, boss!
Ora incomincio a capir il mistero,	Now I begin to understand the mystery,
E a veder schietto tuto il vostro progetto:	and see clearly your whole plan.
A Londra è vero? Voi ministro, io corriero,	Off to London, is it? You as minister, me as courier,
E la Susanna...segreta ambasciatrice.	And Susanna...confidential attachée.
Non sarà, non sarà. Figaro il dice.	It won't happen, it won't happen; Figaro says so.

*

[1] (*allegretto*)
Se vuol ballare, signor Contino...   If you want to dance, dear little Count...

YouTube references. The title which you should search for is given at an appropriate point in each section; they are marked 🖱 followed by the name of the clip, e.g. **1 1 Salome and the cistern**. Only one opera house, Covent Garden, declined to let me upload clips from their DVDs; so for Sergei Leiferkus's performance of Jago's *Credo* directed by Moshinsky (**2.3**), and for the final scene of Zambello's *Carmen* (**6.2**), you will have to seek out copies of the DVDs.

ACKNOWLEDGEMENTS

The translations in this book from French, German and Czech are my own. I have very little competence in Italian, and I am grateful to Rosalind Halton and Paola Favaro (Mozart) and Camilla Russell (Verdi and Puccini) for help in achieving close translations for the operas composed in that language. And I have no knowledge of Hungarian, so I am most grateful that the eminent Bartók scholar Carl Leafstedt has allowed me to use his translation of the sequence from *Duke Bluebeard's Castle* (**6.4**).

The extract from the score of *The Midsummer Marriage* by Michael Tippett, © Schott Music Ltd, Print Rights for Australia and New Zealand administered by Hal Leonard Australia Pty. Ltd. ABN 13 085 333 713 www.halleonard.com.au, is used by permission. All rights reserved. Unauthorized reproduction is illegal.

The extracts from the score of *Peter Grimes* Music by Benjamin Britten Words by Montagu Slater are © 1945 Boosey and Hawkes Music Publishers Ltd. Print Rights for Australia and New Zealand administered by Hal Leonard Australia Pty. Ltd. ABN 13 085 333 713 www.halleonard. com.au, are used by permission. All rights reserved. Unauthorized reproduction is illegal.

ABOUT THE AUTHOR

Michael Ewans holds degrees from Oxford and Cambridge, where he studied Aeschylus for his doctorate, supervised by George Steiner. From 1973 he lectured in Classics, Drama and Music at the University of Newcastle, Australia, including a period as Assistant Dean (Research) in the Faculty of Music, during which he directed chamber opera performances and opera workshops. He retired from the Chair of Drama at the University of Newcastle in 2011, and is now a Conjoint Professor in the School of Humanities and Social Science. He was elected a Fellow of the Australian Academy of the Humanities in 2005. His eleven books include six volumes of translations of Greek drama with theatrical commentaries based on his own productions, and three previous books on opera; *Janáček's Tragic Operas, Wagner and Aeschylus: the 'Ring' and the 'Oresteia'*, and *Opera from the Greek: Studies in the Poetics of Appropriation.*

1

Introduction

This book explores in some detail the types of interaction between text, music and performance in opera. The intended readership consists primarily of singers studying operatic acting and their teachers, stage directors – especially those in the early stages of their careers – and their mentors, and other students of music and of drama. Reading this book and working through the examples with the video clips, students will learn how to improve their own work from my detailed analysis of scenes acted by outstanding singer-actors and directed by equally outstanding directors. I also hope that this work will enable audience members to deepen their understanding of how first music and then stage action illuminate the text of operas.

Much scholarly writing about opera is less effective than it might be because the authors lack a perspective which truly focuses on the *dramatic* elements in opera, and far too many scholars neglect performance. They prefer to focus on historical and contextual studies, or else on analyses which are primarily musical rather than musico-dramatic.[1] Nonetheless, I hope that some musicologists will be interested in this book.

Operas are usually studied as if they simply consisted of a set of notes, words and performance instructions on the written page; but this is false.

---

[1] A notable exception is to be found in the 'synopses' which appear in many of the Cambridge Opera Handbooks. But these, since they provide overviews of whole operas, necessarily lack the kind of detail which is offered in this book. And Warren 1995 discussed some opera scenes in performance, although he was limited by the availability at that time of only a few VHS recordings and the non-existence of YouTube. However he pays insufficient attention to the role of the director, referring for example to 'the Boulez *Ring*' and never naming Chéreau. Similarly, Jonathan Miller gets no credit for his stunning update of *Rigoletto* to New York or Chicago (**5.2**: Warren and I thoroughly disagree on the dramatic value of that quartet!).

More recently Levin (2007) made a determined attempt to get musicologists to take opera performance seriously. His work has borne some fruit in more recent publications, but, like his book, these are academic discussions, addressed by their authors to fellow musicologists, and of very little value to professional practitioners engaged in performance.

An opera only exists when it is realized by singing actors, orchestra and a production team. Rarely, if ever, is the living visual dimension of opera discussed in any but general terms (a director's overall production concept is often described in newspaper and magazine reviews and in performance histories); and it has never, as far as I am aware, been studied in conjunction with an analysis of how the music illuminates the drama. A core element in this book will therefore be detailed analysis of directors' and singers' responses to the text and music.

The composition of an opera which is equally effective as music and as drama is a difficult task, as each composer has to develop for himself or herself a viable personal idiom in which their style of music and their chosen text come together in a perfect synthesis. Only a very small number of composers – Mozart, Wagner, Verdi, Puccini, Strauss and Janáček – have achieved the feat of writing more than four operas which have become firmly established in the standard international repertory; and it is notable that all of them served a considerable apprenticeship, and wrote operas which owed too much to previous composers' styles and were relatively weak, before creating their masterpieces. The exceptions – composers whose first operas are totally assured *dramma per musica* – are rare, and they are almost always men who found one text which was totally aligned with their emotional concerns and met their deepest needs: Beethoven, Bartók, Debussy and Berg.[2]

There are several pre-eminent practitioners of music drama before the mid-nineteenth century, from whom I would single out Monteverdi, Gluck, Mozart and Berlioz; and no one could sanely deny that there is insight into character, situation and emotion in the music of these composers (cf. **2.1, 3.1, 3.2, 5.1, 6.2, 8.1** and **8.2** below). But it has to be recognized, even by lovers of Baroque, Classical and early Romantic opera, that Wagner broke through longstanding barriers with the composition of *Tristan und Isolde* and *The Nibelung's Ring*. He inaugurated a *durchkomponiert* opera, in which there are no separate 'numbers', and equal musical attention is bestowed on every phase of the drama. Wagner also anticipated some of the discoveries of psychoanalysis.[3] So he launched a new direction for opera in

---

[2]Debussy had attempted to compose *Rodrigue et Chimène*, but, again, his idiom in the draft of that opera is undeveloped compared to the shimmering impressionist brilliance which he brought to *Pelléas et Mélisande*. Berg of course went on after the overwhelming success of *Wozzeck* (which is surely the best-received opera written in an avant-garde idiom in the history of the medium) to compose another tragedy of sex and murder, *Lulu*, which is a very great work despite the relative weakness of the unrevised Paris scene (III.1). Cf. **4.3**.

[3]Freud himself was the first to admit that artists can and do anticipate the discoveries of the science of psychology. 'The poets and philosophers before me discovered the unconscious. What I discovered was the scientific method by which the unconscious can be studied' (speech on his 70th birthday, quoted at Trilling 1951: 47). A psychological reading of the *Ring* is presented in Donington 1963. This is a problematic book, since its Jungian analysis is pursued far too far, in disregard for the primary socio-political meanings of the *Ring*; but it cannot be altogether ignored.

two ways; these works demonstrated the possibility of a more continuously intense operatic experience for the audience, and of a very considerable psychological depth conveyed through the music.

Between 1902 and 1905 another barrier was broken, when three very different composers, who could all compose highly flexible music with deft changes of rhythm and tempo, created three great operas based on prose texts rather than on verse libretti. These texts were drawn directly from recent plays which happened to epitomize the three main theatrical styles that were prominent in Europe at the turn of the century. Debussy with *Pelléas et Mélisande* based on Maeterlinck's symbolist play, Janáček with *Jenůfa* from Gabriela Preissová's realist drama *Her Step-daughter*, and Strauss with *Salome* based on a decadent text by Oscar Wilde (from which he forged an expressionist opera) all dispensed with a librettist and set the original play, making only a few minor cuts.[4] These three composers, together with their immediate successors, Bartók (*Duke Bluebeard's Castle*) and Berg (*Wozzeck* and *Lulu*), created psychological music dramas of unprecedented intensity, which premiered between 1902 and 1935. In my view only a few subsequent composers have come near to equalling their achievements, and for that reason they feature prominently in this book.[5]

What does music do when 'applied' (to use Wagner's term) to drama?[6] A good perspective from which to begin is that of a stage director who has experience with straight drama but is approaching his or her first opera production. Such directors will find themselves both restricted and liberated by working in this new medium. Restricted because the principal actions are linked to particular moments in the score, and must be done at prescribed times,[7] and similarly each line of text must be sung to precise notes, which demand a relatively fixed inflexion as opposed to the many different 'readings' which an actor or actress can bestow on any given

---

[4]Cf. Strauss on the inception of *Salome*: 'The Viennese poet Anton Lindtner had sent me this exquisite play and had offered to turn it into a libretto for me. When I agreed, he sent me a few cleverly versified opening scenes, but I could not make up my mind to start composing until one day it occurred to me to set to music *Wie schön ist die Prinzessin Salome heute Nacht* ['How beautiful the Princess Salomé is tonight', Narraboth's opening line in Hedwig Lachmann's German prose translation of Wilde] straight away. From then on it was not difficult to purge the piece of purple passages to such an extent that it became quite a good libretto. Now, of course, that the dance and especially the whole final scene are steeped in music it is easy to say that the play was "simply calling for music". Yes indeed, but that had to be discovered.' Strauss 1974: 150.

[5]The *bel canto* operas of such composers as Donizetti, Rossini and Bellini do not appear in this book, since almost by definition they explore the art of beautiful singing at the expense of a full musical response which illuminates the drama.

[6]*Music Applied to the Drama*, 1879; Wagner 1907: 10, 176–93.

[7]Most composers simply write the stage directions of the libretto above the music to which they wish them to correspond; Berg, a control freak in this regard, as in his directions to musicians, frequently places arrows in his opera scores, which connect the stage directions to a phrase, or in some cases even a particular note, in the orchestra.

words in a playscript – and the speed at which text unfolds in an opera is
almost of necessity much slower than in a play. But the same director is
also, in another way, liberated; with a straight play the actors and director
have to work together for some time in rehearsals to elicit the subtext of
each speech, but in opera the subtext is supplied by the orchestral music;
that music makes sense of and illuminates the action, and it provides any
director who has ears to listen to it with clues to how the drama should
unfold on stage.[8]

This book therefore explores, in scenes from twenty-four operas, how
music illuminates the drama, and how in its turn performance subsequently
responds to and illuminates the drama and the music. The twenty-four
operas have been selected for their excellence as music drama, from a variety
of periods, styles and national operatic traditions. In Chapters two to five
(**Part I: Forms**) I analyse how music illuminates the feelings and thoughts of
characters in different musical forms, from solo aria to ensemble, and the
ways in which singers and directors can in their turn illuminate the text and
the music. In Chapters six and seven (**Part II: Encounters**) I consider how
music can link the characters to their spatial and metaphysical surroundings
respectively – and ways in which specific productions have fully or partially
succeeded in conveying those links. Finally, in Chapters eight and nine
(**Part III: Shaping the Opera**) I discuss how composers may use their music
to give insight into a character as a whole, and to give the outcome of a
tragic opera a growing feeling of inevitability – and, again, how exemplary
singers and directors have responded to these aspects of opera. Of course,
in complex passages, two or more of the functions of music considered
individually in the three parts of this book can be in operation at the same
time; but it is both possible and desirable to separate them for analysis.

As I have already remarked, one dimension that is usually excluded
from the analysis of opera is performance (although quite a number of
recent books and articles discuss performance history, which is not my
main concern). Hornby's excellent book on straight drama, *Script into
Performance*, quotes with approval Susan Langer on the performance of
music: '[it] is as creative an act as composition, just as the composer's own
working out of the idea, after he has conceived the greatest movement and
therewith the whole commanding form, is still creative work. The performer
simply carries it on.'[9] Hornby himself goes on to propose that in drama:
'the director and performer must come to the script with imagination;
imagination is not simply a matter of following what is written down, as if

---

[8]Unfortunately it is all too evident from their productions that some opera directors lack either
the ability or the desire to respond creatively to what the music has to say about the characters
and the action. As a result, they are effectively only staging the libretto, not the opera as a
whole.

[9]Langer 1953: 109.

the script was a blueprint.'[10] But the production must not be the result of the unfettered creativity of an arrogant director, as has happened in many modern 'concept-productions' in the name of *Regietheater* ('directors' theatre'), a disease that has especially infected opera performance in Germany and Austria in recent years, but which has also been inflicted on opera-lovers elsewhere in the world.[11] Hornby again; 'Before and during rehearsals, the director and performers construct an interpretation of the text, *organizing the text into units that are the elements reflected in the performance ... a script is realized (or embedded) in a performance via an interpretation, but that interpretation is not something separate from the script but rather itself a function on it.*'[12]

What is said in these quotations about the script of a play is even more true of the libretto *and its accompanying score* in opera. Audiences cannot receive an opera until the music and the action are realized in performance by stage director and designers, as well as by the conductor, orchestral musicians and singers; accordingly when discussing an opera it is inadequate to concentrate simply on analysing the features to be observed in the score. Further insight must be sought from actual productions; and, with the advent of videotape and subsequently DVD recording, it is now possible to discuss in some detail how individual directors and singing actors have interpreted the text and the music through their stagecraft. This is done with each example studied in this book, and readers can view the performances to which I shall refer, since all but one of these productions has been commercially released.[13]

A production comprises set designs and lighting designs, costume and make-up designs, and movement and blocking. Good directors create a synthesis of these elements which complements and illuminates both the text and the music. Although all of them are important, the main focus in this book will be on how the singers' blocking, movement, facial expressions, gestures and postures interact with the music and the text. These are the crucial elements in conveying meaning through production – though that is not to say that the designers of sets, lighting, costume and make-up are insignificant, and aspects of their work will always be discussed when they are important to the effect of a scene which I am analysing.

The book begins with an example of something rare in opera – an extended section for orchestra when the singing actors are present on

---

[10] Hornby 1977: 99.

[11] Let it be clear that I am not hostile to all post-modernist productions, only to productions in which an arbitrary concept overrides the fundamental themes of the text and music; cf. my warm regard for Pierre Audi's modern-dress *Iphigénie en Aulide*, Olivier Py's extraordinary *Lulu* and Nikolaus Lehnhoff's radical *Parsifal*, **8.1**, **4.3** and **7.3** below.

[12] Hornby 1977: 107; italics in original.

[13] This book does not explore the important question of the relationship between the video director's choices of what to place on the screen and the original stage production. That is a separate issue, which could form the basis for a whole book in itself.

stage, but silent. There are of course many operas containing ballet scenes or *divertissements*; but these almost by definition do not advance the action of the opera, and so will not be discussed in this book. Here, I will by contrast study an interaction which is solely between stage action and orchestral music, and in which the music has much to say about the dramatic situation, and its development during the passage when there is silence onstage.[14] In subsequent chapters I shall add vocal lines into the mix, so we will then study the more complex interactions between various forms of sung text, orchestral music, *mise en scène* and acting.

1.1 *Salome and the cistern* (Strauss/Wilde *Salome* scene 3, conclusion)

Oscar Wilde's two great innovations, in contrast to previous literary treatments of the myth, are that his Salomé demands the head of Jochanaan because he has rebuffed her sexual advances; and that Herod orders her to be killed at the end of the play. The second innovation does not concern us here (although it inspired Strauss to deliver one of the most shocking endings in all opera, cf. **8.3**); the first, Jochanaan's rejection of Salomé's desire for him, precipitates the orchestral music studied here.

After Jochanaan has four times pronounced that Salomé is accursed, he descends back into the cistern from which he came. At this point in Wilde's play Salomé repeats one more time her obsessive 'I will kiss your mouth, Jochanaan, I will kiss your mouth'; and the Page of Herodias pronounces a touching elegy on the young Syrian, Narraboth, who committed suicide in agony when he saw Salomé's lust for the prophet: 'He was my brother, and nearer to me than a brother …'. Strauss cut both these speeches, and a few sentences of dialogue between two soldiers, and replaced them with … nothing. All the characters on stage are silent during a massive eruption by his very large orchestra, which proceeds for just under four minutes until the next event in the play – the entry of Herodes, Herodias and the entire court.

Together with the earlier symphonic passage, which follows Narraboth's order for the grille over the cistern to be opened, at Salome's request, this orchestral sequence is sometimes wrongly described as an interlude.[15] That implies that this music is either simply an orchestral transition to the next scene, without dramatic meaning in itself, or a comment by the composer on what has preceded it; in either case an 'interlude' is music detached from

---

[14] For other examples cf. e.g. Butterfly's overnight vigil in the original two-act version of Puccini's opera, the sub-scene where Elektra digs for the axe in Strauss' opera (110aff.), and Marie's reverie after singing the lullaby in Berg's *Wozzeck* (I.3.404–426).
[15] E.g. Puffett 1989: 53.

the current situation on stage. I shall show by contrast that, during this section where the singers are silent, Strauss creates an orchestral narrative which illuminates the emotions of his principal character, Salome, and the evolution of her feelings and thoughts after Jochanaan has refused further contact with her and returned to his imprisonment in the cistern. My analysis of the dramatic meaning of the music is illuminated by the superb performance of Teresa Stratas, directed at the height of her powers by Götz Friedrich in his 1974 film, with the Vienna Philharmonic conducted by Karl Böhm.[16]

1 1 Salome and the cistern

When Jochanaan tells Salome that he will not see her again, and curses her for the first three times, a motif is heard four times in the orchestra (**1.1.1**), which was first introduced at 'I want to kiss your mouth, Jochanaan' in the confrontation which has just occurred (122.10–11). But its full significance will not become plain until the very end of the orchestral music that is to follow. Strauss is planting a seed, which will in due course become central to the opera.

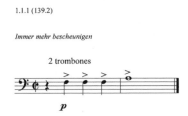

1.1.1 (139.2)

Immer mehr bescheunigen

2 trombones

p

When Jochanaan goes down into the cistern, Strauss accompanies this (logically enough) with a descending version of the music to which the prophet came out (140.9 cf. 65.10ff.); but as this reaches the depths, a principal motif associated with Salome and desire (**1.1.2**) is furiously overlaid onto its embers, in flutes, clarinets and violins, *mit äusserster Leidenschaft* (the Italian indication *molto appassionato* does not demand quite as much expression as the German, which translates as 'with the

---

[16] For an analysis of Stratas's performance of Salome as a whole see 8.3. No other available videorecording of *Salome* comes near to Friedrich's in the musical intelligence of the direction and the dramatic power of the performance. For example, in Luc Bondy's Salzburg Festival (1997) production, Catherine Malfitano as Salome is not even on stage for most of this section, and when she returns at the end she drops a red flower into the cistern during the final sequence involving **1.1.6** and **1.1.7**; Bondy is in no way responding to what the music is saying at that point (see below).

utmost passion'); and it is equally furiously developed throughout figure 141 to express her extreme desire for Jochanaan. At 142 the theme to which she sang 'Nothing in the world is as black as your hair' (107.6ff., **1.1.3**) enters, and now alternates with **1.1.2** in an intense *stretto* symphonic development.

1.1.2 (140.14)

1.1.3 (142.1)

The focus in all this music is on charting Salome's extremely turbulent emotions. The use of these motifs shows first that her passion is the subject of this passage (**1.1.1**) and then that her desire for Jochanaan has been very greatly increased by her overwhelming frustration (**1.1.2** and **1.1.3**). In Friedrich's film, Stratas is first seen in close-up staring, weeping, quivering; at 142.9 she sinks to the ground; at the next reprise of **1.1.3** (2–1 before 143) she extends her hands towards the cistern; then at the next reprise of **1.1.2** she holds the edge of it. As these two motifs are intensely developed over the next few bars her head is bowed down between her extended arms – a position of utter hopelessness (to 143.9).

Here the tempo changes to *Sehr lebhaft* (*molto mosso*) and the second section of the orchestral commentary begins (143.10). Once again Salome is tormented by memories – which are now (**1.1.4**) of Jochanaan's fierce accusations (presumably against Herodes, at 66), and his faith in Christ (130).[17]

---

[17] For Strauss, Jochanaan's denunciation of the Tetrarch and his glorification of Jesus as the only one who can save Salome are two sides of the same coin.

1.1.4 (143.10)

Sehr lebhaft

At this point Friedrich rightly decided to intensify the physical manifestation of Salome's agony; Stratas rolls over and writhes on her back, and at the next repetition of **1.1.4** lays her hand on the cistern. As the *stretto* in the orchestra becomes more powerful (144.8, *immer schneller*), she crawls towards the cistern on hands and knees, and then climbs onto its barred grille at the *sfz* in 145.5. At the *fff* sustained semibreve in 146.2 she takes up a commanding position on top of it, on hands and knees but unbowed – an exhibition of a determination to conquer, and perhaps a foreshadowing of triumph. In the next few bars she raises herself a little, looks down into the cistern with fierce, hooded eyes – and then, when the *stretto* finally reaches its conclusion with the high *fff* C sharp violin *tremolos* of 148.7, suddenly collapses onto it, her hands extended, clasping the hooks which had been used to raise the grille.

Now comes a new motif. It is first heard in the form shown as **1.1.5**, but the duration of both chords and the intervals of the fall from first to second are varied continually in what follows (under persistent *tremolos* on C sharp; the inverted pedal and the bitonality create a deliberately disturbing effect on the listener). Friedrich interpreted this falling motif physically; Stratas twitches and collapses even more at each recurrence of **1.1.5**, so that she ends this section (at 151.5, just before the double bar) utterly prostrate. In this second section, Salome has been tortured still further by her memories (reprises of **1.1.3** and **1.1.1**, but dominated by the introduction and *stretto* symphonic treatment of **1.1.4**), and in Friedrich's production this is symbolized by Stratas's approach on hands and knees to the grille over the cistern, and then her gradual collapse onto it; this is the nearest she can get to Jochanaan. Her frustration leads as the section closes to complete physical collapse.

1.1.5 (148.9)

Sehr schnell

Strauss begins the third, shortest and final section with an utter contrast (double bar at 151.6). For the first time a slow tempo is adopted (*beinahe doppelt so langsam, andante*). Low C sharp tremolos in *divisi* violas are heard above an extended solo for contrabassoon. For eleven bars it keeps returning to the depths, but then the melody grows an upward-pointing *marcato* tailpiece (**1.1.6**), which recurs three times.

1.1.6 (152.3)

(beinahe doppelt so langsam)

contrabsn.

Friedrich rightly interprets this as the beginning of the crucial change in Salome's mood. She is now thinking what she can do, and beginning to rise from the depths of despair; so, in his production, Stratas starts to raise her head on the first occurrence of **1.1.6**, stares intensely, and then gradually rises up after the second repeat, when the almost inexorable C sharp tremolos of the last few pages move, first to D and then to E flat, as the key finally changes.

A momentary distraction now occurs, in the form of a high, jerky melody in E flat clarinet, flute and oboe (**1.1.7**). It is a strange transformation of the opening theme of the opera, which is associated with Salome (1.2–3, quoted as 8.2.1).[18] It dies down after four bars, since it is an anticipation, representing turbulent thought, of what is to follow immediately.

1.1.7 (153.1)

(beinahe doppelt so langsam)

E flat clarinet, flute

---

[18] Carpenter (1989: 105) is right to suggest that Strauss may have been influenced by Berlioz, whose orchestration he greatly admired; this music recalls the cackling E flat clarinet distortion of the beloved's *idée fixe* near the start of the 'Dream of a Sabbath Night' in the *Symphonie Fantastique* (movement V letter E, bars 40ff.). Note that in *Salome* as in the Berlioz symphony a beautiful woman's beautiful theme is caricatured, both by the distortion of the theme and by the use of the squeaky E flat clarinet.

Next comes the culmination towards which this entire orchestral sequence has been leading. Stratas rises during the four bars of **1.1.7** to her full height, but leaning forward and with her arms half extended as if welcoming and accepting a new thought.

That is exactly what Salome is doing. At the moment when **1.1.7** settles onto its final D natural semibreve, brass instruments intone **1.1.8**, which is of course an extension of **1.1.1**. And as this pronouncement concludes, in Friedrich's production, Stratas as Salome is fully erect. She has made her resolve.

1.1.8 (153.5)

(beinahe doppelt so langsam)

But the use of this *leitmotif* here is utterly un-Wagnerian; Strauss breaks the rules of the game. Spectators who are hearing and seeing the opera for the first time will not understand what **1.1.8** signifies; but anyone who has heard the opera more than once will instantly recognize what Salome has decided. Much later in the opera, when Salome has danced the Dance of the Seven Veils and Herodes asks her to declare what she wants as her reward, **1.1.8** is the basis of the melody for her repeated demands *Ich will den Kopf des Jochanaan*, 'I want the head of Jochanaan'.[19] The lust for a kiss, with which the confrontation with Jochanaan ended (**1.1.1**), has now become a lust for Jochanaan's death (**1.1.8**).

With this resolution, the passage for orchestra alone is complete, and with it the third scene. To replace Wilde's spoken transition, which refers backwards rather than forwards, Strauss has used his orchestra to chart Salome's evolving emotions after Jochanaan has rejected her; in doing so he has prepared fully for the interaction between Herodes and Salome which will occupy most of the fourth, longest and final scene of the opera.

---

[19] Cf. e.g. 284.3–5. Note the violent lurch from E flat minor to A major on the last three chords of **1.1.8**, which will later become the last three syllables of 'Jochanaan'. In my view this signifies the strength of her new desire.

1.2 Conclusion

This analysis shows that even when there is no sung text and, in this case, not even any stage directions, operatic orchestral music can still illuminate the emotions and thoughts of characters onstage. It also demonstrates that even music without text provides 'clues to action' which demand illustration on stage in the form of the postures, gestures and facial expressions of the (temporarily silent) singing actors.

Discussion question

As directed by Friedrich, Teresa Stratas physicalizes almost every moment of Strauss's orchestral sequence. Is this overdone? Compare her performance with another, more restrained version of this section, and ask whether or not that second version is less adequate than Stratas's performance to matching the complex and passionate insights into Salome's feelings that Strauss's music provides. (On this issue see further 8.3.)

PART ONE

Forms

2

Arias and Monologues

This chapter discusses sections of scenes where a character is either alone singing to the audience, or addressing a silent onstage audience, or revealing his or her thoughts and feelings to a confidante. Examples will be drawn both from the recitative-aria format of classical opera and from the less formally structured monologues of Romantic and modern opera.

When a singer is singing solo, the inflections of the vocal line normally portray the expressed emotions which go with the text – the character's uppermost feelings; the orchestra portrays inner feelings and thoughts which lie underneath those explicit surface emotions. The orchestra's role is to give depth to the overtly expressed feelings by illuminating the deeper energies behind them. And the director's task is to illuminate words, vocal line and orchestral music through the props, costumes and acting.

2.1 'Great work, boss!' (Mozart/Da Ponte, *Le nozze di Figaro*, no. 3).

Da Ponte created this aria out of almost nothing from Beaumarchais' original play, and for a very good reason. The opera omits the whole of Figaro's diatribe in Act V of the play: 'No, my Lord Count, you shan't have her, you shall not have her! Because you are a great nobleman you think you are a great genius ...'.[1] In this speech Figaro attacks the Count for having a superior status to Figaro, who is by far his mental superior, simply through the accident of his birth. Da Ponte almost certainly omitted this speech because it was the most inflammatory section of a play which had been banned from the Viennese stage for its revolutionary politics; but Moberly was right to argue that the meaning of the music in *Se vuol ballare* is

---

[1] Beaumarchais 1964: 199.

generated by this sentiment.[2] Da Ponte developed the idea for the recitative and aria from one line in Act II of the play ('I'll get hold of him [Chérubin] and teach him his part and then – dance, your Lordship.'),[3] to expand and crystallize the implications of this much earlier scene. And Mozart's music more than restores the power of the inflammatory speech which Da Ponte deliberately omitted; the librettist knew – or at least perhaps hoped – that Mozart would compensate for its absence by his setting of No. 3.

The subject of *Le nozze di Figaro* is a class conflict, supplanted as the opera unfolds by a gender conflict. Figaro joins the class conflict as soon as he discovers that the Count intends to sleep with his bride. *Se vuol ballare*, the first solo aria in the work, is a powerful denunciation of the Count by a Figaro determined to thwart this ambition.[4] It is very surprising that a commentator as subtle and generally wise as Tim Carter should fail to hear the social anger expressed in No. 3.[5] Frits Noske rightly noted the way in which the lower-class characters in *Le Nozze di Figaro* appropriate the dance rhythms of the upper classes;[6] but the minuet in *Se vuol ballare* is not merely a dance appropriate to an aristocrat, as Noske remarks; it is particularly appropriate to Figaro when he is singing about what he proposes to do with that aristocrat. Figaro takes the minuet to himself, not merely in that he sings one; he creates a minuet in Mozart's music, and he intends to make the Count sing and dance to its tune. In performance you can hear the bitterness, the measured, deliberate anger, and the intensity of Figaro's determination to make the Count dance to his guitar.[7]

✐ 2 1 Great work, boss! (Sellars)

✐ 2 1 Great work, boss! (Terfel)

No. 3[8]

FIGARO

(pacing angrily up and down and rubbing his hands together)

2.1.1 Bravo, signor padrone!	Great work, boss!
Ora incomincio a capir il mistero,	Now I begin to understand the mystery,

---

[2]Moberley 1968: 51–2.

[3]Beaumarchais 1964: 133.

[4]The Count reciprocates the mutual feeling of class hatred later, in No. 17. Seventeen of the opera's twenty-eight numbers dramatize class conflict, gender conflict, or both.

[5]Carter 1987. His synopsis does however rightly stress the dance theme in the opera; cf. 51 and notes, 57, 67.

[6]Noske 1977: 34.

[7]Cf. Schmidgall 1977: 98 and 102.

[8]Here, and throughout this book, I print the text as sung, including all repeats both varied and unvaried. This is necessary for study of the musical setting and of productions, but is not normally a feature of most published libretti.

E a veder schietto tuto il vostro progetto:	and see clearly your whole plan.
A Londra è vero? Voi ministro, io corriero,	Off to London, is it? You as minister, me as courier,
E la Susanna...segreta ambasciatrice.	And Susanna ... confidential attachée.
Non sarà, non sarà. Figaro il dice.	It won't happen, it won't happen; Figaro says so.

*

[1] (*allegretto*)

Se vuol ballare, signor Contino,	If you want to dance, dear little Count,
Se vuol ballare, signor Contino,	If you want to dance, dear little Count,
Il chitarrino le suonerò,	I'll play the guitar,
Il chitarrino le suonerò,	I'll play the guitar,
Sì, le suonerò,	Yes, I'll play it,
Sì, le suonerò,	Yes, I'll play it,
Sì, le suonerò. **2.1.2**	Yes, I'll play it.
Se vuol venire nella mia scola,	If you want to come to my school,
La capriola l'insegnerò.	I'll teach you capers,
Se vuol venire nella mia scola,	If you want to come to my school,
La capriola l'insegnerò,	I'll teach you capers,
La capriola l'insegnerò.	I'll teach you capers.
Sì, l'insegnerò, sì l'insegnerò,	Yes, I'll teach you, yes, I'll teach you.
Saprò, saprò, saprò...ma piano...	I'll know, I'll know, I'll know...but quietly...
Piano, piano, piano, piano, piano, piano!	Quietly, quietly, quietly, quietly, quietly, quietly!
Meglio ogni arcano dissimulando	I can better uncover every secret
scoprir pu potrò.	by stealth.

*

[2] (*presto*)

L'arte schermendo, l'arte adoprando,	I'll defend myself with cunning, I'll use cunning,
Di qua pugnendo, di là scherzando,	fighting here, using tricks there,
Tutte le machine rovescierò, rovescierò.	I'll overturn all his schemes, overturn them.
L'arte schermendo, l'arte adoprando,	I'll defend myself with cunning, I'll use cunning,
Di qua pugnendo, di là scherzando,	fighting here, using tricks there,
Tutte le machine rovescierò, rovescierò,	I'll overturn all his schemes, overturn them,
Tutte le machine rovescierò, rovescierò,	I'll overturn all his schemes, overturn them,
Rovescierò.	overturn them.

*

[3] (*allegretto*)

Se vuol ballare, signor Contino,	If you want to dance, dear little Count,
Se vuol ballare, signor Contino,	If you want to dance, dear little Count,
Il chitarrino le suonerò,	I'll play the guitar,
Sì, le suonerò.	Yes, I'll play the guitar.
Il chitarrino le suonerò,	I'll play the guitar,
Il chitarrino le suonerò,	I'll play the guitar,

| Sì, le suonerò, | Yes, I'll play it, |
| Sì, le suonerò. | Yes, I'll play it. |

(*orchestral* presto *as Figaro exits*)

One of the most notable features of Mozart's recitatives is the great sensitivity with which the vocal inflections articulate the emotional positions of the characters. Susanna has just told Figaro that the Count proposes to reinstall the *droit de seigneur* on his estate and exercise it on her. And, as soon as she has left, this recitative lets us hear Figaro thinking himself into the implications of what he has just learned. As he becomes clearer and clearer, his inflections become more and more agitated. At first Figaro tries to meet the situation with irony (bar 2, 'Great work, boss!'), but soon he is increasingly angered and disgusted by the implications of the Count's scheme (3–10). He is particularly concerned about Susanna, and so at 'and Susanna, confidential attachée' Figaro takes a long pause after her name, and the continuo descends fluidly as he broods on her beauty and this impending outrage (10–12).[9] This moment of pathos, for which the singer should temporarily impose a *ritardando*, leads immediately to his determination to thwart the Count (12–14), in which the tempo should be picked up again.

*

Da Ponte's stage direction for this recitative is *pacing angrily up and down the room and rubbing his hands together*; but the singer needs to do more than that if he is to reflect Mozart's music adequately on stage. In the Châtelet production, directed by Olivier Mille, Bryn Terfel as Figaro holds in his right hand the ruler which he had been using in the opening duet to measure the room.[10] He expresses increasing agitation by crossing the stage in bars 6–7, uses his face alone to express (very finely) his anguish on 'and Susanna', and raises the ruler sharply and threateningly to make much of 'it won't happen, it won't happen'. Peter Sellars, by contrast, in his production (which was updated and relocated to Trump Tower, Manhattan) saved his prop for the aria; Sandford Sylvan as Figaro focuses during the recitative on the door of the Count's bedroom. During the vocal pause in bars 6 and 7 he stands on his own sofa bed, extends his hands incredulously at 'off to London, is it?' then goes forward to the door on 'you as minister'

---

[9]To bring out the pathos, the descending line in the bass of the continuo in 8–10 should be played by the cello.

In the vocal line note that B is temporarily flattened on 'segreta' for a touch of emotional colour. This anticipates the key of the aria, which is F major.

[10]I have selected this production and Peter Sellars' for discussion of no. 3, from the quite substantial number of available DVD recordings of *Le nozze di Figaro*, because the directors' approaches to the number are both good (in different ways), and an interesting contrast.

2.1.1 (I.2)

FIGARO; *(pacing angrily up and down the room and rubbing his hands together)*

(8). Sylvan makes much more of the pathos of 10–12 than Terfel, standing very close to the door with head bowed; and, in a markedly original twist, sang from 'it won't happen' to the end very quietly. This understatement was arguably more effective than the customary sudden *forte*; certainly the anger is all there in this quiet but firm resolve, and the movement which Sellars devised for the earlier parts of the recitative, though not what Da Ponte originally had in mind, enhanced Mozart's measured escalation of

Figaro's emotions as he realizes to the full what the Count is intending, and determines that it will not happen.

Figaro launches into his aria without an orchestral introduction. In the opening section he resolves to make the Count dance to his tune, and Mozart makes him imagine doing this to the allegretto of a stately, aristocratic minuet. *Pizzicato* strings evoke the specific instrument which Figaro proposes to play, the guitar; and from bar 20 the horns stop accompanying the minuet and evoke the horns of the cuckold, echoed by a swirl in *arco* violins (**2.1.2**).[11]

2.1.2 (3.20ff)

The aria gains intensity from the repeat of 'if you want to come' onwards, with alternations between *forte* and *piano* in the orchestra, first every two bars, then every bar. 'Figaro's veneer soon wears thin and brute power exerts itself through the *piano* attempts at reserve',[12] and the increasing energies which this creates soon generate the powerful *presto* middle section, a patter song whose climax at the fierce resolve of 'I'll overturn all his schemes' is followed by a brief, ironic reprise of the *allegretto* opening, 'if you want to dance'.

In production, this aria needs a prop. And what could be more natural than to place an actual guitar among the disordered household effects on which the curtain had risen in Sellars' production? Sylvan turns round, smiling with confidence as he begins the aria, then picks up the guitar on the repeat of 'the guitar', and uses it as a prop throughout the next section, first holding it in playing position but soon raising it angrily in the air on the repeat of 'if you want to come', and again on the sudden *forte* on 'capers'. Similarly aggressive moves (though without an actual guitar) are to be seen in Mille's Châtelet production. Terfel mimes guitar playing, with the ruler functioning as an

---

[11] Noske (1977: 5–6) rightly notes the anticipation here of No. 26, at the point in Act IV where Figaro believes that what he feared in No. 3 is actually going to happen, and accordingly the horns of the cuckold dominate the close of that aria.
[12] Schmidgall 1977: 102.

imaginary guitar, then extends it like a dueller's sword on the first repeat of 'if you want to come', and swishes it angrily on the repeat of 'capers'.

Both directors rightly saw the need for a change of action for the rushing semiquavers under the obsessive repeats of 'I'll know'. Terfel drops his ruler and paces angrily up and down. Sylvan approaches the door, once again waving the guitar angrily in the air and only putting it down after 'quietly, quietly...'. Sellars then has his Figaro maintain the relationship with the Count's door by a variety of moves during the *presto*, at one point actually hitting it. Sylvan ends up sitting on the floor, leaning on the door, for the reprise of the returning *allegretto*. Terfel by contrast at the Châtelet uses a new prop after 'quietly, quietly...'. He picks up a wig on a model head, and sings the *presto* to it; on the second 'I'll overcome all his schemes', Terfel actually strikes the head. At the climactic end of the *presto* he holds it up, and then, in the reprise of the *allegretto* minuet, first bows ironically to it, then on 'the guitar', holds it close and caresses it, and finally holds it fiercely during the last few bars, and hits it again after the last word. All of this is extremely effective.

In their different ways these productions illustrate the need to respond in detail to Mozart's music. In *secco* recitative close attention must be paid to the inflexions of the vocal line, but in an aria the orchestral music must also be read as a clue to the emotional dynamics of the character's evolution during the number. This is especially true of an intense aria like this one, whose powerful primary emotions of anger and determination are contained by the minuet for the dancing Count only in the opening *allegretto* (the 'I'll know' section excluded) and its closing reprise. They are by contrast fully unleashed during the central *presto* and in the *presto* exit music.

Discussion question

I think that Sylvan's performance of Figaro's anger with the Count is more introverted than Terfel's. You may agree or disagree. Either way, point out the aspects of the singers' interpretations that support your position. Is one of the two interpretations more true to Mozart's music than the other?

2.2 Wotan confides in his 'will' (Wagner *Die Walküre* II.2)

After the turbulent interlude that marks Fricka's triumphant departure, Wagner's very large orchestra becomes almost silent as Brünnhilde approaches Wotan. The music is hushed to a low *piano* held D on bassoons and bass clarinet – with the ominous threat always hovering that the full orchestra will break out turbulently and violently (as it soon will).

Wotan's monologue is far more complex than Figaro's aria (2.1). He has created a mortal hero, Siegmund, to do what he does not dare to do – to retrieve the ring of power; but Siegmund has consummated an incestuous union with his sister Sieglinde, and then fled with her from the house of her husband Hunding. Wotan's wife, Fricka, goddess of the family, demands that Wotan should let Siegmund die when Hunding catches up with him. Wotan has no choice but to swear that he will do this. His daughter, the Valkyrie Brünnhilde, then finds him and begs him to confide in her.

Figaro has a clear objective in his aria, and it is stated at the end of his recitative: to defeat the Count's plan to take his bride to bed. Wotan by contrast *does not know what he can do*. So the first six sections of this monologue see Wotan gradually agreeing to share with Brünnhilde, who is as she says 'his will', all that is troubling him, and confiding the long backstory to her. This narrative culminates in a terrible outburst that he has been unable to create a free agent [6]; and then he falls into even greater anguish, as he realizes that his enemy, the dwarf Alberich, has been able to create a son and so bring about the destruction of the gods. He longs for 'the end' [7], and then he bitterly and ironically bestows on this son of his enemy 'the empty glory of divinity' [8].

And so Wotan has evolved, through telling his story to Brünnhilde, towards a decision. He orders her to fight for Fricka, and allow Siegmund to be destroyed. But now [9] Brünnhilde rebels, defies Wotan, and evokes the full weight of his fury.

Before English National Opera sang the *Ring* in Andrew Porter's English translation (1970–3), and the subsequent advent of surtitles, Act II scene 2 was regarded as one of the most impenetrable, not to say boring, parts of the *Ring* – especially by those who could not understand the text.[13] It is on the contrary one of the most intense and concentrated scenes in the trilogy,[14] and its two key outcomes – Wotan's bequest of the ring, in bitter despair, to Hagen, and Brünnhilde's rebellion against his command to kill Siegmund – are pivotal to the development of the plot of the remainder of the cycle. How can this scene be staged in such a way as to bring out its deep, inner meaning?

Porges records Wagner's own aims as director for this scene: '… we should be made to feel the emotions of the narrator and at the same time to understand clearly the substance of his narration. Complete understanding

---

[13] Hanslick, who could of course understand the text, had already condemned this scene in 1876 as 'an abyss of boredom', and claimed that even committed Wagnerians thought it was a disaster (Nattiez 1983: 138).

[14] *The Nibelung's Ring* (to give the cycle its full title) is not a tetralogy but a trilogy, even though it comes in four parts. Wagner subtitled the one-act *Das Rheingold* a 'preliminary evening'; *Die Walküre* is the first of the three three-act 'stage festival plays' (*Bühnenfestspiele*) which comprise the main action.

can only be imparted by a performer who, while maintaining a mysterious, sombre tone of voice throughout, manages to *connect* the manifold characterizations demanded by each separate moment.'[15]

Wagner's score, if it is realized in accordance with this ideal in an outstanding performance, provides the basis for a full and intense musico-dramatic experience. But because of the use of a number of *leitmotifs* in the orchestra (Wagner called them 'motifs of reminiscence') to relate what is being sung in this scene to past events in *Das Rheingold* and in earlier parts of *Die Walküre*, it is necessary for both singers and directors to be aware of this musical subtext and respond to it in performance.[16]

The most insightful performance of this scene available on DVD is that by Donald McIntyre and Gwyneth Jones, conducted by Pierre Boulez and directed by Patrice Chéreau, in the Centenary production, which was first seen at Bayreuth in 1976.[17] For comparison, some of the strategies adopted in Harry Kupfer's production, recorded at Bayreuth in 1991–2, will also be discussed.

This particular scene in Chéreau's *Ring* evoked quite a lot of *angst* among traditionalist Wagnerians. Wagner's original setting for Act II was a distant gorge leading forward to a high ridge of rocks, somewhere in the wild mountains. In a stroke of creative genius Chéreau and his set designer, Richard Peduzzi, relocated scenes 1 and 2 to a large room in Valhalla, which has two notable features – a freestanding, full-length mirror, and a ball with a spike on its underside. This ball, suspended on the end of a long wire stretching down from the flies, swings in slow circles over a low circular dais, and symbolizes the unfolding of inevitable fate. With these two simple props, Chéreau went straight to the heart of the scene; the pendulum symbolizes the bonds in which Wotan is now entangled, while the mirror dramatizes the god's introspective brooding.[18] And these two stage props (together with a chair and a coat) give to Chéreau's production

---

[15] Porges (1882) 1983: 55–6; italics in original.

[16] This *caveat* also applies to the scenes from operas by Strauss and Berg, who followed in Wagner's footsteps in creating a complex web of repeated motifs in their music dramas; cf. 4.1, 4.3, 5.4, 8.3 and 9.2. You will find these scenes and whole operas harder to study than the others discussed in this book, but the extra effort will be richly rewarded!

[17] Chéreau's production aroused great controversy in Germany when it was first seen; there was a certain amount of nationalistic hostility to Wolfgang Wagner's decision to invite a French team to Bayreuth for the centenary year. But it marked a massive advance in the staging of the *Ring*, and this came to be realized when it was broadcast worldwide, directed for television from 1981 onwards by Brian Large. For favourable critical assessments of Chéreau's production, see Engstrom 1981, Nattiez 1983 and M. Ewans 1985b and 2015.

I saw the *Siegfried* of Francesca Zambello's San Francisco/Washington State Opera *Ring* during a flying visit to the Bay area in May 2011. If the rest of her cycle equals the interpretative standards of that production, and if the performances are issued on DVD, there will at last be another *Ring* available with the same high directorial intelligence and first-rate staging as Chéreau's.

[18] Cf. Engstrom 1981: 87–8 for another positive evaluation of this design.

points of focus which are not available either in Wagner's original *mise-en-scène* or on Kupfer's bare stage.[19]

✎ 2 2 Wotan and Brünnhilde (1)

[1] Chéreau gets at once to the heart of the emotional situation. Wotan is *sunk in gloomy brooding*, and Brünnhilde is intensely concerned.[20] So the scene begins with Wotan sitting downcast in the chair, while she kneels and pleads with him, looking into his eyes, and a motif of despair sounds out in the cellos:

2.2.1 (346)

Mässig

This was first heard in Act II scene 1, at the point where Fricka begins to win the argument with Wotan and tear away the evasions with which he has tried to defend the incestuous union of Siegmund and Sieglinde (323). In the stage directions when it was first sounded, then, *from this point on Wotan's expression and entire behaviour grow more and more profoundly and terribly dejected.* Plainly therefore this descending theme portrays the process of Wotan's sinking into distress and despair, and that is why it is heard now.

Brünnhilde's gentle pleas arouse Wotan from despair to *a fearful outburst.*

2.2.3 is a principal theme of the trilogy, simply because Alberich's curse, in *Das Rheingold* scene 4, that the ring will bring death to whoever possesses it, dominates the subsequent action, leading as it does to the deaths of Fasolt, Siegmund, Fafner, Siegfried and ultimately Brünnhilde, and the downfall of the gods. The key to understanding this motif is its initial rise, dramatic fall of a major seventh, descent and final rise again,

---

[19] Because of the length of this monologue, I do not print the whole text. The English subtitles on the DGG Boulez/Chéreau DVD are very good.

[20] For a description of this scene in Chéreau's production cf. Nattiez 1983: 138–45. His discussion is detailed, but it does not relate the actions developed in rehearsal by Chéreau, McIntyre and Jones to the leitmotifs in the orchestra, something essential to an understanding of how to perform this scene.

2.2.2 and 3 (348)

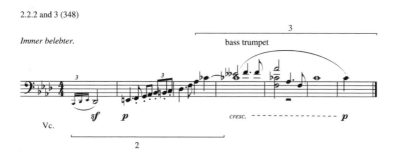

echoing the baleful unfolding of Alberich's text ('As by curse it became mine, accursed be this ring'). Played throughout the trilogy, almost always by brass instruments, it is ominous whenever it is heard. And that curse now drives Wotan to agony; in Chéreau's production he gets up, Brünnhilde tries to hold on to him from behind, he breaks away, and she goes to him and grips him again to try to soothe him.

Wotan fights off Brünnhilde, as the beautiful music associated with the sight of the Rhine gold sounds out distorted (**2.2.4**), followed by **2.2.5**, the aggressive, attacking theme with which Fricka engaged in argument with Wotan in II.1.[21] And he collapses to the ground, as he sings 'I am the saddest of all creatures' to a slight variant of **2.2.6**, the theme which is almost universally known as the 'renunciation of love' motif – although it is more accurately described as an *acceptance of lovelessness and inevitable suffering* theme:[22]

---

[21] E.g. 295, where Fricka sings *boiling over with indignation* (Wagner's stage direction).

[22] Cf. Donington 1990: 111. Alberich accepts lovelessness, not voluntarily, but under the pressure of suffering progressively more unpleasant rejections by the three Rhine daughters. And this theme's grim melodic contour, implying acceptance of inevitable suffering, informs three vital moments in *Die Walküre*. It is heard when Siegmund takes Notung, whose name means both the sword of need and that of misery, and by whose power alone he has any chance to defend his love; again when Sieglinde sings in Act III that she would rather die than live without Siegmund (before Brünnhilde renews her spirits by telling her she is bearing Siegmund's child); finally when Wotan accepts that he must lose Brünnhilde and bequeath her to Siegfried. (*Die Walküre* 214, 765, 1004). This theme is absent from *Siegfried*, whose hero because of his 'innocence' is not forced to make this choice; but in *Götterdämmerung* it recurs with terrible power when Brünnhilde rejects Waltraute's plea, clinging to 'Siegfried's ring', whose allure is about to destroy her marriage (469–70). Wagner commented while composing the end of *Götterdämmerung* Act I: 'when the ring was snatched from her I thought of Alberich; the noblest character suffers the same as the ignoble, in every creature the will is identical' (Wagner, C. 1978: 228; entry for 4/6/1870). Like Alberich and Siegmund, Brünnhilde accepts an instrument of power, and it leads her to a forced marriage and later to the death of her hero.

2.2.4 and 5 (350-1)

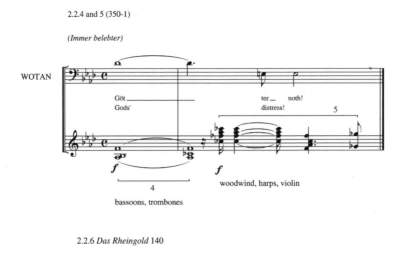

(Immer belebter)

2.2.6 *Das Rheingold* 140

Etwas langsam

By having Wotan collapse under the pressure of this motif, Chéreau indicates that the god is not yet resigned to his fate.[23]

[2] Brünnhilde asks him with a gentle vocal line to tell her what is hurting him; 'I am faithful to you' (356) – an ironic claim, in view of the direction in which the scene will later develop. Here the stage direction is that *she lays her head and hands with loving concern on his knees and breast. Wotan looks long in her eyes, then he strokes her hair with unconscious tenderness.* Kupfer follows this direction fairly closely: Anne Evans leans on John Tomlinson's shoulder and conveys that she is a submissive part of Wotan's will, and Tomlinson actually caresses his Brünnhilde's hair in accordance with the stage direction. Chéreau, however, violates this stage direction to establish his more complex vision of the psychology of the scene; at this point, McIntyre as Wotan, after touching Gwyneth Jones' head affectionately,[24] goes to face the mirror. And, as his monologue begins in near-total orchestral silence, Jones sits erect on the low podium, above which the pendulum hovers, looking at him intensely and *facing the mirror,*

---

[23] By contrast Kupfer has his Wotan – John Tomlinson – (who is kneeling throughout this section) strike the ground with his spear on 'Gods' distress'. This does not dramatize the struggle with his will which the interaction between Wotan and Brünnhilde in Chéreau's production signifies; and then Tomlinson throws his spear to the ground on 'I am the saddest of all creatures'. This is simply a melodramatic gesture.

[24] 'He calms her unease and thanks her for her kindness': Nattiez 1983: 140.

so that when Wotan looks into it, he sees both his own image and that of Brünnhilde behind him. This perfectly symbolizes the relationship between Wotan and his daughter, whom he describes here as 'my will'.[25]

[3] Now Wotan begins to unfold his story, and in Chéreau's production he is metaphorically stripping himself bare; he takes off his eye-patch and faces his full, half-blinded self in the mirror.[26] Only when his narrative reaches the point of telling Brünnhilde that she and the other eight Valkyries were created by his union with Erda [4] does McIntyre face Jones again; he comes close to her, and clasps her as he describes their mission to bring heroes to Valhalla.

[5] But now Wotan begins to unfold the trap in which he is caught; the motif associated with the prophecies of the Wala rises from the depths to convey a new onrush of inexorable fate (2.2.7), as he starts to sing of Alberich's plans.

Chéreau makes his Wotan go away from Brünnhilde at this point, crossing to the far right of the stage. He needs distance as he tries to accept this new threat, and, while Jones kneels on the pendulum base, looking anxious, McIntyre seeks the suppport of the back of his chair, and then clenches his fists at the thought of the threat of battle with the hosts of Nibelheim. (By contrast Kupfer's Wotan stays near his Brünnhilde, holding her close. This is in some ways an appropriate response, but it implies that Wotan is rather more dependent on his daughter than he actually is.) As the section concludes, with the words 'I, who am lord through treaties, am now a slave to them' (380–1), Kupfer's Wotan fittingly – given that the treaties are engraved on Wotan's spear – picks it up and throws it away. In the Chéreau production, by contrast, the focus is on the human emotions felt by these two gods. McIntyre falls to kneel on the ground. Then at the opening of the next section, [6], in which Wotan tells her what the solution is, Brünnhilde goes to comfort him; and, when the new idea of the free hero emerges, they both peer forward into the darkness of the auditorium, as if to see the new hero. Then McIntyre holds Jones' shoulders and sings his vision of the free hero while looking into her eyes – almost as if he knows already that the hero of whom he sings now will become her mate (as of course he does come to recognize in the closing scene of Act III).[27]

This passage climaxes in another outburst: 'O godly distress! Horrible disgrace! In loathing I find always *myself* in everything I have created'

---

[25] On the relationship between Wotan and Brünnhilde, and the ways in which 'Wotan's will' can and does rebel against him at the end of the scene, cf. M. Ewans 1982: 138–41.

[26] This is a much better image than Wagner's original *he gazes steadfastly into Brünnhilde's eyes*, which Kupfer follows. Chéreau's Wotan is looking into his own eyes – including the blinded one! – as well as into hers.

[27] Kupfer introduces physical force here; Tomlinson forces Evans down, bending her backwards, and kneels on top of her. This is unmotivated and quite wrong; physical violence against Brünnhilde must indeed happen in this scene – but not until after she has enraged Wotan by defying his command.

2.2.7 a and b (*Das Rheingold*) 625, 632

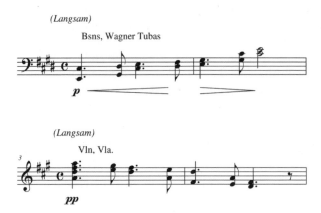

(388–91). And the interaction of motifs here reinforces the feeling that all Wotan's options have been blocked. Once again the distorted version of the motif associated with the Rhine gold (**2.2.4**) sounds out, locked together with a rhythmically animated version of the theme of inexorably rising destiny, **2.2.7** (388–90).

I italicize 'myself' in this quotation because as Wotan sings *mich* – the last word in the outburst in the original German – the full orchestra pronounces a *staccato* chord *ff*, separated by a bar of orchestral silence from what comes before and afterwards; this is a climactic moment. In Chéreau's production, Wotan has once again approached the mirror; and now he turns suddenly, on this chord, to face himself fully in the mirror again – the ultimate moment of self-confrontation. By contrast the problems of the bare stage are nowhere more evident in Kupfer's production than here; having earlier thrown away his spear in anger, his Wotan has no props left except Brünnhilde, so he throws *her* away at this moment. But this is again wrong (cf. note 27); at this stage of the scene it is not Brünnhilde for whom Wotan feels disgust, but himself.

🖉 2 2 Wotan and Brünnhilde (2)

Brünnhilde asks about Siegmund. Wotan admits that Fricka has easily defeated him, and McIntyre holds out his hands in a gesture expressing the absolute futility of what he has tried to do. A new section [7] begins as she asks in horror if he is going to take the victory away from Siegmund, and this leads to the crux of his whole predicament:

[7] **2.2.2** Ich berührte Alberichs Ring, **2.2.8**   I set hands on Alberich's ring:
  gierig hielt ich das Gold!   greedily I held the gold!
  Der Fluch, den ich floh   The curse that I fled
  Nicht flieht er nun mich;   still has not left me;
Was ich liebe, muss ich verlassen, **2.2.9b**   What I love, I must forsake,
  morden, wen je ich minne,   murder the man I cherish,
    trügend verraten,   deceive and betray
    wer mir traut!   the one who trusts me!
  2.2.3   (398–403)

It is precisely because he once possessed the ring, even for a short time, that Wotan must fall.

The music illuminates this; once more the use of motifs of reminiscence expresses the nature of Wotan's anguish. Like his first outburst, this one springs into being with the rising up in the orchestra of **2.2.2** – again, he is trying to break free of Fricka's bonds; but he fails. The first half of the sinister theme, which expresses the dark, hypnotic allure of the ring (**2.2.8**), descends in the orchestra as Wotan sings the first line of the text.

But then, as he sings 'the curse that I fled/still has not left me', an at first surprising theme is heard; the next four lines of text are dominated by the theme which expressed in Act I the outpouring of the first true love to be seen in the trilogy, that of Siegmund for Sieglinde (**2.2.9a**). It was heard again earlier in this scene, to express Brünnhilde's love for him.[28] But it is now hideously distorted, in dissonant music, to express Wotan's distress at having to destroy the son whom he loves (**2.2.9b**).

Wotan's bitterness is so intense because he is forced to accept that his power must come to an end, simply because it has become tainted by the touch of corruption; he finds that his success is undermined by the violence which he has committed to obtain it. And the corruption which this violence has created is so powerful that the destruction which it causes is inevitable.[29] For that reason the baleful theme **2.2.3**, first heard as the setting of Alberich's curse on the ring, concludes this passage (403), expressing the absolute necessity of Wotan's resignation from all earthly power – which he very soon expresses with the greatest intensity; he now wants only one thing – 'the end, the end!' (411–12).

Chéreau illuminates this crucial section very effectively. First, McIntyre, as Wotan, clasps Brünnhilde's shoulders to tell her about the corruption he has suffered by taking the ring from Alberich; then he runs rapidly away, only to have to turn back to her to symbolize how he cannot escape the curse and must destroy the son he loves. He then clasps her shoulders again,

---

[28] 356–7.
[29] Cf. M. Ewans 1982: 135.

2.2.8 (*Das Rheingold* 136)

(*Langsam*)

Ob, E.H, bsn.

2.2.9 a (25-26)

2.2.9 b (401)

(*Schnell*)

woodwinds, brass

wracked by the pain of having inevitably to destroy Siegmund. At this point Wagner directs that Wotan should pass from gestures expressing pain to those of despair; and in response, as **2.2.3** returns, enunciated powerfully by three trombones over a timpani roll, Chéreau deploys a new prop to physicalize the situation. Wotan has been wearing a magnificent dark red cloak; now he takes it off and throws it down, as he bids farewell to his 'lordly pomp' (404–9). And then, as Wotan sings, 'Only one thing I want now: / the end, / the end!' (411–12), on the first 'the end' McIntyre suddenly seizes the wire and stops the pendulum.[30] Only the destruction of the gods will halt the inexorable unfolding of destiny.

---

[30] The use of the cloak and pendulum during this section is far superior to Kupfer's interpretation, in which Wotan swishes his spear wildly during the farewell to his godly glory, then on the first 'the end' rams it into the ground, at which point the earth splits open behind him.

[8] In Chéreau's production, the moment where Wotan bitterly accepts his destiny, and bequeaths the world *in bitter anger* to Hagen, is illuminated by the use of the sumptuous cloak which symbolizes his power and which accordingly he had earlier discarded; as the fanfares rise towards Wotan's ironic blessing of the 'Nibelung's son' McIntyre picks it up, addresses it, kneels with his hands wide out and finally, violently discards it for a second time, on 'may your eager hate gnaw it away'.

2.2.10 a and b (418-9)

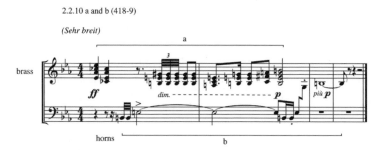

Here the originally seductive sequence of chords, which beckoned the gods towards the security of Valhalla (**2.2.10a**), is bitterly split around the forward-thrusting, spellbinding theme which was first heard when the Rhine gold was illuminated and displayed to Alberich in *Das Rheingold* scene 1 (**2.2.10b**).[31]

[8] So nimm meinen Segen, **2.2.10**	So take my blessing,
Niblungen-Sohn!	Nibelung's son!
Was tief mich ekelt	That which deeply revolts me,
das geb ich's zum Erbe,	I bequeath to you—
der **2.2.10** Gottheit nichtingen Glanz:	The empty glory of divinity:
zernage ihn gierig dein Neid!	May your eager hate gnaw it away!

(418–21)

The symbolism is plain; the power of the forged Rhine gold breaks the serene comfort afforded by Valhalla, so Wotan must accept that the glory of his power is empty.[32]

This may be a *coup de théâtre*, but it does not come near to matching the symbolic meaning which Chéreau achieves when Wotan stops the pendulum.

[31] **2.2.10a** heard first at *Das Rheingold* 183–7; **2.2.10b** first at 105–9.

[32] Wagner himself quoted this passage (1907: 188), and commented as follows: 'after in the course of the drama the simple nature-motive [**2.2.10b**] had been heard at the first gleam of the shining Rhine-gold, then at the first appearance of the gods' castle Valhalla, shimmering in the morning's red, the no less simple motive [**2.2.10a**] had also been heard, and each of these motives had undergone corresponding mutations in very close sympathy with the rising

Wotan began the scene in despair, and this text for his final resignation expresses bitter anger; but the music qualifies this mood. The security of Valhalla is now clearly illusory, and Wotan concedes ('the empty glory of divinity') that his power, his fortress and its heroes were gained by disloyalty and deceit. So there is a new kind of splendour in the music at this moment; noble fanfares build up in the brass, both to 'So take my blessing...' and to 'the empty glory...' (418–19). Wotan began by fighting against his fate; now he accepts it, in bitterness, but also with nobility.

As the scene draws to an end, [9] Brünnhilde refuses to obey Wotan's order to kill Siegmund, and he is furious:

Ha, Freche du!	What, impudent girl!
Frevelst du mir?	Are you rebelling against me?
Wer bist du, als meines Willens	What are you, but my will's
blind wählende Kür?	blind obedient slave? (426–7)

In Chéreau's production, intense violence illuminates the depth of Wotan's rage. Before the first line, McIntyre hits Jones, and she falls back full length on the ground. She puts up a protective arm to shield herself, but after the fourth line he seizes her elbow and raises her body a little off the ground; Jones looks up at him in terror as he menaces her. Soon he thrusts her back onto the ground – just after he has threatened her with the full power of his anger (431),[33] and she cowers through the rest of his verbal attack. Wotan's climactic last lines are:

Besorge, was ich befahl:	Remember what I command:
Siegmund falle!	Siegmund dies!
Dies sei der Walküre Werk!	That is the Valkyrie's work! (434–6)

Chéreau here finely combines the aggression in the music with the implication of this text; McIntyre pushes Jones once more to the ground, on the second line of text, but now with her spear, held horizontally, so leaving it in her hands for her to use against Siegmund before he *rushes away* accompanied by a furious *stretto*. The pendulum remains immobile to the end of the scene, reminding the spectators that, in consigning the

---

passions of the plot, – with the help of a digression in the harmony I could present them knit in such a way that, more than Wotan's words, this tone-figure should give to us a picture of *the fearfully gloomy soul of the suffering god*' (italics mine).

[33] Kupfer also unleashes violence here. His Wotan pushes Brünnhilde to the ground with the butt of his own spear, which she grasps to avoid being hurt further; when she lets go after his threat he kneels on top of her, pressing the spear vertically onto her. But these movements are less effective than those in Chéreau's production, because Chéreau builds the violence towards the visually outstanding response to Wotan's climactic last lines, when McIntyre's Wotan simultaneously both displays his contemptuous anger, by pushing Jones to the ground, and leaves her holding the spear with which she must kill Siegmund.

world bitterly to Hagen, Wotan has begun his journey to full acceptance of 'the end', which he brought upon himself by possessing, even briefly, the Nibelung's ring.

Wagner's music dramas demand great attention to detail; although the action is often slow-moving by the faster time-frames of the twentieth and twenty-first centuries, the music is extremely expressive at every moment, and the use of recurrent themes makes it essential for the director to concentrate on the constantly shifting meanings of the music, and for the singer to understand the musical motifs which are illuminating his character's psyche. Chéreau's production of this scene shows that even the stage design must sometimes be reconceived to reflect the inner meaning of the music drama, and here he felt – in my view rightly – that that could be achieved only by completely replacing Wagner's original *mise-en-scène*.

Discussion questions

- Analyse Chéreau's use of props in this scene – the pendulum, the mirror, the cloak and the eye patch.
- Discuss the use of physical violence by Wotan against Brünnhilde in Chéreau's production and in Kupfer's.
- What are the distinctive features of McIntyre's interpretation of Wotan's torment in this scene?

2.3 *I believe in a cruel God* … (Verdi/Boito *Otello* II.2)

It is not now necessary to argue the old question of whether Jago's *Credo* is 'faithful' to Shakespeare. Schmidgall and Hawes settled that years ago, in the opera's favour; Verdi was right to acclaim his librettist's creation as 'wholly Shakespearian'.[34] What has perhaps been less often discussed is *why* Verdi and Boito felt it necessary to take up only a few hints in the original play and make them into a manifesto of evil. The answer, I think, is simple; this opera is, to a certain extent, an allegorical struggle between good (Desdemona) and evil (Jago) for the soul of Otello.[35] So a librettist (composer of *Mefistofele*) with an interest in exploring the demonic, and a composer working for performance in a strongly Christian cultural context, both felt a compelling

---

[34] Quoted by Hawes (1994: 64). Schmidgall 1990: 240–50, Hawes 1994: 47–68. Cf. also Hepokoski 1987: 181–3.

[35] For this interpretation cf. e.g. Schmidgall 1990: 247–9 and Hawes 1994: 61.

need to dramatize why Jago acts as he does. Similar motivations, I believe, led Britten, Forster and Crozier to put a self-revealing monologue into the mouth of Claggart in *Billy Budd* (another Christian allegory of the struggle between good and evil, this time for the soul of Captain Vere), when there is nothing of the kind in Melville's original novella.

Scene 2

JAGO

(Following Cassio with his eyes)

[1] Vanne; la tua meta già vedo.

Ti spinge il tuo dimone

E il tuo dimon son io,

E me trascina il mio,

Nel quale io credo inesorato Iddio.

2.3.2

[2] Credo in un Dio crudel

che m'ha creato simile a sè,

e che nell'ira io nomo.

2.3.3

[3] Dalla viltà d'un germe

o d'un atòmo vile son nato.

Son scelerato perchè son uomo,

E sento il fango originario in me.

Si! Quest'è la mia fè! 2.3.2

[4] Credo con fermo cuor,

siccome creda la vedovella al tempio

che il mal ch'io penso

e che da me procede

per mio destino adempio.

[5] Credo che il giusto e un istrion beffardo,

e nel viso e nel cuor,

che tutto è in lui bugiardo, lagrima, bacio,

sguardo, sacrificio ed onor.

[6] E credo l'uom gioco d'iniqua sorte

dal germa della culla

2.3.4 al verme dell'avel.

[7] 2.3.2 Vien dopo tanta irrision la Morte.

E poi? E poi?

La Morte è il Nulla,

[8] è vecchia fola il Ciel!

2.3.1

Go. I already see your fate.

Your demon drives you

and I am your demon,

and mine drives me

To what I believe in, an inexorable God.

I believe in a cruel God,

who created me in his likeness,

and whom in my anger I summon.

From the vileness of a germ

Or an atom I was born vile.

I am wicked because I am a man,

and I feel the primal filth in me.

Yes! This is my faith!

I believe with a firm heart,

like a young widow in church,

that the evil which I think

and which emanates from me

is accomplished by my destiny.

I believe that the honest man is a mocking actor,

in his face and his heart,

that all in him deceives – tears, kisses,

glances, sacrifice and honour.

And I believe that mankind is the toy of wicked fate

from the germ of the cradle

to the worm of the grave.

After all this mockery comes Death.

And then? And then?

Death is Nothingness,

Heaven is an old fable!

It has also been questioned whether this monologue is an aria. It certainly does have an introduction which might be called a recitative, followed by a change of key and time signature as the *Credo* itself begins; but it is not an aria in any traditional sense of the word. Two analysts have claimed that it is in ABA' form;[36] but this is fanciful. It is true that the opening motif of the monologue proper (**2.3.2**) returns at the start of section [7]; but it returns chromatically harmonized and relatively quiet – questioning and mysterious, as opposed to its fully diatonic *tutti* presentations at the start of section [2] and the end of section [3] in octaves and *ff tutta forza*; and none of the material in [7] and [8] which follows the transformed return of this theme bears any resemblance to the materials of [2] and [3]. It is better to accept that in Verdi's adventurous late *durchkomponiert* style, separated by sixteen years of operatic silence from his last grand opera (*Aida*), the conventions of the aria form are stretched in a way never before heard in the Italian tradition.

And for this monologue they need to be. Verdi hears and makes real through music the sudden mood-changes implicit in Boito's text. Jago moves rapidly and freely from key to key, constantly disrupting expectations, and the orchestra which expresses his feelings and motivation changes texture, dynamics and orchestration just as suddenly. For just one example consider the sixteen bars that follow the start of the 'aria' proper, C 7ff.[37] Four bars of octave declamation by the whole orchestra (**2.3.2**) *ff tutta forza* in F minor are followed by six bars of woodwind and viola trills, which lead Jago to E flat major. Trills are a characteristic of Jago's vocal line elsewhere in the opera; their being heard in the orchestra reveals, now that he is alone, his unstable, blasphemous and angry feelings. Then a furious *staccato* upward flourish in the piccolo and violins is followed by a semitone shift of key to E major for a new theme *forte, aspramente* ('harshly') in the strings (**2.3.3**), which expresses Jago's surge of emotion and dying fall as his thoughts turn to the insignificance of mankind.[38] Then comes an orchestral silence, and then a repeat of the opening four notes of the same theme, now *ppp*. The impact on late-nineteenth-century Italian audiences of these sudden and violent mood-shifts, which continue throughout the piece, cannot be underestimated; they were accustomed to a much more orderly and stable style of operatic music.[39]

The monologue is in eight sections; we must include the 'recitative' before the *Credo* proper because of the relentless repetitions of **2.3.1**. This motif was quiet and delicate in the first scene, and remained so until its *piano*

---

[36] Hepokoski 1987: 146 and Hawes 1994: 65.

[37] References to the score of this scene are by rehearsal letter and bar after it.

[38] Budden (1981: 358) imaginatively hears in this theme 'echoes of Liszt's and Boito's Mephistopheles, with its suggestion of an infernal dance'.

[39] Hepokoski 1987: 145–8, shows how Verdi's manipulation of tonality also creates uncertainty, frequently sending the listener's ears off on a false trail. But he is so concerned with showing how in his view the music echoes Jago's character as a trickster that he does not engage closely with how the music illuminates the evolution of Jago's emotions during the monologue. Nor does he have much to say about melody, texture and orchestration, which are just as important to the total effect of music as harmony.

appearance one bar before this *fff* breakout – another violent contrast of dynamic and orchestration. These repetitions propel Jago forward to the *tremolandi* under '[what I] believe in, an inexorable god' and so lead to **2.3.2**, which Hawes has called, cautiously, the 'Credo theme', and Hepokoski, more adventurously, 'pillars of negative affirmation'.[40]

2.3.1 (II.2 B12)

(Allegro assai moderato)

Tutti except flutes

2.3.2 (II.2 C7)

Allegro Sostenuto ♩=96

Tutti

Neither of these labels is adequate. Here as always in music drama we are not contemplating a static phenomenon, even an abstract one like those implied by these descriptions; music unfolds through time, and in operatic arias and monologues it illuminates the development of a single character's feelings. What we are hearing as the full orchestra declaims **2.3.2** (and what we should be seeing on stage) is the process of Jago building up his strength to the open affirmation of his creed.

In [2] and [3] this creed unfolds relentlessly. The violent changes of texture, dynamic and orchestration over the first few bars have already been discussed; once the whole of **2.3.3** has been introduced, the first five notes, repeated *ppp* and surrounded by silence, make us hear Jago contemplating the insignificance of man ('from the vileness of a germ/or an atom I was born vile'). Then his increasing animation is shown as this figure is transformed (now once again *forte aspramente*) by the addition of trills to the fourth note (and an oboe adding a touch of bitterness to the otherwise

---

[40] Hepokoski 1987: 146–7, Hawes 1994: 65.

2.3.3 (II.2 D2)

(Allegro sostenuto)

upper string texture). This shows Jago's thoughts growing into 'I am wicked because I am a man' (more violent *tremolandi* expressing his extreme emotion), and so to the return of **2.3.2** which closes the section; once again this motif shows Jago gathering all his emotional strength to declaim: 'Yes! This is my faith!'

For a second time this powerful motif is a springboard – this time for section [4], which begins over a throbbing triplet pulse in cornets and trumpets, with **2.3.3** repeated to show that once again Jago is confronting the insignificance of mankind; but the moods change so remarkably that he goes down from *f* to *ppp* for just a bar and a beat to contemplate the 'young widow in church' to whom he outrageously likens his constancy. From here on, the first four notes of **2.3.3** perform the same function as **2.3.1** in the 'recitative';[41] its repetitions show how his emotions are driving Jago forwards, to [5] ('I believe that the honest man...') where the voice floating through the *tremolandi* indicates the boldness and daring of Jago's belief.[42]

The *tremolandi* and his own vocal energy propel Jago inexorably onwards into [6]; yet again, a variant of **2.3.3** precipitates his thoughts. Now he reaches the last article of his belief; 'I believe that mankind is the toy of wicked fate ...'. Here there are more *tremolandi* under the declamation to illuminate his boldness, and then a sudden tone painting for 'the worm of the grave', showing how Jago imagines us fading away (**2.3.4**).

Now [7] Jago peers into the abyss. The powerful octaves which led him to begin the *Credo* (**2.2.2**) are transformed into a descending chromatic sequence, which makes us hear his deepening thoughts as he contemplates the absurdity of life and the inevitability of death.[43] Then silence and more mysterious chords (now *pp/ppp* for strings alone) surround his contemplation of eternity ('And then? And then?'). The hollow chords descend, dissolve into isolated cello *pizzicati*, and end in a very low C *pppp* on celli and basses, which as if grudgingly rises to D flat. Then there is a longer

---

[41] Note that both of these driving motifs consist of a semiquaver triplet followed by a longer note.
[42] Not, I think his contempt for the honest man (Hawes 1994: 66).
[43] Note the *ppp* timpani and bass drum blow on the last syllable of 'Morte'.

2.3.4 (II. 2 G 1)

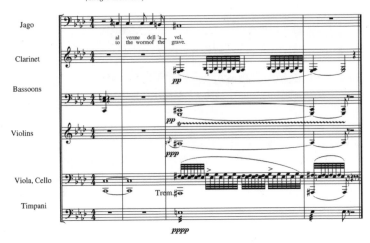

orchestral silence for 'Death is Nothingness'. Silence is of course the perfect realization of Jago's nihilistic thoughts.

And suddenly the orchestra erupts [8]. Here once again, and for the last time, Jago feels the driving emotion of **2.3.3**, which is accompanied by pounding triplets (as at E 1–4), leading to his final mocking blasphemy, 'Heaven is an old fable!' We hear *forte* triplets in the cornets and trumpets, **2.3.3** tossed out by the woodwind over upper string trills, and a *fortissimo tutti* climax for the last word of the piece, 'Ciel!'. The orchestra at first presents a thoroughly false assertion of D flat major, which suddenly loses four flats and becomes the 'true' key of F major just after Jago reaches his blazing top F on this word ('Ciel!'). This wrench is a most effective conclusion to an extraordinary few minutes of music theatre.[44]

*

---

[44] Hawes (1994: 66–7) rightly notes that 'the orchestra here makes Jago's true feelings – what dramatists call the "sub-text" audible'. But she is wrong to then try to claim that the orchestra 'has a further function here, to act as if it were Jago's Evil Genius (her capitals) – perhaps the Devil himself. 'There is something triumphant about [the final] outburst, as if the orchestra were waiting to see if he would deny this one remaining article of faith, and so deliver himself wholly into the hands of Satan.' Although orchestral music can do many things in opera (and they are one of the main subjects of this book) it cannot portray the emotions of someone who is not present – in this case, the Devil. Cf. **6.3** on a similar illegitimate interpretation (by Roger Nichols) of the sounding of the main theme associated with Golaud during the encounter with the departing ship in *Pelléas et Mélisande*.

Boito's Preface to Ricordi's *Disposizione scenica* for this opera warns that 'the crassest of mistakes, the most vulgar error into which any artist attempting this role [Jago] can possibly fall is to play him as a kind of human demon; to give him a Mephistophelean sneer and make him shoot Satanic glances everywhere ... Every word spoken by Jago is on the human level – a villainous humanity if you like, but still human. He should be young and well-favoured.'[45] Budden argues that 'in general he is required to make his effects less by his gestures, in which he should be sparing, but rather by the play of his features', and he cites this remark by the first interpreter, Maurel (who doubtless received much advice from the composer): 'There must be great reserve with gestures; without this the emotional effectiveness of the principal aspects of this superb page of lyric declamation will be reduced.'[46]

These remarks still hold good, even though after over a century of innovation it may well be that there is a rather greater place in a modern production for gesture than the creators and first interpreter of Jago imagined.[47] An exemplary performance of this scene is offered by Sergei Leiferkus in Elijah Moshinsky's 1992 production at Covent Garden.[48]

Leiferkus begins upstage, at the back of five wide shallow steps, after ushering Cassio off left into the upstage wings. The moment Cassio is gone, and before scene 2 begins, Leiferkus's Jago turns away from the literal Cassio and faces forward to address an imaginary one, commanding attention from the top step. This is good stagecraft, since to follow Boito's/ Verdi's direction here, *following Cassio with his eyes*, would lose the 'recitative' section into the wings, and the next six bars give Leiferkus time to come slowly forward. He finally reaches centre front stage during the orchestral outburst of **2.3.2** at the start of **[2]**, so that he is in the strongest possible position to declaim the opening of the *Credo* proper. As **[3]** begins, he complements the text and music with gestures, raising his left hand to his breast with clenched fist during the first occurrence of **2.3.3**, but gradually opening the fist and extending both his hands slightly on 'or of a vile atom...I am born'. Then he uses expressions; first a proud face with chin raised for the powerful return of **2.3.2** at 'Yes! That is my faith', then in **[4]** an ironic expression for 'like a young widow in church'; and once again he half raises his half-clenched left hand, to express the tension in the next line, 'that the evil which I think ...'. In **[5]** 'I believe that the honest man ...' is

---

[45] Quoted in Budden 1981: III 328.

[46] Quoted in Budden 1981: III 357.

[47] Boito's further instructions to 'ladies called upon to play Desdemona' and to prospective Otellos show that with all three principal roles he and Verdi were extremely afraid that melodramatic overacting would ruin their opera. Given the propensities of some late nineteenth-century Italian singers, these fears were probably justified.

[48] Conducted by Georg Solti, but unfortunately with two great singers who do not equal Leiferkus as actors in the other principal roles – Placido Domingo and Kiri te Kanawa.

accompanied by a very intense expression, followed by dismissive left-hand gestures during the list of emotions which the honest man fakes.

In [6], Leiferkus raises both his hands level with his shoulders to accompany the high notes in 'I believe man is the toy of wicked fate', brings them down and clenches his fists as the music drops in pitch and starts to ebb away ('[germ] of the cradle'), and then crosses left and collapses slightly, holding onto the edge of a nearby table for support – to show how Jago's thoughts are now weighing on him – as the orchestral *staccati* fade away to a low C in the violas and cellos at letter G, just before 'to the worm of the grave'. Then the tone-painting of 2.3.4 sees him raise his right hand slightly as he concludes the low A sharp semibreve on '[a-]vel'; Jago is ready and willing to pursue this thought further.

When [7] begins, with the mysterious *legato* chromatic transformation of 2.3.2, Moshinsky and Leiferkus rightly show Jago brooding on the mystery of death. Leiferkus peers forward, then closes his eyes, bows his head and raises his left hand to almost shield his face, to express on stage what the mysterious chords are saying about Jago's feelings. Then, as he sings 'After all this mockery comes Death', he gently lowers the hand, so that it is completely down after 'la Morte'. And the return of the chromatic *legato* chords, now *ppp*, is also heard as questioning. Since 'And then?' first interrupts and then halts the progress of the chords, this is clearly right. Once again Leiferkus peers into the space in front of him, with his head now forward and an almost anguished expression; and the lower part of his left arm is extended with fingers up and open, to reinforce the posture and facial expression with a questioning gesture. He shakes his head slightly after the first 'And then?', and after the second one intensifies the mood by half closing his eyes. But then he opens them again, suddenly, to an almost manic look on 'Nothing', which is sung with a violent change of tone, almost with contempt. Both the facial expression and the tone-quality on these two notes prepare for the final section [8], which begins immediately with an orchestral outburst, followed an agitated bar later by Jago's ultimate blasphemy. Leiferkus's expression changes instantly on the orchestral entry from manic to sane but fiercely intense, and as he hits the final sustained top F of 'Ciel!' (Heaven), he raises his hands up and out to the empty space above (where, for Jago, there is no Christian Heaven), and laughs violently, breaking this pose, the moment he finishes singing.[49]

Perhaps there are more gestures in this interpretation than Boito, Verdi or Maurel would have envisaged as appropriate. But Leiferkus utterly avoids the melodramatic would-be Mephistopheles against whom Boito warned; his Jago is indeed the evil, but definitely human (and handsome), character that Boito envisaged and Verdi set to music; and every gesture

---

[49] The laugh is traditional, though it is sanctified neither by the score nor by the *Disposizione scenica*; Budden 1981: III 359.

and facial expression – perhaps especially those in [6] and [7] – was finely thought through by the director and soloist, to complement and illuminate the text and the music.

Discussion question

Sergei Leiferkus makes considerable use of facial expressions and gestures in this performance. Analyse these; are all of them appropriate to the music and the text?

2.4 'One fine day…' (Puccini/Giacosa and Illica [after Belasco] *Madama Butterfly* Act II scene 1)

In Butterfly's memorable aria, set in the remote and plangent key of G flat major, Puccini demonstrates how clarity and simplicity can lead to greatness.

[1] **2.4.1** Un bel dì, vedremo levarsi un fil di fumo
sul'estremo confin del mare.
E poi la nave appare.
Poi la nave bianca entra nel porto,
romba il suo saluto.
Vedì? È venuto!
[2] Io non gli scendo incontro. Io no.
Mi metto là sul ciglio del colle e aspetto

gran tempo e non mi pesa la lunga attesa.

E uscito dalla folla cittadina un uomo,
Un piccolo punto s'avvia per la collina.
[3] Chi sarà? Chi sarà?
E come sarà giunto che dirà?
Chiamerà 'Butterfly' dalla lontana.
Io senza dar risposta me ne starò nascosta
2.4.2 un po' per celia, e un po' per non morire
al primo incontro, ed egli alquanto in
pena chiamerà;
'Piccina mogliettina, olezzo di verbena',
i nomi che mi dava al suo venire.
[4] **2.4.3** Tutto questo avverà, te lo prometto.
Tienti la tua paura, io con sicura
fede l'aspetto.

One fine day, we'll see a thread of smoke
rising on the far edge of the sea.
And then the ship appears.
Then the white ship enters the harbour,
thunders its greeting.
You see? He has come!
I don't go to meet him. Not I.
I put myself there on the edge of the hill
        and wait
for a long time, and the long wait
        does not weigh on me.

And from the city crowd a man has come out,
a little speck sets out up the hill.
Who will it be? Who will it be?
And when he's come, what will he say?
He'll call 'Butterfly' from the distance.
Without replying I'll hide myself
a bit to tease him, and a bit so as not to die
at our first meeting, and he, worrying
a bit, will call:
'Dearest little wife, perfume of verbena',
the names he gave me on his arrival.
All of this will happen, I promise you.
Hold back your fear, I with firm faith
await him.

A simple but moving melody is introduced right at the start (**2.4.1**). Here the melody sounds tender and visionary;[50] but at the two climaxes of the aria it will be shown to have awesome power. The first occurs when Butterfly imagines Pinkerton calling her name from afar: 'I won't answer and I'll hide myself, / a bit to tease him, and a bit **so as not to die / from our first meeting...**' (**2.4.2**).

Here not quite all of the orchestra is playing (no trombones, harps or double basses), and the dynamic is only *fortissimo*; but at the second and final climax of the aria, as Butterfly reaches her last words, the same melody is declaimed *fff* by the full orchestra. The build-up consists of six bars over which *tremolo* violins and violas crescendo under Butterfly's declaration of faith; and then on Butterfly's last two words (*l'aspetto*, 'I await him'), there is a surging run in the violins and the singer leaps a fifth to a top B flat, the tempo broadening to *Largamente* (**2.4.3**).

The aria's narrative is structured around Butterfly's determination to persuade Suzuki of the reality of her vision – and her almost equal determination to be coy with Pinkerton, and not go to him at once when he comes back to Japan. So gentle play is made with the opening motif during the first phase of the aria [1]. In this section the orchestra rouses briefly and pictorially for *romba il suo salute*, '[the ship] thunders its greeting', and this is followed by two *con passione* bars for the key point of the text, *Vedi? È venuto!* ('You see? He has come!'). After that, [2] follows, in which Butterfly is determined not to go to meet Pinkerton, and imagines herself waiting up on the hill. Puccini accompanies this with delicate sustained woodwind chords, only syncopating the rhythm and slightly increasing the intensity as Butterfly imagines 'a man, a little speck' emerging from the crowded city and climbing the hill towards her. The music remains slow and gentle as Pinkerton is seen calling from the distance – but suddenly rouses itself, *con molto passione,* at **2.4.2**. This is one of those fascinating moments where opera truly diverges from spoken drama, since almost no straight actress would choose to change from gentle diction to grand declamation for 'so as not to *die* at the first meeting ...'. Where understatement would be far more effective in the spoken theatre, the 'great passion' with which Puccini's Butterfly declaims *morire, con forza* and on the same high tonic G flat with which she began the aria, anticipates the ritual suicide with which, after Pinkerton's betrayal, she ends the opera.

The reuse of **2.4.1** from here to the end of the aria unleashes all the emotion that her initial vision contained within itself; Puccini reveals that behind the delicate vision of a distant ship with which the aria began lies the turbulent passion which racks this young woman. So there are now a few

---

[50] Puccini requires the accompanying instruments – a solo violin and a clarinet – to play *pianissimo, as if from the distance,* and the underlying tremolo violins to play like a distant murmur.

bars in which the melody drops delicately, from *p* to *pp* in the orchestra, and down from E flat to D flat, as she completes her vision of the returning Pinkerton. But as soon as this has happened, just before Butterfly turns to address Suzuki directly ('all of this will happen, I promise you'), the orchestra begins its final *crescendo* (**2.4.3**).[51] Tension is whipped up by a horn/bassoon fanfare in bar 10 under *prometto*; from this point on the voice is at the top of and above the stave; and the next three bars are a very powerful *crescendo* in voice and orchestra to the climactic *fff* G flat major tonic chord, spanning the orchestra from heights to depths, and with Butterfly alone on a high B flat. After which the melody fades away in the orchestra over eight bars to silence.

*

---

[51] Notice 'just before'; Puccini uses the orchestra (to be precise, the violin/viola *tremolandi*) to portray how the final thought, Butterfly's declaration of faith to Suzuki, enters her mind a bar before she enunciates it with her voice.

2.4.2 (2.14.9)

🖱 2 4 One fine day (Barker)

The key to interpreting this aria on stage is the tension between the two women, which is Butterfly's motivation for singing it. Suzuki is so doubtful whether Pinkerton will return that, earlier in the scene, Butterfly has physically attacked her and threatened her with death. In her last words before the aria begins Butterfly has bullied Suzuki into tearfully agreeing that he will come back, but Suzuki's doubts have not eased. So a good production of the aria must follow Puccini's direction to the singer of the title role, that she must *act the scene as though it were really happening*. It must also stage carefully Suzuki's reactions to this attempt to persuade her – a classic example of how even a silent witness to a monologue must keep focus and act at all times.

Moffatt Oxenbould's production for Opera Australia, first seen in 1997 with Cheryl Barker in the title role and Ingrid Silveus as Suzuki, was excellent in both these respects. The exigencies of video production mean that for much of the later part of the aria the camera concentrates on Barker's Butterfly and we do not see Silveus, whose focused responses

2.4.3 (2.15. 8)

to Barker were a joy to watch in the theatre; but enough of Silveus's work is visible at the start to establish Suzuki's essential role as a doubting confidante. And the great strength of this production is that throughout the aria Barker makes use of oriental gestures and postures to illuminate the evolution of Butterfly's emotions.

At the start of the aria, the women are kneeling side by side, and Butterfly puts her right arm round Suzuki's shoulders. Silveus looks disbelieving, but at 'a thread of smoke on the far horizon of the sea', as Barker raises a hand towards the vision she is seeing and looks outward into the audience, Silveus responds by looking out, as if trying to see it too – but then sinks her head in despair at 'and then a ship appears'. Only after that, at '[the white ship] enters the port' does she raise her head again, peering out as if trying to believe. Shortly after this, Barker raises the tension, putting her left hand excitedly very close to Suzuki's shoulder at 'You see? He has come!'

In section [2] the acting rightly becomes more animated. At 'I don't go to meet him', Barker withdraws her hand from Silveus and gives a little shake of her head, then smiles confidingly as she approaches 'Not I!' She rises to her feet for the next phase of the narrative, crossing left, away from Suzuki, so that she can take up a stylized, oriental posture of distancing herself from Pinkerton on 'and wait, wait for a long time' – only relaxing her hands at 'from out of the crowded city'. A brief gesture of two fingers close together illustrates 'a little speck'.

For [3], once again a hand extended forward continues to show how Butterfly sees intently what her imagination is conjuring, willing Suzuki to believe it. Then Barker mimes distancing herself from Pinkerton on 'without replying', smiles behind a coy hand on 'a bit to tease him', and of course extends her hands right out on the first climax at 'so as not to die / at our first meeting'. In the spirit of Puccini's overall direction for the aria, she then mimes calling out as she narrates Pinkerton's call to her, and as the second climax approaches Barker turns firmly to address her Suzuki on 'Banish your fears' – but, having made this contact, she delivers the actual climax on *l'aspetto* directly to the audience, with her hands fully outstretched. Oxenbould then overrides the original stage direction. Butterfly stands alone, an isolated figure, as her vision ebbs away in the orchestral music and Barker slowly lowers her hands to her sides. Only when the music has stopped does Silveus (still kneeling) look up at her Butterfly as if she now almost believes in the vision. That is arguably a better representation of the relationship between the two women at the end of this aria than Puccini's original conception that that the two women should *embrace emotionally* after Butterfly has finished singing.[52]

This analysis demonstrates that Puccini both can and should receive as much sensitive response onstage to the changing emotions expressed by his music as other composers who have been held in higher regard as music-dramatists – for example Wagner, Janáček and Berg. Puccini is very much more than a composer of affecting lyric melodies and melodramatic climaxes, and his operas need not just star voices but gifted singing actors. They suffered for far too long from the 'stand and deliver' tradition, simply because this is possible (though highly undesirable) in his operas, whereas it is almost impossible when staging the mature work of the three northern European masters named above.

---

[52] Despite stellar casting (Mirella Freni with Christa Ludwig), Jean–Pierre Ponelle's film shows far less insight into the music drama of this aria than the Australian production. There is far less facial expression and gesture, and as a result the staging does not illuminate the nuances of the music sufficiently.

Discussion questions

- How effective do you think Cheryl Barker's stylized, quasi-Japanese movements and gestures are?
- Discuss how Barker works to make her Suzuki believe in her vision of Pinkerton's return.

2.5 Kát'a's ecstasy (Janáček after Ostrovsky *Kát'a Kabanová*, Act I scene 2)

✒ 2 5 Kát'a's ecstasy (Gustafson)

In this scene Kát'a is alone with Varvara, her friend and confidante. Janáček's stage direction for her first words implies that she has been working at embroidery as the curtain rises. But Nikolaus Lehnhoff, in his 1988 production at Glyndebourne, which was the first that I know of to paint this opera in expressionist colours, rightly saw that the opera centres on the contrast between a repressive indoors and a liberating outdoors. So Nancy Gustafson as Kát'a opens the scene alone, with a blue shawl wrapped around her and standing in the doorway between the oppressive, predominantly dark red and hideously patterned walls of the room and the seductive blue sky of the outdoor world, which can be glimpsed through the door.[53] The monologue which she is about to deliver is crucial to the understanding of the rest of the opera.

In Act I scene 1 we have seen Kát'a coming home from church, submissive to the repressive power of her mother-in-law – but now she is alone with someone she trusts completely, and is therefore free to speak; this is the audience's one chance to learn her inner thoughts and feelings before the action develops irrevocably in the second part of this second scene. Progressive costume change for Kát'a is a central part of Lehnhoff's production concept (see **7.4**). Now she has taken off the black coat which she was obliged to wear to go to church; she is wearing a radiant white dress, symbolizing her innocence and goodness.

Lehnhoff decided that he needed levels for an effective staging of the first part of the scene. And he obtained them by presetting the luggage, which in the opera's original stage directions is brought in later by two servants. This luggage belongs to Kát'a's husband Tichon, whom she will shortly try to persuade not to go away on business, in a confrontation (**4.2**) which leads to the climax of the Act. A large trunk gives Kát'a a

---

[53] The remarkable set and costume designs were by Tobias Hoheisel.

heightened space to stand on for the more ecstatic parts of her monologue; and a smaller suitcase provides something for Varvara to sit or lean on as she is listening.

The musical setting of this monologue divides it into ten sections; each of them – in keeping with Janáček's normal custom – has its own new thematic material.[54]

1.2 *(a room in the Kabanovs' house)*

2.5.1

KÁT'A *(laying her embroidery aside)*

[1] Viš, co mi napadlo?	Do you know what I'm thinking?
VARVARA	
Co?	What?
KÁT'A	
Proč lidé nelětaji.	Why people can't fly.
VARVARA	
Nechápu, co praviš!	I don't know what you mean!
KÁT'A	
Povidám, proč lidé nelětaji,	I was saying, why can't people fly,
tak jako ptáci nelětaji?	fly just like birds?
Víš, zdává se mi někdy, že jsem pták.	You know, sometimes I imagine I'm a bird.
tak tě to láká vzlétnout. Chci to zkusit!	What fun to soar up high. I want to do it!
(makes flying gestures)	
VARVARA	
Co vyvádíš?	You're crazy!
KÁT'A	
Jaká jsem bývala rozpustila!	I used to be a wild girl!
2.5.2 A u vás jsem docela, uvadla.	But here I've pined away.
VARVARA	
[2] Mysliš, že toho nevidím?	Do you think I didn't know?
KÁT'A	
Ach, byla jsem zcela jinši!	Oh, I was quite different then!
Žila jsem, po ničem netoužic,	I lived without a care,
jako ptáče na svobodě! 2.5.1	free as a bird!
(smiling)	
Maminka duše ve mně netušila,	Mother didn't know what was in my heart,
strojila mne jak panenku!	dressed me up like a little doll!
[3]	
Viš, jake sem žila na svobodna?	Do you know how I lived when I was free?

---

[54] This is not of course to say that Janáček never uses recurrent motifs, only that they are deployed much less frequently in his operas than they are in those of, for example, his contemporary Richard Strauss. In this opera, both the eight grim timpani blows, which are first heard early in the prelude (see **4.2**), and the music of the forces of nature in Act III (see **7.4**) are heard repeatedly at crucial moments.

Hned ti to povím.
Vsávala jsem časně, byvoli to v létě,
vyšla jsem ke studánce a umyla se.
Pak přinesu si vodicky,
a všechny, všechny květinky v dome zaleju.

VARVARA
U nás to zrovna tak!

KÁŤA
Potom jsem šla do kostela.
Já k smrti ráda chodila do kostela.
[4]
2.5.3
Bývalo mi, jak bych stoupala do ráje.
Nikoko nevidím, neslyším, času nevnímám,
ani když bohoslužby konce.
[5]
Maminka řikávala, 2.5.4
že na mne všichni hleděli,
co se to se mnou děje!
[6]
A viš, za slunečniho dne, 2.5.5
když s kopule padal takový světelný proud,
a v něm valil se dým jako oblaka,
a stávalo se mi, že jsem v tomto sloupu
vídala lítat anděly,
a zpívat.
[7] *(calms down)*
2.5.6 A já padnu na kolena
a pláču;
a já sama nevim, proč modlim se a pláču.
[8]
Tak mě našli.
2.5.7 A jaké sny se mi zdávaly, jaké sny!
Jak bych viděla zlaté, vysoké chrámy,
a hory a stromy,
a bylo mi, jak bych létala, vysoko létala,
a všude zpivaji hlasy neviditelné...

VARVARA
Kátŏ, co je s tebou?

KÁŤA *(increasingly agitated)*
... a cypreše voní!

VARVARA
Co je s tebou?

KÁŤA *(grasps Varvara's hand: anxiously)*
Nějaký hřich na mne jde!

Well, I will tell you.
I got up early, and if it was summer
I'd go out to the well and wash myself.
Then I'd bring water,
and water all, all the flowers in the house.

You do that here too!

Then I'd go to church.
I could die of happiness going to church.

I felt as if I were rising to paradise.
I saw and heard no one, never knew the time,
not even when the service was ended.

Mummy used to say,
that everyone looked at me,
wondering what was wrong with me!

And then, on a sunny day,
when the light streamed down from the dome,
and the incense floated in it like mist,
it seemed to me that in that pillar of light
I could see angels flying
and singing.

And I fell on my knees
and cried;
And I never knew myself why I prayed and cried.

That's how they'd find me.
And what visions I saw, what visions!
I would see great golden cathedrals
and mountains and trees,
and it was as if I was flying, flying high,
and all around invisible choirs singing...

Kát'a, what's wrong with you?

... and the smell of cypress trees!

What's wrong with you?

A dreadful sin is coming to me!

Jako bych stála nad propastí ...	As if I were standing over an abyss ...
VARVARA	
Co je s tebou děje?	What's wrong with you?
KÁŤA	
Někdo mi do ní strkal,	Someone's pushing me in,
a já nemám za co se chytit.	and I've nothing to catch hold of.
VARVARA *(frightened)*	
Jsi zdráva?	Are you well?
[9]	
KÁŤA	
Zdrava ...	Well ...
Raději bych byla nemocna.	I wish I were ill.
2.5.8 Taková divná touha do hlavy mi leze	Such strange longing creeps into my head
a nikam **2.5.9** nemohu jí uniknout.	and I can't escape from it anywhere.
Začnu přemýšlet	I start to think,
a nemohu myšlenky sebrat.	but I can't put thoughts together.
Jazykem přemílám slova,	I repeat words with my tongue,
ale na mysli tane něco jiného.	but something different rises in my thoughts.
Jako by mi d'ábel našeptával	It's as if a devil were speaking to me
a samé takové nedobré věci	and whispered such terrible things
až je mi hanba před sebou samotnu!	that I am ashamed of myself!
A v noci ...	And at night ...
[10]	
VARVARA	
Co se ti zdava?	What do you dream about?
KÁŤA	
Varjo! Nemohu spat.	Varvara, I cannot sleep.
Pořad mně zní v uchu takové nešeptávání;	I always hear this whispering in my ear
kdosi se mnou tak laskavě mluvi,	someone speaks to me so lovingly,
jak když holub vrká,	as if a dove were cooing,
jak by mne objimal tak vřele, tak vřele,	as if he held me so warmly, so warmly,
horoucně, jak by mne někam vedle a ...	ardently, as if he leads me somewhere and ...
VARVARA *(quickly)*	
Nu a?	Yes, and?
KÁŤA	
A já jdu, a jdu za ním!	And I go, I go with him!

The first section is animated by Janáček's simple yet utterly effective, beautiful evocation of the escape created by flying like a bird (**2.5.1**).

As this sequence in a bright E major reaches its climax at 'sometimes I dream I am a bird. How I'd love to fly! I want to do it!' Gustafson climbs up on the trunk, waving her shawl above her head, at the full extent of her arms. But then Kát'a's mood changes, and she sighs; 'here I've pined away'. Just before these words, Gustafson jumps down and sits on the floor to create a complete contrast for this line of text. Fragments of the flying motif

persist – her thoughts are still about liberation – under her sad vocal line in
E flat minor (**2.5.2**).

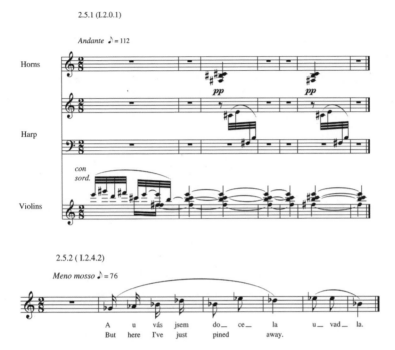

2.5.1 (I.2.0.1)

2.5.2 (I.2.4.2)

Gustafson lowers her face towards the ground, and then raises her head for
[2], when the orchestral sound warms and the birdsong persists (naturally
enough, given the text) on 'I was quite different before, lived without a care,
like a bird at liberty' (on the last five words [four in the original Czech] the
music returns to E major, I.2.5). During the next lines, 'Mother didn't know
what was in my heart, dressed me up like a little doll' she rises gracefully to
her feet, wraps the shawl around her like a dress, and bows gracefully like
a doll, smiling. This is an excellent use of hand props to illuminate the text.

Now a new mood begins. Janáček structures the next sections [3–7]
with a strong echo of the traditional recitative and aria form; realizing that
section [3] is the beginning of a story, Lehnhoff has Gustafson as Kát'a sit
on the trunk and gesture to Varvara to kneel in front of her. She then relaxes
her posture and begins the story – with her legs apart to demonstrate the
freedom in her childhood which she is describing. Warm sustained chords
under Kát'a's opening words represent the simplicity, naturalness and
goodness of her younger self, and her love of nature; and then, after 'I could
die of happiness, going to church' (I.2.7) this 'recitative' blossoms into an
'aria' (sections [4]ff.), beginning with a triplet accompaniment in the flutes
to a moving solo horn melody (**2.5.3**). The mood intensifies at the start of
section [5], which Janáček marks *in ever greater ecstasy*; a clarinet solo

under the triplets (**2.5.4**) shows the increasing power of Kát'a's vision, as
the music returns to a bright sharp key, this time A major.

2.5.3 (I.2.7.4)

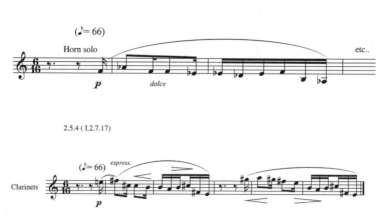

Now Kát'a describes her experiences in church. For this section [6] Janáček
deploys one of his characteristic devices – a considerable separation between
top and bottom instruments; he symbolizes in music the perilousness of
Kát'a's position, as she remembers the sun pouring into the incense-filled
church and her soul rising in response. The triplets from [5] are heard again
as a delicate tracery high in the violins; far below them is a deep pedal chord,
and, in the middle, a rising figuration in celesta and harp (**2.5.5**) is soon
heard, which builds rapidly towards a powerful climax as she describes how
she saw angels flying and then, as the climax is reached (I.2.8.17–18), singing.

2.5.5 (I.2.8.8)

During this music, Gustafson first kneels up on the trunk, with her hands
on her thighs, then with her eyes growing wider gradually rises, until at
the climax ('and singing') she stands erect to her full height, legs apart and
arms spread wide above her; in the moments that she recalls here, she was
free and reaching for the heavens. In this way Lehnhoff matches with the
singer's body the rise of the music to ever-greater ecstasy.

The tempo changes to *meno mosso* as Kát'a *calms down* (Janáček's stage
direction) [7]. The climax is followed by a change of mood; a plaintive

violin solo conveys Kát'a's unexpected inner sadness: 'And I fell on my knees and cried; and I never knew myself why I prayed and cried'. (**2.5.6**)

2.5.6 (I.2.9.1)

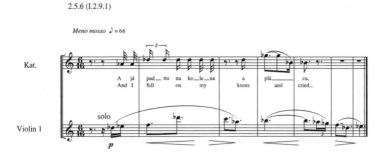

Once again Lehnhoff matches the physicalization to the trajectory of the music, which dies down *diminuendo* and *ritardando* to a *fermata* after these words. Gustafson first lowers her arms to hold her hands out in wonderment at her own state, then kneels with her hands still extended in front of her, and finally, suddenly drops her head and arms to crouch right down. Louise Winter as Varvara then gently pats her back.

Section [8] begins as Kát'a describes her visions – lofty golden cathedrals, and mountains and forests – and once again she imagines herself flying. For this section Janáček creates a simple motif of a major second leap up and then fall (**2.5.7**).

2.5.7 (I.2.10.1)

Once again the flying is symbolized by a new, perilous variant of **2.5.1** which surges along, high in the violins, and is left high, and supported only by violas, when (stage direction *anxiously*) her visions suddenly turn from the heights of flying to the depths of the abyss of sin.

Note that the *music* does not fall to the depths here; even the celli and basses, when they take over the supporting role as the violas join the violins in the hysteria (1.2.12), are on a high D. Janáček portrays Kát'a's perilous position, confronting the abyss, by showing her suspended above it, until Varvara's repeated attempts to bring her back to awareness of her surroundings finally register. The tumult is silent, the tempo slows, and now [9] Kát'a describes her desires, accompanied by an intimate theme in cor anglais and violins (2.5.8), whose warm, gradually rising pattern matches the course of the feelings which are gently but inexorably being aroused within her. In what follows, a little motif in the horns (2.5.9) intrudes to express her confusion – but, even when she sings 'it's as if the devil were whispering [to me]', the cor anglais theme and languorous mood persist, since the devil's temptation is seductive.

2.5.8 (I.2.12.13)

2.5.9 (I.2.12.19)

Then, [10] when she goes on to describe what happens when she lies awake at night, the mood remains sensual until just before the climax, as she describes seeing a man embracing her, calling her, 'and I go, I go with him!'

Lehnhoff decided that this new phase of the monologue [8–10], in which Kát'a's visions are impelling her, demanded a greater physicality than the gentler 'I wish I could fly like a bird', and description of her ecstasy in church, in [1–7]. Continuing to use the raised level of the top of the trunk would not suffice to match this much more intense and passionate music. So, on 'I felt as if I were flying, soaring and flying', Gustafson rushes forward to the front left corner of the stage, then raises her hands up, clasped on the back of her head; and at 'I am falling into some sin', Lehnhoff overrode Janáček's original stage direction that she is *grasping Varvara's hand*: his Kát'a is now well away from Varvara, who looks on in horror and retreats upstage as Gustafson gestures violently, stretching out her left arm and pointing out in front of her. Louise Winter as Varvara comes forward and re-engages with Kát'a (Gustafson is now looking terrified) only when we reach her own lines: 'What's happening to you? Are you all right?'

As we enter section [9] and the tension in the orchestra at last relaxes, Gustafson moves away from Winter, and on 'such strange longing creeps into my head', she bends forward, clasping first her womb and then her breasts, to bring out the sexuality of the desires which she is now describing. In the next few lines of text, Lehnhoff expresses Kát'a's confusion and feelings of weakness by having her lean against the wall for support, but, when Varvara prompts Kát'a to describe her sleepless nights, Gustafson stands with her hands behind her on the wall, staring forward intensely on 'as if a devil were speaking to me' and 'whispered such terrible things'. After Varvara's next question, Gustafson first smiles as she describes the whispering in her ear, then brings her hands up close to her upper body as she sings of how it speaks to her with a voice like a dove. But on the last three lines of the monologue, as the music becomes much more intense, she pulls Varvara upstage towards the door with both hands, then stands in the doorway, clasping the frame, and finally on 'and I go, I go with him' acts this out by actually leaving through it! (After the general pause and *fermata*, as in Janáček's stage direction Kát'a *gradually returns to her senses*, Gustafson of course re-enters the playing space to address Varvara once more.)

So concludes a powerful and imaginative staging, which responds to every one of the shifting moods of the music. That music in its turn dramatizes the feelings and thoughts that lie behind each of Kát'a's emotions as they change and develop during the course of the monologue.

Janáček's opera scores move freely, and rapidly, between heights and depths, fast and slow music, full orchestral sound and very sparse passages; rhythm changes subtly and frequently, and he often modulates abruptly between unrelated keys. All of these features of his music are used to express very quick changes of mood and tone, which in my view reflect not only his musical personality but also the immense changes which happened to the pace and intensity of European life in the early modernist period. (Cf. Berg's contemporary opera *Wozzeck*, and contrast the measured pace and often gradual changes of mood in Wagner.)

The distinguished British director David Pountney once proposed that a director of *Kát'a Kabanová* should perhaps not 'echo the music and create a stage picture which brings the psychological elements to the fore'. He argued instead: 'the work could be most interestingly interpreted along detailed naturalistic lines – in the style of an Ibsen play, for instance. A meticulously detailed and restrained bourgeois setting could create a startling tension with the music; absolute Victorian probity and order on the stage, whilst the music betrays the psychological turmoil underneath.'[55] But it is notable that he did not pursue this idea in either of his own two productions;[56] in both of them there were some realistic period set items (heavy wooden tables, samovars etc. in the indoor scenes), but the designers (Maria Bjørnson and Roger Butlin, respectively) both hung an abstract swirl above the playing area, 'to suggest both the omnipresent river and Munch-like eddies of emotion',[57] presumably with the director's full approval.

---

[55] Pountney 1982: 185 and 186.
[56] For Scottish and Welsh National Operas (co-production) in 1979, and for The Australian Opera in 1980.
[57] Caption for a plate of the Glasgow production at Pountney 1982: 187.

Although both of Pountney's productions had great merits, they were in my view too rigid and static during crucial scenes to match the expressionist intensity and the frequently shifting moods of Janáček's music and his dramaturgy. This composer demands much more physicality, in particular from the singer playing the title role, than Pountney envisaged. Lehnhoff met this challenge, also abandoning the dark Russian realist nineteenth-century gloom in which all too many previous productions of this opera were mired. That 'look' is still maintained in Russian productions of Ostrovsky's original play, but it does not respond adequately to Janáček's setting. There is (or should be) no going back after Lehnhoff's commanding production and Gustafson's performance, which in my view was the first to respond fully to the nature of Janáček's score and his particular synthesis between music and drama.[58]

Discussion questions

- Discuss Lehnhoff's use of space – heights and depths, downstage and upstage – in this scene.
- Analyse Gustaffson's use of her body and her facial expression during the scene. Do you think it does justice to the music and the text?

2.6 *Now the great Bear* ... (Britten/Slater *Peter Grimes*, Act I scene 2)[59]

This short AA[1]BA[2] aria in E major (only twenty-two bars, although mostly *adagio*) is a crucial stage in the development of the audience's under-standing of the title figure. It is Peter Grimes' entrance-aria in I.2, and it establishes his character as a visionary and a mystic in advance of, and to counterbalance, the cruelty to Ellen which he displays in II.1 (see 4.4), and to the boy John in II.2. The onstage audience in the pub responds with incomprehension ('he's mad or drunk') and the Methodist preacher, Bob

---

[58] For discussion of further scenes from this production see 4.2 and 7.3 below.

Do not waste your time (as I have) in viewing the concept production by Christoph Martaler (Salzburg Festival, 1998), which appears to be set in a Soviet-era housing block (!). In this scene the Varvara looks bored, detached and indifferent throughout the monologue, and as it proceeds there are all sorts of distractions, created by other people moving around, (none of them, of course, envisaged in Janáček's *mise-en-scène*) – which pull focus from Kát'a and her predicament. Presumably the director intended this *Verfremdung* (estrangement of the audience); but it is utterly at odds with Janáček's passionately involved music for his heroine.

[59] For a confrontation from this opera see 4.4. For a monologue from this opera see 7.5.

Boles, actually attempts to attack Peter physically; but Britten's music for the aria encourages the opera's audience to make a far more sympathetic evaluation.

A 2.6.1 Now the Great Bear and Pleiades where earth moves
Are drawing up the clouds of human grief
2.6.2 Breathing solemnity in the deep night.

A¹ Who can decipher in storm or starlight
The written character of a friendly fate
As the sky turns, the world for us to change?

B But if the horoscope's bewildering
Like a flashing turmoil of a shoal of herring
A² Who, who, who, who, who can turn skies back and begin again?

We shall compare two excellent performances, by John Vickers directed by Elijah Moshinsky at Covent Garden, and by Philip Langridge directed by Tim Albery for ENO.

The A section is sung over a simple but moving orchestral melody, *pp dolce* (**2.6.1**), which is gently passed in a canon from lower to upper strings during the first two lines of text, after which the singer floats the third line in between the notes of a mystical chord stretching over more than six octaves (**2.6.2**),[60] responding to the fact that the text turns there from description to contemplation.

✐ 2 6 Great Bear (Vickers)

✐ 2 6 Great Bear (Langridge)

Both Vickers and Langridge deliver the A section facing forward, peering into space and ignoring the villagers; but Langridge, as Peter, stands at the top of a steep but short flight of stairs which descend, in Hildegard Bechtler's set design for Albery, from the door into the bar of the Boar Inn, so that his visionary Grimes has the advantage of being able to literally overlook the onlookers; Vickers compensates for his position on a level with the others by opening his hands wide apart in a gesture of contemplation as the aria begins.[61] He also has more movement than Langridge (who remains virtually static) in the A¹ section; Vickers lowers his head in

---

[60] The chord 'represents the star-scape which has transfixed Grimes and indicates the expanse of his vision' according to Seymour (2004: 63).

[61] When he did this, in his oilskins, Vickers' already towering physical presence was enhanced so that he dominated the scene.

the bar of vocal rest as the lower strings re-introduce **2.6.1**, then raises it again to face out again as he begins the second stanza, arms still out, hands apart and now shaking to show the intense emotion in the music (which is not belied by the *pp* dynamic); as the chord-cluster returns for 'As the sky turns', he moves his head from side to side, wracked by his emotion, only relaxing his tense facial expression on the last part of the line, 'the world for us to change' – a goal which this interpretation implies is unachievable.

2.6.1-2 (I.2.76.1)

Both interpreters violently change their demeanour for the five bars of *molto animato* turbulence which comprise the B section. Here Langridge is the more powerful, shaking his head and holding it with his hand as the section opens, then making wild gestures in keeping with the music on 'like a flashing turmoil', and shaking his head again on the penultimate instrumental bar with its four dissonant, descending triplet flourishes. Vickers lowers his head as the first orchestral flourishes of the section are played, makes a violent movement on 'bewildering', and then stands with body erect and a manic expression as the orchestra takes over the turbulence from the voice. This is slightly less effective than Langridge's wild gestures, which prefigure the madness into which Peter descends later in the opera (see my analysis of his interpretation of Peter's demented monologue in the penultimate scene, 6.5). But Vickers is most effective in the final section of the aria; as 2.6.1 returns, now under a very high tonic inverted pedal in the first violins, and in this reprise descending from the second violins to the celli and basses, Langridge conveys all the anguish by vocal tone and facial expression alone. He does this extremely powerfully, but Moshinsky and Vickers, by using the singing actor's body as well, achieve more pathos and therefore a more sympathetic Peter for the audience. Vickers relaxes his posture on the first 'who', but brings his hands together on the third and wrings them in anguish on the fourth and fifth reiterations; then, in a marvellous illumination of the fatalistic question which sums up his life (he has already witnessed the death of one boy apprentice owing to his megalomania, and at the end of Act II a second one will die), he opens his hands wide on '[who] can turn skies back...', extends them to the audience on the last, sustained note of 'back', and ends the aria with head bowed, gradually lowering his hands in despair during the last bar. This performance fully embodies Hans Keller's description of the last stanza: 'he [Peter] seems to divine the inescapable tragedy of his character'.[62]

Discussion question

Body language is central in different ways to both Vickers' and Langridge's performances of this aria. Which do you think is more effective, and why?

2.7 Conclusion

The first aim of this chapter has been to show how in arias and monologues by a diverse range of master-composers the orchestral music illuminates in detail the evolution of the feelings of the principal character. It portrays the unfolding emotions which motivate the thoughts that the character is expressing through the text and vocal line. Then I hope to have shown, by detailed consideration of exemplary productions, that for a good performance the director and singing actor must understand and respond to the text, the vocal line and the instrumental music. Between them they must create expressions, postures and gestures which complement the music, and illuminate in

---

[62] Keller in Brett (ed.) 1983: 111.

their turn, through the medium of stage action, what the character is feeling at each significant moment, as expressed in the text and the music.

In the *Figaro* recitative and aria, both Olivier Mille and Peter Sellars realize that the contrasting successive emotions through which Figaro journeys demand a detailed response in the acting; and both directors also see that the aria needs props to make Figaro's anger with the Count, and his determination to exact revenge, visually effective in production.

Wotan's monologue in *Die Walküre* II.2 demands an environment in which his colloquy with a part of himself, his 'will' Brünnhilde, can be staged in such a way as to bring out its full dramatic complexity. Chéreau and his designer Richard Peduzzi achieved this by the drastic step of relocating the action, and this brought them immense rewards. There is consummate acting from Gwyneth Jones and Donald McIntyre, and that is matched by a highly effective use of props to illuminate the stages through which Wotan passes, from his initial brooding through to the bitter act of consigning of the world to Hagen, and then to his reaction when Brünnhilde rebels. No other staging recorded so far comes close to this in its deep response to Wagner's text and music.

Verdi's *Credo* is an exceptionally dynamic *scena*, and it requires the performer to respond in detail to the libretto, and to the twists and turns of Verdi's constantly surprising setting. Directed by Elijah Moshinsky, Sergei Leiferkus achieves this most effectively.

In 'One fine day ...' Puccini demanded that the singer should *act the scene as though it was really happening*. A narrative such as this requires a visionary response in which the performer embodies at each stage how Butterfly thinks she would respond if and when Pinkerton actually returned. This Cheryl Barker for the most part achieves, under the direction of Moffat Oxenbould.

Kát'a's monologue demands scrupulous attention to the close-knit details of Janáček's musical illumination of the text. Nikolaus Lehnhoff responds closely to the changing moods of the music, and brilliantly uses a single prop, a pair of suitcases, to give the scene the levels which are needed to chart the heights of Kát'a's ecstasy and the depths of her subsequent guilt. He exploits the dynamics of the stage set and Nancy Gustafson's great facial and bodily expressivity to achieve the intensity which the music demands.

'Now the Great Bear ...' may be a short aria, but it is of crucial importance in the opera, with its insight into the mystical side of Peter Grimes. Its sharply delineated ABA structure demands a physical realization which brings out the great contrast between the sections. This need was well met, in fascinatingly different ways, by John Vickers, under the direction of Elijah Moshinsky, and – perhaps not quite so effectively – by Philip Langridge under the direction of Tim Albery.

3

Duets

In duets there is an interaction between two people, and the music must link them together and show how the thoughts and feelings of one person impact on the other person, leading to his or her response. Both partial overlapping and fully singing together, in harmony or unison (with or without sharing a common text), are frequently used to indicate a close affinity between the feelings of the two characters onstage. In this way emotional interactions and connections between characters can be established and explored in opera (and in the musical) in ways which are totally unavailable to the spoken play. To be successful a production of a duet must work out each character's emotional journey, and both analyse and realize, through stagecraft, how the music shows their developing interaction as the duet progresses.

3.1 *The Art of Seduction* (Mozart/Da Ponte *Don Giovanni*, Act 1 scene 9)

This is our first (and only full) opportunity to see Don Giovanni engaged in the occupation which – as he tells Leporello at the start of Act II – means more to him than the food that he eats or the air that he breathes. He takes just under six minutes to turn Zerlina from Masetto's loyal bride into his own compliant victim.

Mozart sets Da Ponte's text in such a way that it is possible, and indeed necessary, for the director to show Zerlina's brief journey from rejection of Don Giovanni to complete acceptance that 'the torment of an innocent love'[1] will be resolved for them in 'marriage' – a word which for Giovanni means something rather different from the legal ceremony that Zerlina doubtless naively imagines. Simultaneously, the director must also show the

---

[1] There is irony in this text; just how 'innocent' is Zerlina's new love, since it involves betraying Masetto?

ways in which Giovanni successfully persuades her to make that journey. To achieve these two essential aims while responding properly to Da Ponte's text and Mozart's music a great deal of action is needed; and there needs to be a very good sexual chemistry between the two singing actors, since the interaction between their characters must be erotic.[2]

Jürgen Flimm directed an excellent production in 2001, filmed by Brian Large and with the music in the secure hands of Nikolaus Harnoncourt. Rodney Gilfrey played Don Giovanni – and he was young and handsome, essential criteria for the title role which are not always possessed by baritones who attempt it;[3] Liliana Nikiteanu was the impressive Zerlina, and their performance made Giovanni's success in conquering Masetto's bride-to-be completely credible. None of the other filmed modern performances comes near to this one in sexual intensity and therefore in dramatic credibility. Cf. e.g. Opera Australia's 1991 production directed by Lindy Hume with Jeffrey Black and Fiona Janes (virtually sexless), or Giorgio Strehler's 1987 La Scala production with Thomas Allen and Susanne Mentzer, in which some sparks fly but the scene as a whole is too stylized. Similarly, Bryn Terfel's interaction with Hei-Kyung Hong in the Met production credited to Zeffirelli (although actually directed by Stephen Lawless in 2000 in Zeffirelli's 1990 designs) does not have much to offer. Terfel sits at a distance from his Zerlina for nearly half the recitative, and she has to hold out her hands towards him on 'these white and fragrant fingers'. There is much interweaving of hands during the early part of the *duettino*, and byplay with a rather obviously symbolic apple, from which Giovanni induces Zerlina to take a bite at the end. It all looks rather artificial.

It is fascinating to compare Flimm's relatively recent production with that filmed at the Salzburg Festival of 1954, with Herbert Graf directing Cesare Siepi and Erna Berger, under the baton of Wilhelm Furtwängler. There is everything to be admired about Graf's selection of movements and gestures; Zerlina walks away from Don Giovanni when resisting him, and comes nearer when she is succumbing; and the last few bars are the accompaniment to a hearty kiss. But times, and in particular the conventions of representing sexual attraction onstage, have changed since 1954, so to modern eyes the whole encounter is rather coy – which is not at all appropriate for realizing today the scene which Da Ponte and Mozart created![4]

---

[2] Unfortunately this basic *desideratum* for a scene of sexual conquest quite often fails to be met. As for example in Peter Sellars' production, where Eugene Perry as Giovanni sat moodily, far away from his Zerlina, throughout the recitative, and there was relatively little physical interaction between them even in the *duettino*.

[3] For an analysis of Gilfrey's whole performance as Don Giovanni see **8.2**.

[4] Remember that Da Ponte wrote this libretto in the evenings (simultaneously with two others for Martini and Salieri during the day), inspired by a bottle of Tokay to his right, a box of Seville snuff to his left, and the company on demand of his housekeeper's very compliant sixteen-year old daughter! (Da Ponte 1967: 175–6).

🖉 3 1 Don G seduces Zerlina

Scene 9

DON GIOVANNI AND ZERLINA

DON G Alfin siam liberati, Zerlinetta gentil,

da quel scioccone: che ne dite, mio ben,

so far pulito?

ZER Signore, è mio marito.

DON G Chi? Colui?

Vi par che un onest'uomo, un nobil Cavalier,

com io mi vanto, possa soffrir che quel visettto d'oro,

quel viso inzuccherato, da un bifolcaccio

vil sia strapazzato?

ZER Ma signor, io glie diedi parola di sposario.

DON G Tal parola non vale un zero;

Voi non siete fatta per esser paesana;

3.1.1 un altra sorte vi procuran

quegli occhii briocconcelli,

quei labretti si belli, quelle dittuce candide e odorose;

parmi toccar giuncata, e fiutar de rose.

ZER Ah non vorrei ...

DON G Che non vorreste?

ZER ... alfine ingannata restar;

Io so che raro colle donne voi altri cavalieri

siete honesti e sinceri.

DON G Eh, un'impostura dell gente plebeia!

La nobilità ha dipinta negl'occhi l'onestà.

Orsù, non perdiam tempo;

in questo instante io ti voglio sposar.

ZER Voi?

DON G Certo, io.

Quel casinetto è mio;

soli saremo, e là, giocello mio, ci sposeremo.

No. 7 Duettino

DON G 3.1.2 Là ci darem la mano, là mi dirai di si;

At last we're free, my sweet Zerlina,

of that buffoon. What do you think,

my dear, rather neat?

Sir, he is my husband.

Who? Him?

You can't suppose an honest man,
   a noble Knight

like me, could allow this golden
      little face,

this sweet face, to be spoiled

by an oaf like that?

But sir, I promised to marry him.

Such promises are worth nothing;

you were not fated to be
      a peasant girl;

another destiny awaits you thanks to

those mischievous eyes,

those beautiful lips, these white
      and fragrant fingers;

as soft as cream, and smelling
      like roses.

Oh, I don't want ...

What don't you want?

... to find myself deceived in the end;

I know that you fine gentlemen
      are rarely

honest and sincere with women.

Oh, a lie put around by the
      common people!

Nobility has honesty painted
   in its very eyes.

Come, let's not waste time;

I want to marry you right now.

You?

Yes, I.

This little house is mine;

We'll be alone, and there, my jewel,
   we'll marry.

There we will join hands, there you
   will say yes;

Veni, non è lontano, partiam, ben mio, da qui.	Come, it is not far, let's go, my love.
ZER Vorrei, e non vorrei, mi trema un poco il cor;	I want to, and don't want to, my heart trembles a little;
Felice, è ver, sarei, ma può burlarmi ancor,	It's true, I should be happy, but he might be tricking me,
ma può burlarmi ancor,	he might be tricking me,
DON G Vieni, mio bel diletto;	Come, my darling;
ZER Mi fa pieta di Masetto;	I'm sorry for Masetto;
DON G io cangierò tua sorte.	I will transform your life.
ZER Presto non son più forte,	Now I'm no longer strong,
non son più forte,	I'm no longer strong,
non son più forte.	I'm no longer strong.
DON G Vieni, vieni!	Come, come!
Là ci darem la mano,	There we will join hands,
ZER Vorrei, e non vorrei,	I want to and don't want to,
DON G là mi dirai di si;	there you will say yes;
ZER mi trema un poco il cor;	my heart trembles a little;
DON G partiam, ben mio, da qui.	Let's go, my love.
ZER ma può burlarmi ancor.	he might be tricking me.
DON G Vieni, mio bel diletto;	Come, my darling;
ZER (entering on 'diletto') Mi fa pieta di Masetto;	I'm sorry for Masetto;
DON G (entering on '(Ma)-setto') io cangierò tua sorte;	I will transform your life;
ZER (entering on 'tua') presto non son più forte,	now I'm no longer strong,
non son più forte,	I'm no longer strong,
non son più forte.	I'm no longer strong.
DON G andiam, andiam!	Let's go, let's go!
ZER Andiam!	Let's go!
DON G and ZER (together) Andiam, andiam mio bene,	Let's go, let's go my darling,
a ristorar le pene	to remedy the torment
d'un innocente amor.	of an innocent love.
Andiam, andiam mio bene,	Let's go, let's go my darling,
a ristorar le pene	to remedy the torment
d'un innocente amor.	of an innocent love.
3.1.3 DON G Andiam!	Let's go!
ZER Andiam! Andiam!	Let's go! Let's go!
DON G Andiam!	Let's go!
DON G and ZER (together) Andiam, mio bene, andiam	Let's go, my darling, let's go
le pene a ristorar	the torment to remedy
d'un innocente amor.	of an innocent love.

(They walk towards Giovanni's house, embracing each other.)

Recitative

Don Giovanni starts the recitative already establishing an emotional closeness to his 'Zerlinetta gentil';[5] so Flimm rightly begins with his holding her hands, and staring into her eyes.[6] Giovanni then tries too coarsely to dispose of her feelings for Masetto, so she breaks away on 'Sir, he is my husband'. But Giovanni recovers rapidly, and starts to praise the beauty of her face; this charms Zerlina, who has been moving away from him; she stops suddenly on 'this sweet face'. However she is still resisting him ('But sir…'), so she resumes folding her cloth, and then begins to leave. After a wicked laugh, Giovanni once again turns on the flattery, and at 'those beautiful lips' (where the vocal line, **3.1.1**, invites a caressing tone) he succeeds; Nikiteanu as Zerlina turns towards him, and gives him a look full of meaning:

3.1.1 (I.9.16)

Gilfrey as Giovanni therefore now initiates the next stage of the seduction, starting to praise Zerlina's 'white and fragrant fingers, as soft as cream'.

---

[5] In Flimm's production Zerlina is wearing a white dress, with a bridal veil on her head. She holds the tablecloth from the wedding feast, which she has been folding, and a bouquet of flowers. These props will be used in the scene.

[6] Cf. Strehler's production, where Giovannni boldly holds Zerlina's face in his hands on 'this golden little face'. But the rest of the scene does not build adequately onwards from this early physical contact.

He takes Nikiteanu's hand gently, caresses his own cheek with it (standing very close to her), and then kisses it. Her mouth is very close to his at this point, but this Giovanni wisely refuses to push his luck at such an early stage of the seduction by stealing a kiss. Zerlina's text now shows that she does not know what she wants; on 'Oh, I don't want ...' Nikiteanu breaks away from Gilfrey – but not very far, and this expresses in stage action her divided feelings.

Giovanni dismisses the infidelity of the nobility as 'a lie put around by the common people' – in Flimm's production, raising his hand to his heart for emphasis. But now it is time for him to make a move ('Come, let's not waste time'). Gilfrey takes her bouquet from his Zerlina, and kneels to propose marriage, offering one of the flowers back to her. This has a great effect on Zerlina; Nikiteanu clasps the flower to her breasts, leaves him, crosses to the right of the stage, and leans on the set for support. Then, as he invites her to be alone with him in the 'little house', she faces him, clearly moved. In response Gilfrey raises and extends his hand to her as Don Giovanni concludes the recitative – and keeps this pose into the start of *Là ci darem la mano*, in this way supporting the opening words of the *duettino* with an almost literal gesture.

Duettino

3.1.2 (1.9 no.7 duettino, 1)

The most notable feature of the first bars of the *duettino* is that Zerlina accepts (although with variations in melodic contour) the tempo, rhythm and harmony of the opening melody (**3.1.2**). This shows that Giovanni has made considerable progress during the recitative. Nikiteanu first raises her hand towards her Giovanni, to match his, but then lowers it and turns away on 'my heart trembles a little'. Her divided emotions at this stage are rightly reflected in a half turn back towards him on 'I should be happy', followed by a turn away, to address the audience, on 'but he might be tricking me'.

Giovanni now escalates the pressure, as Mozart makes his words more forceful with an *mf tutti* in bar 19. Accordingly, 'Come, my darling' leads in Flimm's production to physical contact. Giovanni crosses round Zerlina, comes close and seizes her arm. When she tries to break away on 'I'm sorry for Masetto', he keeps hold of her, and suddenly turns her round so that she is in his arms, very close. She leans on his shoulder as she confesses her weakness, and he responds to this early hint of imminent victory by taking off her bridal veil and throwing it away. At the end of 'I'm no longer strong' Zerlina makes another, forceful attempt to break away, but he keeps hold of her hand, runs his own hands up her arm (Zerlina still facing away from him), and then comes very close, embracing her from behind. Note that Mozart has himself escalated the intensity in this section, showing that the seduction has now progressed considerably further; in the repeat of *Là ci darem la mano* from bar 30, Zerlina interrupts between the phrases of Giovanni's song with the repeated phrases of her own initial response. On the repeat of 'my heart trembles a little' Nikiteanu's Zerlina, almost overcome, breaks away and leans once again against the set.

Now, Mozart increases their closeness yet again. They move in the next section from alternating lines, which at the start of the aria were sung completely separately (30–8), to overlapping with each other (38–43). In Flimm's production Giovanni responds to this further increase in intensity by taking off his coat, then caressing Zerlina's hair briefly as he urges her for the last time: 'I will transform your life'. With her final confession of weakness, Nikiteanu's Zerlina breaks away, also for the last time; but Giovanni has heard that her resistance is almost gone, and tells her *Andiam! Andiam!* 'Let's go! Let's go!' On *Andiam!* Gilfrey sits down on a chair, and sits Nikiteanu on his knees in front of him. This Zerlina does not resist, and her echoing of his one word, *Andiam*, signals the final conquest.

Tempo and time signature (but not key) change for the closing *allegro*, in which the two characters are so united in feeling that they sing the same words together in harmony. And Flimm invented movements which match this perfectly. The couple begin with their heads very close, then Zerlina rises slowly and turns to face Giovanni during the first strophe, and at the end of it takes the initiative for the first time in the scene. This is very good direction. No Zerlina in other recorded productions takes the initiative at all in physical terms in this scene, and that is an opportunity lost to respond to the music of the closing *allegro*, which shows that there is now not only a harmony but an equality of desire between them both.

Accordingly, under Flimm's direction, when Giovanni attempts to rise from his half-kneeling position, Nikiteanu as Zerlina puts him down again with a gentle pressure of her hands on his shoulders, and stands caressing him, slowly taking his jacket off during the second strophe. As this strophe ends, and Mozart's music moves into a dance-like figure, **3.1.3** (Rushton hears it as a pastorale),[7] Gilfrey's Giovanni regains the initiative; he takes his Zerlina by the waist, stands up, and holds her, to mark that his conquest is total.

3.1.3 (1.9 no.7 duettino, 64 ff.)

They are now complete equals in desire. So in Flimm's production Zerlina once again takes the initiative. She caresses Giovanni's face; he smiles as she started to undo his shirt buttons, and, as the third and final strophe ends, the director symbolizes that they now both want to be united. Gilfrey pulls Nikiteanu's blouse down off her shoulders, and in reply she gives him a languorous kiss the moment the singing is over. Given this escalated level of close physical interaction (much sexier than any other production available on DVD!), Gilfrey does not merely conclude the scene – as in Da Ponte's stage directions, and in all other productions I have seen – by walking towards the summerhouse, arms entwined with his Zerlina's. As **3.1.3**, the dance of the seduction's endgame, sounds for the last time in the orchestra, this Giovanni picks up his very willing Zerlina and begins to carry her off in his arms. Unfortunately for Don Giovanni, however, he does not get very far; Donna Elvira interrupts them, and all of this highly successful seduction has been for nothing.

In this duet, Mozart's throughline is the conquest of Zerlina by Don Giovanni. The music shows *both* the emotions which he is projecting at her *and* her increasingly accepting response, which leads them, in the Duettino, from singing separately at first through gradually increasing interaction, to the final section in which they sing the same melody and the same words at the same time. Flimm's production illuminates and complements each stage of this musical process.

---

[7]Grove Music (electronic resource) *s.v. Don Giovanni.*

Discussion question

Choose one other performance of this *duettino* and compare it with that of Gilfrey and Nikiteanu. I think theirs stands out because of the sexual chemistry generated by the actors, and the director's detailed response to the changes in Mozart's music as the seduction proceeds. Do you agree? Give reasons for your view.

3.2 'On Such a Night ...' (Berlioz after Virgil Les Troyens IV, no. 37)

The examples in this chapter are evenly divided between two duets which show the progression as two people fall in love – or in Don Giovanni's case, in lust – (3.1 and 4.3) – and two duets which show the harmony between two characters who are already in love (3.2 and 3.4). Didon and Énée consummated their love during the Royal Hunt and Storm which opened Act IV, and now on a moonlit night they sing of their ecstasy. But at the end of the scene their hope of continued bliss is totally and almost brutally undermined, as they leave the stage, by the sudden appearance of Mercure, who strikes on Énée's shield as if on a gong, and solemnly pronounces the word 'Italie' three times.[8]

The purpose of this duet in Berlioz's dramatic scheme is to demonstrate the intensity and closeness of their relationship, so that his audience can understand why Didon breaks out into passionate rage and subsequently commits suicide when Énée abandons her in Act V.

✏ 3 2 Didon & Énée

No. 37 Duet

(Moonlight)

DIDON & ÉNÉE

Nuit d'ivresse et d'extase infinie!	Night of intoxication and infinite ecstasy!
Blonde Phoebé, grands astres de sa cour,	Golden Phoebe, great stars of her court,
Versez sur nous votre lueur bénie;	Turn on us the blessing of your rays;

---

[8]Note the violent changes when Mercure appears (136) – of key (from the duet's G flat major to D major then E minor), dynamic, texture and orchestration – trombones, ophicléide, timpani and percussion, unheard previously in the number, now enter *ff*.

Fleurs des cieux, souriez à l'immortel amour!

Flowers of the heavens, smile on our immortal[9] love!

DIDON

Par une tel nuit, le front ceint de cytise,

On such a night, her forehead wreathed with laburnum blossom,

Votre mère Vénus suivit le bel Anchise
Aus bosquets de l'Ida.

Your mother Venus followed handsome Anchises to the groves of Ida.

ÉNÉE

Par une telle nuit, fou d'amour et de joie,
Troïlus vint attendre aux pieds des murs de Troie

On such a night, maddened by love and joy,
Troilus came to wait at the foot of the walls of Troy

La belle Cressida.

For beautiful Cressida.

DIDON & ÉNÉE

Nuit d'ivresse et d'extase, ô nuit,
d'ivresse et d'extase infinie!
Blonde Phoebé, grands astres de sa cour,
Versez sur nous votre lueur bénie;
Fleurs des cieux, souriez à l'immortel amour!

Night of intoxication and ecstasy, oh night
Of intoxication and infinite ecstasy!
Golden Phoebe, great stars of her court,
Turn on us the blessing of your rays;
Flowers of the heavens, smile on our immortal love!

ÉNÉE

3.2.1 Par une telle nuit la pudique Diane
Laissa tomber enfin son voile diaphane
Aux yeux d'Endymion.

On such a night chaste Diana
Finally let her diaphanous veil fall
In the sight of Endymion.

DIDON

Par une telle nuit le fils de Cythérée
Accueillit froidement la tendresse enivrée
De la reine Didon!

On such a night the son of Venus
Received coldly the intoxicated tenderness
Of Queen Didon!

ÉNÉE

Et dans la même nuit, hélas! l'injuste reine
Accusant son amant obtint de lui sans peine

And that same night, alas, the unjust queen
Accusing her lover obtained from him without difficulty

Le plus tendre pardon.

The most tender pardon.

(They go slowly upstage, embracing each other, and then disappear as they sing.)

DIDON & ÉNÉE

(excitedly) Ô nuit d'ivresse et d'extase infinie!
Nuit d'ivresse et d'extase,
Ô nuit d'ivresse et d'extase infinie!
Blonde Phoebé, grands astres de sa cour,
Versez sur nous votre lueur bénie;
Fleurs des cieux, souriez à l'immortel amour!

Oh night of intoxication and infinite ecstasy!
Night of intoxication and ecstasy,
Oh night of intoxication and infinite ecstasy!
Golden Phoebe, great stars of her court,
Turn on us the blessing of your rays;
Flowers of the heavens, smile on our immortal love!

---

[9]This word is sung only by Didon, not by Énée, both here and in the remaining stanzas. J. Ewans (1980: 284–5) rightly notes the irony: 'At this stage in *Les Troyens* Dido believes that her relationship with Aeneas will be as enduring as their love is ecstatic.'

| Souriez à l'amour, souriez à l'amour! | Smile on our love, smile on our love! |
| Souriez à l'amour, souriez à l'amour! | Smile on our love, smile on our love! |

(At the moment when the two lovers, no longer visible, end the duet in the wings, Mercure
suddenly appears in a moonbeam not far from a broken column on which hangs Énée's armour.
Approaching the column he strikes with his wand two blows on the shield, which produces a long
and mournful sound. Then, extending his hand in the direction of the sea, the god repeats in a
serious voice:)

MERCURE

| Italie! Italie! Italie! | Italy! Italy! Italy! |

(he disappears)

The text is designed for music in *rondo* form.[10] It is framed by a set of three choric stanzas ('Night of intoxication and infinite ecstasy!'), in which Didon and Énée invoke the moon and stars to bless their love. This opening line is initially heard only once; in the first repeat of this stanza it is set twice; in the second and final reprise it is set three times. And this progressive elaboration towards the final stanza is matched at the end of that stanza: with Didon's *immortel* omitted, the last phrase 'smile on our love' is sung four times as the couple disappear into the distance.

In between these stanzas, Berlioz famously borrows from the artist whom he most revered, apart from Virgil and Gluck: Shakespeare. At the opening of Act V of *The Merchant of Venice*, the lovers Lorenzo and Jessica exchange three-line stanzas beginning with the half-line 'in such a night as this...' and referring to lovers from Greek myth – Troilus, Thisbe, Dido and Medea in that order. Then the pattern is broken by a return to the present; Lorenzo's next stanza refers to Jessica running away to him at Belmont from her father's house in Venice. In reply Jessica accuses him of vowing fidelity to her many times – but falsely; and Lorenzo completes the sequence, before they are interrupted by the arrival of Stephano:

> In such a night
> Did pretty Jessica, like a little shrew,
> Slander her love, and he forgave it her.

Berlioz' lovers give only three examples, not four, and only one is carried over from Shakespeare; they are, in order, Venus, Troilus and Diana. Then, paralleling Shakespeare's final development, Didon accuses Énée of responding coldly to her tenderness, and Énée replies much like Lorenzo (adding an extra stanza and so breaking the pattern):

---

[10] '... always coming back to the same thing yet always free to make new discoveries. It seems as if it could go on for ever, and we don't want it to stop – which makes the intervention of Mercury all the more shocking.' Kemp 1988: 38.

Et dans la même nuit, hélas! l'injuste reine	And that same night, alas, the unjust queen
Accusant son amant obtint de lui sans peine	Accusing her lover obtained from him without difficulty
Le plus tendre pardon.	The most tender pardon.

Under the first choric stanza the music (in the remote key of G flat major, which Kemp describes with reference to this duet as 'warm [and] forgetful')[11] undulates gently in muted violins; to show their intimacy, Didon and Énée sing almost exactly the same text together, and for the first three words they begin in harmony, after which their vocal lines decorate the text with separate but closely interweaving inventions. A similar pattern is followed in the second setting, but with a different accompaniment and new vocal decorations.

To understand the music of the settings of the intervening solo 'on such a night' stanzas, and of the final duo recapitulation of 'night of intoxication', we can gain insight from the stage realization by Yannis Kokkos. His production was performed and recorded at the Théâtre du Châtelet, Paris in 2009. It would recommend itself on musical grounds alone; Sir John Eliot Gardiner presided in the pit over the splendidly named *Orchestre Révolutionnaire et Romantique* playing on period instruments. He met all Berlioz' instrumental demands – which include an ophicléide, a choir of saxhorns ranging from *suraigu* ('shrill and high-pitched') to contrabass, and exotic percussion instruments; and he conducted his large forces with authority and power. The three leads are strongly cast, Susan Graham as Didon, Gregory Kunde as Énée and Anna Caterina Antonacci electrifying as Cassandre (see **6.1**); all sing eloquently.[12] And an Énée who sounds unstrained by the high tessitura of the role, which taxed even Domingo, is a rare find indeed. They also look the parts and act very well. There is none of the 'stand and deliver' by implausibly portly singers which characterized some past productions of this opera; and Kokkos's production is highly effective and theatrically gripping.

In this scene he is not afraid to leave his singers still where that matches the music; so Didon and Énée begin the duet on the end of a couch stage right, seated side by side and looking up towards the sky. They only move as the first stanza comes to an end; during the instrumental *coda* they turn to look at each other, and then, to initiate the seduction game of 'on such a night …' (for that is what it is), Graham, as Didon, leaves her Énée and walks to stage left as she begins to sing about the love of his parents Venus and Anchises, gently swishing her diaphanous floor-length wrap

---

[11] 1988: 115. It is also the key of Puccini's aria for Madama Butterfly, 'Un bel di', cf. **2.4**.

[12] Antonacci also returns as Cassandre at the end of the opera to prophesy the future of Rome (*Fuit Troia: stet Roma!*). Gardiner and Kokkos use the last part of Berlioz' original finale, on which see Macdonald 1988: 63–5.

as she goes. Naturally enough, therefore, Kunde follows her across as he begins his responsive stanza (Troilus). He takes her hand and clasps it as he concludes with 'beautiful Cressida', and for the second choric stanza they face forward, she behind him with her hands on his chest and shoulder. The whole stanza is delivered more intimately than the first, as they stay very close and touch each other throughout.

The accompaniment to Énée's Diana stanza, with its whirling, eddying scales and trills, is much more erotic than the music previously heard – and this makes sense, since it refers to Diana's disrobing for Endymion.

3.2.1 (4.37.72)

Kokkos brilliantly accompanies this by having his Didon cross back towards the couch, throw off her robe exactly when Énée sings of Diane doing the same, and twirl around bare-armed in what apparently is her only remaining garment, a long and beautifully flowing silk shift.[13] For her intense and passionate responding stanza, singing of Énée's alleged coldness towards her, as the orchestral music continues to flow – now in descending groups of six semiquavers – Graham sits on the couch, and extends her hand to her Énée as if trying to seduce him out of this coldness. And she wins the game, since Kunde crosses to come to her while singing Énée's equally passionate response, and she lies down, holding him, as the stanza concludes.

---

[13] Kokkos designed the sets and costumes himself.

More trills lead into the final vocally intertwined stanza, which is marked to be delivered *avec exaltation*. And Kokkos declines to fulfil the stage direction for the couple to start leaving at this point, in order to bring out the increased intimacy which in his production the game of 'on such a night' has created. On the first line of the final stanza Énée clasps Didon's hand across her recumbent body; she only sits up on 'Golden Phoebe'; then, as the music soars (to top C flat for Énée), they are soon caressing each other, heads together. Finally, Didon stands, on the first phrase of the closing movement – 'Smile on our love'; on the third and last repeat they embrace; and after the final notes of the duet they kiss.

Kokkos evidently did not want to waste the duet's lovely woodwind *coda* (129–35) on an empty stage. Only as it begins do the entwined couple turn and head upstage, Didon picking up her previously discarded wrap as they go. Mercure is heard, but not seen, as they disappear into the distance; but Énée's ship lights up in the background during the final bars, giving visual reinforcement to the need for him to abandon Didon.

Discussion question

Analyse how the movements which Kokkos devises for his two principals show an ever-closer relationship between their characters as the duet progresses.

3.3 Love in a garret (Puccini/Giacosa and Illica, *La Bohème* Act 1)

The enduring popularity of this opera is undoubtedly due to the immense pathos of Mimì's death in the final scene; but that scene itself would not have the impact which it does in the theatre if the depth of the love between Rodolfo and Mimì had not been established in the duet which concludes Act I.

Puccini responded with commanding lyricism to the text which his librettists gave him; and this scene is so powerful because Giacosa and Illica have compressed into what became fourteen minutes of music all the phases of two young people falling in love.

🖉 3 3 Love in a garret Luhrmann

🖉 3 3 Love in a garret Zeffirelli

(Mimì stoops to the floor, continuing to search for the key; at this moment Rodolfo reaches her and as he also stoops, his hand encounters hers.)

MIMÌ *(surprised)*

Ah!   Ah!

RODOLFO *(holding Mimì's hand, with a voice full of emotion)*

[1]Che gelida manina,   What an ice-cold little hand,

Se la lasci riscaldar.   let me warm it up.

Cercar che giova? Al buio non si trova.   What good will searching do? In the dark
                                             it won't be found.

Ma per fortuna è una notte di luna,   But fortunately it is a moonlit night,

e qui la luna l'abbiamo vicina.   and here we have the moon near us.

(Mimì tries to withdraw her hand.)

Aspetti signorina, le dirò con due parole chi son,   Wait, mademoiselle, and I'll tell you in
                                             a couple of words who I am,

chi son, e che faccio, come vivo.   who I am and what I do, how I live.

Vuole?   Would you like that?

(Mimì is silent. Rodolfo releases her hand, drawing back she finds a chair, into which she sinks, overcome by emotion.)

[2] Chi son? Chi son? Sono un poeta.   Who am I? Who am I? I am a poet.

Che cosa faccio? Scrivo.   What do I do? I write.

E come vivo? Vivo.   And how do I live? I live.

In povertà mia lieta   In my cheerful poverty

scialo da gran signor   I squander like a great lord

rime ed inni d'amore.   verses and hymns of love.

Per sogni e per chimere   Through dreams and illusions

e per castelli in aria   and castles in the air

l'anima ho milionaria.   I have a millionaire's soul.

3.3.1 Talor dal mio forziere   Sometimes from my treasure chest

ruban tutti i gioelli   (1a) two thieves steal all the jewels,

due ladri, gli occhi belli.   some beautiful eyes.

V'entra con voi per ora,   They came in with you just now,

ed i miei sogni usati,   and my usual dreams

ed i bei sogni miei   and my lovely dreams

tosto si dileguar!   vanished at once!

3.3.1 Ma il furto non m'accora   But the theft does not upset me

poichè, poichè v'ha preso stanza   (1b) because, because sweet hope

la dolce speranza.   has moved in.

Or che mi conoscete,   Now that you know me,

parlate voi.   you speak.

Deh! Parlate. Chi siete?   Come, speak. Who are you?

Vi piaccia dir?   Would you like to say?

MIMÌ *(She hesitates, then decides to speak.) (Still seated, in a simple way)*

[3]Sì.   Yes.

Mi chiamano Mimì,   They call me Mimì,

ma il mio nome è Lucia.   but my name is Lucia.

La storia mia   My story

è breve. A telo o a seta   is short. On linen or silk ricamo in casa e fuori...

I embroider at home or outside ...

Son tranquilla e lieta,

I'm contented and happy,

ed è mio svago

and it is my delight

far gigli e rose.

to make lilies and roses.

Mi piaccion quelle cose

Those things give me pleasure

che han sì dolce malia,

which possess such sweet enchantment,

che parlano d'amor, di primavera,

which speak of love, of spring,

che parlano di sogni e chimere,

which speak of dreams and illusions,

quelle cose che han nome poesia.

those things that have the name poetry.

Lei m'intende?

Do you understand me?

RODOLFO (moved)

Sì.

Yes.

MIMÌ

Mi chiamano Mimì,

They call me Mimì,

il perchè non so.

I don't know why.

[4] Sola, mi fo

All alone

il pranzo da me stessa.

I prepare my meal by myself.

Non vado sempre a messa,

I don't always go to mass,

ma prego assai il Signor.

But I pray a lot to the Lord.

Vivo sola, soletta,

I live alone, quite alone,

là in una bianca cameretta,

there in a little white room,

guardo sui tetti e in cielo,

I overlook the roofs and the sky,

(she rises)

ma quando vien lo sgelo

but when the thaw comes

il primo sole è mio,

the first sunlight is mine,

il primo bacio dell'aprile è mio!

(2)the first kiss of April is mine!

Il primo sole è mio!

The first sunlight is mine!

Germoglia in un vaso una rosa

In a vase a rose comes into bloom

foglia a foglia la spio!

I watch it petal by petal!

Così gentil

How sweet is

il profumo d'un fior!

the scent of a flower!

Ma i fior ... ch'io faccio, ahimè, non hanno odore!

But the flowers that I make, alas, have no fragrance!

Altro di me non le saprei narrare:

I don't know what else to tell about me:

Sono la sua vicina

I am your neighbour

che la vien fuori d'ora a importunare.

who comes to bother you at a bad time.

SCHAUNARD (from the courtyard)

[5] Ehi! Rodolfo!

Hey there! Rodolfo!

COLLINE

Rodolfo!

Rodolfo!

(At the shouts of his friends, Rodolfo is annoyed.)

MARCELLO

Olà. Non senti?

Hallo! Don't you hear us?

(Rodolfo, getting more annoyed, gropes his way to the window and opens it, leaning out a
    bit to answer his friends in the courtyard. From the open window rays of moonlight enter,
    which brighten the room.)

Lumaca!	Slowcoach!
COLLINE	
Poetucolo!	Scribbler!
SCHAUNARD Accidenti	Damn
Al pigro!	the idler!
RODOLFO *(at the window)*	
Scrivo ancor tre righe a volo.	I'm dashing off three more lines.
MIMÌ *(approaching the window a little)*	
Chi son?	Who are they?
RODOLFO	
Amici.	Friends.
SCHAUNARD	
Sentirai le tue ...	You'll hear your ...
MARCELLO	
Che te ne fai lì solo?	What are you doing there alone?
RODOLFO	
Non son solo. Siamo in due.	I'm not alone. There are two of us.
Andate da Momus, tenete il posto,	Go to Momus, keep a seat,
ci saremo tosto.	we will be there shortly.

(He remains at the window to make sure that his friends are going.)

MARCELLO, SCHAUNARD and COLLINE *(more and more in the distance)*

Momus, Momus, Momus,	Momus, Momus, Momus,
zitti e discreti andamocene via.	Let's go silently and discreetly.
Momus, Momus,	Momus, Momus,
MARCELLO	
Trovò la poesia.	He's found his poetry.
SCHAUNARD and COLLINE	
Momus, Momus, Momus!	Momus, Momus, Momus!

(Mimì stands wreathed in moonlight near the window; turning, Rodolfo sees her and contemplates her in ecstasy.)

RODOLFO

[6]

O soave fanciulla ...	Oh lovely girl ...

MARCELLO *(in the far distance, but as if shouted out)*

Trovò la poesia.	He's found his poetry.
RODOLFO ... o dolce viso	... oh sweet face
di mite circonfuso albar lunar,	surrounded by gentle whiteness
	of the moon,
in te ravviso	in you I recognize
il sogno ch'io vorrei sempre sognar!	the dream that I would like to dream
	for ever!
3.3.1 Fremon già nell'anima	Already through my soul quiver
le dolcezze estreme.	the greatest of delights.
MIMÌ	
3.3.1 Ah! Tu sol comandi, amor!	Ah! Love, you alone command!
Tu sol comandi, amore!	Love, you alone command!

RODOLFO (putting his arm around Mimì)

Fremon già nell'anima	(3) Already through my soul quiver
le dolcezze estreme ...	the greatest of delights ...

MIMÌ (on the verge of yielding)

Oh! Come dolci scendendo	Oh, how sweetly his flattering words
Le sue lusinghe al core.	descend into my heart.
Ah! Tu sol comandi amor!	Ah! Love, you alone command!

RODOLFO (in octaves with Mimì's last line)

... nel bacio freme amor!	... love quivers in a kiss!

(RODOLFO kisses Mimì)

MIMÌ (withdrawing)

[7] No, per pietà!	No, please!

RODOLFO

Sei mia!	You're mine!

MIMÌ

V'aspettan gli amici ...	Your friends are waiting for you ...

RODOLFO

Già mi mandi via?	Are you sending me away already?

MIMÌ

Vorrei dir ... ma non oso ...	I want to ask ... but I don't dare ...

RODOLFO (gently)

Di'!	Say!

MIMÌ (coquettishly)

Se venisse con voi?	What if I came with you?

RODOLFO (surprised)

Che? ... Mimì?	What? ... Mimì?

(suggestively)

Sarebbe così dolce restar qui.	It would be so nice to stay here.
C'è freddo fuori.	It's cold outside.

MIMÌ (with great abandon)

Vi starò vicina! ...	I'll stay beside you!

RODOLFO (lovingly helps Mimì put on her shawl)

E al ritorno?	And when we get back?

MIMÌ (mischievously)

Curioso!	We'll see!

RODOLFO (with tender gallantry)

Dammi il braccio, mia piccina!	Give me your arm, my little darling!

MIMÌ (gives her arm to Rodolfo)

Obbedisco, signor!	I obey you, my lord!

(They go arm in arm to the door.)

RODOLFO

Che m'ami di'!	Say that you love me!

MIMÌ (with abandon)

Io t'amo!	I love you!

(They go out.)

[8] RODOLFO and MIMÌ *(off-stage, gradually dying away)*
Amor! Amor!   (4) Love! Love!
(Curtain)

In the first section Rodolfo, pretending to search for Mimì's missing key, achieves his first aim, that of establishing physical contact with her. And his holding her hand has a powerful effect on Mimì; at the end of the section she is silent, unable to answer his question, and the stage direction is that she *sinks into a chair, overcome by emotion.*

In [2] to [4] first Rodolfo and then Mimì sing very different mini-arias, in which they describe themselves to each other. The result is that they are revealed as having a close affinity; both seek poetry and 'dreams and illusions' (Mimì's words are an exact echo of Rodolfo's); and both are poor but happy.

Just as Mimì finishes her story, Rodolfo's friends call up to him from the courtyard [5]. The interruption actually helps Rodolfo and Mimì to become much closer than would otherwise be possible, if Rodolfo had needed to respond immediately after Mimì's downbeat closing recitative; during the exchanges between Rodolfo and his friends, Mimì comes near the window, and as they go away *stands wreathed in moonlight; turning, Rodolfo sees her and contemplates her in ecstasy.* The effect of her beauty as it is now revealed, after the dim light of the earlier parts of the scene, emboldens Rodolfo to declare his love [6]. Mimì responds equally ecstatically, and is now *on the verge of yielding.* In Puccini's setting, as the duet reaches its climax Rodolfo and Mimì share the same music for the first time.

Then Rodolfo pushes his suit too far [7]. He kisses Mimì, but she retreats from him; she is not ready for physical love yet. But she is interested, and proposes a compromise: take me to Momus, and we'll see what happens afterwards. Rodolfo responds appropriately, changing from passionate suitor to gallant escort; they exchange two lines of elegant banter. [8] Then, as they make their way to the door, arm in arm, he asks if she loves him; and now Mimì has no hesitation in responding – *with abandon* – that she does. In a magical final touch, their departing voices are heard offstage singing the one word 'Amor!' in harmony.

Puccini's music for this duet seems like a continuous stream of melody;[14] but there are four strategic moments of great intensity (I shall call them 'climaxes', although not all of them are loud), of which the first and third are linked by shared material:

---

[14] *La Bohème* is *durchkomponiert*; the 1982 Met audience for the Zeffirelli/Levine production discussed below showed great disrespect for both the artists and the opera by applauding after Rodolfo's and Mimì's short accounts of themselves, which are component parts of a continuously developing scene.

1   1 (a) ([2]; 32.8ff.) Rodolfo: 'Sometimes from my treasure chest /
    two thieves steal all the jewels / these beautiful eyes'.

    1 (b) This passionate melody (2.3.1) is repeated at 33.3ff. – 'but the
    theft does not upset me, because, because sweet hope has moved
    in'.

    Both these passages are scored *p*, but the second crescendos to a
    forte top A flat (optional, but taken in preference to the alternative
    E flat by the Rodolfo in both the recordings to be discussed).

2   ([4]; 38.5ff.) Mimì: 'the first kiss of April is mine'.

3   ([6]; 41.9ff.) Mimì and Rodolfo sing in octaves the melody from
    the first climax, 2.3.1 – the first time they sing together. Their parts
    are marked *f con anima*; the orchestra is marked *fff largamente
    sostenuto*; his text is 'Already through my soul quiver / the greatest
    of delights', while hers is 'Love, you alone command!'.

4   [8]; 43.14) The final climactic moment finds the singers offstage,
    singing the word 'Love' *piano* as their voices fade into the distance.
    The orchestra is playing *ppp/pppp*, with exquisite chords of C
    major leading to the fall of the curtain.

*

A good production of this scene must make psychological sense of the
two characters' journeys through the details of the music to the total love
of the third and fourth climaxes. We shall study Zeffirelli's classic 1982
production at the Met, set in the original period with Teresa Stratas and
José Carreras, in comparison with the celebrated update to 1957 in Baz
Luhrmann's 1990 production for Opera Australia, with Cheryl Barker and
David Hobson.

Often small details are highly effective in communicating the gradual
growth of affection between Mimì and Rodolfo. Section [1], for example,
demands a decision on a simple but important issue. Rodolfo takes her
hand, at the start of the *andantino affettuoso*, but when should Mimì
withdraw it? Both Zeffirelli and Luhrmann decided that Puccini's original
position for the direction is too late. (In the score she tries to withdraw
her hand at 30.23, and he only finally releases it at 31.36, 'would you like
that?'.) In both of these productions[15] she withdraws her hand during the
delicate descending harp figurations starting at 31.11, after his 'in the dark
it won't be found'. But in both cases eye contact is maintained despite her
withdrawal from physical contact.

Puccini originally intended Mimì to try to withdraw her hand at 30.23,
because Rodolfo's next line after that moment ('Wait, mademoiselle …')

---

[15] And also in John Copley's 1982 production at Covent Garden.

clearly implies that she does something indicating a desire to leave. In Zeffirelli's staging she rises and actually goes nearly to the door; Rodolfo blocks her exit and begs her to hear his story, and after 'Would you like that?' Stratas indicates assent by going to the far end of the table and sitting down. In Luhrmann's version, the relationship does not come that near to ending before it begins. Barker tries to rise to get away, but Hobson gently restrains her with his hand; she sits down again with her hands in her lap as he makes his request, and then simply nods slightly and smiles to give her consent.

In section [2] Luhrmann makes much better use of set and movement than Zeffirelli. On his opening words 'Who am I? Who am I?' Hobson gets up and moves away from his Mimì, who relaxes on the floor. He sits briefly on the bottom step of Marcello's painter's ladder, but then climbs up it – very appropriately – as he sings about his 'castles in the air'. So then he is sitting on the top step, a long way above Barker (who is still sitting on the floor) as he declares how she has captured his heart and builds to the first strategic climax (1a) ('sometimes from my treasure chest …'), praise for her beauty which makes Barker smile after 'some beautiful eyes'. He remains in this commanding position through to the second and final climax of his mini-aria (1b) – the same melody in the orchestra, *crescendo* to 'sweet hope' on a top A flat. Only then does he descend, coming to kneel down close to his Mimì to ask her about her story.

Zeffirelli's treatment of Rodolfo is more conventional and less effective. The only prop used is a long table surrounded by chairs, and Carreras sings much of the aria at the opposite end of it from Stratas, mainly facing out towards the audience – although he does half-turn towards Stratas on 'sometimes from my treasure chest …'[16]. A nice touch is that Stratas's Mimì looks visibly nervous at 'some beautiful eyes' – more uncomfortable with Rodolfo's flattery and near-declaration of love than Barker's Mimì in the Sydney production. However, Zeffirelli's production of this section only warms up after 'But the theft …', where Carreras goes closer to Stratas, and she leans her head far back in joy as he hits his high note on '(sweet) hope!'

[3–4] In Mimì's narration, however, Zeffirelli does not build on the closeness to Mimì which Rodolfo has achieved by the end of section 2. After a few moments sitting on the table near Mimì (where he should have stayed), Carreras goes away from her, gets a chair and sits down at the far end of the table as she sings 'My story / is short'. By contrast Hobson sits down on the floor close to Barker, looking intently at her. And Luhrmann builds on this closeness; just after 'I live alone', this Rodolfo extends his hand to her in sympathy; then she stands up and takes it, letting it go,

---

[16] The distance between the singers in this production, separated by the length of the table, seems much further than the vertical distance in Luhrmann's staging. For a man to be above a woman with whom he is falling in love is more intimate than being horizontally distant from her – and the table acts as a barrier.

gently, on 'and the sky'. Now Barker is standing for the first time in the scene, ready for her first big moment; and she faces forward, ecstatic, as she sings *con grande espansione* that 'the first kiss of April is mine' (**climax 2**). Hobson's Rodolfo lies on the floor, looking up in wonder and delight at this passionate young woman. Mimì may not know it, but both the text and the music of this declaration show that she is searching for love.

Less dramatically, Stratas remains seated throughout her mini-aria; but she is a great singing actress, and even when confined in this way she does wonderful things to interpret her words and music. For example, on '(the first kiss) of April is mine' she first clasps her hands, then opens them out as if to grasp April's first kiss in her hands, then draws them in to pull it to her body. In the next section she mimes the growth of the flowers with her hands on the table, gently letting her imaginary artificial flowers drop to the floor as she laments that they have no perfume.

[5] The interruption by the other Bohemians stages itself. In Zeffirelli's production the garret has a small balcony at the side. Rodolfo and Mimì both go out on it to look down as she sings 'who are they?' but Stratas then goes inside while Rodolfo tells his friends to go on ahead to Momus; she needs to be near the window at the back of the garret, ready to be illuminated by the moonlight when Rodolfo comes back inside. Luhrmann's garret has no balcony; Rodolfo goes out of the door onto the roof of the building to get rid of his friends, and Mimì follows him. She is shown in all her beauty by the giant red fluorescent sign reading *L'AMOUR* which is on the roof, and has just now been illuminated; it will stay as a striking backdrop to the love which flowers from now until the end of the Act.

[6] When Rodolfo begins 'O lovely girl', there are only seven bars of *Largo sostenuto* before Mimì joins him and they sing together in octaves at the third high point of the scene; here the orchestra is marked *fff largamente sostenuto* as it reprises the climactic melody from Rodolfo's mini-aria (3); **3.3.1**.

Both the productions under analysis are good, and the acting is superb; but in my judgement Luhrmann has made a much better preparation for this moment where Rodolfo and Mimì sing together and accept the power of passion. There has been a greater sense in the earlier sections of the scene that love is taking hold of them both, and this entitles him to the bold but brilliant touch of having the French word for Love displayed in red – the obvious colour of passion – from the start of section [6] to the fall of the curtain.

Now that mutual passion has been acknowledged, the rest of the Act is relatively straightforward. In Zeffirelli's version Stratas turns to her Rodolfo smiling happily as he begins his address to her with 'Oh lovely girl', and they take each other's hands, arms extended at full length, as their voices join together. In Luhrmann's production Hobson stands behind Barker, with his hands clasped round her; both face the audience until in the last words of the duet he turns her towards him ready for a kiss.

[7] As is common in the first stages of desire, Mimì may have declared herself but is still not quite ready for physical lovemaking. So in

3.3.1 (I.41.9-12)

both productions she withdraws from the kiss, as specified in the stage directions;[17] Barker, indeed, actually pushes her Rodolfo away; but, as warm sustained chords of desire rise in the orchestra (41.2–5), she then has to move to restrain Hobson's disconsolate Rodolfo from walking away on 'Are you sending me away already?' – a nice touch. The physical contact is the opposite way round in Zeffirelli; Carreras grips Stratas from behind on 'You're mine!', and it is she who disengages and walks away, on 'your friends are waiting for you …'. This is a more obvious staging than Luhrmann's, but is nevertheless almost equally effective.

In both productions the outcome is (almost) the same. From Mimì's hesitating request to accompany Rodolfo to Café Momus, the music is heading for her declaration, *with great abandon*, 'I'll stay beside you …!', which both sopranos sing with intensity, and very close to their respective Rodolfos. In a lovely touch of coquetry, Stratas gives her Rodolfo a peck on

---

[17] In Copley's production, Mimì withdrew even before Rodolfo had a chance to kiss her, which is making her reticence too extreme. Mimì is a Parisienne living *la vie de Bohème*, not an English convent schoolgirl – as her coquettishness will prove almost immediately.

the cheek after 'We'll see!', and she makes a deep curtsy on 'I obey you, my lord!' – playing to the full the game of gallantry with which the lovers are for now restraining their physical desire. Then, 'Say that you love me' and 'I love you' are played very close, after which Carreras ushers his Mimì out.

Luhrmann, directing with a lighter touch, allows his lovers not to be solemn right to the end; after Mimi acknowledges that she loves him, first they gaze into each other's eyes, then they break apart, and Barker's Mimì giggles, secure in her new love, just before they leave.

[8] The orchestra plays to an empty stage, as the lovers' ecstatic voices recede *perdendosi* into the distance. Luhrmann's red neon *L'AMOUR* sign shines out against a starry night sky, while Mimì and Rodolfo sing this same word in Italian – a magical ending, as translucent C major triads speak of the innocence and purity of this young love. Rodolfo's jealousy, Mimì's infidelities and her death from consumption are all far off in the future of Acts III and IV.

Discussion question

Discuss how each of the two directors, Zeffirelli and Luhrmann, use positions on the stage, and stage business, to chart the journey of Mimì and Rodolfo from first meeting to declaring their love. I think Luhrmann's staging of the scene is superior; do you agree or disagree? Give reasons for your choice.

3.4 Jenůfa and Laca alone (Janáček after Preissová *Jenůfa* Act III scene 3)

This piercingly beautiful scene is the only chance which the audience has to see Jenůfa and Laca alone between their muted, shocked engagement at the end of Act II and the terrible dénouement of the opera, which makes extreme demands on the emotional and moral strength of both of them. The interaction here shows how they have grown in strength since the events of Act II, and is therefore crucial to understanding their reactions during and after the Kostelnička's confession in scene 10.

Janáček's first masterpiece has only recently received adequate interpretations on DVD and VHS. Nikolaus Lehnhoff's Glyndebourne production in 1989 is a disappointment after his outstanding *Kát'a Kabanová* of 1988 (see **2.5**, **4.2** and **7.3**), whose deep insight it lacks. Tobias Hoheisel's set for Act 1 does not give the spaciousness which the outdoor scene requires; and Lehnhoff has a most eccentric idea which ruins the ending; village men start to smash up the furniture in the Kostelnička's house, and this is a perverse distraction from the final duet, where the text and the music are totally focused on how Jenůfa and Laca come to be united at last. The 2005 Barcelona production was a disaster on stage, and in the pit, since Olivier Tambosi burdened the opera with a highly disruptive overriding 'concept', and Peter Schneider conducted J. M. Dürr's by then utterly discredited 1969 edition, which retains all the cuts and extensive reorchestrations that Janáček's old enemy Karol Kovařovic forced on the composer as a condition of his accepting the opera for production in Prague in 1916.

Stéphane Braunschweig's staging in 2009 at the Teatro Real, Madrid, is powerful precisely because of its sparse, minimalist staging – although some may find it hard to accept a virtually set-less production of an opera which was based closely on a highly realistic play. For the third Act, for example, all we see is two sets of backless pews, extending with a central aisle almost up to the back of the stage – evoking not the Kostelnička's house in which Preissová set the scene but the church to which the wedding party should subsequently be going. Ivor Bolton's passionate conducting of Janáček's original score complements the stark power of the staging.[18]

The best production is the most recent, performed without international stars but to very high standards by the local ensemble at Malmö, Sweden. Marco Ivanovic conducts, eliciting startlingly authentic primary tones from the orchestra, and Orpha Phelan's multi-level staging is exciting – although the updating to the post-Second World War period takes the action out of the original setting, in which Jenůfa's unmarried pregnancy drives her to thoughts of suicide, into one where this is far less plausible.

🖋 3 4 Jenůfa and Laca Braunschweig

🖋 3 4 Jenůfa and Laca Phelan

JENŮFA

19[19] 3.4.1 Vidiš, Laco, ja to tušila,	You see, Laca, I knew
že to každému napadne,	that everyone would notice
jak jsem to na zdavky nastrojena.	the way I'm dressed for my wedding.
LACA *(taking a posy from his jacket pocket)*	
Jenůfka, já ti přece kytičku donesl ...	Jenůfa, I at least brought you some flowers ...
20 Je až z Belovce od zahradníka.	all the way from Belovec, from the gardener.
JENŮFA	
Děkuji ti Laco!	Thank you, Laca!
LACA	
Tu bys nevzala, tu bys nevzala?	You won't take them, you won't take them?
Jenůfka!	Jenůfa!

---

[18] And if my ears do not deceive me, he has restored some short orchestral passages which even the near-definitive Mackerras/Tyrrell edition does not include.

[19] These numbers are the rehearsal figures of the score.

JENŮFA

Och Laco, takové nevěsty	Oh Laca, such a bride
ty sis nezasloužil, nezasloužil!	you don't deserve, don't deserve!

(She pins the flowers to her bodice.)

LACA

21 Ó dětino, už mi o tom nemluv!	Childish creature, don't say that to me again!
Mne jen to ranou udeřilo	It struck me hard
v tu prvni chvili, ·	in the first moment,
jak mi to tetička řekly,	when Auntie told me about it,
ale potom hned jsem ti to odpustil!	but then I forgave you right away!
22 Však se já na tobě tak mnoho provinil,	I've done so much wrong to you,
celý život tobě to musím	I must spend all my life
vynahrazovat, celý svůj život,	making it up to you, my whole life,
celý svůj život, celý svůj život!	my whole life, my whole life!

JENŮFA

23 Tak mi je líto tebe, tak mi je líto tebe!	I'm so sorry for you, so sorry for you!
Tys při mně stal v neštěstí,	You stood by me in my misfortune,
ty, misto Števa.	you, instead of Števa.

LACA

Já vim, žes Števu lúbila ...	I know that you loved Števa ...

JENŮFA

Tys při mně stal v neštěstí,	You stood by me in my misfortune,
ty, misto Števa.	you, instead of Števa.

LACA

... jenom když včil už naň nemysliš.	... even if you don't think about him now.
Já nosil srdce zášť na Števu!	I had hatred in my heart for Števa!
A o všechno bych ho byl nejraději 24 připravil.	And I would have liked to rob him of everything.
Ale tys mi nakázala	But you insisted
abych se s nim udobřil.	that I should make it up with him.
25 Já uz jsem to všechno zlé v sobě překonal,	I've overcome all the evil in myself,
všechno, 26 **3.4.2** že tys s mnou, že tys s mnou!	all, now you are with me, now you are with me!
27 Števu jsem, jak se patři, pozval	Števa, as is right, I invited
na naši svatbu, na naši svatbu, na naši svatbu.	to our wedding, to our wedding, to our wedding.
Slíbil, že dojde jako bratr i s Karolkou.	He promised he would come like a brother – and with Karolka.
28 A hen...už jsou tu!	And now ... here they are!

For most of the scene a sinuous, graceful orchestral line underlies the voices – in celli (supported by a bassoon) and then for a few bars (19.5–9) clarinets, before the celli resume their course.

This continuous line, whichever of them is singing, tells us of the deep affinity between Jenůfa and Laca right from the outset (19); **3.4.1**. And

3.4.1 (III.3.19.1)

then the celli persist beneath the gentle descending phrases of four notes in oboes and *pizzicato* violins, as Laca hesitantly offers her a posy of flowers (20). This is a pivotal moment; Laca is attempting to re-make the trauma of the end of Act I, where, too, he offered Jenůfa a posy – but accompanied it then with the violence of slashing her cheek with his knife. When Jenůfa accepts *this* posy and pins it onto her dress, it symbolizes the security which their relationship has now achieved. That security and the ever-unfolding cello line which binds them together persist during 21, even though Laca expresses mild irritation with her and goes on to dwell on how he was affected by the news that she had had a child by Števa (21.2ff.).[20]

The passion in the string line now becomes more animated, as the violins take over the seamless melody at 22 in loose counterpoint with the lower instruments, which are also highly expressive (the marking here is *dolce*). And this pair of interlocking lines continues to bind the couple together, as Laca resolves to devote his whole life to Jenůfa, and she overlays his vocal line with her expression of her sympathy with him. The sinuous and passionate string lines temporarily become a rough *ostinato* when Laca admits to his jealousy of Števa (23.7ff.); but this is a *recul pour mieux sauter*: the upper strings descend rapidly in two tumultuous bars (end of 24) as Laca describes how Jenůfa insisted that he should be reconciled with

---

[20] Janáček uses recurrent motifs only rarely in *Jenůfa*; this is one place where he does. As Laca describes his shock in the first moments, the orchestra recalls the heavy pairs of falling chords which were first heard in Act II when the Kostelnička told Jenůfa that her child had died (II.98.12–99.2).

his brother; and the gathering *crescendo* at the start of 25 leads to a *tutti* with glorious descending brass (26) as Laca sings how, now he is with her, he has overcome all the evil in himself.

Moral growth is the central theme of *Jenůfa*;[21] accordingly this declaration is the climax of the scene, the moment to which it has been leading. Laca is now secure in the strength which this relationship has given him.[22] After the passion is spent, there is a solemn peace at 27.3ff. as he announces that he has invited his brother to the wedding; and the scene ends with transitional phrases in 26 as they await the imminent arrival of Števa and Karolka.

*

Only one of the four staged recordings does justice to the scene. Tambosi and Lehnhoff are in different ways ineffective, and even Braunschweig, whose production has many striking points elsewhere (see 5.5), fails to do justice to what the music is saying.

In Braunschweig's production, Amanda Roocroft in the title role and Miroslav Dvorský as Laca are costumed in funereal black. So too are the rest of the wedding party, doubtless for contrast with the totally white outfits which the 'happy' couple, Števa and Karolka, turn out to be wearing when they arrive; this symbolism is overdone. As the scene begins, Jenůfa and Laca are alone, sitting in the two front pews, separated by the aisle. These positions are at odds with the music, and even more so since Roocroft does not face her Laca during the first few lines, not even when he offers her his flowers. She faces forward, with her hands in her lap.

In this production, the flowers are not a small posy but a large bouquet – the only splash of colour on the stage. And Roocroft's Jenůfa declines to take them – a directorial decision which defies the stage direction, removes the important connection between this moment and the end of Act I, and disregards the clear implications of the music. Disconsolate, Dvorský, as Laca, takes the flowers away, and after 'Childish creature' (21.1) directs most of his lines out to the audience throughout his reliving of his suffering and his desire to make it up to her for hurting her. Dvorský uses his hands and arms expressively during this passage – at 24, for example, as Laca's music heads for its glorious climax, Dvorský raises his right hand to his chest on 'I've overcome all the evil in myself', and clasps both hands to his chest on 'now you are with me!'. But why is this glorious declaration sung facing forward, and so far from the woman whom Laca has loved since childhood and who has transformed his life by promising to marry him?

---

[21] M. Ewans 1977: 35 and 68–9.
[22] However, under the stress of the dénouement, he will relapse a little, asking Jenůfa if she has lost her senses when she forgives the Kostelnička; III.11.68.6–7.

3.4.2 (III.3.25.5)

Where is the interaction with Jenůfa, which both the text and the music demand? He remains detached from her, until a loud knocking offstage heralds the arrival of Števa and Karolka.

Gabriela Preissová created this moment away from others to show that Jenůfa and Laca have surmounted the tragic events of their past, and been enriched by each other's love, prior to the terrible test which they will undergo with the discovery of Jenůfa's dead baby (5.5) and the Kostelnička's confession. Janáček responds to her text with music which affirms the depth of the bond between them, by its sinuous, continuous orchestral lines almost throughout, and by the many passages where there is close interaction of the voice parts. And the climax, Laca's triumphant declaration of how having Jenůfa with him has transformed his personality, set to descending fanfares under upper string descending *tremolandi* (**3.4.2**), speaks of an emotional closeness which demands an equal physical closeness between Laca and Jenůfa, to match on stage the drama in the pit and in the vocal line. After all the text is 'now you *are with me*'!

Only Orpha Phelan rises properly to this moment. In the Malmö production Daniel Frank as Laca takes hold of Erika Sunnegåardh's Jenůfa from behind at 'But you insisted …', and as the upper instruments begin the build-up towards the fanfares she turns, they embrace just before 'I have overcome all the evil in my heart', and he sings ecstatically over her shoulder, holding her tightly, 'all, now you are with me!'. Only after the passion is spent does he gently release her, first caressing her neck.

Once this essential physical contact has been established for the climax, the director should work backwards to think out the interaction earlier in the

scene. This Orpha Phelan has clearly done. The important stage direction
that Jenůfa take the posy is accepted, and the action is performed – in
contrast to any previous recording – where Janáček prescribes it, at 20.7
(though Jenůfa does not subsequently pin it to her dress, as she already
wears a festive leaf). Then the moment of dissent between the couple is
well conveyed; Laca crosses right and faces away from her at the start of 21
('Childish creature...', as he relives the moment when he heard that Jenůfa
had given birth to Števa's baby [21]), but then Jenůfa crosses and goes round
to face him as he sings 'but then I forgave you right away!'. This puts her
in a good position for the ensuing *dolce* music in which Laca resolves to
devote his life to making up for the wrong that he has done to her, she pities
him, and their voices intertwine (22–3). Rightly, again, Phelan makes Jenůfa
move a bit away from Laca when he speaks of his hatred for Števa, but from
there on, as the text becomes solely concerned with their feelings for each
other, an increasing physical closeness develops, as described above, and
leads the couple up to the tight embrace which the climax requires.

Discussion question

Examine the details of the singing actors' postures and gestures in Orpha
Phelan's response to the words and music of this duet. Does she lead up
convincingly to the climactic embrace at the end? If so, how?

3.5 Conclusion

In duets, the one orchestra is chronicling the unfolding emotions of both
characters, and so showing the effects which the words and actions of
each character are having on the other. These analyses have shown, among
other things, how composers express the development of two characters'
feelings for one another by the sharing of musical material, not only in the
orchestral fabric but also by gradually increasing the interlocking of voices
through overlapping, singing simultaneously, and – when they are truly
united – by the sharing of the same text.

All of this must be reflected in stage action which illuminates the pattern
of developing feelings expressed by the text and the music. In particular,
the growth of physical displays of affection and intimacy must be shown
on stage. This can be done in various ways, and I have analysed how gifted
directors have chosen gestures, postures and positions for each stage of
the unfolding action which make sense of what the text and the music are
saying about the two characters and their developing relationship.

In the Mozart, Jürgen Flimm has worked out in considerable and effective
detail how in the recitative Don Giovanni charms Zerlina with a mixture
of flattery and braggadocio. Mozart then structures the *duettino* to show

an ever-increasing closeness between the couple, and the movements and gestures in Flimm's production physicalize this aspect of the music, with an especially notable ending in which Zerlina rightly takes the initiative.

Berlioz' great duet for Didon and Énée demands both a physical realization of the 'intoxication and infinite ecstasy' in the returning stanzas of the *rondo*, and a realization that the three episode pairs of stanzas, 'on such a night', are a seduction-game. In his production, Yannis Kokkos stages the gentle gradations of Berlioz' music masterfully, responding to the emotions expressed by the characters in each stanza, and so makes completely credible the mutual ecstasy of the final *avec exaltation* stanza. He even leaves the couple onstage during the woodwind coda, kissing and only then departing, to intensify the sudden contrast when Mercure summons Énée to Italy.

'What an ice-cold little hand' is justly one of the most admired duets in the Italian repertory. It is very demanding for the director and the singing actors, since in just fourteen minutes of music Rodolfo and Mimì must progress from being total strangers to being ecstatically in love. Both the productions studied here devise effective postures and gestures to illuminate this journey, but Luhrmann has a greater sense than Zeffirelli of how relative positioning of the two singers can match the music and convey the essential stages of this mutual discovery of love.

The interaction between Jenůfa and Laca demands a development of closeness which it receives only in Orpha Phelan's Malmö production. Janáček binds his characters together with a wealth of subtle detail, in both the vocal lines and the orchestra, and directors must concentrate on and respond to this music as they stage the journey to Laca's triumphant declaration of how Jenůfa's love has given him inner strength and nobility, which must be accompanied by a close embrace.

4

Confrontations

These are scenes where two characters are in one-to-one conflict. By convention, characters in an opera can hear the emotion conveyed in another's vocal line but cannot hear the orchestral commentary underneath the music which another character is singing, and so – particularly in the Strauss and Janáček examples discussed as **4.1** and **4.2** – the composer can exploit for dramatic effect the inability of one participant in a confrontation to know the inner feelings and thoughts of the other.

When directing such scenes in spoken tragedy, I have often asked the actors to imagine the concept of an invisible cord linking them, so that each character pulls the other in turn. In opera this invisible cord is made audible in the orchestral music. It is the role of the director to clarify on stage the ebb and flow of the conflict, and the reasons for the victory of one character, if this eventuates.

4.1 Elektra and Klytämnestra (Strauss/ Hofmannsthal *Elektra*)[1]

Klytämnestra dismisses her attendants with their torches, and the stage is darkened for this sinister confrontation between a murderess and her vengeful daughter. Strauss's huge orchestra lies almost silent in the pit while Klytämnestra approaches Elektra – ready, however, to break out in its full power at the dramatic climaxes. This tremendous scene shows Strauss's ability to compose *durchkomponiert* music drama with very long spans; the music flows continuously for over seventeen minutes, and there is only one musico-dramatic break. The first part [1] is entirely concerned with dreams and sacrifices. Because of her need for release from torments, the Queen is

---

[1]For a study of this opera and its relationship to Sophocles' drama see M. Ewans 2007: 81–104. For a study of the increasing inevitability of Elektra's death see **9.2**.

deluded into thinking that her daughter is genuinely trying to help her by telling her what sacrifice will cure her ghastly dreams and waking visions; Elektra relishes apparently being helpful, while actually foreshadowing the return of Orest.[2] Then [2] Elektra takes advantage of Klytämnestra's new closeness to ask her to let Orest come home. This rapidly leads to a furious row; Klytämnestra first denies that she is afraid of Orest, and then threatens to maltreat Elektra until she reveals what sacrifice is needed so that she can sleep again. At this point Elektra *springs out of the darkness towards Klytämnestra, coming ever nearer to her, and becoming ever more threatening;* she brings to vivid life her vision of the avenger pursuing Klytämnestra, and reaches three consecutive intense emotional and musical climaxes as she imagines her own triumph when Orest murders their mother (125–8).

[2a] But Elektra's triumph is cruelly undermined. Hofmannsthal creates a shocking *peripeteia*, and the invisible cord which at this point binds mother and daughter close together, *eye to eye,* Elektra *in wild intoxication* and Klytämnestra *breathing horribly in her fear,* is about to be broken. In the second of the great orchestral *tuttis* which punctuate this opera almost like the choruses of Sophocles' original Greek tragedy, the Confidante brings Klytämnestra some whispered news – which we will soon learn is that 'Orest is dead', and so she need fear no more. Maidservants come out with more and more torches so that once again light fills the stage – a light which symbolizes Klytämnestra's new knowledge, but which is delusory because that 'knowledge' is false. She absorbs the news, and *her tension gives way to an evil triumph* (in almost all productions she then laughs maniacally, almost hysterically, at Elektra); Strauss now transfers to Klytämnestra's exaltation in her own triumph the motif (5.1.7c) with which he had portrayed Elektra's fantasy of triumph. As the maids follow the queen into the palace, Elektra is once again left in near-darkness, while her sister Chrysothemis enters running, *howling loudly like a wounded beast,* and shrieking that Orest is dead.

🎵 4 1 El:Klyt part 1

(Only a feeble light from the interior of the palace shines through the vestibule onto the courtyard and here and there illuminates the figures of the two women.)

(KLYTÄMNESTRA descends: softly) 4.1.1

[1] Ich habe keine guten Nächte. 4.1.2 Weißt du kein Mittel gegen Träume?

I have no good nights. Do you know no remedy against dreams?

ELEKTRA *(moving nearer)*

---

[2]Remember that Chrysothemis told Elektra that Klytämnestra is disturbed because she has dreamt about Orest (122.1–2). That auspicious news is the reason why Elektra has resolved to stage this confrontation.

Träumst du, Mutter? **4.1.3**

KLYTÄMNESTRA

Wer älter wird, der träumt.
Allein, es läßt sich vertreiben.
Es gibt Bräuche.
Es muß für alles richt'ge Bräuche geben.
Darum bin ich so
behängt mit Steinen, denn es wohnt in jedem
ganz sicher eine Kraft.
Man muß nur wissen, wie man si nützen kann.
Wenn du nur wolltest,
du könntest etwas sagen, was mir nützt.

ELEKTRA

Ich, Mutter, ich?

KLYTÄMNESTRA *(breaking out)*

Ja, du! Denn du bist klug.
In deinem Kopf ist alles stark.
Du könntest vieles sagen, was mir nützt.
Wenn auch ein Wort nichts weiter ist!
Was ist den ein Hauch?
Und doch kriecht zwischen Tag und Nacht,
wenn ich mit offnen Augen lieg', ein Etwas
hin über mich. Es ist kein Wort, es ist
kein Schmerz, es drückt mich nicht,
es würgt mich nicht,
nicht ist es, nicht einmal ein Alp, und dennoch,
es ist so fürchterlich, daß meine Seele
sich wünscht erhängt **4.1.4** zu sein, und jedes Glied
in mir schreit nach dem Tod, und dabei leb'ich
und bin nicht einmal krank: du siehst mich doch:
sie' ich wie eine Kranke? Kann man denn
vergehn, lebend, wie ein faules Aas?
Kann man zerfallen, wenn man gar nicht krank ist?

Zerfallen wachen Sinnes, wie ein Kleid,
zerfressen von den Motten? Und dann schlaf'ich
und träume, träume, daß sich mir das Mark
in den Knochen löst, und taumle wieder auf,

und nicht der zehnte Teil der Wasseruhr
ist abgelaufen, und was unterm Vorhang
hereingrinst, ist noch nicht der fahle Morgen,

nein, immer noch die Fackel vor der Tür,
die gräßlich zuckt wie ein Lebendiges

Do you dream, mother?

He who grows older, dreams.
But still, they can be driven out.
There are rites.
There must be fitting rites for everything.
That is why I am
so hung with precious stones, since there
lives in every one most certainly a power.
One just has to know how to use them.
If you only wanted to, you could
tell me something which would help me.

I, mother, I?

Yes, you! For you are wise.
In your head everything is strong.
You could tell me much which would help me.
Even if a word is nothing more!
What then is a breath?
And still, between day and night,
when I lie with open eyes, a Something
crawls over me. It is not a word, it is
not a pain, it does not press me,
it does not choke me,
it is nothing, not even a nightmare – but yet,
it is so terrible, that my soul
begs to be hanged, and every limb
in me screams out for death, and still I live
and am not even ill: for you can see it:
do I look like a sick woman? And can one
perish living, like a rotten corpse?
Can one decay, when one is not sick
at all?
Decay with all one's senses awake, like a
dress devoured by moths? And then I sleep
and dream, dream, that the marrow
in my bones is dissolving, and I stagger up
again,
and not the tenth part of the water-clock
has run away, and that which grins into the
room from under the curtain is not
yet the pale morning,
no, just the torch in front of my door,
which flickers horribly as if it were alive

und meinem Schlaf belauert.	and eavesdrops on my sleep.
Diese Träume müssen	These dreams must have
ein Ende haben. Wer sie immer schickt,	an end. Whoever keeps sending them,
ein jeder Dämon läßt von uns, sobald	every demon leaves us, as soon
das rechte Blut geflossen ist.	as the right blood has flowed.

ELEKTRA

4.1.5 Ein jeder!   Every one!

KLYTÄMNESTRA *(wildly)*

Und müßt ich jedes Tier, das kriecht und fliegt,	Even if I must draw blood from every beast
	that creeps or flies,
zur Ader lassen und im Dampf des Blutes	and in the steam of blood
aufsteh'n und schlafen gehn wie die Völker	rise up and go to sleep, as do the people
des letzten Thule im blutroten Nebel:	of distant Thule in their blood-red mists:
ich will nicht länger träumen.	I will no longer dream.

ELEKTRA

Wenn das rechte	When the right
Blutopfer unterm Beile fällt, dann träumst du	blood-offering falls under the axe, then will
nicht länger!	you dream no longer!

KLYTÄMNESTRA *(very hastily)*

Also wüßtest du mit welchem	And so you know with which
Geweihten Tier …?	consecrated beast …?

ELEKTRA *(smiling mysteriously)*

Mit einem ungeweihten!   It is not consecrated!

KLYTÄMNESTRA

Das drin gebunden liegt?   It lies bound within?

ELEKTRA

Nein! Es läuft frei.   No! It roams free.

KLYTÄMNESTRA *(eagerly)*

Und was für Brauche?   And what are the rites?

ELEKTRA

Wunderbare Bräuche,	Wonderful rites,
und sehr genau zu üben.	and very strictly to be observed.

KLYTÄMNESTRA *(vehemently)*

Rede doch!   Tell me, then!

ELEKTRA

Kannst du mich nicht erraten?   Can you not guess my thought?

KLYTÄMNESTRA

Nein, darum frag'ich.   No, that is why I ask.

(as if solemnly imploring ELEKTRA)

Den Namen sag'des Opfertiers!   Speak the name of the sacrificial beast!

ELEKTRA

Ein Weib.   A woman.

KLYTÄMNESTRA *(eagerly)*

Von meiner Dienerinnen eine, sag'!	One of my serving women, say!
Ein Kind? Ein jungfräuliches Weib? Ein Weib	A child? A virgin? A woman

das schon erkannt vom Manne?

who is truly known by men?

ELEKTRA *(quietly)*

Ja! Erkannt!

Yes! Known!

Das ist's!

That's it!

KLYTÄMNESTRA *(pressing on)*

Und wie das Opfer? Und welche Stunde?

And how should this offering be?
And at what hour?

Und wo?

And where?

ELEKTRA *(quietly)*

An jedem Ort, ze jeder Stunde
des Tags und der Nacht.

In any place, at any hour
of day and night.

KLYTÄMNESTRA

Die Bräuche sag'!

Tell me the rites!

Wie brächt' ich's dar? Ich selber muß –

How do I make the offering? I myself must -

ELEKTRA

Nein. Diesmal

No. This time you do not go out

Gehst du nicht auf die Jagd mit Netz und mit Beil.

to the hunt with net and axe.

KLYTÄMNESTRA

Wer denn? Wer brächt es dar?

Who then? Who makes the offering?

ELEKTRA

Ein Mann.

A man.

KLYTÄMNESTRA

Ägisth?

Aegisth?

ELEKTRA *(laughs)*

Ich sagte doch: ein Mann!

Did I not say a man!

KLYTÄMNESTRA

Wer? Gib mir Antwort.

Who? Give me an answer.

Vom Hause jemand?

Someone from the household?

Oder muß ein Fremder herbei?

Or must a stranger come here?

ELEKTRA *(staring at the ground, as if far away)*

Ja, ja, ein Fremder. Aber freilich
ist er vom Haus.

Yes, yes, a stranger. But truly
he is from this house.

KLYTÄMNESTRA

Gib mir nicht Rätsel auf.

Set me no riddles.

Elektra, hör mich an. Ich freue mich,
Daß ich dich heut'einmal nicht störrisch finde.

Elektra, listen to me. I am pleased
That today for once I do not
find you stubborn.

4 1 El:Klyt part 2

ELEKTRA *(softly)*

[2] **4.1.6** Läßt du den Bruder nicht nach Hause,
Mutter? **4.1.7a**

Won't you let my brother
come home, mother?

KLYTÄMNESTRA

Von ihm zu reden hab' ich dich verboten.

ELEKTRA

So hast du Furcht vor ihm?

KLYTÄMNESTRA

Wer sagt das?

ELEKTRA

Mutter,

Du zitterst ja!

KLYTÄMNESTRA

Wer fürchtet sich

vor einem Schwachsinnigen?

ELEKTRA

Wie?

KLYTÄMNESTRA

Es heißt,

er stammelt, liegt im Hofe be den Hunden,

und weiß nicht Mensch und Tier zu unterscheiden.

ELEKTRA

Das Kind war ganz gesund.

KLYTÄMNESTRA

Es heißt, sie gaben

ihm schlechte Wohnug, und Tiere

des Hofes zur Gesellschaft.

ELEKTRA

Ah!

KLYTÄMNESTRA (with drooping eyelids)

Ich schickte

viel Gold und wieder Gold, sie sollten ihn

gut halten wie ein Königskind.

ELEKTRA

Du Lügst!

Du schicktest Gold, damit sie ihn erwürgen.

KLYTÄMNESTRA

Wer sagt dir das?

ELEKTRA

Ich seh's an deinen Augen.

Allein an deinem Zittern seh'ich auch,

daß er noch lebt. Daß du bei Tag und Nacht

an nichts denkst als an ihn. Daß dir das Herz

verdorrt vor Grauen, weil du weißt; er kommt.

KLYTÄMNESTRA

Was kümmert mich, wer außer Haus ist?

I have forbidden you to speak of him.

You're afraid of him, then?

Who says that?

Mother,
you're trembling!

Who is afraid
of a feeble-minded boy?

What?

They say,
he stammers, lies in the yard with the dogs,
and can't tell man from beast.

The child was completely healthy.

They say that he was given
poor living-quarters, and the animals
in the yard for company.

Ah!

I sent
much gold and gold again, for them to treat
him well as a child of kings.

You lie!
You sent gold for them to strangle him.

Who tells you that?

I see it in your eyes.
And from your trembling also I can see
that he still lives. That you by day and night
think of nothing else but him.
That your heart
is diseased by terror, since you know;
he comes.

What does a man matter, who is not in
this palace?

Ich lebe hier und bin die Herrin. Diener
hab'ich genug, die Tore zu bewachen.
Und wenn ich will, laß ich bei Tag und Nacht
vor meiner Kammer drei Bewaffnete
mit offenen Augen sitzen.
Und aus dir
bring' ich so oder so das rechte Wort

schon an den Tag. Du hast dich schon verraten,

daß du das rechte Opfer weißt und auch
die Bräuche, die mir nützen. Sag'st du nicht
im Freien, wirst du's an der Kette sagen.

Sagst du's nicht satt, so sagst du's hungernd. Träume

sind etwas, das man los wird. Wer dran leidet

und nicht das Mittel findet, sich zu heilen,

ist nur ein Narr. Ich finde mir heraus,
wer bluten muß, damit ich wieder schlafe.

ELEKTRA *(with a spring out of the darkness towards KLYTÄMNESTRA, coming ever nearer to her,*
and becoming ever more threatening)

Was bluten muß? **4.1.7 a & b** Dein eigenes Genick,

wenn dich der Jäger abgefangen hat!
Ich hör'ihn durch die Zimmer gehn, ich hör'ihn

den Vorhang vor dem Bette heben:
wer schlachtet
ein Opfertier im Schlaf? Er jagt dich auf,
schreiend entfliehst du, aber er, er ist hinterdrein:

er treibt dich durch das Haus!
Willst du nach rechts,
da steht das Bett!
Nach links, da schäumt das Bad
wie Blut!
Das Dunkel und die Fackeln werfen
schwartzrote Todesnetze über dich –

(KLYTÄMNESTRA trembles with speechless terror)
Hinaus die Treppen durch Gewölbe hin,
Gewölbe und Gewölbe geht die Jagd –

I live here and I am the mistress. I have
enough servants to watch the doors,
and if I want, then every day and night
I can make three armed men sit in front of
my room with open eyes.
And out of you
some way or another I shall force the
  right word

just when I need it. You have
  betrayed yourself –

you know the proper offering and also
the rites, which will help me. If you won't
say it when free, then you
  will speak in chains.

If you won't say when full, you'll say it
  starving. Dreams

are something that one can get rid of.
Someone who suffers them

and does not find the means
  by which to cure himself

is just a fool. I will find out
who must bleed, that I can sleep again.

What blood must flow? From your
  own neck,

the moment that the hunter has trapped you!
I hear him going through the rooms,
I hear him

lifting up the curtain from the bed:
who kills a sacrificial victim
in its sleep? He hunts you up,
you flee screaming,
  but he, he is right behind;

he drives you through the house!
If you turn right,
there stands the bed!
Turn left, there is the bath
foaming like blood!
The darkness and the torches cast
their nets of death in black and red
  all over you –

Down the steps and through the vaults,
vaults and vaults the hunt goes on –

Und ich! **4.1.7c** Ich! Ich! Ich! Ich, die ihn dir geschickt, **4.1.8**	And I! I! I! I! I, who sent him to you,[3]
Ich steh da **4.1.7c, 4.1.8** und seh' dich endlich sterben!	I stand there and see you die at last!
Dann träumst du nicht mehr, dann brauche ich	Then you will dream no more, then I will need
nicht mehr zu träumen, und wer dann noch lebt,	no more to dream, and all who still live then,
der jauchzt und kann sich seines Lebens freun!	they will exult, and can enjoy their lives!

(They stand together eye to eye, ELEKTRA in wild intoxication, KLYTÄMNESTRA breathing horribly in her fear.

[2a] **4.1.8, 4.1.7c, 4.1.7a** *At this moment the entrance hall is lit up. The CONFIDANTE comes running out. She whispers something in KLYTÄMNESTRA'S ear. She appears at first not to understand properly. Gradually she pulls herself together. She commands 'Lights'. SERVING MAIDS run out with torches and place themselves behind KLYTÄMNESTRA. KLYTÄMNESTRA commands 'More lights!' Even more SERVING MAIDS come out and place themselves behind KLYTÄMNESTRA, so that the yard is full of light and a reddish-yellow gleam plays around the walls. Now her appearance changes gradually and her tension gives way to an evil triumph.* **4.1.3** *She has the message whispered to her again and as she does so keeps her eyes fixed on ELEKTRA.* **4.1.7c** *Her whole body satiated with wild joy, she raises both hands threateningly against ELEKTRA.* **4.1.7c** *Then the CONFIDANTE picks up her staff and KLYTÄMNESTRA hurries into the house, leaning on them both, hastily, greedily, and picking up her robe at the steps. The MAIDS with the lights run in after her as if pursued.)*

We shall study this scene as directed on film by Götz Friedrich, in a remarkable set by Josef Svoboda and with Leonie Rysanek in the title role and Astrid Varnay as Klytämnestra (cf. **9.2**). No other recorded version comes close to this one in its understanding of how to stage the developing interaction between the two women.

Hofmannsthal does not describe Elektra's appearance in a stage direction; he does not have to. She is almost invariably portrayed as barefoot, wearing a ragged dress which expresses visually how she is neglected and mistreated, and that dress is often (although not in Friedrich's production) black, to symbolize her role as the bringer of death. By contrast, Hofmannsthal's highly expressionistic stage direction for Klytämnestra's appearance needs to be quoted: *her sallow, bloated face, in the glaring light of the torches, appears even paler over her scarlet robe ... the Queen is completely covered with precious stones and talismans. Her arms are full of armlets, her fingers bristle with rings. The lids of her eyes appear unnaturally large, and it seems to cost her an unspeakable effort to keep them open.* And very soon after she enters she describes herself as 'just a living corpse like a wasted field' (138.3–139.1). Klytämnestra's internal moral decay, the fact that she is

---

[3] Here the DVDs take a standard theatre cut of 35 lines. See note 3.

wracked with guilt and fear, has to be matched in her outward appearance.[4] As costumed and made up by Pet Halmen for Friedrich's production, Astrid Varnay is bloated in body and face; she also wears the excess weight of jewels and talismans required by Hofmannsthal and Strauss, and has huge dark circles around her eyes, which she uses to great expressive effect. Her Klytämnestra is visibly decaying, cruel – and fearful.[5]

This is necessary to the effect of the scene. Only Klytämnestra's need for release from a deep psychological malaise which has corroded her body could lead her to trust for a moment the daughter whom she has recently imaged as a snake and a nettle (133, 139.1). But she does, and Elektra knows how to play on her mother's insecurity. So, as the first part of the scene unfolds, Friedrich gradually brings the two women closer together.

[1] Dreams and sacrifices

We actually hear Klytämnestra's jewels clink in Strauss's score as she goes down towards Elektra (177). Each time this music is repeated, Friedrich has Varnay clutch at the jewels and talismans (180.1–3: 181.7ff.).

4.1.1 (177.1)

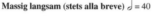

2 harps, glockenspiel,
pizz. strings

---

[4]When she sings 'I am not even ill ... do I look like a sick woman?' (189–90), the audience should think 'yes you do!'

[5]Contrast for example Waltraud Meier's appearance in Nikolaus Lehnhoff's 2010 production at the Salzburg Festival. Her only jewellery was a pair of earrings, and she was slim and stylish in a red fur coat over a close-fitting dress, and wearing designer sunglasses. There was no trace in her appearance of the decay which Hofmannsthal wanted his Klytämnestra to embody in her physique, costume and make-up.

Lehnhoff's production of *Elektra* has many weak points, not the least being that Elektra does not dance herself to death! It simply lacks the blazing energy which characterizes Friedrich's film. And, in our scene, there is a strange lack of engagement and contact between the two principals, which is totally at odds with the drama contained in the music; also it is hard to see the purpose of many of the movements. (At least there is some degree of contact between them at the start of section two.) This *Elektra* is very disappointing in the light of the marvellous insights which Lehnhoff brought to *Kát'a Kabanová* (see **3.5**, **5.2** and **8.3**), *Parsifal* (**8.2**) and his Salzburg Festival production of Schreker's masterpiece *Die Gezeichneten* (2005).

And then we hear a bitonal chromatic descent which portrays Klytämnestra's insomnia and the pain of her nightmares:

4.1.2 (178.1)

This motif becomes important over the next few minutes, together with another:

4.1.3 (178.6)

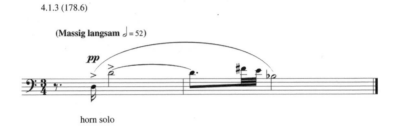

horn solo

This motif is associated with Klytämnestra's dream, since it was first heard at 119–21 when Chrysothemis told Elektra about the dream, and then at 151 when Elektra tells Klytämnestra that she '[is] always like a person in a dream'. After this scene it is next heard when Elektra marvels to Orest that he is prepared to commit matricide alone (172a). By then it has been transferred from the dream of revenge to the actuality; it is very prominent while Elektra lures Ägisth into the palace (201a 5ff.).

These motifs predominate, together with expressive chromatic melodies, as Klytämnestra gradually achieves greater confidence that Elektra can help her. In Friedrich's production, Rysanek, as Elektra, looks with murderous intensity at Klytämnestra throughout her description of her sufferings. Meanwhile Varnay, who sits down on a stone seat as Klytämnestra admits her old age at 179, shows great acting skills during the celebrated, almost atonal passage (186–7) about the Something which creeps up on Klytämnestra while she is trying to get to sleep; her eyes open wide, she shakes her head slightly in disbelief that this can happen to her, she clenches her hands, she shakes her head again with eyes almost closed on 'it's nothing, not even a nightmare' (187.7–188.1); then her eyes open fearfully, and as the description develops ('every limb in me screams out for death', 188.6–189.2) she leans back, ever more tense, as her fear takes hold. Meanwhile the falling chromatic figures derived from **4.1.2** are joined by a new motif:

4.1.4 (188.1)

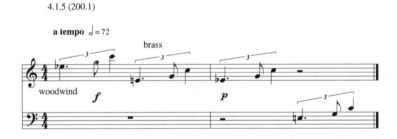

This fiercer agitation in Klytämnestra's psyche, as depicted in the orchestra, justifies Friedrich in escalating the pain expressed in Varnay's posture. Finally **4.1.2** explodes into a fierce sequence of dissonant *ff* downward scales (after 'devoured by moths', in 193), and Varnay's fearful look changes to agony as she raises her head, eyes wide, and then inclines it to one side, eyes closed in pain. Now, Elektra, who has been watching her intently while leaning on a rock, gets up and comes nearer to Klytämnestra (195) – but not all the way; for some reason which I do not understand Rysanek lies down on the ground (still looking intently at Klytämnestra) at 197, then at 199 stares at the ground as if seeing Agamemnon's spirit.[6]

Development of **4.1.4** leads to a climax (Klytämnestra has a sustained top G on 'as soon as the right *blood* has flowed'), and Elektra comments sardonically. At this point one of the main motifs of the opera is heard:

4.1.5 (200.1)

This was first heard when Elektra in her monologue imagined herself, her brother and sister dancing in triumph after their vengeance has been achieved (56); and it will predominate in the closing scene of the opera

---

[6] A shadow, which looks very much like Agamemnon, was seen against a rock during 197. The important role which the spirit of Agamemnon plays in Friedrich's film as a whole is discussed at **9.2**.

as Elektra dances herself to death. Its role here is to tell the audience that the Train-Bearer was right to tell Klytämnestra that 'she [Elektra] means it maliciously' and 'her every word is falsehood' (143, 154); it underlies much of the next few minutes (206, 207, 210, 212, 214), and it reflects, together with reprises of **4.1.3**, how Elektra is obsessed with the revenge throughout Klytämnestra's wild tirade. The shed blood which Klytämnestra imagines in the next few lines of text will be her own, and Strauss signals this by the appearances of **4.1.5** under Elektra's comments now, long before Elektra's imagining of Orest's pursuit and her own triumph in the second half of the scene (which calls for different music).

'I will no longer dream' (202.5–7) spawns another outburst of **4.1.2**, the chromatic descent which evokes how Klytämnestra's nightmares torment her. Just before this point Friedrich rightly has Varnay get up from her seat and go much nearer to Rysanek; Klytämnestra's suffering has led her to be completely enmeshed in the delusion that Elektra can help her, so she goes to her to seek that help. **4.1.3** on solo horn and heckelphone, as Elektra sings 'when the right blood-offering falls under the axe...' (203.4–5), tells the audience just how wrong she is.

Rysanek continues to be on all fours; so when she wants to get near to her Elektra, Varnay has to go down on her knees, facing Rysanek but maintaining a slight height advantage. As Klytämnestra continues to ask her questions (and the triumphal dance keeps coming back in the orchestra to accompany each of Elektra's answers) during 205 she crawls towards Elektra, trembling with anticipation. It is as if Elektra is reeling in a fish on a line.

Elektra stands after 'wonderful rites, and very strictly to be observed' (206). This is sung to a variant of **4.1.5**; the triumph to come is never far from Elektra's thoughts. To regain some advantage, Klytämnestra soon stands as well and pursues her; the women are very close as she implores Elektra, extending her hands, to tell her who the sacrificial woman should be. **4.1.1** in the orchestra (208) tells the audience that it will be herself.

When Klytämnestra wants to know who will make the offering (212.6), Elektra turns away, and stays turned away as her thoughts turn to Orest; Klytämnestra looks at Elektra but Elektra will not look at her, even when she begs for no more riddles. And now, in Friedrich's interpretation, Klytämnestra is totally dependent on Elektra. As Klytämnestra tells her daughter how pleased she is that today Elektra is not being stubborn (215.6ff.), Varnay caresses Rysanek's face, chin and arms, kneels down, embraces her, and leans on her bosom. She has the illusion of affinity with her daughter – but it is on Elektra's terms; this is shown by a sinister little solo horn reprise of **4.1.3** just before 216, while the music is running down to a full stop. The invisible cord has drawn Klytämnestra so tightly into Elektra's web that she is forced to endure what is about to happen.

[2] The return of Orest

The opening phrase of a very memorable theme sounds out as an oboe solo:

4.1.6 (215.16)

This music expressed Elektra's deep love for her father, when it first appeared in her monologue (**9.2.3**; 45.9ff.); its appearance now, as Elektra is about to ask for her brother to return home, is the first stage of the transfer of the theme from love for her father to love for her brother, which will be completed in Elektra's beautiful address to Orest after he has returned and she has recognized him (148a ff.). It appears now, and on the next two occasions that she sings in this section, to underline how her hopes lie with Orest.

Meanwhile a new motif is beginning to appear. As Elektra ends her challenge to Klytämnestra to let Orest come back, **4.1.7a** appears in the bassoons (216.4):

4.1.7 a and b (229.10)

4.1.7a is derived from the fanfares accompanying Elektra's vision of Agamemnon returning (**9.2.2**; 42.4ff.); as she saw Agamemnon coming back then, she feels that Orest is coming back now. And Klytämnestra is affected by this; in Friedrich's production she is rightly made to draw back a little from Elektra when these notes have sounded – but not too far, as she is still bound close to her daughter by the events of section [1]. She claims that she paid money for Orest to be looked after like a son of kings; but Elektra furiously challenges this – Rysanek turns and faces Varnay closely, and Varnay's Klytämnestra is stunned, eyes wide, looking sickly. **4.1.3** and **4.1.7a** continue to sound in the orchestra, for obvious reasons, as Elektra diagnoses that her mother's terror is 'since you know: he comes'. Klytämnestra begins her assertion to the contrary with some confidence;

Varnay reflects this, but the anxious hand that she had put up to her throat as Elektra sang 'that your heart is diseased by terror' remains there, to signal Klytämnestra's underlying unease.

Klytämnestra concludes her challenge to Elektra: 'I will find out who must bleed, that I can sleep again' (228) with another torrent of falling chromatic triplets (4.1.2) – now signalling the torrent of blood which she seeks, rather than the sleepless suffering with which this motif was originally associated. Klytämnestra ends with a climactic top G sharp on 'sleep'; but in Friedrich's production she turns away, eyes shut and in pain; this is no victory, and she is still tied relentlessly to Elektra, who immediately begins her powerful imagining of Klytämnestra's death.[7]

At this point 4.1.7a flares out *fortissimo* in the trombones, and is immediately followed by its new and violent tailpiece 4.1.7b in strings and woodwind. This is a savage attack on Klytämnestra (who is now lying on the ground), and Rysanek's Elektra looks down at her mother with enormous power, while Klytämnestra looks up at her in shock. Again, here, Friedrich rightly insists on the physical closeness of the bond between these enemies; very soon Varnay is leaning right back, closing her eyes under the intensity of the attack, and by 234 Rysanek is close on top of her, and Varnay's Klytämnestra opens her eyes in pain at 235, 'there stands the bed!' They remain in these positions, with Elektra dominant, and Varnay obeys to the full the stage direction just before 237, *trembles with speechless terror.*

Then Elektra rises to her triumph – in Friedrich's production, Rysanek does that literally, leaning upwards and backwards on 239 as she begins to celebrate, and 4.1.7c, a new set of three chords derived from 4.1.7b, blazes out in the brass and woodwind; it is followed closely by 4.1.8, her original dark invocation in the opening monologue to Agamemnon (horns and trombones at 36.6ff.), which is now played as a motif of triumph. Again (cf. 4.1.3) what was premonition then now becomes envisaged actuality.

After the cut, resuming at 255, both these motifs blaze out again to propel Elektra to three successive sustained top notes; A flat, A sharp and a devastatingly triumphant long-held final top C.

They stand together eye to eye, ELEKTRA in wild intoxication, KLYTÄMNESTRA breathing horribly in her fear. Hofmannsthal prescribes

---

[7]The following attack on Klytämnestra would be all the more powerful if it were performed in full, as it was in Solti's 1967 audio recording with Nilsson and Resnik. 35 lines of intense text by Hofmannsthal, with a remarkable setting by Strauss, are usually cut in theatre productions, together with part of the second Chrysothemis scene and a few lines after the recognition of Orest, to enable sopranos to survive a live performance of one of the most demanding roles in the repertory. And this section (240–54) is cut on all DVDs of the opera. It is a great pity that Karl Böhm did not conduct the complete score in Friedrich's film; Rysanek could have sung it in the studio in short takes, and it would have made this great swansong, the culmination of a lifetime's devotion to Strauss (Böhm recorded the music for the film at 87, only months before his death) even greater.

4.1.7 c and 4.1.8 (255.1)

(so schnell und deutlich als möglich)

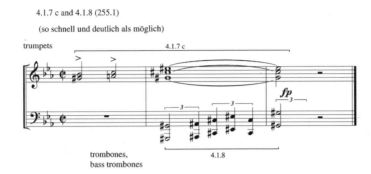

that the two women should be extremely close, but he does not prescribe the relative heights. Friedrich rightly keeps Klytämnestra a little lower, with Elektra radiant in her triumph and hatred, as **4.1.8** sounds out first in lower then in higher instruments to symbolize that Agamemnon lives in the person of his avenger (259.1–3). Klytämnestra is still bonded to Elektra, and the closeness which she developed towards the end of part one of the scene has now turned in part two into an horrific bond with an Elektra who has vividly prophesied her death.

[2a] And suddenly this intense tension is released. Elektra's motif of triumphant attack (**4.1.7c**) is followed at 260 by three groups of **4.1.7a** in trumpets and trombones, which sound like war whoops; but at that precise moment the interior of the palace is lighted up. During the ensuing *tutti* the Confidante whispers in Klytämnestra's ear, and she gradually changes from Elektra's cowed victim to attaining a triumph, in which she appropriates for herself first **4.1.3** (several times) and then finally at the ultimate climaxes (270, 271–2) even **4.1.7c**. The invisible cord which bound the mother and daughter together breaks instantly after Elektra's orchestral whoops of triumph; at 260.5 the music dissolves into agitated figurations, as serving maids with lights illuminate the scene with the literal and metaphorical light of this sudden *peripeteia*. Friedrich stages [2a] with masterful crowd control, and a measured build-up to Klytämnestra's hysterical laughter at 265–6. As the scene ends, our last vision is of Varnay laughing out loud at Elektra from the security of a first floor window in her smooth, gleaming metallic palace façade – which, in Josef Svoboda's design, lies in extreme contrast to the blackened rubble and ruins in the courtyard to which Elektra has been banished and in which the main action takes place.[8]

---

[8]Lehnhoff has an idea here, which does not really work because it is not true to the music. In his production no maids appear at the end of this scene, only the Confidante and the Trainbearer; and Klytämnestra is too sick after the stress of section [2] to call for lights herself, let alone to laugh at Elektra. The Confidante and Trainbearer do both these things for her before they take her inside, almost too weak to move. This is an understandable attempt to

Discussion question

Discuss in detail the performances in this scene of both Astrid Varnay and Leonie Rysanek. Do their postures and gestures respond adequately to Strauss's extraordinary, motivically complex music and to the roller-coaster emotional journey which Hofmannsthal makes both characters undergo?

4.2 Kát'a and Tichon (Janáček/Ostrovsky, *Kát'a Kabanová*, Act I scene 2).

This example is again from *Kát'a Kabanová* I.2 (cf. **2.5**) – but later, as Kát'a tries to persuade her husband Tichon not to go away from home on business. She is desperate because she knows that if he goes she will succumb to the temptation to see Boris, with whom she has fallen in love; but Tichon – who has already been shown in I.1 to be a weakling and a drunkard – is naïve, and almost impervious to her state. The music shows them uneasily yoked together; quite simply, Tichon is trying to leave, and Kát'a is trying to make him stay. Their contrasting musical materials are juxtaposed, and collide; Kát'a's increasing desperation, expressed in the orchestra as well as in her passionate vocal lines, becomes more and more evident to the audience, and even affects the insensitive Tichon.

Once again we study an excerpt from *Kát'a Kabanová* in Nikolaus Lehnhoff's 1988 Glyndebourne production, with Nancy Gustafson in the title role and Ryland Davies as Tichon.

✔ 4 2 Kát'a and Tichon

[1] **4.2.1** *(TICHON enters right, dressed for a journey.)*

KÁTA *(Falls on TICHON and embraces him.)*

Tišo, Tišo, neodjíždej!	Tichon, Tichon, don't go away!

VARVARA

Zbláznila jsi se!	You're going crazy!

(exit)

(Glaša and Fekluša enter right, carrying luggage.)

FEKLUŠA *(to Glaša)*

4.2.2 Na dlouho jede?	Is he going for long?

GLAŠA

Ne na dlouho.	No, not for long.

---

bring out how totally Elektra has defeated her mother, but it greatly weakens the power of the *peripeteia*; Strauss composes in the *tutti* a complete 90° turn for Klytämnestra, from abject subjection to exultant rejoicing, and this must be reflected on stage.

(exeunt centre)

KÁTA

Tišo, neodjíždej!!   Tichon, don't go away!

Holoubku můj!   My dearest dove!

Neodjíždej!!   Don't go!

TICHON

Nelze, Kát'o!   That's not possible, Kát'a!

Jak nepojedu, když maminka posílá?   How can I not go, if Mother sends me?

KÁTA

Vezmi mne také s sebou! Vezmi mne!   Then take me with you! Take me!

TICHON *(releases himself from her embrace)*

Není to možné!   It can't be done!

KÁTA

Proč by nebylo možné?   Why should it be impossible?

Což pak už mne nemáš rad?   Don't you love me any more?

TICHON

[2] Ne, mám tě rad!   No, of course I love you!

Ale z takové otročiny člověk by utekl   But from such a slave-life a man
                                                          would desert

od ženy krasavice nevím jaké   the most beautiful of women

a máli člověk po celý život takhle žít   and faced with spending his
                                                          whole life like this,

uteče 4.2.3 i od ženy!   he'd even leave his wife!

KÁTA *(shocked)*

Jak tě mám pak mít ráda,   How am I to love you

když taková slova mluvíš?   when you say words like this?

TICHON

Slova sem, slova tam!   A word here, a word there!

Kdo se v tobě vyzná?   Who can understand you?

KÁTA *(in tears)*

Kam se já, ubožka, poděju?   Where can I turn in my misery?

Kdo se mne zastane?   Who will support me?

TICHON

Přestaň!   Stop this!

KÁTA *(goes up to her husband and nestles against him)*

[3] Tišo, holoubku,   Tichon, my dearest dove,

kdybys zůstal doma, nebo mne vzal s sebou,   If you stayed at home, or took me
                                                          with you,

tolik bych tě měla ráda,   I would love you so much,

tak bych tě laskala!   fondle you like this!

Tišo, komu mne tady necháš?   Tichon, who are you leaving me to?

TICHON

Nevyznám se v tobě, Kát'o!   I can't understand you, Kát'a!

Jindy člověk slove ze tebe nedostane – a ted'?   At other times a man can't get
                                                          a word out of you – and now?

KÁTA
Tišo, komu mne zanecháš?

TICHON
[4] Vždť viš, že jinak nelze.
Jaká tedy pomoc?

KÁTA
Tišo, stane se bez tebe neštěsty!

Stane se neštěsty.
(suddenly) Viš tedy, co?
Žádej ode mne nějakou strašlivou přísahu,

TICHON
Jakou přísahu?

KÁTA
4.2.4 Nu takovou: že za tvoji nepřítomnosti
za žádnou cenu s nikým cizím ani nepromluvím,

nikdoho nespatřím
že ani pomyslití neopovážím se,
kromě na tebe.

TICHON
Ale nač to? Nač to?

KÁTA
[5] Pro pokoj mojí duše, prokaž mi to milost!

TICHON
Jak pak můžeš za sebe ručit?

KÁTA (falls to her knees)
[6] Abych ani otce, ani matky
vícekrát nespatřila;
abych nez pokání umřela, jestli že –

TICHON (lifting her to her feet)
Nu, copak?
Co děláš?
Vždyť je to takový hřích.

KABANICHA (offstage)
Je čas, Tichone.
(KÁTA and TICHON freeze)
(enter KABANICHA)

Tichon, who are you leaving me to?

Look, it's got to be like this.
So what help is there?

Tichon, something dreadful will
    happen without you!
Something dreadful will happen.
So, d'you know what?
Make me swear a terrible oath,

What kind of oath?

Like this; that when you're not here
for no price will I say a word
    to any stranger,
or look at anyone,
or even dare to think about anyone,
except you.

But why? Why?

For the peace of my soul,
    do me this kindness!

But how can you be sure of yourself?

May I never see
my father and mother again;
may I die without confession, if I –

Now, what's this?
What are you doing?
Look, this is such a sin.

It's time, Tichon.

Janáček composes the confrontation as a conflict between unrelated musical blocks; Kát'a's emotions are opposed to Tichon's resistance, which is symbolized by the troika bells evoking his imminent journey (4.2.2). All the other motifs are hers. But Tichon cannot understand why she is so anxious for him to stay, and he is deaf to the sheer desperation which the audience can hear sounding out of Kát'a's orchestra. Janáček's scene focuses his fullest tragic powers on Kát'a's journey from agitation to absolute desperation – even though Tichon, too, has his own quiet misery (the repetitive jingle of the troika music oppresses him with the suffering of his servile life, and the business trip which he must make at his mother's order).

[1] At the end of the previous section, Varvara has suggested that Kát'a should meet with the man she loves, and a violent *forte* motif expresses Kát'a's agitated rejection of this:

4.2.1 (I.2.17.1)

Because Kát'a's only hope of not giving way to temptation is for Tichon to stay, this motif accompanies Kát'a now as she almost hysterically clasps Tichon and falls on his neck, alternating with agitated semiquavers in violins and clarinet or flute, which maintain a high level of instability throughout much of the scene. Then comes the troika-bell motif **4.2.2**, which not only symbolizes Tichon's journey but is also a fast variant, heard already in the prelude, of the eight ominous timpani blows that appear at crucial moments in the opera. This recurring motif is not, as it has inevitably been labelled, a 'fate theme'; I believe with Daniel Muller that it symbolizes in music the binding power of the iron circles of tradition in 1860s Russian society – a force which in their different ways all the young characters in the opera are trying to escape.[9]

In Lehnhoff's production Kát'a first clasps Tichon as soon as he appears, then falls on his neck as **4.2.2** sounds for the first time – in this relatively mild form with oboe (it is transferred during the next few bars to the horns). Kát'a's first appeal, using the endearment 'my dove', which she will employ again later in the scene, fails; as Tichon sings over her with 'That's not possible, Kát'a', Lehnhoff rightly has Davies pull away and try to disengage from his Kát'a; but the leaping motif **4.2.1** still breaks out – albeit a little calmer – and Gustafson won't let go of him; Kát'a's agitation is still evident in the violins' swirling semiquavers, and its cause – the troika motif – sounds out clearly in a solo horn (18.18–19).

---

[9]'la vielle Russie, le cercle de fer de la tradition', Muller 1930: 63 (English version in Tyrrell 1982: 168). Cf. M. Ewans 1977: 109–10 and Tyrrell 1982: 22–3.

4.2.2 (I.2.18.1)

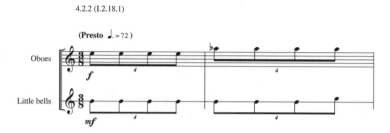

Tichon sings 'It can't be done!' as he breaks from her embrace. In Lehnhoff's production, this is his second attempt to free himself; and Lehnhoff is right to have made Tichon try to break from Kát'a earlier, since for Tichon to have suffered her feverish embrace from his entry right through to this point would be implausible. Two more bars of **4.2.1** express the agitation which she feels because of his continuing refusal, and then Kát'a suddenly tries a new tack: 'Don't you love me anymore?' – four short bars of gentle 3/8 *adagio*. Gustafson sits down on the trunk to indicate Kát'a's apparent subordination; she first turns her eyes downward, looking defeated, as she sings in the first two *adagio* bars – and then, as the orchestra continues to depict her emotions by itself, she looks up at him in appeal, eyes wide.

[2] But the appeal doesn't work. Davies as Tichon has been checking his briefcase to make sure all is ready for departure. Now he puts it down and tells her how he feels, putting on his coat as he does so. To show that he, too, is oppressed the troika music dominates his first four bars, followed by agitated string and woodwind semiquavers as Tichon is roused to emotion and declares how he hates this 'slave-existence' which would destroy a man's love. Gustafson's Kát'a hears and sees this with horror – tense, with staring eyes and arms rigid behind her (she is still sitting on the trunk, relatively the weaker of the two). Three more bars of troika bells separate 'and faced with spending his whole life like this...' from the punch-line 'he'd even leave his wife'. This precipitates absolute terror in Kát'a; it is as if she is staring into an abyss.

4.2.3 (I.2.18-1)

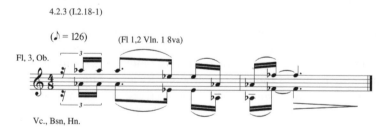

This new and powerful motif will be used to devastating effect, together with **4.2.2**, in the last bars of the Act, once the separation from Tichon which Kát'a fears now has become reality and she has collapsed under the pressure of Kabanicha's triumph. The stage direction here is *shocked*, and Gustafson turns away, unable to bear having to face Tichon; her expression is anguished, and she clenches her hands together under her chin because of the tension. Tichon is indifferent; in Lehnhoff's production he first buttons up his coat, then picks up the small suitcase. He tells her to stop.

[3] Kát'a resolves on one more attempt at intimacy to persuade Tichon, yet again calling him her 'dove' (fig. 21, *moderato*). In the stage directions she *goes up to her husband and nestles against him*; in Lehnhoff's production Gustafson does more. As Kát'a's very warm music unfolds *dolce* in the violins, with solo woodwind instruments, Gustafson gets up, goes across to her Tichon, and sits him down on the trunk – trying to reverse the previous power relationship – before embracing him. Davies as Tichon faces forward, away from her, while she is cuddling him. He is resisting her affection – and in the music Tichon even interrupts to sing against her, showing that he is suspicious of this sudden warmth. Kát'a makes the most explicit statement yet of why she is so anguished – 'Tichon, who are you leaving me to?' – but he detaches himself from her, fairly brutally, in the last bars before 22.

[4] He refuses absolutely to do what she wants; 'it's got to be like this'. Tichon in Lehnhoff's production faces away from Kát'a, avoiding eye contact; Gustafson, as Kát'a, now escalates the situation by running to block the door, warning that 'something dreadful will happen' – more high semiquaver triplets, under which **4.2.2** and a variant of **4.2.3** are heard, maintaining the high tension as she proposes to swear a 'terrible oath'. And this generates a new, extremely trenchant motif.

4.2.4 (I.2.23.1)

Tichon is buckling under the pressure. Varvara has already denounced him (at the end of I.1) as a drunkard, and in Lehnhoff's production Davies as Tichon now tries to get a drink from his hip-flask – but it is empty, so he throws it away. This is good stage business; it shows that Tichon has no escape from the pressure of Kát'a's desperation. **4.2.4** is tossed between groups of instruments, under clarinet trills and violin tremolos, until Tichon simply demands: 'why?' With this, **4.2.4** blasts out very forcefully, *forte* in trombones, tuba and lower strings; he has brought Kát'a's desperate urgency to a crashing halt.

[5] This leads to yet one more strong contrast of mood, tempo, rhythm, orchestration and dynamics; Kát'a makes a gentle plea, to a beautiful melody in the violins, which is echoed in a few moments of peace after she has stopped singing by violins *dolcissimo*, now with harp chords. Gustafson plays Kát'a now as looking sadly at Tichon, her hands at her sides – she has almost no emotional reserves left with which to make such a heartfelt plea. Davies as Tichon simply picks up his suitcase during these moments of peace in Kát'a's soul, rejecting her – then drops it again and takes off his hat in exasperation, as he sings 'But how can you be sure of yourself?' and walks away. This destroys her last hope.

[6] And now Kát'a is totally desperate. The violence of **4.2.4** is back as Kát'a *falls to her knees*. In Lehnhoff's production this does not happen until after she has sung her first four bars – and she does not simply drop to her knees in a space by herself; Gustafson's wide eyes are used to great expressive effect as she clutches onto her Tichon and falls to her knees holding him tightly, while she makes more and more desperate oaths. Tichon is then directed to *lift her to her feet*; and Lehnhoff makes much of this. While Kát'a was kneeling and clasping him, Davies as Tichon lowered a hand and *almost* caressed her hair; now, when he raises her up, he touches her cheek and is about to embrace her – when a sudden angry blast on the trombones and tuba (in the last bar of I.2.24) heralds the arrival of his tyrannical mother Kabanicha, and he moves hastily away from his wife. The ebb and flow and sudden mood-changes of Janáček's music have displayed to the audience the invisible cord which has held Kát'a and Tichon in an anguished interaction throughout this confrontation. Now it has been snapped by the arrival of Tichon's mother.

As soon as Kabanicha's voice is heard, before she has even entered, the troika bells ring out unimpeded, with a nice decorative flute accompaniment; Kát'a has lost. And by a hideous irony Kabanicha now requires Tichon to make Kát'a swear on oath to all the things he refused to let her swear for herself.[10] At the end of that next, penultimate, sub-scene Kát'a, who has already been pushed to her emotional limits by this confrontation with Tichon, breaks down, and Janáček, armed with all the powerful musical materials which have been deployed in the confrontation between Kát'a and Tichon, then heads inexorably for one of his most powerful Act-curtains.

Discussion question

Lehnhoff adds a lot of stage business (especially for Tichon) to the confrontation between Kát'a and Tichon, and he also overrides two stage directions. Why does he do this? Is he justified?

---

[10] Janáček contrived this by a brilliant rewrite, reversing the order of two sub-scenes in the original Ostrovsky play. M. Ewans 1977: 118; Tyrrell 1982: 58.

4.3 Lulu masters Dr Schön (Berg/Wedekind *Lulu* Act 1 scene 3)

🖋 **4 3 Lulu Graham Vick**

🖋 **4 3 Lulu Olivier Py**

Sonata continuation

4.3.1 DR SCHÖN

(drawing himself up threateningly and going up to Lulu)

Wie kannst Du die Szene gegen mich ausspielen?

> How dare you act out that scene against me?

LULU

Sie haben recht, daß Sie mir zeigen, wo ich hingehöre,

> You're right to show me where I stand,

indem Sie mir vor Ihre Braut tanzen lassen.

> by letting me dance in front of your fiancée.

DR SCHÖN

Bei deiner Herkunft ist es ein Glück für dich, vor Anständigen Leuten aufzutreten.

> With your origins it's a privilege for you to appear in front of decent people.

LULU

Oh, ich weiß es wohl, was aus mir geworden wäre,

> Oh, I know well what might have happened to me,

4.3.2 wenn sie mich nicht davor bewahrt hätten.

> if you hadn't looked after me.

DR SCHÖN

Bist Du denn heute etwas and'res als damals?

> Have you changed since then?

LULU

Gott sei Dank, nein!

> No, thank God.

DR SCHÖN

Das ist echt!

> Typical!

LULU

Und wie überglücklich ich dabei bin!

> And how happy I am about that!

DR SCHÖN *(throwaway gesture)*

Wirst Du jetzt tanzen?

> Will you dance now?

LULU

Vor wem auch immer es sei.

> In front of anyone who's there.

DR SCHÖN

Also dann auf die Bühne!

> OK, then get on stage!

LULU *(imploring like a child)*

Nur eine Minute, ich bitte; ich kann mich gar nicht aufrecht halten. Man wird ja klingeln ...

> Just a moment, please; I can't stand upright. They will ring the bell ...

DR SCHÖN *(after a short pause)*

Was wollte der Prinz hier?

> What did the Prince want here?

LULU

Er nimmt mich nach Afrika.

He's taking me to Africa.

DR SCHÖN

Nach Afrika?

To Africa?

LULU

Sie haben mich ja zur Tänzerin gemacht,
damit einer kommt,
der mich mitnimmt.

You made me into a dancer,
so someone might come
and take me with him.

DR SCHÖN

Doch nicht nach Afrika!

But not to Africa!

LULU

Warum haben Sie mich denn nicht in Ohnmacht
fallen lassen?

Why didn't you just let me fall down
when I fainted?

4.3.5 DR SCHÖN

Weil ich leider keinen Grund hatte,
an deine Ohnmacht zu glauben.

I'm afraid I had no reason
to believe in your faint.

LULU

Sie hielten es unten nicht aus …

You couldn't bear it …

DR SCHÖN

Ich weiß zu gut, das Du unverwüstlich bist.

I know too well that you're
indestructible.

LULU

Das wissen Sie also doch?

So you know that after all?

DR SCHÖN (flaring up)

Sieh mich nicht so unverschämt an!

Don't look at me so brazenly!

LULU

Es hält Sie niemand.

No one is making you stay.

DR SCHÖN

Ich gehe sobald es klingelt.

I'll go when the bell rings.

LULU

Sobald Sie die Energie dazu haben!

When you have enough strength of
mind!

Wo ist ihre Energie?
Sie sind seit drei Jahren velobt:
warum heiraten Sie nicht?

Where is your strength of mind?
You've been engaged for three years:
why don't you get married?

DR SCHÖN

Glaubst Du denn wirklich, daß Du mir im Wege stehst!

Do you really think that you
stand in my way!

LULU

Geh'n Sie, um Ihre schuldlosen Braut,
willen lassen Sie mich allein!
Eine Minute doch, und Sie werden schwach!

Go then, for the sake of your innocent
fiancée, leave me alone!
One more minute, and you'll be weak!

DR SCHÖN

Schweig! In acht Tagen bin ich verheiratet!

Shut up! In eight days I will be
married!

Komm mir derweil nicht zu Gesicht.	Keep away from me till then.
LULU	
Ich will meine Türe verschließen. Sie müssen	I will lock my doors. You must now feel
sich jetzt rein fühlen,	that you are pure,
sonst können Sie das Kind in seiner	or you won't be able to marry that
Unschuld gar nich heiraten.	innocent child.
DR SCHÖN	
Willst Du, daß ich mich an Dir vergreife!	Do you want me to lay hands on you!
LULU	
Heiraten Sie sie: dann tanzt sie in ihrem kindlichen	Marry her: then she will dance in
Jammer vor mir, statt ich vor ihr.	front of me in her childish sorrow, not me in front of her.
DR SCHÖN *(raises his fist)*	
Verzeih' mir Gott...	God forgive me...
LULU	
Schlagen Sie mich!	Hit me then!
DR SCHÖN	
(screams) Fort, fort!	Out, out!
(runs to the door)	
Aber wohin? Zu meine Braut? Nach Hause?! ...	But where? To my fiancée? Back home?! ...
Wenn ich zur Welt hinaus könnte!	If I could escape from the world!
LULU	
Sie wissen zu gut, daß ...	You know too well that ...
DR SCHÖN	
Schweig!	Shut up!
LULU	
... daß Sie zu schwach sind, um sich von mir	... that you are too weak to cut
loszureißen ...	yourself loose from me ...
DR SCHÖN *(completely exhausted, he has collapsed into the chair on the left of the table in the centre)*	
Oh, oh, du tust mir weh!	Oh, oh, you are hurting me!
LULU	
Mir tut dieser Augenblick wohl – ich kann nicht sagen, wie!	This moment makes me feel – I cannot say how good!

Last sonata-reprise

DR SCHÖN	
Mein Alter! Mein Welt!	My old age! My world!
(sobbing)	
Das Kind, das schuldlose Kind!	The child, the innocent child!
LULU	
Er weint. Der Gewaltmensch weint!	He weeps. The tycoon weeps!
Jetzt gehn Sie aber bitte ...	Now please go ...
DR SCHÖN	
Ich kann nicht ...	I cannot ...

LULU

zu ihr ...	to her ...

DR SCHÖN

Ich kann jetzt nicht zu ihr.	I cannot go to her now.

LULU

Hinaus mit Ihnen!	Go away!

DR SCHÖN *(gesture of helplessness)*

LULU

Schicken Sie mir den Prinzen.	Send the Prince to me.

DR SCHÖN *(in a hollow voice)*

Sag' mir um Gotteswillen: was soll ich tun ...	For God's sake tell me: what should I do?

(Linking idea) 4.3.3

LULU *(She gets up; her shawl remains on the chair. She pushes aside the costumes lying on the centre table.)*

Hier ist Briefpapier.	Here's some paper.

DR SCHÖN

Ich kann nicht schreiben ...	I can't write ...

LULU *(standing upright behind him, leaning on the back of his chair)*

Also schreiben Sie!	Write!

DR SCHÖN

Ich kann nicht ...	I can't ...

Letter Duet 4.3.4

LULU *(dictating)*

'Sehr geehrtes Fräulein ...'	'Esteemed young lady ...'

DR SCHÖN

Sehr geehrtes Fräu ...? Ich nenne sie Brigitte.	'Esteemed young ...'? I call her Brigitte.

LULU *(with emphasis)*

...'Sehr geehrtes Fräulein ...'	'Esteemed young lady ...'

DR SCHÖN *(writing)*

Mein Todesurteil!	My death sentence!

LULU

'... Nehmen Sie Ihr Wort zurück.' 'Ich kann es mit meinem Gewissen ...'	... 'You must take your promise back.' 'My conscience ...'

(gesture from Lulu, when Dr Schön puts down his pen and gives her an imploring look)

Schreiben Sie: 'Gewissen nicht vereinbaren, Sie an mein fürchterliches Los zu fesseln ...'	Write: 'my conscience does not allow me to bind you to my dreadful fate ...'

DR SCHÖN *(writing)*

Du hast ja recht! Du hast ja recht!	Yes, you are right! You are right!

LULU

'Ich gebe Ihnen mein Wort, daß ich Ihrer Liebe ...'	'I give you my word that I am not worthy ...'

(Dr Schön turns to her again)

Schreiben Sie: 'Liebe unwürdig bin'.	Write: 'not worthy of your love'.

Diese Zeilen sind Ihnen ein Beweis. Seit drei Jahren	These lines are a proof for you.
versuche ich, mich loszureißen;	For three years I have tried to make
ich habe nicht die Kraft dazu.	myself free; I don't have the strength
	to do it.
Ich schreibe Ihnen an der Seite der Frau,	I write to you from the side
die mir beherrscht.	of the woman who is my master.

(Dr Schön puts the pen down.) (commanding gesture from Lulu)

Vergessen Sie mich!	Forget me!

(Dr Schön picks up the pen and writes.)

'Doktor Ludwig Schön.'	'Dr Ludwig Schön.'

DR SCHÖN *(sobbing out loud)*

O Gott!	Oh God!

LULU

Ja, kein: O Gott.	No 'oh God'.

(with emphasis)

'Doktor Ludwig Schön.'	'Doctor Ludwig Schön'.

(Dr Schön writes)

'Postskriptum:'	'Postscript:'

DR SCHÖN *(to himself)*

Postskriptum?	Postscript?

LULU

'Versuchen Sie nicht, mich zu retten.'	'Do not try to save me.'

Coda

DR SCHÖN *(breaks out)*

4.3.2b Jetzt – kommt – die Hinrichtung ...	Now – comes – the execution ...

(collapses into himself)

(gentle ringing of a bell)

(While Lulu gets ready for her dance number, the curtain falls.) **4.3.2a**

Berg's continuous flow of music (interrupted only by Dr Schön's brief attempt at a breakout at 1278–2) relentlessly binds together these two bitter adversaries in the combat of sex and death – Wedekind's tiger and his snake[11] – as Lulu masters the man whom she has been aiming to marry since before the opera began, and whom she will in Act II describe as 'the only person I have loved' just after shooting him five times (II.1.564–7/8).

Beherrscht, 'masters', in the last sentence of the letter to Dr Schön's fiancée which Lulu dictates, is the key word of the scene. It begins with Dr Schön in power – or at least feeling himself to be – and so, as the characters from the previous sextet exeunt, his *Hauptstimme* (principal theme) **4.3.1**,

---

[11] While the Animal Trainer describes his menagerie in the Prologue, Dr Schön's motif (**5.3.1**), flashes out in the lower brass at bar 22, as the Trainer foreshadows exhibiting his tiger. Soon after that Lulu is actually brought on as the Trainer's snake, and he sings an elegy on her fatal beauty (44ff.).

leaping high with its bold assertion of masculine strength, emerges, and sounds again to begin this scene.

4.3.1 (1.3.1209)

Vln., Ob.

But the fatal bond between Schön and Lulu is underscored very soon, at 1219–20, as Lulu sings that she knows what would have happened to her if he had not taken care of her.

Here Berg combines two of the most important motifs in the opera (**4.3.2**). One (**a**) is the *Hauptrhythmus*, which was first heard in the Prologue, just before the Animal Trainer introduces Lulu, his deadly snake (43–4); its meaning then rapidly becomes clear, in scene 1, when it accompanies the *Melodrama* in which the Medical Specialist, finding his wife and the Painter in an intimate embrace, dies of a heart attack (I.1.96). It takes a similarly dominant role when the Painter himself commits suicide in I.2 (percussion solo, 1.2.745ff.). And it closes each Act of the opera: at the end of this scene when Dr Schön correctly foresees his coming execution; at the end of Act II when Alwa ignores Lulu's reminders that she poisoned his mother and shot his father, and buries his face in her lap – so dooming himself in turn; at the end of Act III, after the deaths of Lulu and the Countess Geschwitz at the hands of Jack the Ripper. It is not, as traditional commentators would have it, a 'Fate theme';[12] it is specifically a theme associated with the inexorable deaths which Lulu causes, first of her lovers and finally of herself.

The other motif (**b**) is equally filled with emotional meaning. It is a fragment from the post-Mahlerian *Lento* in D flat major, which was first heard as the closing theme of the Sonata, when Lulu told Dr Schön in I.2 (615ff.) that if she belongs to any one man in the world it is he, because he rescued her from the streets. So the recall here is natural, given what Lulu is singing here. **4.3.2b** was then developed at length in the interlude between Act I scenes 2 and 3, which begins with Lulu's last words to Dr Schön, 'you'll marry me now' ringing in the audience's ears (I.2.954–5). It is music of overwhelming melancholy; like **4.3.2a**, it also speaks of death.[13] Dr Schön's decision ten years or so earlier to feed and clothe the

---

[12] E.g. Redlich (1957: 194), quoted with approval by Perle 1985: 207.

[13] It is finally recapitulated at length towards the end of Act III, as Lulu, now a London prostitute, begs Jack the Ripper (doubled by the singer who played Dr Schön) to sleep with her, even offering to pay *him* to spend the night with her (III.2.1235ff.).

4.3.2 a and b (1.3.1219)

twelve-year-old girl who sold flowers outside the Alhambra Café between midnight and two, and tried to steal his watch, will cause his destruction because of the intense emotional bond between them, and the appearance here of these two themes together signifies that the outcome of this scene will be his death. Dr Schön will assert himself later in the scene (1248–50, where he declines to believe that Lulu's onstage faint was anything but fake [**4.3.5**]); but his battle against his infatuation with her will soon prove to be lost. To the most agonized music that has accompanied him so far in the opera, he attempts to escape from her, but realizes that he has nowhere to go (1278–83). This is the first climax in the scene; his failure to find a way out is symbolized by a catastrophic descent in the orchestra, from the heights of flutes and violins (top G flat) to the lowest depths of tuba and piano (bottom D, augmented by a *fortissimo* outburst on the tam-tam). Soon after this comes the recapitulation ('last reprise') of the Sonata, in which Schön's noble theme (**4.3.1**) is still to be heard (e.g. right at the start, I.3.1289–90), but is emasculated as his resistance crumbles.

At the end of that comes a 'linking idea' (I.3.1298), as Lulu finds paper for Schön to write the letter breaking off his engagement. As with our last example, Berg here puts together two ideas from earlier in the opera, one in solo violin and the other in clarinets and violas.

These are two major musical themes from scene 1, which like the Mahlerian *lento* discussed above have been imprinted on the audience by being developed in an interlude, this time that between Act I scenes 1 and 2. The idea heard on solo violin (**4.3.3a**) was the melody of Lulu's Canzonetta at I.1.258ff., when she hoped that the Medical Specialist would come back to life. **4.3.3b** is the melody of the Canon, which was first heard in the first scene as Lulu teased, and the Painter pursued her (I.1.156ff.). It was then developed at length in the interlude after she successfully transferred herself

4.3.3 a and b (1.3.1298)

(Allegro energico Tempo 1)

from the dead Medical Specialist to the Painter (Trio; Canon, I. 367ff.).[14] It represents the playful side of Lulu's erotic power; her conquest of the Painter in the first scene of the opera was indeed playful, but for this melody to return now, together with the melody from the Canzonetta which she sang just after the Medical Specialist's death, associates this moment with conquest and death.

The new Canon of the Letter Duet (**4.3.4**) which now follows is also slightly playful,[15] but naturally has an underlying air of insistence, as Lulu imposes her dictation on Dr Schön.[16]

---

[14] It is also heard as a bridge theme in the Sonata exposition, I.2.554–86, where Lulu tells Dr Schön how blind the Painter is.

[15] It is a strange Letter Duet; Lulu sings the words and Dr Schön silently writes them, with occasional protests, so it is not really a duet in any normal sense of the word. One part in the Canon is actually inaudible, as it consists of the words as Dr Schön writes them, shortly after Lulu sings each phrase. Berg writes actual notes for these unheard words! Berg is always meticulous, but sometimes he goes too far with his precise instructions. This is one such instance.

[16] Its theme was first heard for fifteen bars in 1.2 (650–5), accompanying the heated argument between Lulu and Dr Schön in which Lulu denied she was jealous of 'the child' (Dr Schön's fiancée Charlotte, who as he acidly points out is only one year younger than Lulu herself). That argument led the Painter to interrupt his work to find out what has happened, at which point there is a mini-explosion of **4.3.2b** in violins, violas and horns (I.2.666). This anticipates the way in which the Letter Duet (and the whole Act) will similarly end with a Coda which begins with an outburst of that theme.

4.3.4 (1.3.1303)

And at the end, after the humiliating postscript has been extracted from an already totally demoralized Dr Schön, the orchestra gathers ominously for the second climax of the scene, the *Lento* Coda. Once again the intense passion of the *Lento* theme, **4.3.2b**, rises in the orchestra, *molto espressivo*. It was the coda of the first Sonata; its role as the Transformation Music made it effectively the coda to the whole of Scene 2; and it appears now as the Coda to the entire Act, symbolizing that Dr Schön's inability to resist Lulu is about to destroy him. 'Now … comes … the execution'; and it literally will, at the end of Act II scene 1. So the orchestra reaches a climax of searing dissonance (1357 beat 1), and then heads softly but with menace towards the crushing *forte Hauptrhythmus* **4.3.2a** in brass, piano and bass drum, as the curtain falls. Lulu has wrecked Dr Schön's planned wedding, and only death will now release him from the binding power which she holds over him.

*

The three available DVDs of *Lulu* offer an opportunity to study the development of production over the last thirty-five years. Wedekind wrote a 'monster-tragedy' in two parts – *Earth Spirit* and *Pandora's Box* – in which men and women are like wild animals, and lurid sex and violence are the subjects of every scene. Berg then set his own brilliant condensation of the two plays with all the very considerable sensuality, and highly expressive dissonance, which his mature musical idiom commands. The work of both men demands an appropriate response in performance.

A literal adherence to the *mise-en-scène* envisaged in Berg's 1930s stage directions can be seen in John Dexter's 1980 production,[17] the first staging of the complete opera at the Met, conducted by James Levine. Julia Migenes is costumed for this scene in a long flowing dress, quite unsuitable for the kind of show that would go with Alwa's kitschy jazz-band music – or for the stunning effect that Lulu should make on Alwa when she emerges from behind the changing screen in her 'ballet costume' at I.3.1020. Franz Mazura, a veteran player of Dr Schön, is in full evening dress and white

---

[17] Costumes and sets by Jocelyn Herbert.

tie.[18] The movements generally follow the stage directions, with some effective gestures added (e.g. Lulu embraces Dr Schön while she is *imploring like a child* that she is still too weak to go back onstage). When Schön raises his fist against her ('God forgive me ...'), Migenes falls at his feet in a melodramatic gesture, hands extended in supplication – and in a nice touch Schön, after rushing to the door, finds that he is confronting his image in a mirror, on 'But where?'. Clearly, what he sees confirms that there is nowhere for him to go.

The Letter Duet is played very straight; Dr Schön sits at a table, with spectacles on to signal his age and vulnerability. Lulu stands on his left, later crossing behind him, with a wine goblet in her hand, from which she drinks triumphantly the moment he has written down the postscript. During the Coda, she takes the completed letter and folds it. Mazura, as Dr Schön, marks the searing climax at I.3.1358 beat 1 simply by letting his pen fall, which is in no way an adequate response to the text or the music, and he remains seated at the table in a state of shock when Lulu exits.

Graham Vick's Glyndebourne production (1996) was unfortunately set in a minimalist design, by Paul Brown, consisting of large bare brick walls and an open staircase. But the acting is much more responsive than in Dexter's production to the animal desires which surge (in the spirit of the Animal Trainer's Prologue) throughout Berg's setting of this scene. Christine Schäfer is a very attractive Lulu, and she *is* dressed as one might expect for Alwa's show; a sleeveless, glittering silver top which shows plenty of cleavage, a tutu, panties and white, patterned stockings with suspenders. Schäfer's total ease with this revealing costume says much about the sexual dynamics of Lulu's dominance over so many men in the course of the opera. For example, her acting of the *imploring like a child* lines at I.3.1230ff. is much more erotic than that of Migenes. This Lulu holds Dr Schön tightly, and runs her hands sexily down his chest while gazing intensely into his eyes. Then, knowing that these moves have had an effect, she breaks contact and walks away from him before replying to 'What did the Prince want here?' and sitting down casually. After that, there is plenty of movement towards and away from each other to illustrate the ebb and flow of the conflict, and the increasingly strong grip which Lulu has on Dr Schön.

Schäfer's Lulu is highly provocative at 'Marry her; then she will dance in her childish sorrow before me ...', holding out her hands in mock entreaty.

---

[18] It must be admitted that, although imposing, Mazura's Schön is not particularly sexually attractive. It is hard to see the tiger in him, or to imagine either Lulu or Charlotte falling in love with him for his looks alone. Maybe the power that he wields, as a rich newspaper baron, is the attraction? (The ageing newspaper tycoon Rupert Murdoch wooed and won the much younger and then very beautiful Wendy Deng for his third wife – though she later divorced him.)

This motivates Wolfgang Schöne's Dr Schön to break out violently;[19] he very nearly hits his Lulu at 1278, where Berg only requires that he should raise his fist. Similarly, at 'If I could escape from the world', he hurls a chair in his anger and frustration, while Lulu stands happy and at ease. For the top B on '[I cannot say how] *good* (I feel)' she holds her hands up and out, expressing through gesture the extreme joy, which is very much there in her music.

This Dr Schön is defeated by the time of 'For God's sake tell me: what should I do?'. Schäfer's Lulu had sat down on a chair a few moments before (at 'to her ...'), and now Schöne kneels down on the floor beside her and looks closely into her eyes, expressing Dr Schön's helplessness. Vick is quite rightly reluctant to break this significant pose, so Dr Schön produces a pen from his pocket and, as if by magic, finds a clipboard with paper on it under Lulu's chair. (This is not very realistic; but *Lulu,* for all the detailed descriptions of décor in the stage directions, is very far from being a realistic opera.) Dr Schön writes his letter kneeling on the floor, and resting the clipboard on Lulu's beautiful and very much exposed thigh; this position exemplifies his sexual dependence on her.

In the Coda she takes the clipboard and letter from his hands. Dr Schön bows down on 'execution', and at the dissonant climax at the start of I.3.1358 sinks his head onto Lulu's thigh – a powerful image of how her sexuality has conquered him. When Lulu leaves, in the last two bars, Dr Schön collapses his head and arm onto the chair.

In Vick's production, the uninspiring (and uninspired) sets are greatly offset by the sexual power which Schäfer's Lulu wields over Dr Schön in this scene (and, elsewhere in the opera, over others). But for truly deep illumination of *Lulu* we need to study the work of avant-garde *enfant terrible* Olivier Py. DGG released a DVD of his production at the Gran Teatre del Liceu in Barcelona in 2011. It stars Patricia Petibon as a very powerful, predatory Lulu, and Ashley Holland as Dr Schön – maybe looking a bit young to be Alwa's father, but highly effective nonetheless.

Py's production is visually stunning.[20] In this scene, Alwa's show is going on continuously on an upper level in the background. Rightly reflecting in twenty-first century terms the tackiness of Alwa's jazz-band music (as heard earlier in I.3), the dances are raunchy strip-club stuff, with both male and female dancers performing erotic choreography under red lights, bare-chested and bare-legged. In contrast to this, Lulu's own costume is expressionistic, and not sexy at all.[21] She has been dancing in a black

---

[19] Schöne is dressed for this scene in a lounge suit, much less formal than was Mazura.

[20] It is also very expressionistic, and its disregard for Berg's original *mise-en-scène* may be too much for some viewers. But cf. **8.3** on Teresa Stratas's performance as Salome in Götz Friedrich's film, set against Strauss's original expectations. The same principles apply here.

[21] This makes Alwa's overwhelmed reaction when she comes out after changing at I.3.1020 a lot harder to understand than in Vick's production, but that is a relatively small price to pay for what Py gains.

body suit with the bones of a white skeleton sewn onto it, and wearing a death's head mask, which she has discarded for this scene. In this way, Py and his set-and-costume designer, Pierre-André Weitz, get to the heart of what Wedekind – and even more powerfully Berg, with his use of the *Hauptrhythmus* **4.3.2a** in this scene and throughout the opera – are telling us. Lulu brings death to all who fall under her spell – and ultimately to herself. And in Py's production the means which she uses, sexuality, is constantly on display on the upper stage almost throughout I.3.

In Py's conception this scene is a dance of death, a ferocious sex-combat of truly Strindbergian dimensions. As it begins, Lulu is kneeling on the floor, and in his fury Holland's Dr Schön seizes her by the hair at 1215 ('with your background...'); Petibon puts both hands up to her head to break his grip, but fails. Where a *throwaway gesture* is prescribed for Dr Schön at the end of 1225, this Schön actually throws his Lulu to the floor; but then for '[I'll dance] in front of anyone who's there' she defiantly raises a leg, showing him her crotch. He still has some resistance left, so he pushes the leg down violently and breaks away from her.

Rather than having physical contact with Dr Schön during the *childishly imploring* 'Just a moment, please ...', as in both previous productions, Petibon stays on the floor, and collapses to the ground after 'they will ring the bell...', pretending to be totally abject; she only breaks this pose and stands up in the 'short pause' of the following bars.

There is much more violence to follow. Lulu goes to Schön and holds him on 'Why didn't you just let me fall down when I fainted?'; but then the orchestra changes from picturing the faint (**4.3.5a**) to focusing on the impact of Schön's violent reaction (**4.3.5b**):

4.3.5 (1.3.1246)

Py rightly hears the assertive masculine power surging in the orchestra in **4.3.5b**, so his Dr Schön turns Lulu around, grabs her from behind, and they are grappling with each other, locked in love-hate, until Lulu gets the upper hand with her counter-attack on 'Where is your strength of mind?' Here, she pushes him away and raises a fist threateningly, and her anger mounts until 'Go then ...', where she throws something (the object is not really visible on the DVD). But, when she taunts him with 'one more minute and you'll be weak!', once again Dr Schön's violent reaction ('Shut up!') is physicalized; he grabs her fiercely and throws her to the floor, as he sings of his determination to be freed from her by his marriage. Lulu crawls away from him.

In the light of the physical sex-combat so far, the like of which had never been seen before in a production of *Lulu*, you might expect fireworks for the break-out where in Berg's stage direction (following Wedekind) Dr Schön *raises his fist* towards Lulu and then attempts to leave. And you get them. Holland as Dr Schön raises not his fist but a chair, which he threatens to bring down on Lulu's head – but then he throws it away in frustration, and she laughs.

That was Dr Schön's last chance to escape. But he has nowhere to go; Lulu has won. So now Py rightly has him fall to his knees for 'But where?', and on her next line Lulu goes behind him and pushes him down onto all fours.

This sets up the most powerful image in the scene. To symbolize her absolute victory, Petibon mounts on top of her Dr Schön's back and grabs his hair – as he grabbed hers, earlier, but in a far more demeaning posture for the victim. Then, as she hits the top B on '[I cannot say how] *good* (I feel)', expressing her extreme pleasure in this moment of triumph, Petibon raises her hands high in the air. So too did Schäfer as Lulu in Vick's production, but this is a far more powerful victorious gesture, when Lulu is riding on Dr Schön's back, than when she is simply standing at a distance from him.

Petibon gets off when Lulu tells Dr Schön to send the Prince to her, and walks away laughing. But Py is not finished with this powerful image. And he has one more expressionistic surprise in store. As the Linking Idea begins (4.3.3. after 'What should I do?'), a young woman in a bridal dress appears stage right. She represents Dr Schön's aristocratic fiancée, Charlotte Marie Adelaide von Zarnikow ('I call her Brigitte', Dr Schön tells Lulu at I.3.1305),[22] and she watches the dictation of his letter to her with increasing anguish.

Petibon's Lulu now continues to treat Dr Schön with contempt. She throws the writing paper at him, walks around him as he writes, and then

---

[22] Berg changed the name in Dr Schön's line from the fiancée's real first name, 'Charlotte', which is spoken at this point in Wedekind's original, to 'Brigitte'. He thereby extended Wedekind's giving of pet names to young women, which commodifies them as objects of desire, from Lulu (who in the course of the first two Acts is variously called Nelly, Eva and Mignon by different lovers) to Dr Schön's fiancée.

at 'My conscience...' 'Write:' pushes him from kneeling erect down to all fours again. She mounts on top of him once more as he exclaims 'Yes, you are right!', and as she dictates 'I give you my word...' she closes her eyes in ecstasy; she then makes her dominance even more complete (if that is possible!) by casually lifting up one leg to rest her right foot on his back. (By this stage the bride is looking appalled.) Only when Lulu has Dr Schön's signature does Petibon get off Holland's back, and she takes up a position between him and the bride.

And now for the final shock, Py's staging of the *lento* Coda. As soon as she has finished dictating the postscript, Petibon goes to the bride and tears off her bridal dress, leaving her in her underwear. Then, as Schön pronounces his death sentence, still kneeling with the letter in his hand, Lulu crosses left, taking the bridal dress with her, checks her appearance in the mirror of her dressing table, and then goes up the stairs to the dance stage. In the last two bars the bride collapses, and as the *Hauptrhythmus* brings the music to a close Lulu – now on the front of the raised stage – holds the bridal dress, the symbol of Schön's marriage, up at arm's length, with contempt, first to the stage audience which has been watching Alwa's show, and then, as the curtain falls, turning round with blazing eyes, to the opera's audience in the auditorium.

So ends a stunning physicalization of Berg's intense sex-combat, a fight for survival between two fierce antagonists, who both have everything to lose if they do not prevail. The Animal Trainer's snake defeats his tiger by the means she knows best – 'to entice, to seduce, to poison and to murder – without you even feeling it' (I.Prologue.50–5). Despite his desperate attempt to break away, Dr Schön is now linked to Lulu by unbreakable chains. And Py has illuminated her mastery to the full.

Discussion question

Which staging of this confrontation do you think is more appropriate to Berg's music – Graham Vick's relatively traditional (but still striking) version, or Olivier Py's avant-garde approach to the scene? Give reasons for your choice – and in particular consider the much more violent physicality of Py's production, and the appearance of Dr Schön's fiancée as a silent extra in the closing minutes.

4.4 Not going to church (Britten/Slater *Peter Grimes* Act II scene 1)

This section of Act II scene 1 is a pivotal scene in Britten's first opera. Here Peter admits that 'my only hope depends on you. / If you take it away what's left?', and then loses that 'only hope' by striking Ellen in a fit of rage, seen by enough of the Borough inhabitants to precipitate action against him, and leading to fresh tragedy at the end of the Act.[23]

We shall examine how the connection between Peter and Ellen, and the movement to its decisive rupture, is portrayed in the text, in the music, and on stage in the performances by Jon Vickers and Heather Harper, directed by Elijah Moshinsky at Covent Garden in 1981, and by Philip Langridge and Janice Cairns, directed by Tim Albery at English National Opera in 1994.[24]

♨ 4 4 Not going to church Vickers

♨ 4 4 Not going to church Langridge

In musico-dramatic terms the scene, as Britten has composed it, divides into five sections.

CHOIR *(off)*
[1] O all ye works of the Lord, bless ye the Lord;
O ye Sun and Moon, bless ye the Lord;
O ye Winds of God, bless ye the Lord;
Praise Him and magnify Him for ever.
PETER GRIMES enters.
PETER
Come boy!
ELLEN
Peter – what for?
CHOIR *(off)*
O ye Light and Darkness, bless ye the Lord;
O ye Nights and Days, bless ye the Lord;
O ye Lightnings and Clouds, bless ye the Lord;
Praise Him and magnify Him for ever.
PETER
I've seen a shoal. I need his help.
ELLEN
But if there were then all the boats

---

[23] In several parts of the scene an offstage chorus is heard participating in a church service, but, despite that, this study appears in this chapter rather than in 6, 'Noises Off', because the characters on stage here do not interact in any way with the church music from offstage. At moments, however, the audience will register ironic connections between what is being sung in the church and what is happening outside.

[24] Act II scene 1 of *Peter Grimes* has been the subject of a detailed analysis, Matthews 1983. But the author rightly describes it as 'an examination of the music'; the relationship of the musical phenomena which he picks out for study to the developing stage action is not his concern.

Would fast be launching.
PETER
I can see the shoals to which the rest are blind!
CHOIR *(off)*
O ye Wells, bless ye the Lord;
O ye seas and floods, bless the Lord;
O ye Whales and all that move in the waters;
Praise Him and magnify Him for ever.
ELLEN
This is a Sunday, his day of rest.
PETER
This is whatever day I say it is.
Come boy! Come boy!
CHOIR *(off)*
O all ye Fowls of the Air, bless ye the Lord;
O all ye Beasts and Cattle, bless ye the Lord;
O all ye Children of Men, bless ye the Lord;
Praise Him and magnify Him for ever.
CHOIR *(off)*
O ye Servants of the Lord bless ye the Lord;
O ye holy and humble, bless ye the Lord;
Ananias, Azarias, Misael, bless ye the Lord;
Praise Him and magnify Him for ever.
ELLEN
You and John have fished all week
Night and day without a break.
Painting boat, mending nets, cleaning fish, now let him rest!
PETER
Come boy!
ELLEN
But your bargain?
PETER
My bargain?
ELLEN
His weekly rest.
PETER
He works for me, leave him alone, he's mine.
CHOIR *(off)*
Glory be to the Father, and to the Son, and to the Holy Ghost,
As it was in the beginning, is now and ever shall be,
World without end. Amen.
ELLEN
Hush!
Hush, Peter! Peter! Hush, Peter! Hush, Peter! Hush, Peter!
(speaks to PETER, away from the boy)

[2] **4.4.1** This unrelenting work,
This grey unresting industry,
What aim, what future,
What peace will your hard profits buy?
PETER
Buy us a home, buy us respect,
And buy us freedom from pain
Of grinning at gossip's tales.
Believe in me, we shall be free.
CHOIR *(in church)*
[3] **4.4.2** I believe in God the Father Almighty,
Maker of heaven and earth,
And in Jesus Christ his only son, our Lord,
Who was conceived ...
ELLEN
Peter, tell me one thing,
Where the youngster got that ugly bruise?
PETER
Out of the hurly burly.
ELLEN O your ways
Are hard and rough beyond his days.
(ELLEN goes to PETER and puts her hand on his arm.)
Peter, were we right, were we right in what we planned to do?
Were we right, were we right?
PETER
Take away your hand.
(then quietly)
My only hope depends on you,
If you take it away what's left?
ELLEN *(moves unhappily away from him)*
[4] Were we mistaken when we schemed
To solve your life by lonely toil?
(AUNTIE is seen peering through the "Boar" window.)
PETER *(in anger)*
Wrong to plan!
Wrong to try!
Wrong to live!
Right to die!
(BOLES and KEENE walk down the street.)
(They stop for a moment to listen.)
ELLEN
Were we mistaken when we dreamed
That we'd come through and all be well?
PETER
Wrong to struggle!

Wrong to hope!
Then the Borough's right again!
ELLEN
Peter, you cannot buy your peace,
You'll never stop the gossips' talk,
With all the fish from out the sea.
We were mistaken to have dreamed.
Peter! We've failed, we've failed.
(PETER cries out as if in agony. Then strikes ELLEN,
whose work basket falls to the ground.)
CHOIR *(off)*
[5] Amen!
PETER
4.4.3 So be it! – And God have mercy upon me!
(PETER drives the boy fiercely out in front of him.)
(ELLEN goes out the other way, weeping.)

[1] The first section is set as declamatory vocal lines, detached from the underlying E minor harmony of the choir and organ. There is no meeting of minds between Ellen and Peter, as she wants to keep the boy, John, resting and he wants to take him out to sea. The church service is a continuous accompaniment until the end of the *Gloria* is followed by Ellen's repeated outcries of 'Hush, Peter!' These cries end the increasingly angry argument.

[2] So now Ellen can start to reason with him. And with the choir and organ silent the main orchestra can, and does, illuminate the feelings which they both bring to the dispute. For a few moments they are talking as we can imagine they have talked before (remember the *a capella* duet at the end of the Prologue, after the inquest).

[3] But the gulf between them is opening, precipitated by the 'ugly bruise' which Ellen found on the youngster's neck, and which Peter does not deny is his doing. The music (see below) expresses Peter's growing anger as she presses him further 'were we right in what we planned to do? Were we right, were we right?' and he pushes her hand away violently. But then, as if frightened that the connection between them will be broken, he pleads with her *dolce semplice*.

[4] Ellen, however, is still smarting from the rejection. She asks twice 'were we mistaken when we schemed (1) / dreamed (2) …?', and at the third and decisive repeat turns this into 'We were mistaken …'. Her gentle *arioso* line over solo harp is in stark contrast with Peter's rejection of her questioning, which is set to violent and jagged *con forza* vocal lines over a rough instrumental accompaniment. Peter is so disturbed by the direction which Ellen is now pursuing that he bursts in at the end of her first question, then abrasively sings his next denial over her next question. Here the *staccato* brass chords (**4.4.2**), which have portrayed the increasing tension as the argument nears its climax, become exceptionally prominent.

Then Ellen admits defeat, and a gentle solo violin reflection on her melody separates 'we were mistaken to have dreamed ...' from 'Peter! We've failed, we've failed!' – with an agonized octave leap on the last 'we've',[25] which precipitates turmoil in Peter, who first cries out *as if in agony* and then strikes Ellen, all in two bars of jagged and ugly music which mark the breaking of the relationship.

[5] At this moment the chorus in the church intones 'Amen!' *fortissimo* in octave F naturals, supported by the full organ. Peter accepts this as a verdict on the irrevocability of what he has done, and sings 'So be it...' followed by a new *leitmotif* on the exit line 'and God have mercy upon me!' This outburst will underlie much of the rest of the opera.

*

[1] As the chorus, accompanied by the organ, sings an unsettled and fast setting of the *Benedicite* (*allegro agitato*), the conflict begins. Both Vickers and Langridge respond to the almost gestural quality of Grimes' vocal lines by acting this section in an extremely intense and determined manner. And in both productions Ellen shows her equal determination not to let the boy go; both Ellens restrain the boy when he instinctively tries to obey Peter's first 'Come boy!'. Then in Moshinsky's production Vickers, who began the scene a long way upstage and on the opposite side from Ellen and the boy, comes very close to them on 'This is whatever day I say it is! Come boy!'; here it looks as though he is going to take the boy by force. Harper holds the boy firmly to prevent him from going to Grimes, and this is good because the music shows that Ellen intensifies her resistance at this point – the vocal line for her response, 'you and John have fished all week ...' is marked *marcato*.

Both singers playing Grimes make a grab for the boy on the *con forza* climax of the argument: 'He works for me, leave him alone, he's mine!'. Cairns, as Ellen, seems to have more power over Langridge's Grimes – two outstretched warning hands are enough to stop Langridge's advance; in contrast, Vickers actually takes the boy from Harper and hauls him upstage – but the intensity of Ellen's outcry on top B flat ('Hush, Peter') distracts him, and he pushes the boy away so that he can confront her. Langridge's Grimes is also intimidated by this outcry; he retreats and turns away as his Ellen sings these words for the last time, and so is facing away from her as section two begins.[26]

---

[25] The octave leap is the largest given to Ellen, even in this moment of pain. Peter, by contrast, is quite often made to sing the dissonant minor ninth as an emblem of his distress and his much less restrained passion, cf. e.g. 'Wrong to plan?'

[26] In section two Ellen is supposed in the stage direction to be speaking to Peter *away from the boy*, but Albery keeps the boy close to her in his production; he is after all a vital stakeholder in the argument between the grown-ups, and in both productions the apprentice acts very well his silent but appalled observation of the adult conflict on whose outcome he is totally dependent.

[2] Now Ellen begins to try to persuade Peter, and with the choir and organ silent we hear in the orchestra the feelings in their minds; for Ellen, who sings *tenebroso*, there is a correspondingly dark echo of her line in oboe and bassoon, with a sudden *staccato* downslide in lower strings at the end of each phrase, almost a shudder of distaste for the unrelenting work: **4.4.1**.[27]

4.4.1 (II.1.15.7)

As Peter engages with her question and attempts to persuade her, he is accompanied by restless *tremolos* which speak of his agitation and tension, and a sinister bass line, which climaxes in 'Believe in me, we shall be free!' *con forza* – on which the chorus re-enters, singing F natural against his F sharp, declaring that they have faith in a power who is for them more worthy of belief than Peter: 'I believe in God the Father Almighty ...'.

Langridge begins the section facing away from his Ellen, but the quiet intensity of 'This unrelenting work ...' forces him to cross over to be close to her, sitting beside her on the bench before he tries to persuade her with 'Buy us a home ...', which Langridge accompanies with intense persuasive gestures. Vickers by contrast remains distant from his Ellen throughout, giving him the chance to make rhetorical gestures as he tries to sell her the idea that they will gain a home, respect and freedom from gossip as the reward for his efforts.

[3] In a fine invention, Moshinsky has Harper, as Ellen, gently shaking her head as the *Credo* begins; she has not accepted Peter's vision of the future, and is gearing herself up for the next round of the confrontation, in which the gulf between them will widen. Britten symbolizes this by the intrusion just before the chorus fades of an ominous figure, which will

---

[27] In Moshinsky's production, you can see this distaste in Harper's facial expression.

grow in intensity as the gap between Ellen and Peter widens; it consists of a rhythmic F natural pedal in the horns (**4.4.2a**), together with snap staccato chords in the trombones, which gradually rise in pitch (**4.4.2b**).

4.4.2 (II.1.16.2)

This combination will underlie the whole of section [3], growing louder towards a vicious climax after 'Take away your hand', and still remaining under the vocal line, but more quietly, to undermine Peter's subsequent plea 'My only hope ...'.

The two productions have opposite approaches to 'tell me one thing'; in Albery's, Cairns sends the boy away just before these words, as if Ellen is clearing the decks before actually accusing Peter of child abuse; the boy goes and sits in a corner until Peter drags him off at the end of the scene. By contrast, Harper goes to the boy and opens his jacket, confronting Peter directly with the evidence. Both Peters are defensively angry, with big arm gestures, as they give their evasive answer, 'Out of the hurly burly';[28] but now, with 'were we right?' Ellen's anxious repeated question leads her (unwisely) to attempt a moment of intimacy.

In the stage directions, she *goes to Peter and puts her hand on his arm* as she begins this *arioso* sequence; but both productions rightly opt for a more instant, impulsive reaction by Peter, so neither Ellen touches him until the fourth and last 'were we right?', which occurs the moment before he sings 'Take away your hand!'[29] When Langridge sings this, Cairns withdraws her hand as if it were burning, clenches it and puts it up to her mouth, and then gradually lowers it – all the while looking extremely agitated. This is excellent preparation for what Ellen will do after his plea ('if you take it

---

[28] Vickers sang instead 'How should I know?' which does not seem to me to be an improvement on Slater's original text.

[29] In the duet at the end of the Prologue, hand contact was made almost a symbol of their friendship: 'Your voice out of the pain / Is like a hand / That I can feel and know: Here is a friend' (Prologue fig. 9).

away, what's left?);[30] when, after two slow bars of the ominous undertow and snap chords (**4.4.2**) she sings again, it is with words that will lead to the breakdown of their relationship.

[4] For, now, Britten intensifies the dispute by giving Ellen and Peter entirely opposed music. 'Were we mistaken ...' is a mini-*arioso* in regular semiquavers, marked *dolce*, over *pp* harp figurations. By contrast, Peter's angry and rhythmically irregular retorts are accompanied by *fz* chords with demisemiquaver flurries after them in D major, far removed from the flat keys in which Ellen has been singing; and when he sings over her, trying to override her, their two musics are simply jammed together bitonally.

This leads to a menacing *fortissimo* return of the brass pedal (still obses-sively on F) and *staccato* snaps (**4.4.2**). The gap between the two characters is widening, and there is only a tenuous connection left. Ellen now absolutely opposes Peter's plan ('Peter, you cannot buy your peace ...'). For this, Cairns is facing forward, still not looking at her Peter. They have both been sitting on the bench since 'Buy us a home ...'. Moshinsky however has Vickers break and move away to physicalize the gulf that has now opened between the two. As she begins 'We were mistaken ...' Harper lowers her head and turns it away from Vickers, but then – as the solo violin broods briefly on her melody before 'Peter! We've failed!' – she gets up and crosses towards him, almost crying.

Neither Peter leads up to the moment when he hits Ellen by excessive physical movement. Clearly both directors wanted to prepare for the surprise of the blow by letting Peter's growing agitation during section [4] be conveyed almost entirely through facial expressions (and these are very effective, especially from Langridge) – although Vickers does make a dramatic gesture of contempt on 'then the Borough's right again!'. This makes the actual climax all the more powerful; during the two bars of vocal silence and extreme *tutti* orchestral agitation immediately after Ellen's last 'we've failed' (17.1–2), Langridge suddenly rushes forward to deliver the outcry of pain directly to the audience, then turns and goes back upstage equally quickly to the bench to hit Ellen on the side of the face; she falls stunned to the ground. Vickers' Grimes simply lashes out at Ellen, grabs the boy, pauses for a moment, and then leaves the stage, holding the boy tightly.

[5] The invisible cord has been snapped in the two bars of extreme agitation. Now the irrevocable nature of that moment is crystallized as the choir and organ, who have been silent for several minutes, break out into a triumphant 'Amen', in unison, and on the F natural, which has been a pedal note for much of the music since the horn part in **4.4.2** took it over from their *Credo*. Peter then pronounces sentence on himself: 'So be it, and

---

[30] In the stage directions at this point she *moves unhappily away from him*; both Moshinsky and Albery want the two characters close together for section [4], and therefore disregard this.

'God have mercy upon me!' He knows that his violence has lost him the one person who cares for him.

This vocal line cascades down into the B flat major which has been described as the Borough's key.[31] It will predominate in the extended ensemble scene which follows, when the village community comes out from church; indeed much of the music of that next part of the scene is based thematically as well as tonally on **4.4.3**.

4.4.3 (II.1.17.3)

To pronounce this self-judgement Vickers, having gone off, has to come on again, deliver it as if it were an afterthought, and then leave again – all the while still gripping the boy tightly in both hands, and so without an arm free for gesture. This is not very effective. In Albery's production, Langridge does take hold of the boy on 'Amen!'; but he keeps his left hand free, and makes far more of this moment. He faces up towards God with a manic expression on his face, and holds a defiant finger up to the heavens on 'So be it'. This is a great interpretation, taking *Peter Grimes* into the same territory as Ibsen's *Master Builder Solness* (1893), where the title figure made a bargain with God, challenged Him and lost his life for it.

Discussion question

The scene between Peter and Ellen culminates in physical violence, when Peter strikes Ellen. Which production, Moshinsky's or Albery's, makes this irrevocable climactic action seem more inevitable?

4.5 Conclusion

In all of these four scenes of confrontation the musical fabric acts as the invisible cord which binds together the conflicting characters, but in fascinatingly different ways. In *Elektra,* Klytämnestra's delusion that Elektra can help to free her from her fears binds her so closely to her daughter

---

[31] Matthews 1983: 184. Seymour 2004: 69 claims that B flat-F-E flat-C is the Borough's tonal area.

that she is unable to escape from their bond when in the second part of the scene Elektra ferociously prophesies her mother's death in gory detail. The bond, finally, has them close together at the final climax of the scene, Elektra triumphant and Klytämnestra shaking with terror; it is only broken by the news that frees Klytämnestra from her fear. Friedrich's production charts all the stages of this development in the movements and gestures of his two singers, paying special attention to their relative positioning as the confrontation unfolds.

In the scene from *Kát'a Kabanová*, Kát'a increases the bond which ties Tichon to her despite his deafness to her mounting desperation, which the audience hears in the orchestral parts while she is singing. In Lehnhoff's very insightful staging, Tichon is finally about to respond with intimacy to his wife's pleas when a sudden brass chord snaps their bond, announcing the arrival of his mother Kabanicha, which freezes all communication between Kát'a and Tichon. But Janáček's use of strongly opposed musical materials for husband and wife, during the scene itself, implies that, even if they had been left alone for a few more minutes, Kát'a could not have persuaded her husband to stay.

In *Lulu* I.3, Dr Schön makes spirited attempts to break out of his emotional and psychological bond to Lulu, but the invisible cord attaches him to her so firmly that when these attempts culminate in his 'break-out' ('Out, out!') it pulls him back; he realizes immediately that he has nowhere to go. Then we watch Lulu binding him irrevocably to her in the Letter Duet, which, like the scene in which Elektra visualizes her mother's death, binds the two characters together as victor and victim. All of this was well staged by Graham Vick, but Olivier Py's avant-garde, expressionistic staging brings the animalistic power struggle and the eventual defeat of Dr Schön far more vividly before the audience's eyes.

In *Peter Grimes*, the audience watches with dismay as Peter demolishes the only bond he has with anyone. Britten shows this with a highly effective technique; music is shared between Ellen and Peter during the earlier parts of the scene, but later (similarly to the Janáček scene) there are implacably opposed blocks of sound for Peter's increasing anger and Ellen's rising despair, which at the climax provokes him to violence. Although very different in their physique and in their approach to the role, both Vickers and Langridge interact powerfully with their respective Ellens (Harper and Cairns), and both productions physicalize effectively the way in which the rift develops between the friends until Peter strikes Ellen and destroys his only hope.

5

Ensembles

'In this sextet the text is secondary.' Alban Berg, footnote to the ensemble at *Lulu* I.3.1177ff.

'I hope they all know what they're screaming about!' Pangloss, speaking after a brilliant parody of complex ensemble singing in Bernstein's *Candide*.

Ensembles are the most problematic element in music drama. The composer faces two difficulties: first – as these quotations highlight – that of keeping words intelligible, when several soloists (sometimes with chorus) are singing different texts; and then that of trying to use the orchestra to illuminate deep feelings when several characters are simultaneously singing vocal lines which express different surface emotions. Ensembles therefore often find directors at a loss; can they do more with the singers than simply placing them across the front of the stage and letting them 'stand and deliver', without making an already complex situation even harder to understand?

Wagner vigorously opposed the ensembles of traditional opera in his theoretical works of 1848–50, and there are none in the texts of *Das Rheingold*, *Die Walküre* and (before the closing love duet) *Siegfried*; but he notoriously reintroduced them, to the scorn of Bernard Shaw, in *Götterdämmerung*.[1] Wagner had taken over most of the text for this 'stage festival play' from the libretto for an independent 'grand heroic opera' in traditional style entitled *Siegfried's Death*, which he had written before he began to formulate his new vision of the proper relationship between words and music. As he rewrote *Siegfried's Death* to become the text for *Götterdämmerung*, he did not remove any of the ensembles, but simply added or rewrote some crucial scenes (the Norns, Waltraute's plea, Hagen's watch and Brünnhilde's final monologue) to emphasize the cosmic dimensions which the story had now acquired through the creation of its three

---

[1]Shaw 1923 (1967): 54–6.

prequels.[2] Accordingly, as Shaw noted, after a first 'lapse' into duet as Siegfried and Brünnhilde celebrate their new love at the end of *Siegfried*, *Götterdämmerung* itself contains a love duet, a chorus of vassals, an oath-swearing duo, and a revenge trio (5.4). Not to mention a death-aria for Siegfried.

Few subsequent major composers of opera have denied themselves (and their audiences) the musical pleasures of ensemble writing, even in works which are definitely *dramma per musica*. Debussy and Bartók were extreme purists, who tolerated almost no overlapping of vocal lines; but Strauss included the comic quintet for the Jews in the otherwise ensemble-free *Salome*, and ensembles proliferate in his operas from *Der Rosenkavalier* onwards. Berg, after composing the sextet cited above in Act I of *Lulu*, went on to create in the Paris scene (III.1) a concerted section so complex and unintelligible that he himself called it the 'rhubarb' ensemble. Janáček, however, after what he described as a lapse with the decision to compose a quartet with chorus in Act I of *Jenůfa*,[3] confined conventional ensembles thereafter to the superficial spa-goers in Act I of *Destiny*, and to his comic opera *The Excursions of Mr. Brouček*; but he did compose the extraordinary, highly original ensemble when the villagers turn on Jenůfa in Act III of her opera (5.5). On the more conventional British scene, Britten and Tippett were still writing in the 1940s and 50s large ensembles, including some with chorus as well as soloists, in the full Verdian manner; and, although after *The Midsummer Marriage* Tippett hardly used the chorus, he still wrote trios, quartets, quintets and sextets; similarly, Britten's decision to found the English Opera Group and write a series of chamber operas removed from much of his later work large ensembles with chorus such as can be heard in *Peter Grimes* and *Billy Budd*, but did not preclude him from writing ensembles for soloists.

5.1 A cruel departure (Mozart/Da Ponte *Così fan tutte*, I.4, no.6)

Of course, no Wagnerian inhibitions restrained Mozart, who wrote his late masterpieces as heir to a tradition of operatic ensembles, and over fifty years before Wagner's arguments for the primacy of text in music drama. But in the three Da Ponte comedies Mozart faced a challenge; he needed to overcome the difficulties of ensemble to provide through his music the psychological penetration which the text demanded.

---

[2] Cf. M. Ewans 1985a: 85–7.
[3] '[It was] something of a concession to an effective musical motif which I would hardly allow myself today.' Quoted in Tyrrell 1992: 58.

🎵 5 1 A cruel departure

GUGLIELMO

[1] Sento, o Dio, che questo piede　　　　O God, I feel that this foot
È restio nel gir le avante.　　　　　　　Is faltering in its move towards her.

FERRANDO

Il mio labbro palpitante　　　　　　　My lips tremble
Non può detto pronunziar.　　　　　　I cannot utter a word.

DON ALFONSO

5.1.1 Nei momenti i più terribili　　　　In the most terrible moments
Su virtù l'eroe palesar.　　　　　　　The hero reveals his courage.

FIORDILIGI & DORABELLA

[2] Or che abbiam la nuova intesa,　　　Now that we have understood the news,
Or che abbiam la nuova intesa,　　　　Now that we have understood the news,
A voi resta a fare il meno.　　　　　　You are left to do one small thing.
Fate core, fate core, a entrambe in seno　Be brave, be brave, and in our breasts
Immergeteci l'acciar,　　　　　　　　Plunge the steel,
Immergeteci l'acciar.　　　　　　　　Plunge the steel.

FERRANDO & GUGLIELMO

[3] Idol mio, la sorte incolpa,　　　　　My idol, fate is to blame,
Se ti deggio abandoner.　　　　　　　If I have to abandon you.

DORABELLA

[4] Ah, no, no, non partirai!　　　　　Ah no, no, you will not leave me!

FIORDILIGI

No, crudel, non te ne andrai!　　　　　No, cruel one, you will not go!

DORABELLA

Voglio pria cavarmi il core!　　　　　I would sooner tear my heart out!

FIORDILIGI

Pria ti vo' morire ai piedi!　　　　　I would sooner die at your feet!

FERRANDO *(aside to DON ALFONSO)*

[5] Cosa dici?　　　　　　　　　　What do you say?

GUGLIELMO *(aside to DON ALFONSO)*

Te n'avvedi?　　　　　　　　　　Don't you realize?

DON ALFONSO *(aside to the two men)*

Saldo, amico; *finem lauda*.　　　　　Steady, my friend; 'praise the outcome'.

FIORDILIGI, DORABELLA, FERRANDO, GUGLIELMO & DON ALFONSO

[6] Il destin così defrauda　　　　　　Thus Destiny confounds
Le speranze de'mortali.　　　　　　　The hopes of mortals.
Ah, chi mai fra tanti mali,　　　　　　Ah, who ever amid so many ills,
Chi mai può la vita amar?　　　　　　Who can ever love life?
Chi, chi, chi, chi, chi mai può la vita amar?　Who, who, who, who, who can ever
　　　　　　　　　　　　　　　　　love life?

DORABELLA

[7] Ah, no, no, non partirai!　　　　　Ah no, no, you will not leave me!

FIORDILIGI

No, crudel, non te ne andrai! | No, cruel one, you will not go!

DORABELLA

Voglio pria cavarmi il core! | I would sooner tear my heart out!

FIORDILIGI

Pria ti vo' morire ai piedi! | I would sooner die at your feet!

FERRANDO *(aside to DON ALFONSO)*

[8] Cosa dici? | What do you say?

GUGLIELMO *(aside to DON ALFONSO)*

Te n'avvedi? | Don't you realize?

DON ALFONSO *(aside to the two men)*

Saldo, amico; *finem lauda.* | Steady, my friend; 'praise the outcome'.

FIORDILIGI, DORABELLA, FERRANDO, GUGLIELMO & DON ALFONSO

[9] Il destin così defrauda	Thus Destiny confounds
Le speranze de'mortali.	The hopes of mortals.
Ah, chi mai fra tanti mali,	Ah, who ever amid so many ills,
Ah, chi mai fra tanti mali,	Ah, who ever amid so many ills,
Chi mai può la vita amar?	Who can ever love life?
Chi, chi, chi, chi,	Who, who, who, who,
[10] Chi mai può la vita amar?	Who can ever love life?
Ah, chi mai può la vita amar?	Ah, who can ever love life?
Chi mai può la vita amar?	Who can ever love life?
Chi mai può la vita amar?	Who can ever love life?
Chi mai può la vita amar?	Who can ever love life?
Chi mai può la vita amar?	Who can ever love life?
Chi mai può la vita amar?	Who can ever love life?
Chi mai può la vita amar?	Who can ever love life?

Mozart secures clarity by different means in different sections of this quintet. In [1] and [3] the young men imitate each other's line in succession over a simple and quiet accompaniment, and the asides of [5] and [8] are composed similarly; in [2] the young women sing almost every note in harmony (Dorabella has a small decoration in bar 28); then in [4] and [7] they sing separately, and they do so in turn and with parallel feelings. When all five characters sing together, in the quintet proper of [6] and [9], the text is clearly articulated by having at least two singers at a time singing it to the same melody in harmony with each other. Even in the climactic closing section, [10], where there is much decoration, this practice continues.

Like almost every number in *Così fan tutte*, this quintet demands very considerable subtlety from the composer and from the stage interpreters. In Da Ponte's scenario, every character is overacting. Guglielmo and Ferrando both know perfectly well that their departure for military service is a fiction, but they present this decree of 'fate' as seriously as if it were the tragic truth rather than a game, part of their wager with Don Alfonso. For their part Fiordiligi and Dorabella sing that they cannot bear their lovers' cruel departure, with an excess of passion (in both words and music) – although both had, as recently as the recitative after no. 3, confessed to a desire for a bit of fun today. As for Don Alfonso, he has just donned a totally false tragic mask in no. 5, where he declared to the two young women that the news he was bringing (of the men's supposed summons to active service) was too much for him to bear to tell. This was for the sole purpose of playing on their emotions, when he finally divulged his news in the following recitative, to make ready for the young men's arrival. Now, in this quintet, he simply tells his partners in the wager that the sisters' doleful responses are very far from giving them a win in their bet on female fidelity – and the subsequent course of the opera, with its many twists and turns of plot and emotions, amply justifies this comment. Then he joins, cynically but with gusto, in the pessimistic text of the concerted sections [6] and [9–10].

We shall study Mozart's setting in conjunction with the production by Jürgen Flimm, whose excellent staging of the scene where Don Giovanni seduces Zerlina was the subject of analysis in 3.1.[4] Flimm sensibly updates the action of Così to about the late nineteenth century, which enables his actors to avoid the eighteenth-century period dress, wigs and all, which can distance a modern audience from full empathy with the characters, given that this comedy is a good deal more artificial than Le nozze di Figaro or Don Giovanni.[5] He also presents a steady approach to the quintet, avoiding the gross overacting which can be seen in this scene in Peter Sellars' notorious updated production (Da Ponte's characters are themselves overacting [see above]; but the singing actors must not themselves go over the top, especially this early in the opera, or the effect of this subtle comedy is ruined).[6] There is plenty of action in Flimm's staging of the quintet, but he does not hesitate to allow moments of stasis where they are appropriate.

---

[4]See also 8.2. One of the singers is also in this production of Così; Liliana Nikiteanu, excellent in Don Giovanni as Zerlina, joins Cecilia Bartoli as Fiordiligi to give very strong casting to the two sisters whose complex emotional journey is the lynchpin of the opera. And the music is once again in the secure hands of Nikolaus Harnoncourt. The only problem with the cast of this Così does not concern us here; Agnes Baltsa does not have the sassiness and youthful energy which Despina's part (especially her two arias) demands.

[5]The period setting and costumes in the productions by Michael Hampe at La Scala and John Eliot Gardiner at the Châtelet, together with the mannered, very stylized approach to movement, make Così fan tutte a distant experience for the modern audience. Some may miss in Flimm's production the lush scenic spectacle of the outdoor settings, with distant views of the Neapolitan coast, which are the painted background for this scene in both these productions; but his more severe setting is part of an approach which makes the whole drama much more evocative of empathy with the characters.

[6]Sellars' production has some nice moments, and the contemporary setting in 'Despina's Diner' is an inspired modernization; but in Act II his Fiordiligi and Dorabella see through the Albanians' disguises, which totally undermines the text and the music. For a good critique of the Sellars Da Ponte trilogy see Littlejohn 1990 – although he is more sympathetic than I am to the 'choreographed' movements during the ensembles, which for me are far too stylized and mechanical for these emotionally fluid comedies.

[1] Two disconsolate young men enter the stage, one after the other.[7] Both carry rifles, and their military overcoats are draped over their other arms. Mozart charts their doleful attempts to move and speak with hesitant figurations in both voices and orchestra, and in Flimm's production, after coming in at Don Alfonso's invitation to see their beloveds, they stand paralysed at the places where they first came to a stop after entering the stage. That they are acting a part is apparent to the audience, but this is done carefully; we can believe that it is not apparent to the sisters.

Flimm's setting for this scene is the 'school for lovers' of Da Ponte's subtitle.[8] In the opening scene, Guglielmo and Ferrando were members of a small class of male pupils learning cynical maxims about love from Carlos Chausson's Don Alfonso, who is presented as a formidable nineteenth-century academic, dressed very formally in black, and with magnificent eyebrows used to much effect throughout the opera. Now, he is sitting at his desk, and he reads 'in the most terrible moments ...' from a textbook which he has in his hand. This matches the pedantry of his syncopated but ponderous rhythm:

5.1.1 (I.4 no.6, 14-17)

[2] Now, the young women sing for the first time, and the contrast with section [1] is considerable. Their text is a demand that their lovers plunge daggers into their breasts, but the music, with its gentle woodwind swirls (19, 21) and the final disintegration of their vocal lines into notes separated by pauses (29 – as if they are panting for breath as they languish) shows that despite the minor inflections of their music Fiordiligi and Dorabella are actually rather less desperate than you might deduce from their words alone.

Flimm restrains the acting during the delivery of these lines. As performed by Bartoli and Nikiteanu, the emotion is understated. This is right, since despite the text the music here does not justify passion or hysteria (there will be plenty of both later, as the opera unfolds).[9]

---

[7] In Flimm's production, Olivier Widmer sings Guglielmo and Roberto Saccà sings Ferrando.

[8] *Così fan tutte* was usually performed, in Italy in the nineteenth century, with *La Scuola degli amanti* as the actual title. Brown 1995: 166.

[9] Many period costume productions very much overstate the emotion here, by having the sisters frantically grab their soldier lovers' swords and threaten immediate *hari-kiri*. This even happens in Nicholas Hytner's Glyndebourne production (2006).

[3] The young men pretend to try to calm down any agitation that the sisters may be feeling, by presenting the claim that 'fate is to blame' in the same hesitant music (Mozart) and deadpan style (Flimm) as [1].

[4] Of course in reality Guglielmo and Ferrando are hoping to provoke extravagant declarations from their ladyloves, and that is what they now receive. Flowing violin semiquavers increase the tension in the music as the sisters break out passionately, now not together but in succession, echoing and outdoing each other's sentiments. Flimm rightly responds to this with action; Dorabella, who sings first, breaks away to the right of stage and then leans, suffering, on the wall after declaring that she 'would sooner tear [her] heart out'; Fiordiligi has an agonized expression as she too breaks her pose and moves. She crosses to left front, so that the young women end the section at opposite sides of the stage, well forward from their lovers.[10]

[5] The young men, having watched this reaction, have now approached Don Alfonso at his desk. More detached little rhythmic figures, not dissimilar to those in [1], are exchanged between voices and orchestra as they claim progress towards winning the bet, and Don Alfonso tells them that it is as yet a long way from over.[11] The repression which is evident in the dry music of these asides calls for, and duly generates, a much more passionate music in the next section.

[6] The five characters are now united in sentiment for the first time in the quintet. Flimm responds by creating a few moments of rest; he has a nice tableau with the two young women at opposite sides of the forestage, their respective lovers upstage of each of them but further in from the wings, and Alfonso at his desk further upstage and slightly to the right of centre (balanced by his blackboard, also upstage but to the left). This is good, because the audience's ears now need to absorb the interplay of the voices, which are marked *sotto voce*. Fiordiligi and Dorabella lead off in harmony, and are accompanied by restless violin semiquavers just like those which accompanied them in [4]; this shows that the despair in the face of destiny, the subject of the text of this ensemble, originates from them. As indeed it should, because the three male members of the quintet know perfectly well that destiny has nothing to do with what is currently happening, and there is in reality no departure for the sisters to despair about. Nonetheless, the conspirators join in the proceedings. However, their dotted rhythms are jerky in contrast to the smooth lyric lines of Fiordiligi and Dorabella, although at one point (bar 52) Ferrando – as if trying to match and exceed their grief – imitates and extends their decoration of 'le speranze' ('hopes').

---

[10] Contrast Hytner's production, where the sisters end this section very close to their lovers, Fiordiligi even kneeling at Guglielmo's feet and clasping his knees. This makes the men's coming interchange with Don Alfonso in [5] hard to stage credibly – the sisters have to be in tears so they don't notice the conversation, since it occurs immediately above their heads.

[11] In Chausson's delivery, Don Alfonso sings the last *'finem lauda'* extremely firmly, almost derisively.

This leads to a passage (54ff.) where all five singers are united in the melody of their declaration of the final part of the text – 'Who can ever love life?' – a melody which is a compromise between the passion which the young women sought and the more rhythmically irregular style of the three men.[12]

So far in [6] Flimm has kept the singers static. But he correctly realizes that the text of this concerted section means a lot to the young women, and nothing much at all to their lovers and Don Alfonso. So he has Dorabella collapse to a kneeling position when the music reaches an anguished *fermata* on 'chi?' ('Who?', bar 64). This is in preparation for the next bar, where she leads the music straight into the next section.

[7] This is a reprise of [4]; Dorabella stops the ensemble and breaks out passionately, followed immediately by Fiordiligi. Bartoli as Fiordiligi matches her stage sister's agitation in her gestures (although she does not fall to the ground); but, in an inspired production decision, the cruelty of all this is shown, as Guglielmo, behind the women's backs, retreats upstage and smiles, satisfied with his lover's anguished reaction, and the young men once again suggest [8=5] that Don Alfonso must admit defeat.

[9] Mozart achieves musical completeness by following [8] with [9] as [6] followed [5]; the repression in the dry asides of [8] generates a musical demand for the return of the warm concerted section to head into the finale. Once again the young women lead off, with the semiquaver accompaniment and with ornamentation (which once again Ferrando imitates); and once again the men signal their detachment from the sentiment by the jerky rhythms of their counter-setting of the text. But, soon, in Flimm's production, the male lovers' detached observation is broken on stage. As the recapitulation nears its end (87–9), Guglielmo approaches Fiordiligi, and as the coda begins ([10], bar 90), he embraces her from behind and then caresses her hair. Following his lead, Ferrando then goes forward towards Dorabella (who is still kneeling on the floor), and in the decisive moments when first he, and then the other men, finally adopt the gentle, flowing semiquaver descents from the sisters' melody (101ff.), he approaches her, kneels down beside her, and leans his head on her shoulder. After that, as the number comes to an end, she reaches a hand up to him, which he takes. These loving movements respond well to the last change in the male vocal line, and the resulting tableau suits the mood of the instrumental tailpiece

---

[12] Because their musical styles are so different, it is good to separate the sisters physically from their lovers, as Flimm does, here, and in all but the last moments of the reprise [9], where there are musical reasons for a few moments of closeness (see below). Hytner's choice to have the young men close to and consoling their respective girlfriends throughout both these concerted sections does not bring out the difference between the men and the women in their *attitude* to the text here, so it is a less satisfactory staging. And with the soldiers already close to and consoling their loved ones, Hytner cannot respond to the important change in the music of section [9] at 101ff., as Flimm does.

to the quintet.[13] It also creates a strong contrast when the sudden offstage side-drum roll, which usually begins the next scene, breaks this stage picture.[14] More importantly, it provides an essential counter-balance to the cynicism with which Guglielmo and Ferrando, following Don Alfonso's orders, have manipulated their lovers' emotions in the quintet. The delicate balance in the young men's behaviour between love and manipulation, which Flimm shows well in his direction of this quintet, is fundamental to any good production of *Così fan tutte* as a whole.

Discussion question

Does Mozart succeed in giving clarity to the feelings of all the individual characters in this quintet? And does Jürgen Flimm's staging clarify the psychological journey which four of the five characters undergo?

5.2 Lust and treachery (Verdi/Piave *Rigoletto* III.3, no.16)[15]

This justly famous quartet[16] raises acutely the problems of ensemble.

✎ 5 2 Lust and Treachery

(*GILDA and RIGOLETTO in the street, the DUKE and MADDALENA on the
ground floor*)

DUKE

[1] Un dì, se ben rammentomi,	One day, if I remember well,
O bella, t'incontrai ...	Beautiful lady, I met you ...
Mi piacque di te chiedere	It pleased me to ask about you
E intesi che qui stai.	And I found that you live here.
Or sappi che d'allora	You must know that since then

---

[13] The important change in the music at 101ff. is missed or disregarded not only by Hytner but also by Hampe, in whose production the sisters sing this passage away from their lovers, kneeling at Don Alfonso's feet. This is very much at odds with the music.

[14] Flimm and Harnoncourt cut the recitative and duet for the two young men, which follow no. 6 in the complete score, and so go straight to the drum-roll which summons the young men to depart. This cut is quite common in staged performance, and indeed is marked as optional in the Ricordi vocal score – although not in the *Neue Ausgabe Sämtliche Werke*, so it has no authenticity.

[15] In the published full score no. 12.

[16] 'One of the highlights not only of *Rigoletto* but of all Italian opera'; Osborne 1969: 243. When Godefroy published his book on the Verdi operas in 1975, there had been over one hundred recordings of the quartet.

Sol te quest'alma adora.	My soul loves you alone.
GILDA	
Iniquo!	Villain!
MADDALENA	
Ah! ... Ah! ... e vent'altre appresso	Hah! ... Hah! ... perhaps now he is forgetting
Le scorda forse adesso?	The twenty others around?
Ha un'aria il signorino	The young gentleman has the air
Da vero libertino ...	Of a true rake ...
DUKE	
Si ... un monstro son ...	Yes ... I am a beast ...
(tries to embrace her)	
GILDA	
Oh padre mio!	Oh father!
MADDALENA	
Lasciatemi,	Let go of me,
Stordito.	You're crazy.
DUKE	
Ih, che fracasso!	Oh, what a fuss!
MADDALENA	
Stia saggio.	Be sensible.
DUKE	
Eh tu sii docile,	And you be docile,
Non farmi tanto chiasso.	Don't make so much noise to me.
Ogni saggezza chiudesi	All wisdom is lost
Nel gaudio e nell'amore.	In joy and in love.
(he takes her hand)	
La bella mano candida!	What a beautiful white hand!
MADDALENA	
Scherzate voi, signore.	You're joking, sir.
Son brutta.	I am plain.
DUKE Abbracciami.	Embrace me.
GILDA	
Iniquo!	Villain!
MADDALENA	
Ebbro! ...	You're drunk! ...
DUKE	
D'amore ardente.	With passionate love.
MADDALENA	
Signor, l'indifferente,	My indifferent sir,
Via piace canzonar?	is it your pleasure to jest?
DUKE	
No, no, ti vo' sposar ...	No, no, I want to marry you ...
MADDALENA	
Ne voglio la parola ...	I want you to give me your word ...
DUKE *(ironically)*	

Amabile figliuola!   Delightful girl!

RIGOLETTO *(to GILDA who has seen and heard everything)*

E non ti basta ancor? ...   Is this not enough for you?

MADDALENA

Ne voglio la parola ...   I want you to give me your word ...

GILDA

Iniquo traditore!   Villain, deceiver!

Iniquo traditore!   Villain, deceiver!

MADDDALENA

Ne voglio la parola ...   I want you to give me your word ...

Ne voglio la parola ...   I want you to give me your word ...

DUKE

Amabile figliuola!   Delightful girl!

Amabile figliuola!   Delightful girl!

RIGOLETTO

E non ti basta ancor? ...   Is this not enough for you? ...

E non ti basta ancor? ...   Is this not enough for you? ...

DUKE

[2] Bella figlia dell'amore,   Beautiful daughter of love,

Schiavo son de'vezzi tuoi;   I am the slave of your charms;

Con un detto sol tu puoi   With just one word you can

Le mie pene consolar.   Comfort my pain.

Vieni e senti del mior core   Come, and feel the rapid beats

Il frequente palpitar.   Of my heart.

Con un detto sol tu puoi   With just one word you can

Le mie pene, le mie pene consolar.   Comfort my pain, my pain.

MADDALENA

Ah! Ah! Rido ben di core,   Hah! Hah! I laugh with all my heart,

Chè tai baie costan poco;   for such compliments cost little;

Quanto valga il vostro gioco   What value your flattery has,

Mel credete, sò apprezzar.   Believe me, I understand.

Sono avvezza, bel signore,   I am familiar, fine sir,

Ad un simile scherzar,   With flirting like this,

Mio bel signore.   My fine sir.

Ah! Ah! Ah! Ah!   Hah! Hah! Hah! Hah!

Rido il cor.   My heart laughs.

Il vostro gioco sò apprezzar.   I understand your flattery.

DUKE

Con un detto sol tu puoi   With just one word you can

Le mie pene, le mie pene consolar.   Comfort my pain, my pain.

Bella figlia dell'amore,   Beautiful daughter of love,

Schiavo son de'vezzi tuoi;   I am the slave of your charms;

Con un detto sol tu puoi   With just one word you can

Le mie pene, le mie pene consolar.   Comfort my pain, my pain.

Vieni e senti del mior core   Come, and feel the rapid beats

Il frequente palpitar.	Of my heart.
Vieni, vieni, vieni.	Come, come, come.
GILDA	
Ah, così parlar d'amore	Ah, words of love like this
A me pur l'infame ho udito!	I have heard this traitor say to me!
Infelice cor tradito,	Betrayed, unhappy heart,
Per angoscia non scoppiar.	Do not break from anguish.
Perché, o credulo mio core,	Why, oh my credulous heart,
Un tal uom dovevi amar?	Did you have to love a man like this?
Infelice cor tradito,	Betrayed, unhappy heart,
Per angoscia non scoppiar.	Do not break from anguish.
RIGOLETTO *(to GILDA)*	
Taci, il piangere non vale;	Quiet, your tears are in vain;
Ch'ei mentiva or sei secura ...	Now you know for certain he was lying ...
Taci, e mia sarà la cura	Quiet, and let it be my task
La vendetta d'affrettar:	To hasten the vengeance:
Sì pronta fia, sarà fatale;	Yes, it will be soon, it will be fatal;
Io saprollo fulminar.	I am going to strike him down.
Taci, e mia sarà la cura	Quiet, and let it be my task
Taci, Taci.	Quiet, quiet.[17]

Once the Duke has led into the quartet proper [2] with his first presentation of 'Bella figlia dell'amore ...' ('Beautiful daughter of love ...'), the voices sing completely in concert, overlapping and interplaying in so complex a way that the words are almost completely inaudible, even in the most accurate and careful of performances. And, since the vocal lines present the very diverse emotions of four people with totally different attitudes to the situation, Verdi wisely keeps the orchestral accompaniment extremely simple – although that is not to say that it is without interest.

The modern technology of surtitles in the opera house, or subtitles on videotape and DVD, cannot be used to solve the problem of the inaudibility of the words, since the four parallel texts are sung simultaneously. Unable to post all the texts at once during such ensembles, surtitle and subtitle compilers often post none of them.

For the distinguished musicologist Roger Parker, this quartet is great *dramma per musica*:

> If '*La donna*' is the best-known melody in *Rigoletto*, the Quartet which follows is the finest from a musico-dramatic point of view...The main movement, '*Bella figlia dell'amore*', although conventional in that it begins with a long tenor solo, is original in the way it retains the musical

---

[17] This is a fairly full but not complete transcription of the quartet text. In the last four stanzas, which are sung in close ensemble, there is a great deal of repetition.

identity of the four soloists. The slight exaggeration of the Duke's ardent love-song sets a perfect perspective for the other three characters; Maddalena's wayward, chattering line; Gilda, at times with short, breathless phrases, at times rising lyrically above the others; Rigoletto, his insistence on vengeance keeping him firmly rooted to the bass line. It is a measure of Verdi's integrity that, even at the climax and coda, these musical personalities are maintained; in this sense, the Quartet is a perfect example of the new composer we find in *Rigoletto*.[18]

I can agree with Parker that the listener certainly hears the differences in vocal style between the four characters in the quartet, which reflect very well the strong differences between their characters and between their current emotions. But the diverse responses of Maddalena, Gilda and Rigoletto to the Duke's seduction of Maddalena cannot be understood in the theatre, because almost all their words cannot be heard; so the sensitivity of Verdi's vocal setting cannot be appreciated by a spectator but only by a student armed with a score. And only the Duke's emotions can be clearly understood, since following *ottocento* convention he, as the tenor, leads off section [2] with a solo presentation of the words, which he will subsequently repeat in the ensemble.

*

Even the best directors cannot solve this problem. A justly celebrated production of *Rigoletto* is Jonathan Miller's updating to the world of the American Mafia in the 1950s, sung in English at the English National Opera in 1982 and subsequently revived and recorded.[19] Miller's production is excellent in every way, but he is not able to make the interactions in section [2] of this quartet comprehensible to the audience. In Miller's staging, the Duke is flirting with Maddalena inside a bar, and Gilda and Rigoletto are watching through the windows from the cold street outside, as the stage directions prescribe. When the quartet proper begins [2], the Duke at first caresses Maddalena's arm, then puts a bold hand down to her thigh at the brief moment when his voice is heard alone and he begins to sing *Bella figlia* again (341),[20] before once more caressing her arm; when she laughs at him (342) Maddalena moves a little apart from him, and she breaks away more fully when she repeats this

---

[18] Parker in John (ed.) 1982c: 23. Other authorities on Verdi praise the quartet, also focusing on the individuality of the vocal lines; cf. Budden 1973: 504–5, Godefroy 1975: 215, and Osborne 1969: 243 ('This is the kind of thing that opera is uniquely equipped to do, and no one has done it more magnificently than Verdi'). The problem which I address here seems not to have occurred to any of these writers.

[19] Miller used a very good, but free English, singing translation by James Fenton, which is published in John (ed.) 1982c. But I retain my practice of printing a much closer translation.

[20] In the absence of rehearsal figures, references are to the pages of the orchestral score.

laugh after he has intensified his ardour with a sustained top A flat (348); she then goes behind the bar so that it separates them. Meanwhile, as Gilda expresses more passionately how totally she has been betrayed, Rigoletto puts his arm round her. When the quartet has drawn to a close, the Duke embraces Maddalena, while Rigoletto tries to console Gilda.

This is about all that can be done. Unlike any other sequence analysed in this book, the quartet proper can only be staged in the broadest terms, because so little of the text is intelligible that only the most basic postures and gestures can be used to illuminate the overall emotional situation of the characters. And as they repeat the text of their stanzas, this simply sets in stone the emotional positions which they have adopted. There are few details for the director to respond to, since nobody develops at all during the quartet, and indeed Miller can be criticized for letting his Maddalena yield to the Duke's embrace after the music stops, since her text and music have consistently denounced him and ridiculed him for the unprincipled seducer that he is.[21] This quartet is marvellously composed *as music*; it builds steadily and consistently towards the climax just before the end, and it is a great aural experience for all who love the sound of the classically trained singing voice. But it is not, *pace* Parker, a musico-*dramatic* experience. An ensemble composed like this – and there are many such, in most periods and styles of opera – cannot be true *dramma per musica*. Ensembles of this kind frustrate those of us who expect more than just pleasant sounds from this most expensive and potentially most powerful of stage media; and they simply baffle and disappoint those others who come to opera from straight drama, prepared to be converted to the richness of the new medium.

Discussion question

Can anything be done in production which will clarify the feelings which the four characters in Verdi's quartet express in their texts and vocal lines?

5.3 Death in the cards (Bizet/Meilhac and Halévy *Carmen* III.2, no. 20)

Carmen believes in the truth of what the cards say; and they have already told her that she and Don José will die – as she has just said to him. And the reading of the cards which she accepts in this trio greatly heightens the audience's (as well as her) expectation that her broken affair with Don José will indeed lead to death for them both.

---

[21] However, Miller might be justified in retrospect; when we next see Maddalena, she is in love with the Duke.

Bizet composes this trio with very great clarity. There is no question of any of the words being inaudible – Frascita and Mercédès, when they sing together, either alternate or sing the same words in harmony; thus Bizet is able to illuminate with the orchestra all the different moods implied by the text. He brings out the essence of the trio, which is of course the contrast between the good fortunes which Frascita and Mercedes find in their cards – with several pleasant comic touches – and the grim reading which leads Carmen, on picking up the card of death, to sing what is almost a mini-aria, section [6]. The lighter readings frame the darker in an almost ABA form [2] and [4] recapitulated at [7], before they are all brought together in the coda [8], where each of the three gypsies accepts her fate.

✎ 5 3 Card scene Noble

✎ 5 3 Card scene Zambello

(FRASCITA and MERCÉDÈS spread cards before them.)

MERCÉDÈS

[1] Mêlons!   Shuffle!

FRASCITA

Mêlons!   Shuffle!

MERCÉDÈS

Coupons!   Cut!

FRASCITA

Coupons!   Cut!

MERCÉDÈS

Bien, c'est cela!   Good, that's done!

FRASCITA

Bien, c'est cela!   Good, that's done!

MERCÉDÈS

Trois cartes ici,   Three cards here,

FRASCITA

Trois cartes ici,   Three cards here,

MERCÉDÈS

Quatre là!   Four there!

FRASCITA

Quatre là!   Four there!

FRASCITA & MERCÉDÈS

[2] Et maintenant, parlez, mes belles,   And now, dear cards, speak to us,

De l'avenir, donnez-nous des nouvelles,   of the future, tell us some news,

FRASCITA

5.3.1 Dites-nous qui nous trahira!   Tell us who will deceive us!

MERCÉDÈS

Dites-nous qui nous trahira!   Tell us who will deceive us!

FRASCITA

Dites-nous qui nous aimera!

Tell us who will love us!

MERCÉDÈS

Dites-nous qui nous aimera!

Tell us who will love us!

FRASCITA & MERCÉDÈS

Parlez, parlez, parlez, parlez!

Speak, speak, speak, speak!

Dites-nous qui nous trahira!

Tell us who will deceive us!

Dites-nous qui nous aimera!

Tell us who will love us!

FRASCITA

Parlez!

Speak!

MERCÉDÈS

Parlez!

Speak!

FRASCITA

Parlez!

Speak!

MERCÉDÈS

Parlez!

Speak!

FRASCITA

[3] Moi, je vois un jeune amoreux,

I see a young lover,

Qui m'aime on ne peut davantage.

Who loves me, no one could love me more.

MERCÉDÈS

Le mien est très riche et très vieux,

Mine is very rich and very old,

Mais il parle de marriage!

But he talks about marriage!

FRASCITA *(haughtily)*

Je me campe sur son cheval,

I sit astride his horse,

Et dans le montagne il m'entraîne!

And he takes me off to the mountains!

MERCÉDÈS

Dans un château presque royal,

In a castle fit for a king,

Le mien m'installe en souveraine!

Mine installs me as queen!

FRASCITA

De l'amour à n'en plus finir,

In this never-ending love,

Tous les jours, nouvelles follies!

Every day new extravagances!

MERCÉDÈS

De l'or tant que j'en puis tenir,

As much gold as I can hold,

Des diamants, des pierreries!

Diamonds, jewels!

FRASCITA

Le mien deviant un chef fameux,

Mine becomes a famous chief,

Cent hommes marchent à sa suite!

A hundred men march in his train!

MERCÉDÈS

Le mien ... le mien ... en croirai-je mes yeux?

Mine ... mine ... can I believe my eyes?

Oui. *(joyfully)* Il meurt!

Yes. *(joyfully)* He dies!

Ah! Je suis veuve et j'hérite!

Ah! I am a widow and I inherit!

FRASCITA & MERCÉDÈS

[4] Parlez encor, parlez, mes belles;

Speak again, speak, dear cards;

De l'avenir, donnez-nous des nouvelles.

of the future, tell us some news.

FRASCITA

5.3.1 Dites-nous qui nous trahira!   Tell us who will deceive us!

MERCÉDÈS

Dites-nous qui nous trahira!   Tell us who will deceive us!

FRASCITA

Dites-nous qui nous aimera!   Tell us who will love us!

MERCÉDÈS

Dites-nous qui nous aimera!   Tell us who will love us!

FRASCITA & MERCÉDÈS

Parlez, parlez, parlez encor!   Speak, speak, speak again!

Dites-nous qui nous trahira!   Tell us who will deceive us!

Dites-nous qui nous aimera!   Tell us who will love us!

MERCÉDÈS

Fortune!   A fortune!

FRASCITA

Amour!   Love!

CARMEN

[5] Voyons, que j'essaie à mon tour.   Let's see, I will take my turn to try.

(CARMEN *turns up the cards on her side.*)

Carreau! Pique!   Diamonds! Spades!

La mort!   Death!

J'ai bien lu ... moi d'abord,   I have read well ... first me,

Ensuite lui – pour tous les deux, la mort!   Then him – for both of us, death!

[6] **5.3.2** En vain pour éviter les réponses amères,   In vain to avoid bitter responses,

En vain tu mêleras,   In vain you will shuffle,

Cela ne sert a rien, les cartes sont sincères,   It's useless, the cards are sincere,

Et ne mentiront pas!   And do not lie!

Dans le livre d'en haut si ta page est heureuse,   If your page in the book of heaven is happy,

Mêle et coupe sans peur;   Shuffle and cut without fear;

La carte sous tes doigts se tournera joyeuse,   The card under your fingers will turn out to be
                                                              joyful,

T'annonçant le bonheur!   Telling you of happiness!

Mais si tu dois mourir,   But if you have to die,

Si le mot redoubtable   If the dreadful word

Est écrit par le sort,   is written by Chance,

Recommence vingt fois, la carte impitoyable   Try twenty times, the pitiless card

Répétera: **5.3.3** 'la mort!'   Will say again: 'Death!'

Oui, si tu dois mourir,   Yes, if you have to die,

Recommence vingt fois, la carte impitoyable   Try twenty times, the pitiless card

Répétera: 'la mort!'   Will say again: 'Death!'

(*turning up the cards*)

Encor! Encor!   Again! Again!

Toujours la mort!   Always death!

FRASCITA & MERCÉDÈS

[7] Parlez encor, parlez, mes belles;   Speak again, speak, dear cards;

De l'avenir donnez-nous des nouvelles.   of the future, tell us some news.

FRASCITA

5.3.1 Dites-nous qui nous trahira!   Tell us who will deceive us!

MERCÉDÈS

Dites-nous qui nous trahira!   Tell us who will deceive us!

FRASCITA

Dites-nous qui nous aimera!   Tell us who will love us!

MERCÉDÈS

Dites-nous qui nous aimera!   Tell us who will love us!

CARMEN

Le désespoir!   Despair!

FRASCITA & MERCÉDÈS

Parlez encor! Parlez encor!   Speak again! Speak again!

Dites-nous qui nous trahira!   Tell us who will deceive us!

CARMEN

La mort! La mort!   Death! Death!

FRASCITA & MERCÉDÈS

Dites-nous qui nous aimera!   Tell us who will love us!

CARMEN

Encor! La mort!   Again! Death!

MERCÉDÈS

[8] Fortune!   A fortune!

FRASCITA

Amour!   Love!

CARMEN

Toujours la mort!   Always death!

MERCÉDÈS

Fortune!   A fortune!

FRASCITA

Amour!   Love!

CARMEN

Toujours la mort!   Always death!

MERCÉDÈS

Encor!   Again!

FRASCITA & MERCÉDÈS

Encor!   Again!

FRASCITA, MERCÉDÈS & CARMEN

Encor!   Again!

Encor!   Again!

5.3.4

*

There are two outstanding modern productions of *Carmen*; both star Anna Caterina Antonacci, who is mesmerizingly intense in the title role (cf. also **6.2**); one is by Adrian Noble for the Opéra Comique, the other by

Francesca Zambello for Covent Garden. Both stagings show great insight into how to illuminate the text and the music of this trio through stage action, but Noble gains a key advantage when he chooses to stage section [6] with Carmen placed centrally behind the low bench on which the cards have been laid, and Frascita and Mercedes kneeling at each side of it, framing her.

The scene is the gypsy camp. In Zambello's production, Carmen dismisses Don José during the opening music; he is not seen later in the number. Noble by contrast has Don José caress and try to kiss Carmen at this point; she rejects this and moves away from him. But in this production he *is* seen later in the trio, to great effect; his move to the sidelines now is temporary, and he is within earshot to hear Carmen read the death card. Zambello has Frascita and Mercédès reading the cards on a fur coat laid on the ground centre stage in the light of an oil lamp; Carmen leans against a nearby pillar. By contrast, in Noble's production Antonacci, when she comes forward in [4], kneels behind the bench, between Mercédès and Frascita.

[1] The first section begins with patterns of two groups of four semiquavers per bar pulsating in the strings. These persist right through to the end of this section, the moment when Frascita and Mercédès have laid out the cards and ask them to speak. As I hear it, the primary purpose of this pattern is to depict the excitement of the two gypsies as they shuffle and cut the cards, which is rightly shown in their demeanour by the singers in both productions; light woodwind flourishes complete the picture.

[2] Bizet's sense of humour shines through in the *leggiero* music for 'tell us who will deceive us / love us' (5.3.1).

In both productions the acting here is relatively restrained; the directors rightly want to restrain their singers' enthusiasm and their comic gifts until they actually read the cards.

[3] This is pure comedy, as each of the two gypsies seeks to upstage the other with the lover whom the cards are predicting for her. The music here is light and delicate, to allow the humour of the text to shine through; and Noble rightly uses slight overacting here, to bring out the comedy of the reading. Virginie Pochon, Noble's Frascita, after turning her card, flicks her hand proudly as she boasts of a lover 'who loves me, no one could love me more'; and in her next line she mimes riding the horse, with a leg up on the card table. To match this, Annie Gill as Mercédès, seeing that she is to be installed as a queen, does a sassy pelvic swing with her hands on her hips, holds out her hands when she sings that she will be given jewels – as if the jewels are already on her fingers[22] – and triumphantly rises fully erect, taking off and waving her hat, at the comic climax – with a deliciously decorated vocal line from Bizet – 'Ah! I am a widow and I inherit!' (all

---

[22] Norah Amsellem as Mercédès also makes this hand gesture in Zambello's production.

5.3.1 (III.2 no.20, 46-56)

the other gypsy women have gathered round to hear this). This is a better performance of the section than in Zambello's production, as the singers playing the gypsies display altogether more comic energy.

[4] Bizet frames the comic reading [3] with a slightly varied repeat of [2], in which Frasquita and Mercédès shuffle and cut the cards again. In Zambello's production, Carmen has been standing nearby, watching them read the cards with a mild interest; but in Noble's production Carmen takes an interest only now; she pushes her way through the crowd to them.

At the end of the section, Frascita and Mercédès summarize in one word what they expect to get – Mercédès a fortune, Frascita love. This is a preparation for the coda [8], and Bizet ends the section by repeating the semiquaver flow from [1], which symbolizes the constant change as the cards are shuffled. It now runs down and fades out, to lead to the ominous moment when Carmen intervenes.

[5] Carmen, in both productions, demands the cards and is given them. In Zambello's, she puts down a garment a little separate from the rug on which the others had previously laid the cards, kneels behind it and lays out her cards; this leaves her right of centre. By contrast, in Noble's production she is also on her knees – but she is not bending over the cards.

She is kneeling up, with back erect, between the two other women at centre stage – a better position, as it gives her more focus. The section plays itself; fragments of semiquavers alternate with violent chords as Carmen turns up the cards, of which the third is Death. Antonacci reacts with appropriately strong emotions in both productions.

[6] The orchestral underlay is full of pathos (**5.3.2**).

5.3.2 (III.2 no.20, 192-7)

However, Susan McClary is right to point out the divergence between the vocal and the orchestral music: 'Carmen sings with a halting, stagnant accompaniment that resembles a funeral dirge. Yet her melody roams free as she courageously confronts her fate.'[23] And to respond to the seriousness of this moment Noble has Carmen rise fully to her feet. (For Zambello she remains kneeling, but erect.) In both productions Antonacci uses her facial mobility and her hands here to great expressive effect, with very fine detail movements throughout. Note especially how in Noble's production her hands are tight together, clenched, for 'try twenty times'. Just after that, at 'the pitiless card will say again: Death!', the music adds a little figure in the strings to signify the coming of the end (**5.3.3**).

---

[23] McClary 1992: 101.

5.3.3 (III.2 no.20, 224-231)

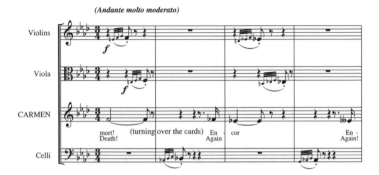

In Zambello's version Carmen responds to this; Antonacci raises both hands, puts one hand hard down on the death card, on 'Death!', and then slaps it one more time on each repeat of the next word, 'Again'. Finally, in both productions she looks upwards – as if to a saving deity who does not exist in the world of this opera – on the last line of the section – 'Always death!'

[7] Bizet now counterbalances the tragedy by bringing back an unvaried repeat of the two fortunate gypsies' song from [2] – but, now, Carmen's fateful comments in her rich mezzo are heard beneath the other singers, undermining but not overcoming the gaiety above. In Zambello's production, Carmen goes away from the cards soon after this section begins – but at 'tell us who will deceive us / love us' the two others surround her, with a happiness that profoundly irritates her – a fine effect; Carmen only escapes towards the end of the section, when she crosses away from them to the front left of the stage, all the time singing 'Again! Despair! Death! Death! Again!'. In Noble's production, less effectively, Carmen goes away to front right as soon as this section begins, and the others stay at the bench with the cards.

[8] Section [8] is the coda of the trio; the semiquaver runs and Frascita/ Mercédès' light woodwind figurations recur for the last time, both to provide ring-composition back to [1–2] and also to show that the number is reaching its conclusion. The fates of all three women are now decided, and they sing in summary what the cards have told them; Mercédès sings 'Fortune!', Frascita sings 'Love!' and Carmen sings 'Always death!'. The light woodwind motifs, which accompanied Mercédès and Frascita in [2], return cruelly to accompany this; they are indifferent to Carmen's fate. But then, in the final bars, the music, which had seemed to be running down to a quiet ending, suddenly rouses itself to a tragic climax. Frascita and Mercédès sing 'Again!', and are joined in the final vocal bars by Carmen, where all three sing this word two more times, *f* and *ff*; and in the fierce orchestral coda there are embers of a light motif associated with Carmen in Act I, (**5.3.4a**) – now heard, ominously, in the lower instruments; but the stress is on the music of Carmen's dirge (**5.3.4.b**).

5.3.4 (III.2 no.20, 270-6)

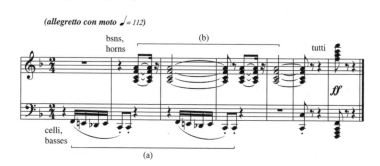

Noble illuminates this. Unlike Zambello, he has not banished Don José to outer darkness during the trio; as section [8] begins, he is to be seen in a prominent position front of stage, left, staring at Carmen with great hostility across the full width of the stage. The cards have spoken the truth.[24]

Discussion questions

- This section gives a number of different reasons to prefer Noble's staging of the card scene to Zambello's. Do you agree?
- Analyse Antonacci's acting performance of the title role in the two versions of the scene, comparing what she does in both productions, one with the other.

---

[24] Zambello has Mercédès, feeling Carmen's pain, cross to her in sympathy during the closing bars. This is a nice touch, but it does not address the central drama of the opera, as Noble does at this point. Nor is there justification for it in the music.

5.4 Siegfried must die! (Wagner, *Götterdämmerung* II.5)

This trio portrays an unholy alliance, temporarily entered into by three people with very different and totally incompatible interests. Wagner's dramatic strategy is to build up intensity gradually, from the relatively calm dialogue before Hagen first proposes to Gunther that 'your only hope is Siegfried's death', until the voices of Brünnhilde, Gunther and Hagen are united – first in their decision that 'Siegfried dies!' and then in their prayers to Wotan and (in Hagen's case) to Alberich. Then the energies generated by the trio itself are discharged in the closing orchestral *tutti* as the bridal procession of Siegfried and Gutrune comes onto the stage.

✎ 5 4 'Siegfried must die!'

HAGEN

Dir Hilft kein Hirn,	Brains won't help you,
dir hilft keine Hand:	hands won't help you:
Dir hilft nur – Siegfrieds Tod!	Your only hope is –Siegfried's death!

GUNTHER *(seized with fear)*

Siegfrieds Tod!	Siegfried's death!

HAGEN

Nur der sühnt deine Schmach!	Only that atones for your disgrace!

GUNTHER *(staring in front of him)*

Blutbrüderschaft	Bloodbrotherhood
schwuren wir uns!	we swore to each other!

HAGEN

Des Bundes Bruch	Blood now atones for
sühne nun Blut!	the breach of the bond!

GUNTHER

Brach er den Bund?	Did he break the oath?

HAGEN

Da er dich verriet.	When he betrayed you.

GUNTHER

Verriet er mir?	Did he betray me?

BRÜNNHILDE

Dich verriet er,	He betrayed you,
Und mich verrietet ihr alle!	And you have all betrayed me!
War ich gerecht,	If I were to have justice,
alles Blut der Welt	all the blood in the world
büßte mir nicht euren Schuld!	would not atone for your guilt!
Doch des einen Tod	But that one man's death

taugt mir für Alle: will suffice me for all:
Siegfried falle   Siegfried dies
Zur Sühne für sich und euch!   to atone for himself and you!

HAGEN *(turning to GUNTHER: secretly)*

Er falle – dir zum Heil!   He dies – and you are saved!
Ungeheure Macht wird dir,   Enormous power will be yours,
gewinnst du von ihm den Ring   if you get the ring from him
den der Tod Ihm wohl nur entreisst.   which death alone will take from him.

GUNTHER *(softly)*

   Brünnhildes Ring?   Brünnhilde's ring?

HAGEN

Des Nibelungen Reif.   The Nibelung's ring.

GUNTHER *(with a heavy sigh)*

So wär es Siegfrieds Ende!   So it will be Siegfried's end?

HAGEN

Uns allen frommt sein Tod.   His death profits us all.

GUNTHER

   Doch Gutrune, ach!   But, oh! Gutrune
   der ich ihn gonnte!   to whom I gave him!
Straften den Gatten wir so,   If we punish her husband like this,
wie bestünden wir vor ihr?   how can we face her?

BRÜNNHILDE *(starting up in rage)*

   Was riet mir mein Wissen?   What did my knowledge tell me?
   Was wiesen mir Runen?   What help were my runes?
   Im hilflosen Elend   In my helpless misery
   achtet mir's hell   I clearly see
Gutrune heist der Zauber   Gutrune is the name of the spell
der den Gatten mir entzückt.   that enticed my husband away.
   Angst treffe sie!   I want her to suffer!

HAGEN *(to GUNTHER)*

Muß sein Tod sie betrüben,   Since his death will make her grieve,
verhehlt sei ihr die Tat.   the deed shall be hidden from her.
   Auf muntres Jagen   Let's set out tomorrow
   ziehen wir morgen.   on a lively hunt.
Der Edle braust uns voran,   The noble fellow will dash on ahead of us,
ein Eber bracht'ihn da um.   a boar will bring him down.

GUNTHER

   So soll es sein!   So shall it be!
   Siegfried falle!   Siegfried dies!

BRÜNNHILDE

   So soll es sein!   So shall it be!
   Siegfried falle!   Siegfried dies!

GUNTHER

5.4.1 Sühn'er die Schmach,   He will atone for the disgrace
   die er mir schuf!   that he made me suffer!

HAGEN

5.4.1   Sterb'er dahin,   He shall die then,
der strahlende Held!   the radiant hero!

BRÜNNHILDE

5.4.1   Sühn'er die Schmach,   He will atone for the disgrace,
die er mir schuf!   that he made me suffer!

HAGEN

Mein ist der Hort,   The hoard is mine,
mir muß er gehören.   I must possess it.

GUNTHER & BRÜNNHILDE

Des Eides Treue   The faith of the oath
hat er getrogen: he has betrayed:

HAGEN

mir muß er gehören: I must possess it:

GUNTHER & BRÜNNHILDE

mit seinem Blut   with his blood
büß' er die Schuld!   he atones for his guilt!

HAGEN

D'rum sei der Reif   that's why the ring
ihm entrissen!   must be seized from him!

GUNTHER & BRÜNNHILDE

Allrauner,   All-knowing,
rächender Gott!   avenging god!

HAGEN

Alben-Vater,   Father of the dwarves,
gefallner Fürst!   fallen prince!

GUNTHER & BRÜNNHILDE

Schwurwissender   Keeper of oaths
Eideshort!   guardian of vows!

HAGEN

Nachthüter!   Guardian of the night!
Niblungenherr!   Lord of the Nibelungs!

GUNTHER & BRÜNNHILDE

Wotan!   Wotan!
Wende dich hier!   Turn your eyes on us!

HAGEN

Alberich!   Alberich!
Achte auf mich!   Listen to me!

GUNTHER & BRÜNNHILDE

Weise die schrecklich   Make your terrible
heilige Schar   holy army

HAGEN

Weise von neuem   Once again make
der Niblungen Schar   the army of Nibelungs

GUNTHER & BRÜNNHILDE

	hierher zu horchen	listen here
	dem Racheschwur!	to the oath of vengeance!
HAGEN		
	dir zu gehorchen,	listen to you,
	des Reifes Herrn!	the lord of the ring!

(As GUNTHER turns vigorously towards the palace with BRÜNNHILDE, the bridal procession coming out of it meets them. Boys and girls, waving branches of flowers, leap joyously in front. SIEGFRIED is carried by the troops on a shield, GUTRUNE on a chair. On the rising ground at the back serving men and maids on various mountain tracks are bringing sacrificial implements and animals to the altars, and decking them with flowers. SIEGFRIED and the troops sound the wedding call on their horns. The women invite BRÜNNHILDE to let them escort her to GUTRUNE'S side. BRÜNNHILDE looks blankly at GUTRUNE, who beckons to her with a friendly smile. When BRÜNNHILDE is about to draw away impetuously, HAGEN quickly stands in her path and forces her towards GUNTHER, who seizes her hand again, and then allows the men to raise him up on a shield. As the procession, hardly interrupted, starts to move again towards the hill, the curtain falls.)

As you can see from the lines beside the text which indicate overlap, Wagner was anxious to preserve as much audibility as he could while still indicating the unanimity of the three characters. When they begin to sing together, he sets the text in pairs of lines, in each of which the characters have a very similar intent and parallel words – different of course because Hagen is invoking Alberich while the others appeal to Wotan. Furthermore the text is not set in harmony or unison, but with a considerable number of overlapping entries, responding to the interplay between the three characters' expressed emotions.

Wagner uses his orchestra here to depict the dominance of Hagen over his weak half-brother and even over the vengeful Brünnhilde. Hagen's baleful motif of a falling minor second sounds ominously throughout, from the initial proposal to kill Siegfried through to the others' acceptance of it ('So shall it be / Siegfried dies!', which Brünnhilde actually sings with Hagen's falling second sounding twice in her vocal line, 907) to the last few bars before the curtain falls. And another motif (**5.4.1**), closely associated with the plotting of the Nibelungs ever since it depicted the creeping aggression of Alberich's curse on the ring in *Das Rheingold* scene 4 (563–4), now appears in syncopated triads to increase the three characters' involvement in the decision to kill Siegfried. It first appears here under Gunther's 'He will atone for the disgrace / that he made me suffer', and this shows how much Hagen is influencing his half-brother.

Then the energies of the trio are reinvigorated five times by the recurrence of a rising scale of *staccato* semiquavers in the violins; and finally – as the ensemble reaches its climax – the three characters are twice closely united by singing in harmony or in imitation over string *tremolos* (912–15, 916–18). The first time that this happens, at 'the faith of the oath / he has

5.4.1 (II.5.908-9)

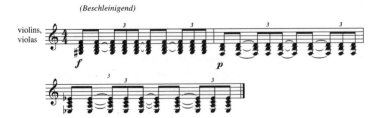

betrayed', is the moment where the unholy alliance is fully forgèd, leading to the united prayers of all three to their respective gods (for Brünnhilde and Hagen, the appeal is directly to their own fathers).

*

These characteristics of the music indicate that the director must use his or her positioning of the singers to make a statement about the power relationships between the characters. Patrice Chéreau is very disappointing in his staging of the trio; he simply lines the characters up – Brünnhilde stage right, Hagen centre and Gunther left – and has them 'stand and deliver' (in a way that is most uncharacteristic of the rest of his production of the *Ring*); the only movement before Siegfried's entry is Gunther raising his hands when he invokes Wotan. By contrast, Harry Kupfer stages the Act on an ugly but highly practical set, which consists of two sets of metal stairs rising backwards from forward left and right diagonally towards a high platform at centre, which is a little behind half way to the back of the stage; and he uses movement and relative positioning to bring out his vision of the relationship between the three.

This vision is fascinating. In the preliminary stages of dialogue Brünnhilde (Anne Evans with long, very striking red hair) pulls focus from the two men. She looks on with disdain as Gunther (at first lying helpless on the ground) feebly resists Hagen's proposal, and she climbs the stairs to dominate by delivering 'He betrayed you / And you have all betrayed me!' from the platform. She then descends for 'Siegfried dies / to atone for himself and you', and seizes Hagen's spear to emphasize the point. Hagen however wrestles it from her, and crosses right to persuade Gunther – who, in this production, rather than responding *with a heavy sigh* to the thought of Siegfried's death, actually looks quite excited by the idea, which helps to explain why it is he who leads off the trio in a few moments' time.

Brünnhilde's fury as she realizes what Gutrune has done to her impels her to seize Gunther by the lapels and wrestle him to the ground, herself falling to her knees as she does so.[25] Then, after Gunther has begun the trio proper with 'So shall it be ...', she pushes him to the ground as she begins to echo his words, then seizes Hagen's spear when she begins to sing 'He will atone for the disgrace ...'. Given the dominance of an Alberich/Hagen motif (5.4.1) in the orchestra, the resulting posture correctly expresses the power relationship at this point; all three are together, with Hagen standing, Brünnhilde on her knees but half erect, holding Hagen's spear, and Gunther on the floor. This pose is held throughout the first occurrence of the *tremolos* that bind them close together; but then, as Brünnhilde begins her prayer to Wotan ('all-knowing, avenging god'), Hagen too kneels and Gunther half rises, so that the spear is held horizontally by all three of them, expressing their equality as they supplicate their respective gods.

After that, Kupfer gives the dominance to Brünnhilde. As the second passage of *tremolos* begins, while Gunther addresses Wotan by name, she rises up and places the spear across the backs of the two kneeling Gibichungs, standing erect between them. By this I think Kupfer means to convey that, although Hagen's plotting propels this scene, the ultimate victory will lie with Brünnhilde when she eases her father's anguish by destroying Valhalla and returning the ring to the Rhine daughters. So she remains in this triumphal position until the arrival of the wedding party leads to an instant break-up of the tableau.

From the moment when Hagen sings the last note of the trio, there are precisely 31 bars of *noch etwas bewegter (un poco più animato)* from a tempo which was already fast. There is no way in which all the detail of Wagner's closing stage directions can be realized during this short time. Both Chéreau and Kupfer opt for just a wedding procession on foot (no one is sitting aloft on a shield or a chair); no servants pour in from the surrounding countryside with sacrificial animals, no boys and girls leap joyously as they lead the happy couple onstage, and there are no onstage horns sounding a 'wedding call'. There is, however, a certain amount of organized chaos in both productions, when the crowd arrives, during which Chéreau makes two excellent points: Siegfried greets Gunther by embracing him, and Gunther shows that he is far from comfortable with returning the embrace to a blood-brother whose death he has just prayed for; and – following an important stage direction – Hagen then seizes the reluctant Brünnhilde and takes her forcibly to Gunther's side. Kupfer, unfortunately, does not make his Hagen do this. Instead he has Gunther attempt to take Brünnhilde's hand at the top of the stairs (while a very naïve-looking Gutrune cavorts merrily with Siegfried on the stage below); Brünnhilde breaks angrily away from Gunther, and they run down opposite flights of stairs before following the

---

[25] This means that she can hear the plot to kill Siegfried during a hunt the next day. This was probably not Wagner's conception of that moment; however, it is not Brünnhilde but Gutrune from whom the plot has to be hidden.

procession out separately. Hagen is left alone front centre in both productions – quite rightly, as throughout the closing bars his baleful minor second
fall sounds again and again; and in Kupfer's production he drives the butt
of his spear onto the ground on the final chord.

Discussion questions

- Is Wagner successful in the musical devices that he uses to try to
  keep the words of all three voices audible, despite the overlaps and
  occasional unisons that he uses during this trio?
- Do you think that Harry Kupfer has charted the changing power
  relationships during the trio correctly? Give reasons for your answer.

5.5 'Stone her!' (Janáček/Preissová *Jenůfa* III. 6–10)

In this intense sequence, which precipitates the dénouement of *Jenůfa*,
Janáček created a highly original ensemble using a series of *ostinati* to
build to an extraordinary climax. Nothing quite like it had ever been done
before; and it so happens that the texts, which Janáček chose for his later
tragic operas, never gave him the opportunity to create anything similar
again. In the later operas he uses the chorus sparingly, but to considerable
effect (especially in *From the House of the Dead*), but there is no situation
comparable in dramatic tension with this sequence of scenes, in which a
recognition leads to an entire chorus demanding the death of the heroine.[26]

While the Grandmother blesses the bride and groom, a descending figure
of four notes, repeated in each bar, steals into the orchestral textures to
accompany her.

5.5.1 (III.6.43.1)

---

[26] The comparison with *Kát'a Kabanová* III.1, which I made in my book on the Janáček operas
(M. Ewans 1977: 63–4), is wrong. Kát'a's confession is precipitated by the storm and by
her conscience, and the chorus comments simply as a group of spectators rather than as an
active participant. Also Janáček does not build up to the climax of that scene by a cumulative
sequence of different *ostinati*, as here in *Jenůfa*.

Janáček rarely uses recurrent motifs; but this one has been heard before, and, despite the gentle orchestration here, it is highly ominous. Played aggressively by the horns, it was the accompaniment to the terrible moment in II.5 (71.2–3) when the Kostelnička, totally deranged, fetched Jenůfa's baby from her room to take it out and murder it.[27] And now, when the Grandmother's blessing is finished, and the bridal pair kneels before the Kostelnička to receive her blessing too, it comes back again as an *ostinato* in the violins. After two bars of that, a noise is heard outside, and voices can be distinguished. The return of **5.5.1** from Act II makes all too much sense; someone has murdered a baby. From this point onwards, the build-up to the final moments, in which Jenůfa has collapsed and Laca prepares to take on the villagers, who have turned into a raging mob threatening to kill her to avenge the infanticide, is inexorable. And the pressure on the Kostelnička to confess gradually becomes overwhelming.

Not every word can be heard towards the end of this ensemble; but Janáček makes sure that even in the pandemonium at the climax of section [6] the two essentials can be heard; Jenůfa's voice soaring in agonized grief over the top of the ensemble, followed, when she falls silent, by Laca's threats high in the tenor range, and below them the villagers, with their relentless cries of 'Stone her!' The only virtually inaudible soloist is the Mayor, reluctantly facing his apparent duty to arrest Jenůfa for infanticide. And this is dramatically right; he is simply being overwhelmed by the mob, both onstage and in the music.

✎ 5 5 Jenůfa 'Stone her!'

(Bride and groom kneel before the Kostelnička. She raises both hands. There is a noise outside.
  The Kostelnička shrinks back in terror. In the tumult outside two voices can be distinguished.)

A WOMAN

[1] 5.5.1 Chud'átko!	Poor little one!
Nějaká bestyja uničila díte!	Some beast has killed a baby!

A MAN

Která bezbožnica to urobila?	What godless person did it?

KOSTELNIČKA

Co díte?	What child?

JANO *(running in)*

[2] Rychtáři,	Mayor,
hledají vás!	they're looking for you!

---

[27] It also returned at the end of the Act, while the Kostelnička makes her first unsuccessful attempt to bless the union of Jenůfa with Laca (II.119.ff.); at the moment when the wind blows her window open she sings 'it is as if Death is forcing his way in'. Indeed he will, here and now, in Act III.

MAYOR

A co je? Cože to?   What's happening? What is this?

KOSTELNIČKA

Co s dítětem tam křičejí?   What are they crying out about a child?

ŠTEVA

Co se děje?   What's happening?

JANO

Vy to ješte nevite?   You don't know yet?

Vy to ješte nevite?   You don't know yet?

Sekáči z pivovaru   Some pickmen from the brewery

našli pod ledem přimrlzé díte!   found under the ice a frozen-to-death baby!

VILLAGERS *(outside)*

5.5.2 Ó hrůza! Ó hrůza! Ó hrůza!   Terrible! Terrible! Terrible!

JANO

Nesou ho na desce,   They're bringing it on a plank,

je jako žive v peřince,   it's like a live child on a pillow,

v povijáku,   in swaddling clothes,

na hlave červenou pupinu.   a red cap on its head.

To je na hrůzu, to je na hrůzu,   This is terrible, this is terrible,

lidé nad tím nařikaji,   people are weeping at the sight,

nad tím nařikaji.   weeping at the sight.

[3] 5.5.3 Ó poběžte,   Oh come along,

ó poběžte!   Come along!

KOSTELNIČKA

Jenůfa ...   Jenůfa ...

(Jano runs off; after him the MAYOR and his WIFE, the guests, the SHEPHERDESS,
LACA and JENŮFA. Only ŠTEVA stands rooted to the spot, and near the bed the
KOSTELNIČKA and the GRANDMOTHER.)[28]

... neodbíhaj,   don't leave me,

ó neodbíhaj!   oh don't leave me!

5.5.4 ... Držte mne, braňte mne!   Hold me, protect me!

GRANDMOTHER

Ale dcero moje!   But my daughter!

KOSTELNIČKA

Držte mne, braňte mne!   Hold me, protect me!

GRANDMOTHER

Ale dcero moje!   But my daughter!

KOSTELNIČKA

Držte mne, braňte mne!   Hold me, protect me!

GRANDMOTHER

Dcero, zase blouzniš, blouzniš!   Daughter, you're raving again, raving!

---

[28] This and the next stage direction are strange, as the scene is not the bedroom but the living room of the Kostelnička's house, and there is no specification for a bed to be in this room at the start of Act III (or, for that matter, Act II).

KOSTELNIČKA

To jdou pro mne, pro mne!	They're coming for me, for me!

(She sinks onto the head of the bed and convulsively clutches the backrest, observing the action fearfully.)

[4] *(ŠTEVA runs off and KAROLKA runs into him at the door. She seizes him by the hand.)*

KAROLKA

Števo, to je ti strašne ...	Števa, this is awful ...
svatba pokažena ...	the wedding's ruined ...
Já byt nevěstou,	If I were the bride,
plakala bych.	I'd be in tears.

JENŮFA *(outside)*

Ó Bože, můj Bože,	Oh God, my God,
to je můj chlapčok, můj chlapčok!	that is my baby, my baby!

ŠTEVA

Jak by mi ten křik nohy pod'tal,	That screaming is making my legs weak,
a úzko je mi včil.	and now I feel afraid.

[5] *(LACA leads JENŮFA indoors. She tears herself away.)*

LACA

5.5.5 Jenůfka, Jenůfka!	Jenůfa, Jenůfa!

JENŮFA

Pust'mne!	Let me go!

LACA

Vzpamatuj se,	Pull yourself together,
vzpamatuj se!	pull yourself together!
Co tě hrozného napadlo?	What is this terrible idea?
Lide to slyši!	People are listening!

JENŮFA

Pust'mne!	Let me go!

LACA

Ó vzpamatuj se,	Oh pull yourself together,
vzpamatuj se!	pull yourself together!

JENŮFA

Pust'mne,	Let me go,
to je Števuška můj chlapčok, 5.5.1 můj, můj!	that is Števuška my baby, mine, mine!

(Enter the MAYOR, in his hands a swaddling cloth and a red cap. The others follow him.)

(The door stays open. People are staring in.)

[6] Ha, vidíte,	Ah, look,
Jeho poviják, jeho čepčáček!	his swaddling cloth, his little cap!
Sama jsem ho ze svych pantlí popravila!	I made it myself with my own ribbons.

MAYOR'S WIFE

Slyšíš rychtáři,	Do you hear, mayor,
Oni o tom vědi!	They know about it!

JENŮFA

Ej, lidé,	Oh, all of you,
5.5.1 kterak jste ho dopravili?	how could you bring him like this?

Bez truhelky,	No coffin,
bez věnečku!	no wreath!
OLD WOMAN	
Ježiši Kriste! Ježiši Kriste!	Jesus Christ! Jesus Christ!
JENŮFA	
Co mu pokoja nedáte?	Why couldn't you give him peace?
OLD WOMAN	
Tak utratila svoje dítě!	So she killed her own child!
JENŮFA	
Kdesi ve sněhu a ledu	Somewhere in the snow and ice
s ním gúlali!	they dragged him out!
MAYOR	
To už jsem snad bar bez pánů	I think I don't need a boss
na stopě!	to be on the right track!
Já musím byt prvni ouřad ...	I must first do my duty ...
VILLAGERS	
6.5.6 Kamením po ni! Ježiši Kriste!	Stone her! Jesus Christ!
Kamením po ni! Ježiši Kriste!	Stone her! Jesus Christ!
Zabila dítě!	She killed her baby!
JENŮFA	
Števo, mlynáři,	Števa, miller,
běž na nima, honem běž,	go after them, go quickly,
to je tvoje ditě!	it is your child!
MAYOR	
... a, a raděj bych se neviděl!	... but, but I wish I could disappear!
VILLAGERS	
Kamením po ni! Kamením po ni!	Stone her! Stone her!
Jistě to dovezla z Vídně!	She must have brought it back from Vienna!
LACA	
Jenom se odvažte	No one dare
někdo se jí dotknout!	to touch her!
Život vás to bude stat!	It'll mean your death!
VILLAGERS	
Kamením po ni! Kamením po ni!	Stone her! Stone her!
Kamením po ni! Kamením po ni!	Stone her! Stone her!
Kamením po ni! Kamením!	Stone her! Stone!
LACA	
[7] 5.5.7 Pěstí vás dobiju!	I'll finish you off with my bare fists!
KOSTELNIČKA	
Ještě jsem tu já! Vy ničeho nevíte!	I am still here! You know nothing about it!

Sections [1] and [2] are entirely underpinned by the agitated *ostinato* of 5.5.1, now in the first violins over *tremolandi* in the other strings. As the chorus sings (offstage) for the first time, another motif is heard in their voices and the horns:

5.5.2 (III.7.46.1)

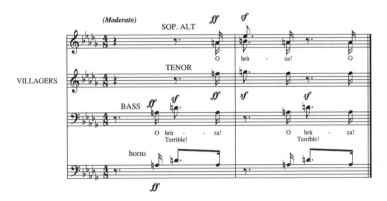

This too has been prefigured towards the end of the last scene, when it suddenly intruded in the horns and undermined the good humour with which the Mayor invited the Kostelnička to pronounce her blessing (III.6.43.9–10); yet another anticipation becomes reality.

Jano's agitated, breathless narration is propelled along by the power of the constant repetitions of **5.5.1** in the violins, and by *staccato* chords and phrases in the woodwind.

In section **[3]**, almost everyone rushes out, leaving only Števa, the Kostelnička and Grandmother Buryja. Then a new *ostinato* is heard as the Kostelnička begs Jenůfa not to go:

5.5.3 (III.8.47.1)

But Jenůfa has already left, and the Kostelnička turns to her mother for support. This sequence is accompanied by fierce, dissonant quintuplets tossed between violins and celli, which suggest a violent, self-enclosed hysteria which will need subsequent release (**5.5.4**).

[4] This motif persists, in a slightly milder form, when Karolka comes back into the room. But as soon as Karolka has sung 'if I were the bride, I'd be in tears', the actual bride – who has much more reason to weep than Karolka can possibly imagine – bursts out with the recognition that it is her

5.5.4 (III.8.49.1)

baby. Now Števa has good reason for his fear, and this *ostinato* reaches a strong climax as Jenůfa's emotions lead to her return to the house.

[5] The tension continues to build as Laca vainly tries to calm the distraught and utterly determined Jenůfa. Their emotional tug-of-war is expressed very vividly in a new pair of *ostinati*, one in violins with oboe and the other in lower strings with trombones and bassoons – while the timpani, not yet heard in this ensemble, add to the intensity by beating out the rhythm of the upper *ostinato*:

5.5.5 (III.9.51.1)

Jenůfa wins the fight with Laca, and this is heralded by two trumpets playing **5.5.1**, muted but *marcato*. The truth has been spoken, and there is no going back.

[6] When the Mayor comes in, with the baby clothes which Jenůfa recognizes at once, Janáček increases the tension a notch further by setting the new *ostinato* for this section against continuously repeated rhythmic patterns in horns and violas, which soon come to dominate most of the orchestra, with the addition from 54.2 onwards of **5.5.1**, now forcibly played in accented notes first by the oboe and then by horns in octaves. When the villagers first sing 'Stone her!' – with a desire for instant rough 'justice' which originates, by the way, with the men, and is only gradually taken over first by the altos and then by the sopranos – all the elements are in place to drive the music through to the end. The energies that are now unleashed are extraordinary (**5.5.6**), and all Janáček has to do in the last few bars is to add in the rest of his orchestra, with almost all parts playing one of these three patterns.[29]

---

[29] There are also demisemiquaver swirls in second flute, second clarinet and second violins, which increase the tension even further.

5.5.6 (III.10.55.1)

[7] (5.5.7) It takes a sustained outcry on top B flat for Laca to halt the momentum of this music, and reach a stalemate with the mob which is threatening Jenůfa with death – a stalemate that can only be broken by the Kostelnička's confession.

✻

Staging this ensemble is an advanced exercise in *Personenregie*. Each of the characters must be in exactly the right place at the right time if the stage action is to illuminate Janáček's musical ordering of the events. Although I have been critical of Stéphane Braunschweig's staging of the duet earlier in this Act (see **3.4**), his handling of this scene is exemplary and, combined with Ivor Bolton's passionate conducting of the music, makes for the overwhelming effect that the composer clearly intended to achieve with this, the first of three great climaxes in the closing scenes of *Jenůfa*.

5.5.7 (III.10.55.10)

Braunschweig begins, obviously rightly, with Jenůfa and Laca kneeling each side of the centre line downstage, and the Grandmother moving to front centre, facing the audience over their heads as she blesses them. In a nice touch, Karolka – who is not sitting with her fiancé (Števa is standing further back, for reasons which will soon become obvious) – sheds a tear during the blessing. As it takes place a large crucifix of red light is seen above the back door. Is God looking on at the events? In view of Janáček's pantheism and total rejection of Christianity, this would be an unfortunate reading. I think that the colour red signifies not the blood of Christ but the blood of the baby, while the cross signifies the religious beliefs of the villagers, which will be transcended at the end of the opera.[30]

Then the disturbance begins [1–2]. The Mayor invites the Kostelnička to pronounce her blessing, but, in this production, she is never to raise her hands over the couple; as the *ostinato* of **5.5.1** begins in the violins, she stands paralysed by fear. And then the individual female and male voices, which are in the stage directions supposed to be heard from outside, enter the stage rapidly as visible characters to sing their lines – a good idea, not least for audibility.

Jano follows them almost immediately, and comes right forward to front centre to tell the news. Braunschweig has the boy seeking to leave after

---

[30] Cf. M. Ewans 1977: 65–9.

the main part of his message has been delivered (on the words 'a frozen-to-death baby'); he and Jenůfa try to go outside at this point, but Laca restrains them and makes Jano tell him the rest. This increases the power of the second part of [2], and doubles Jenůfa's motivation for going outside immediately at the start of [3]; she is now so determined to see that she is through the door almost before Jano and Laca register that she has gone, and follow her.

[3] Now comes Števa's moment. As the Kostelnička tries to call Jenůfa back, he is standing on a bench near the back, and his ominous, perhaps even accusing, presence prevents her from going after her stepdaughter.[31] Her suffering in [3] is so acute that she leans up against the set, far left. The Grandmother advances slowly towards her daughter (she walks with the aid of a cane), and gently touches her back. There is no way she can provide the embrace and the protection that the Kostelnička is asking her for. Indeed, no one can.

[4] When Karolka returns she tries to get Števa to join her, but he remains rooted to the spot. So she comes to the front alone and sits on the front right bench, in her white clothes – for a neat symmetry with Jenůfa when *she* comes back in, almost immediately, all in black, and sits on the front left bench.

[5] Laca follows Jenůfa in, and he in turn is followed rapidly by the crowd. Braunschweig brings them in one section earlier than the stage directions prescribe, so Laca's reproach, 'people are listening', is literally true;[32] he stands behind Jenůfa and tries to bully her into silence – but she breaks away and fights him off.

[6] The Mayor, now in all his top-hatted dignity, enters with the swaddling cloth and cap disdainfully perched on the end of his stick. He holds them out to Jenůfa, who seizes them and kneels at the front, clasping them, during the recognition. In a particularly nasty touch, the Old Woman who first calls on Christ and then accuses Jenůfa of infanticide now stands close behind her, and raises a large wooden cross aggressively above her.

[7] Števa just stands ineffectively as Jenůfa pleads with him for help, holding out the baby's clothes to him. But Laca moves between her and the crowd. He pushes back the Old Woman with the cross and threatens all the villagers by taking a stand between them and Jenůfa, who is caught up in

---

[31] In The Australian Opera's first production of *Jenůfa*, directed by John Copley (1974, and often revived), Robert Gard as Števa lifted his right hand at this moment and pointed at the Kostelnička, with an expression which implied that he has guessed the truth.

[32] Braunschweig is able to get the villagers on very fast, as is desirable, because of his non-naturalistic set with multiple entries through the wings. This part of the scene has always been difficult with naturalistic sets, in which the Kostelnička's living room has only one outside door. (There is a parallel problem with the villagers' exit near the end of the opera, which also has to be fast.) Lehnhoff, for example, being stuck with a very solidly built realistic set, has to get some of the male villagers to climb in through the windows! This is very clumsy.

passionate grief at the front of the stage.[33] The villagers advance threateningly from all sides. Jenůfa collapses, hiding her face in the baby clothes, just before Laca's final line brings the music to a crashing halt. And then from the sidelines the Kostelnička pulls everyone's focus to her by beginning her confession. This is exactly how the last section of the ensemble should be staged.

Discussion question

Analyse the movements of Jano, Jenůfa, Laca, Števa and the Kostelnička during Braunschweig's staging of this ensemble, and discuss how these movements are related to developments in the orchestral music and to the increasing aggression of the villagers.

5.6 Conclusion

Ensembles are the most perilous aspect of opera. On the one hand, there is the sheer visceral excitement of several solo voices singing together over an orchestra, sometimes with a chorus as well; on the other, there is the danger of losing musico-dramatic clarity and setting insoluble problems for directors.

Both Mozart and Bizet ingeniously structure their ensembles so that audibility is preserved and the orchestra can still illuminate the successive contrasted moods of the text. Verdi, on the other hand, abandons audibility, and with it *dramma per musica*, in the famous quartet from *Rigoletto*. In their place we have a static dramatic situation which does not change during the number, while spectators are given the purely musical pleasure of hearing four contrasted voices singing simultaneously four very different emotions over what is of necessity a fairly simple accompaniment.

Despite the size of the *Ring* orchestra and the rich textures which are normal in *Götterdämmerung*, Wagner composes his trio with care not to overwhelm the singers. In the invocations some words are bound to be lost, as Brünnhilde and Gunther are praying to Wotan while Hagen calls upon Alberich; but their texts parallel each other in syntax and meaning, and there is much overlapping (rather than singing different words precisely simultaneously), so nothing essential is lost.

In the sequence from *Jenůfa*, Janáček's highly original procedure of ramping up the tension by unleashing a succession of different *ostinati*, each more powerful than the last, ensures that only the Mayor's words cannot be

---

[33] Quite rightly Jenůfa is heard to be sobbing during the silence before the Kostelnička begins to sing.

heard clearly in the climactic final section – and, since he is being ignored on stage by all the other characters, this makes perfect musico-dramatic sense. Three elements predominate in the music: the villagers' terrifying demands for Jenůfa's immediate death, her passionate outcries and Laca's determination to defend her – all of which are easily heard under the baton of a good conductor.

In production, ensembles need above all careful placing of the characters to bring out their relative power. In the quintet from *Così fan tutte*, Jürgen Flimm uses blocking to underscore consistently the fundamental point that the soldiers are playing a game at the expense of their fiancées – and also the fact that the news that they are 'going to war' does indeed elicit from Fiordiligi and Dorabella the passionate reactions for which they had hoped. Behind the young women's backs, Guglielmo is seen in this production hailing these reactions as proof of success in the wager; but Flimm is right to balance this with a closing section in which Ferrando goes to Dorabella and shows his genuine emotional attachment to her.

Similarly, in the *Carmen* trio both Zambello and Noble realize very effectively the contrast in the text and the music between Frascita's and Mercédès' joyful readings of the cards and Carmen's experience of turning up the death-card, a fate on which she broods in what is almost a mini-aria. Both productions have fine interpretative touches, but Noble's decision to position Antonacci, as Carmen, first kneeling erect and then standing, centre stage, for this section – flanked on each side by the other two gypsies seated on the ground – is superior; and his use of Don José as a baleful presence, who hears the reading and stares murderously at Carmen at the end of the trio, is highly effective.

Even a stage director as talented and inventive as Jonathan Miller can do almost nothing with the Verdi quartet. After the Duke's lead-in nobody can hear what the four characters are singing (apart from the odd word here and there); and even if the words were audible there is no development in their emotional positions. Miller does what he can – which is not very much; a little flirtatious business between the Duke and Maddalena, while Rigoletto supports Gilda as they watch from outside. Some other directors surrender completely, and just let the four singers 'stand and deliver'.

Wagner's trio raises the question of power relationships. By simply placing the three singers across the front of the stage, Chéreau gives up. But there is an important question here, on which the director must take a stance: as the trio ebbs and flows, which, of Hagen and Brünnhilde, is dominant at each point? Kupfer does address this issue, and he gives dominance at the climax of the trio proper to Brünnhilde – while rightly hearing that, after the bridal procession enters, Hagen's baleful semitone fall comes to predominate in the orchestra. This demands that Hagen should hold the audience's attention as the curtain falls – which he does, in both productions.

Janáček's original way of constructing the recognition scene in *Jenůfa* demands precise *Personenregie* to make the overwhelming effect which it deserves. In Braunschweig's production, that is what it gets. When he overrides the stage directions by bringing on all the villagers as soon as Laca drags Jenůfa back inside rather than in the next section as prescribed, this is sensible; it enhances the tension between the couple. Movements and gestures are near perfect for all the soloists, especially Amanda Roocroft in the title role, and Miroslav Dvorský as Laca.

PART TWO

Encounters

6

Noises Off

This chapter analyses scenes where there are events taking place offstage, and the music of the offstage event is heard to be interacting with the music of the onstage characters. Several powerful scenes in opera use this device, and we shall study five of them. In the first scene to be considered, the people involved in the offstage event actually appear after a while on the stage, together with the brass band which is accompanying them; in the other scenes the offstage people and/or events are invisible to the audience throughout, but still have an effect on the onstage characters. Orchestral sound unites the 'noises off' with the characters onstage; so the composer establishes a dialogue between the music heard from offstage, and the music of both the characters singing onstage and the orchestra in the pit. And the stage director has to establish an interaction between the onstage characters and the offstage events in visual parallel to the dialogue in the music.

6.1 Cassandre and the Trojan Horse (Berlioz *Les Troyens* after Virgil, Act I no. 11 [Finale])

Les Troyens is Grand Opera on the largest scale; and Berlioz deploys very substantial forces to portray the Trojans bringing the Horse into the city, the action that leads to their downfall the following night, in Act II. Backstage in the far distance is a brass ensemble, which comprises a small high-pitched saxhorn, two trumpets, two cornets, three trombones and an ophicléide; the first sopranos and the basses of the chorus also begin by standing in the far distance with them. This instrumental ensemble is instructed to come nearer to the stage, when the sopranos and basses also come nearer at bar 46; but it is never seen. Then there is a band of eight saxhorns, ranging down from soprano to contrabass; this band will appear onstage at the climax together with the chorus, accompanying the cortège. Finally there is an ensemble of three oboes and six to eight harps, standing in for the 'flutes of Dindyme' and the 'Trojan lyre', which are mentioned in the libretto. This ensemble is in one of the wings, and the second sopranos, the contraltos and the tenors begin to sing from a position next to it. And of course there is the rest of the orchestra, in the pit. Berlioz rather optimistically suggested that the conductor would achieve ensemble by using an electric metronome with three wires (presumably linking to remote metronomes placed in front of each ensemble); but this music, with its quadraphonic effect, must have been almost impossible to play accurately until the advent of television monitors.

✎ 6 1 Cassandre and the Trojan Horse

No. 11 FINALE

[1] *(The procession is heard in the far distance.)*

DISTANT CHORUS

Du roi des dieux, ô fille aimée,

Oh beloved daughter of the king of the gods,

CASSANDRE *(alone at the front of the stage)*

De mes sens éperdus ...

Of my distracted senses ...

CHORUS

Du casque et de la lance armée,

Armed with a helmet and a spear,

CASSANDRE

... est-ce une illusion? ...

... is this an illusion?

CHORUS

Sage guerrière, guerrière aux regards doux!

Wise warrior, warrior whose look is gentle!

CASSANDRE

Les choeurs sacrés d'Ilion! **6.1.1**

The sacred choirs of Ilion!

CHORUS

À nos destins sois favorable,

Be favourable to our destiny,

Rends Ilion inébranlable!

Make Troy invincible!

CASSANDRE

Quoi! ... Déjà le cortège!

What! ... The procession already!

CHORUS

Belle Pallas protége nous!

Beautiful Pallas, protect us!

(The choristers of the first group come a bit nearer to the stage.)

CASSANDRE

Au loin je l'aperçois!

I see them in the distance!

L'ennemi vient!

The enemy is coming!

L'ennemi vient et la ville est ouverte!

The enemy is coming and the city is open!

Ce peuple fou qui se rue à sa perte

This crazy people which goes to its destruction

Semble avoir devancé les ordres de son roi!

Seems to have forestalled the king's orders!

(We hear the procession nearer.)

CHORUS

[1] Du roi des dieux, ô fille aimée, **6.1.2**

Pallas de la casque et de la lance armée,

Pallas protégé nous!

Sage guerrière, guerrière aux regards doux!

Entends nos voix, vierge sublime!

CASSANDRE

L'éclat des chants augmente.

CHORUS

Au son des flûtes de Dindyme

Se mêler au plus haut des airs.

Au son des flûtes de Dindyme

Se mêler au plus haut des airs.

Que la trompette Phrygienne,

Unie à la lyre Troyenne...

CASSANDRE

L'énorme machine roulante s'avance!

CHORUS

... te porte nos pieux concerts!

Unie à la lyre Troyenne...

(The whole CHORUS comes onstage, and stands to right and left upstage during the passage of the horse and the procession which follows it.)

... te porte nos pieux concerts!

CASSANDRE

La voici!

CHORUS

Du roi des dieux, ô fille aimée,

Du casque et de la lance armée,

Sage guerrière, guerrière aux regards doux!

Souriante guirlande

A l'entour de l'offrande

Dansez heureux enfants,

Dansez heureux enfants!

Semez, semez sur la ramée

La neige parfumée,

La neige parfumée

Des muguets du printemps.

Pallas! Pallas! Protège nous!

Semez, semez sur la ramée

La neige parfumée,

La neige parfumée

Des muguets ...

[2] *(a sound is made by cymbals in the wings)*

Oh beloved daughter of the king of the gods,

Pallas armed with a helmet and a spear,

Pallas protect us!

Wise warrior, warrior whose look is gentle!

Hear our voices, sublime virgin!

The sound of the songs is getting louder.

To the sound of the flutes of Dindyme

Blend your songs as loud as you can.

To the sound of the flutes of Dindyme

Blend your songs as loud as you can.

Let the Phrygian trumpet,

United with the Trojan lyre...

The enormous machine on wheels is coming!

... carry to you our devout music!

United with the Trojan lyre...

... carry to you our devout music!

Here it is!

Oh beloved daughter of the king of the gods,

Armed with a helmet and a spear,

Wise warrior, warrior whose look is gentle!

Smiling garland

Around the offering

Dance, happy children,

Dance, happy children!

Spread, spread on its branches

The perfumed snow,

The perfumed snow

Of the lilies of the valley of spring.

Pallas! Pallas! Protect us!

Spread, spread on its branches

The perfumed snow,

The perfumed snow

Of the lilies of the valley ...

BASSES

| Qu'est ce donc? | What is it? |

(The chorus shows agitation in different ways; some women leave as if to see what's going on offstage, and return almost immediately.)

CASSANDRE

| Jupiter! | Jupiter! |

BASSES

| Et pourquoi ce mouvement d'alarmes? | And why these alarmed movements? |

CASSANDRE

| On hésite! ... Et la foule s'agite! | They're hesitating! ... And the crowd is restless! |

CHORUS

| Dans les flancs du colosse on entend un bruit d'armes ... | Inside the colossus we can hear the noise of weapons ... |

CASSANDRE

| On s'arrête ... | They're stopping ... |
| Ô Dieux! Si ... | Oh gods! If ... |

BASSES

| Présage heureux! | Happy omen! |

TENORS

| Chantez enfants! | Sing, children! |

(The singing resumes, now stronger than before.)

CHORUS

| Fiers sommets de Pergame | Proud summits of Pergamon |

(The singing gets less loud little by little as it gets lost in the distance.)

(The chorus follows the procession and exits.)

D'une joyeuse flamme	With a joyful flame
Rayonnez triomphants,	Blaze out triumphantly,
Rayonnez triomphants,	Blaze out triumphantly,
Rayonnez triomphants,	Blaze out triumphantly,

(The chorus is in the wings.)

| Rayonnez triomphants! | Blaze out triumphantly! |

CASSANDRE

[3] Arrêtez! Arrêtez!	Stop! Stop!
Oui, la flame, la hache!	Yes, fire, the axe!
Fouillez le flanc du monstreux cheval!	Open up the side of the monstrous horse!
Laocoon! Les Grecs ... il cache	Laocoon! The Greeks ... it's hiding
Un piège infernal!	An infernal trap!
Ma voix se perd ...	My voice is going ...
Plus d'espérance! ...	No more hope! ...
Vous êtes sans pitié, grands dieux,	Great gods, you are without pity
Pour ce people démence!	For this deluded people!
Ô digne emploi de la toute puissance!	What a noble use for all your power!
Le conduire à l'abîme en lui fermant les yeux! ...	To lead them into the abyss while closing their eyes! ...

(She hears the last sounds of the triumphal march, which are still audible and then suddenly stop.)

Ils entrent, c'en est fait,	They're going in, it's done,

(She listens.)

le destin tient sa proie!	destiny grasps its prey!
6.1.3 Soeur d'Hector, va mourir	Sister of Hector, go and die
sous les débris de Troie!	under the ruins of Troy!

(exit)

(curtain)

The scene divides into three parts. There is a long and steady *crescendo* over the first part to the first climax, the entry of the full chorus and the saxhorn band at 112. The hymn to Pallas continues at full strength until the moment when a clash of several pairs of cymbals is heard from the wings (157). Just before this, the saxhorn band has left the stage. The second part begins when the chorus overcomes its momentary fears and reads the sound as a happy omen; the Trojans resume singing *now with more* éclat *than before*, and their deeply ironic prayer for the 'proud summits of Pergamon' to 'blaze out triumphantly in joyful flames' (Troy will burn this very night) continues undiminished until after they leave the stage. They fade into the distance. In the final section, Cassandre, still desperately trying to stop the cortège, is left alone to conclude the scene as she began it.

*

Once again we study a scene from *Les Troyens* in the production by Yannis Kokkos (cf. **3.2**). Anna Caterina Antonacci is the electrifying performer in the role of Cassandre. Kokkos's bare set comprises a raised platform right across the middle of the stage; a few steps lead down to the forestage, while a larger number of steps allows singers to descend almost out of sight behind it. And behind that lowered space, at the rear of the playing space, is a large screen; this can reflect the action upstage, and also present other images to the audience – in this scene, projections of the walls of Troy and of the Horse's head.

The first offstage brass band strikes up the Trojan March confidently in B flat major. In Kokkos's production the curtains are closed behind the forestage as the scene begins. Cassandre is, by Berlioz' explicit direction, downstage and alone when the scene begins; she had collapsed, weeping in agony, at the end of no. 10. Antonacci, who is lying supine when the music of no. 11 begins, raises her upper body to look around in puzzlement as the band establishes the melody in bars 8ff., looks up to the sky in disbelief as the chorus began to sing at 18, and utters her first words, doubting her own sanity, in 22. Cassandre begins on a repeated A flat, which has no place in the tonality of the distant sounds that are now reaching her, and the audience's, ears; and her vocal lines over the next few minutes, as she absorbs the shock of what is happening, are leaping and irregular, with agitated rhythms.

The main orchestra supports Cassandre's view of the unfolding event. This stance is taken up even before she sings her first words, since the little groups of five semiquavers in bars 5–7, after the ominous *frisson* of the tremolo strings in 1–4, are confirmed at 62–3 to be part of Cassandre's agitation. And the orchestra repeatedly counters the even and inexorable flow of the march with brief but dramatic, unpredictable interjections – for example:

6.1.1(I.11.29-31)

These interjections culminate in a pair of fierce comments when the second brass band begins to play, the choirs have come nearer and Cassandre realizes with horror that the Trojans have anticipated Priam's orders and are bringing in the enemy. This happens just before they launch into a triumphant re-presentation of their hymn to Pallas (**6.1.2**).[1]

Cassandre is so shocked at this point that she is reduced almost to silence. But what is she shocked by? Berlioz does not bring on the full chorus and the saxhorn band until 112ff. And if we were to follow his second thoughts, we would not see the Horse at all; in his final conception we are not watching the actual procession of those who are taking the Horse into the city, but just a chorus which is accompanying that procession. Berlioz did originally provide stage directions for the Horse to appear: *The gigantic Horse appears and crosses the theatre. It is hauled by a multitude of ropes covered with streamers of various colours and hauled by the crowd. Incense burns on portable altars. The singing returns, louder than before.* However,

---

[1]Kemp (1988: 25) writes correctly that: 'the erratic but persistent emotional shocks that seize her are voiced in the orchestra ...' (cf. also p. 120).

6.1.2 (I.11.75-8)

in the libretto which is now attached to the manuscript full score, Berlioz struck out this stage direction and wrote that the procession is 'invisible to the spectator'. Macdonald notes that 'the scene was never staged in Berlioz's lifetime, so he never had the opportunity to judge the rightness of his own decision'.[2] The stage direction in the Bärenreiter *Urtext* edition is ambiguous, but implies that the audience sees the Horse: *The whole chorus comes onstage, and stands to left and right upstage during the passage of the Horse and of the procession which follows it.* Kemp argues that Berlioz's second thoughts should be overridden: 'the music for the scene indicates

---

[2]Macdonald 2007: 57.

that the horse *should* be seen. It is a carefully planned crescendo, culminating when the full performing resources are heard for the first time and with Cassandra singing "La Voici" ['Here it is!', bar 114] ...'.[3] He is right.

Kokkos brings the procession on stage. He gradually starts to show the chorus both to Cassandre and to the audience, beginning about 29–30, and the Horse is disclosed at 66. The result is that the audience sees the procession and the Trojan rejoicing at the same time as they do Cassandre's reactions to them; and this greatly assists the dramatic impact of the music. To reinforce this effect, Antonacci as Cassandre wears a long and flowing white dress, while all the other Trojans wear quasi-uniform browns, greens and greys. One very striking young woman in white, at the front of the stage, pulls the audience into her conflict with the self-assured mass upstage, who are clad in completely contrasting, drab colours to offset the happiness which we see in their actions and facial expressions.

So, in Kokkos's production, at the first substantial orchestral outburst (quoted above as **6.1.1**), the curtains open while Cassandre sings 'the sacred choirs of Ilion'. Cassandre looks upstage, and sees flaring torches. As she crawls upstage towards them, at 'I see them in the distance' the lights come up on the other Trojans, and soon she can see more and more people, dancing and waving their torches. Just after Cassandre has sung 'the enemy is coming and the city is open', Kokkos responds to this cue; the scenery at the back of the stage half opens, and reveals the head of the Horse. Meanwhile, Antonacci runs around in despair of 'this crazy people', and Kokkos clearly (and rightly) links the orchestral outburst quoted as **6.1.2** to her anguish; on 75, she turns round and sees the Horse, surrounded by welcoming Trojans.

During the next section, while Cassandre is relatively quiet, members of the crowd embrace each other. Antonacci watches them, lifting her left hand up to the side of her face in great anxiety after she sings 'the sound of the songs is getting louder' – just after the third instrumental group (oboes and harps) has been added to the textures accompanying the Trojan hymn. Another severe *fortissimo* comment by the main orchestra in bar 105 illuminates Cassandre's terror; 'the enormous machine on wheels is coming'. Here Antonacci extends a hand out to the audience to symbolize her character's anguish; and now, for the climax, the saxhorn band enters, all the instrumental and vocal resources are deployed and the whole (double) chorus occupies the main (raised) part of the stage to deliver the full-volume repeat of their opening hymn, 'Oh beloved daughter of the king of the gods ...'.[4]

The orchestra remains in its previous role, commenting from Cassandre's perspective. Four loud chords mark how she feels the irony of 'warrior

---

[3] Kemp 1988: 157.
[4] The Bärenreiter *Urtext* vocal score states that 'a hundred additional choristers are necessary'. Eliot Gardiner fielded both the Châtelet's resident chorus and his own Monteverdi Choir for Kokkos's production, and they filled the stage completely.

whose look is gentle' addressed to Pallas (124); at the next orchestral intervention (128) Antonacci – downstage, while behind her the Trojans are singing, embracing, smiling and some even dancing – lifts her hands up, closing her eyes in despair; and in between the next two orchestral comments (130 and 140–1) she raises her hands to block her ears to the hymn, and stays that way until the singing is abruptly stilled by the clash of arms inside the Horse. For a moment at that point Cassandre has hope – Antonacci runs a couple of steps forward, hand extended as if in prayer, on 'Oh gods!'. But Cassandre's hopes are dashed: the basses hail the sound as a happy omen, and the song resumes.

Cassandre is now in absolute despair. Antonacci raises and extends her arms in appeal on 'Stop! Stop!'. But it is too late; the chorus has gone into the city. She crosses the stage violently on 'Laocoon! The Greeks!'. Then she clasps her belly in anguish on 'no more hope!' before addressing the gods, with fierce gestures to illuminate her anger and bitter irony. Finally, as the distant sound of the last band becomes silent, and in orchestral silence, Cassandre proclaims 'destiny grasps its prey!'. Antonacci lowers her hands gently; it is the end.

For Cassandre's exit line, Berlioz reuses an orchestral phrase – sustained chords with *appoggiaturas* – which has already been heard, early in the scene, to express her agitation (cf. her very first entry at 22). Sinister and brooding, it now expresses her final resignation to fate. And after an electrifying top G she leaves (**6.1.3**).

Or so Berlioz prescribes; the fairly static singers of the nineteenth century would depart immediately after delivering their climactic top note, hoping to be recalled for applause after the orchestral coda had run its course and the curtain had fallen. But there is no need for a modern director, with a physically active and highly expressive actress at his disposal, to send Cassandre off so abruptly. By delaying her exit, director and singer can explore in movement the powerful statements with which the orchestra now discharges the tension that has accumulated over this scene (and indeed over this whole Act). After all, it is only now, with the bands and chorus offstage and silent, that the main orchestra can devote itself *totally* to portraying Cassandre's emotions; so why not complement physically what the orchestra is saying?

So at 224 Antonacci runs wildly upstage, and as the music descends and becomes quieter (but *not* slower; the tempo is *Allegro agitato assai*, and the broken crotchets flow inexorably after 229), she runs downstage again, in terrible distress. Finally in 238ff. she runs upstage again, and holds up her hands in horror at the Horse, whose baleful face has remained in the background right up to this point, waiting for this very moment. On the penultimate three bars of rapid *crescendo*, the city walls close, shutting the Horse inside, and under the pressure of the devastating final *fortissimo* chord (B flat and F sounded by most of the orchestra, but with a flattened third [D] in flutes, oboes, violas and trombones) Antonacci as Cassandre

6.1.3 (I.11.232-8)

collapses to the ground. This is masterly stagecraft, completing a version of the scene which responds totally to Berlioz' music.

Discussion question

Analyse how Anna Caterina Antonacci's movements as Cassandre illuminate the pathos of her vision that the Horse's entry into Troy will destroy the city.

6.2 The death of Carmen (Bizet/Meilhac and Halévy *Carmen*, Act IV [Finale])

This scene presents a straightforward but highly effective use of an offstage chorus (and some trumpets and trombones). The three substantial choral stanzas and single cry of 'Victoire' (numbered [1], [2], [3] and [2a] in the text below) progressively intensify Don José's anguish at Carmen's absolute rejection of him; and she is spurred to greater defiance by the same offstage music and text that drives him to desperation, as the crowd in the bullring hail the victory of her new lover Escamillo. The librettists set up a parallel between Escamillo's dispatch of the bull in the ring and Don José's murder of Carmen outside it, and one of the productions which I shall discuss

(Adrian Noble's) even uses a set which reminds the audience of the inside of a bullring, so reinforcing the parallel.

✒ clip not available

JOSÉ *(desperately)*

Ah! Ne me quitte, Carmen,

Ah! Ne me quitte pas!

CARMEN

Jamais Carmen ne cédera!

Libre elle est née et libre elle mourra!

CHORUS *(from the bullring)*

[1] Viva! Viva! La course est belle,

Viva! Sur le sable sanglant,

Le taureau, le taureau s'élance!

Le taureau, le taureau qu'on harcèle

En bondissant s'élance, voyez!

Frappé juste, juste en plein coeur!

Voyez! Voyez! Voyez! Victoire!

(Hearing the cries of the crowd in the amphitheatre applauding Escamillo, Carmen makes a gesture of delight.)

(Don José does not once take his eyes off her. As the chorus finishes Carmen moves towards the bullring.)

JOSÉ *(barring her way)*

Où vas-tu?

CARMEN

Laisse-moi!

JOSÉ

Cet homme qu'on acclame,

C'est ton nouvel amant!

CARMEN *(trying to get past)*

Laisse-moi, laisse-moi!

JOSÉ

Sur mon âme,

Tu ne passeras pas,

Carmen, c'est moi que tu suivras!

CARMEN

Laisse-moi, Don José! Je ne te suivrai pas.

JOSÉ

Tu vas le retrouver, dis,

(with fury)

Tu l'aimes donc?

CARMEN

Ah! Don't leave me, Carmen,

Ah! Don't leave me!

Carmen will never give in!

Free she was born and free

    she will die!

Viva! Viva! The contest is good,

Viva! Bleeding on the sand,

The bull, the bull charges!

The bull, the bull they have goaded

Leaps to the charge, look!

Stricken right, right in the heart!

Look! Look! Look! Victory!

Where are you going?

Let me pass!

This man they are cheering,

He's your new lover!

Let me pass, let me pass!

On my soul,

you will not pass,

Carmen, it's me you will follow!

Let me pass, Don José! I will not follow you.

You're going to meet him, tell me,

You love him then?

Je l'aime,	I love him,
Je l'aime, et devant la mort même,	I love him, and in the face of death itself,
Je répéterai que je l'aime.	I will say again that I love him.

CHORUS *(from the bullring)*

[2] Viva! Viva! La course est belle,	Viva! Viva! The contest is good,

(Carmen again tries to enter the amphitheatre. Don José stops her again.)

Viva! Sur le sable sanglant,	Viva! Bleeding on the sand,
Le taureau, le taureau s'élance!	The bull, the bull charges!
Voyez, voyez, voyez, voyez!	Look, look, look, look!
Le taureau, le taureau qu'on harcèle	The bull, the bull they have goaded
En bondissant s'élance, voyez!	Leaps to the charge, look!

JOSÉ

(violently)

6.2.1 Ainsi, le salut de mon âme	So, the salvation of my soul
Je l'aurai perdu pour que toi,	I will have lost for you,
Pour que tu t'en ailles, infâme!	For you, bitch, to go
Entre ses bras, rire de moi.	Into his arms, to laugh at me.
Non, par le sang, tu n'iras pas!	No, on my life, you will not go!
Carmen, c'est moi que tu suivras!	Carmen, it is me you will follow!

CARMEN

Non! Non! Jamais!	No! No! Never!

JOSÉ

Je suis las de te menacer!	I am tired of threatening you!

CARMEN *(furiously)*

Eh bien! Frappe-moi donc, ou laisse-moi passer.	All right! Kill me then, or let me go past.

CHORUS *(fanfares offstage)*

[2a] Victoire!	Victory!

JOSÉ *(out of his mind)*

Pour la dernière fois, démon,	For the last time, fiend,
Veux-tu me suivre?	Will you follow me?

CARMEN *(tearing a ring from her finger and hurling it at him)*

Non! Non!	No! No!
Cette bague, autrefois, tu me l'avais donnée ...	This ring – once, you gave it to me ...
Tiens!	Take it!

JOSÉ *(drawing his knife, moves in on Carmen)*

Eh bien, damnée ...	For that you die ...

(Fanfare behind the scene. Carmen attempts to escape, but Don José catches up with her at the entrance of the amphitheatre, he stabs her; she falls and dies.)

CHORUS *(from the bullring)*

[3] Toréador, en garde, 62.2 Toréador!	Toreador, on guard, Toreador!
Toréador!	Toreador!
Et songe bien oui songe en combattant	And remember well, yes remember as you fight

(Don José, horrified, falls on his knees beside her.)

Qu'un oeil noir te regarde	That a dark eye is looking at you
Et que l'amour t'attend, Toréador,	And that love is waiting for you,
l'amour t'attend.	Toreador, love is waiting for you.
(The crowd re-enters the stage) **6.2.1**	
JOSÉ	
Vous pouvez m'arrêter ... C'est moi qui l'ai tuée.	You can arrest me ... It is I that killed her.
Ah! Carmen! Ma Carmen adorée!	Ah, Carmen! My adored Carmen!
(curtain)	

Just before we first hear the chorus of spectators [1], Carmen has declared that 'free she was born and free she will die'. As she hears them hailing Escamillo's victory, Carmen *makes a gesture of delight*, and as the chorus finishes she *moves towards the bullring*, which she has not tried to do so far in the scene. Don José also reacts to the first chorus; he watches her intently throughout, and at the end he physically bars her way and prevents her from going in. In the libretto this is the first violence that he inflicts on her; up until this point he has simply been pleading with her to return to him.

Each choral interjection has consequences. Don José now accuses Carmen of being Escamillo's lover, and she not only declares this to be true but also sings that 'in the face of death itself / I will say again that I love him'. This is not the first mention of death in the scene, but it is the first time that she expresses her readiness to defy Don José even in the face of death – which is in fact what she will do later in the scene.

Now the chorus sings for the second time [2]. And this time neither Carmen nor Don José listens passively to the whole stanza before taking action. She tries to go in to the bullring during the chorus, and again he physically restrains her. Then at the end of the stanza, as Don José further intensifies his reaction by singing *violently* that he has lost the salvation of his soul for nothing, a powerful motif, first heard towards the end of the Prelude, breaks out *ff* in the upper instruments:

This is an aural representation of Don José's intense passion for Carmen.[5] Here, the appearance of **6.2.1** after the second choral stanza shows that

---

[5] See below, **9.1**, for a full discussion of this theme and its appearances earlier in the opera.

this second hearing of the action in the bullring has driven Don José to a new and dangerous level of intensity of frustrated desire, reflected both in his tormented vocal line and in the repeated injections by the orchestra of **6.2.1**. And this brings Carmen to make, *furiously,* a challenge which escalates the danger to her: 'All right! Kill me then, or let me go past'.

At this point [**2a**] the chorus hails Escamillo with the one word 'Victoire!', preceded by a trumpet fanfare. Don José is now *out of his mind,* and Carmen makes her death virtually inevitable by hurling his ring at him. Don José responds only with the briefest of words: 'For that you die...',[6] and the third choral outburst [**3**] seals his resolve. In the music Bizet once again, as with **2a**, accompanies with a fanfare; but this one is sombre, with trombones joining the trumpets in a rhythmic pulse. And as Don José kills Carmen an intense counter-melody to the Toreador song emerges, reflecting both his tormented soul and the tragedy of her death:

6.2.2 (IV.2 No. 27, 191 ff.)

At the moment when Carmen is dead and the chorus concludes its final stanza (with the hideous irony that they are promising Escamillo that he will receive Carmen's love after the bullfight), **6.2.1** breaks out once again in the woodwind and violins, as Don José begs to be arrested and confesses his guilt; then the strings surge and recede in an intense sequence of *tremolos,* rising and falling in dynamics, which drives the opera to its final curtain.

*

Directors must show their Carmen and their Don José to be reacting to the 'noises off' which represent through music the events inside the bullring; the real *corrida* in there and the tragic one between man and woman which the audience sees being played out in front of them interact in the ways which I have analysed above, and each choral outcry precipitates a raising of the intensity of the conflict between Don José and Carmen, which must be brought out in production.

The most powerful version of this scene available on DVD is that directed by Francesca Zambello at Covent Garden in 2007, using spoken

---

[6]This is a freer translation than I usually permit myself in this book. But the literal 'Oh well, damned one!' is terrible English.

dialogue as in the original. Anna Caterina Antonacci is as electrifying in the title role as she is in the trio (5.3) and as Berlioz's Cassandre (6.1), and Jonas Kaufmann is outstanding as Don José.

The scene is effectively set by the absolute contrast in their appearances; Don José looks as if he has been sleeping rough (as he probably has) – shaggy-haired, unshaven, with a ragged shirt open to show his chest and the hilt of a large knife protruding from his boot, while Carmen is dressed up for her new lover's bullfight, wearing full Spanish formal dress, with a mantilla in her hair and a crucifix at her throat. And, in Zambello's production, the duel between them has already become physical before chorus [1] is heard. Just beforehand, Don José had pulled off Carmen's mantilla and loosened her hair, and was holding her tightly to him as he made his plea, *desperately*, for her not to leave him. Antonacci's Carmen not only breaks away to make her reply but also pushes him to the ground. She, too, is on her knees at 'free she will die!' So they are both on the ground as chorus [1] begins, and they both rightly turn upstage immediately to register the new sounds which they are hearing from backstage. During the chorus Carmen tries to get up and go inside, but Don José catches her by the legs and makes her fall to the ground again. They then struggle there, right through to her declaration just before chorus [2] that she loves Escamillo. At that point she breaks away from Don José, grabs his shoulder and then pushes him away to register her defiance as the second chorus begins.

Her response to chorus [2] is to wave to friends who are visible, cheering Escamillo, in the crowd at the top of the high bullring wall, which stretches across the back of the stage. Kaufman's Don José is relatively static during this chorus, but he is still affected by their stanza and Carmen's pleased response to it; as 6.2.1 bursts out at the end of the chorus, he seizes her by the hair, and as he sings his anger about losing his soul so that she, 'infâme' (which I have translated as 'bitch') can go to Escamillo, he pulls her head down by the hair and then pushes her to the ground; during the struggle he too falls to the ground, at 'on my life'. On 'No, no, never!' Antonacci crawls away from him, and with her next words of defiance she stands up.

Don José is at this point still on the ground. But as the chorus shouts 'Victoire!' [2a], he gets up and seizes her by the hands. They wrestle again, but Carmen breaks away again on 'No! No!' and gets some distance before throwing the ring. Her death follows the stage directions; after 'For that you die …' Antonacci's Carmen tries to leave, but during chorus [3] Don José seizes her (on the first phrase of 6.2.2) and stabs her (on the second; this precise response to the music is excellent). In a macabre touch, as the chorus comes to an end and 6.2.1 sounds out in the full orchestra, Don José smiles as if about to kiss Carmen, while she is dying in his arms. Then he caresses her face, kisses her dead lips the moment he has finished singing, takes out the flower which he has kept and drops it on her body, and is kneeling in supplication as the curtain falls. In violation of the stage directions, the crowd does not come onstage. It may be unrealistic for Don José not to have soldiers approaching to take him into custody as he sings 'You can arrest me ...', but the entry of others at this point always pulls focus very badly from the tragic couple and from the passionate music, which focuses on Don José and Carmen right up to the fall of the curtain, and in a modern production (where we no longer expect full late nineteenth-century levels of realism) this way of directing the ending is superior.

Antonacci is also the star of Adrian Noble's 2009 production, in which *Carmen* returned at last to the stage of the Opéra Comique, restored by Sir John Eliot Gardiner to its original form, with spoken dialogue and period instruments, and entirely rethought away from the genre of Grand Opera to which it has almost always been wrongly consigned – which is all to the good. However, it presents a less effective version of this scene, primarily because Andrew Richards is a gentler Don José. Early in the scene, during his lyric pleading before the chorus is heard, he was more visionary than Kaufmann is in Zambello's tougher production; but he is less powerful later on as his character is supposed to become more maddened – leaving Antonacci with less violence to react to as Carmen. And the characters' responses to the choral stanzas are muted – in fact there is no response by either of them to the first one, until the very end of it, when Carmen looks up as if reacting to the crowd. Unlike Zambello's characters, who after chorus [1] are fighting on the ground, this Don José simply seizes his Carmen, who breaks away easily when she confirms that she loves Escamillo; at this point, rather than attacking Carmen, Richards holds his hands to his head and writhes in torment. Then as chorus [2] is heard he remains away from her; he goes up to the edge of the set, agonized by Escamillo's success, and thumps on the outer wall of the amphitheatre.

However, even this more introverted Don José has to move towards murder. So as **6.2.1** bursts out for the first time in the scene he picks up the blanket, which he had draped round him as the scene began, and waves it threateningly; this is ominous, because in this production he will use the blanket to choke Carmen before stabbing her. And as she hears 'Victoire!' [2a] Carmen looks up in joy, a good response to the offstage music.

The murder is done late; only on the third development in the melody of **6.2.2** does Don José tie the blanket around Carmen's throat, and he does not stab her in the stomach till the outburst of **6.2.1** at the end of the chorus.

Following Zambello's lead, Noble leaves the stage to the tragic pair alone right to the end of the opera; and there is an extraordinary ending. Don José lets Carmen fall to the ground as he begins singing 'you can arrest me...' and as he finishes his last note Don José touches the corpse between her legs under her dress, first with his hand and then with his mouth, before crawling up the body to lie over her, caressing her head, as the curtain falls. This certainly shows that Don José physically adores Carmen, as his last word in the opera attests; but I find the explicit necrophilia somewhat disconcerting.

This is a much-recorded opera, and some of the earlier performances on DVD continue to have merit. For example, in Francesco Rossi's 1984 film, Domingo as Don José responds immediately when the first chorus is heard, turning his head abruptly towards the amphitheatre; and immediately it is over he fights violently with Julia Migenes-Johnson, as Carmen, in the doorway leading to the bullring. Violence intensifies between them when [2a] is heard, but, like Carreras in Paul Mills' 1989 Met production, Domingo in the film stabs his Carmen too early, on 'For that you die', which fails to recognize that the offstage fanfare and the start of the final chorus are the final straw for Don José.[7] By contrast, Zeffirelli's 1978 production at the Wiener Staatsoper (also with Domingo, but with Obratsova as Carmen) rightly follows the stage directions and has Don José stab Carmen during chorus [3]. But Zambello's production offers a far more intense staging of the conflict than do the earlier versions, and thus its response to Bizet's passionate music is much more appropriate to the early twenty-first century, in which the theatre as a whole has become much more physical than it was thirty or so years ago.

Discussion question

In this scene the choral 'noises off' intensify Don José's agony; analyse how in Zambello's production Kaufmann's and Antonacci's reactions to these sounds add to the inevitability of Carmen's death. Is the amount of groundwork in this production an excessive physicalization of their conflict?

6.3 *Hoé! Hisse hoé!* (Debussy/Maeterlinck *Pelléas et Mélisande* Act I scene 3)

There are two obvious symbols in Maeterlinck's *Pelléas et Mélisande*, obvious because they are thoroughly embedded in western society; the crown (signifying royalty), and the wedding ring. But, apart from these, the symbols in the play are not static objects, to be contemplated, interpreted and assigned a translatable meaning or signification. If this were possible it would defeat the whole aim of Maeterlinck's symbolic dramas, which is precisely to go beyond the surface aspects of human life which can be expressed rationally in words – to explore what Maeterlinck called 'psychological action – the workings of the subconscious; to throw light upon the existence of the soul ... to hush the discourse of reason and sentiment, so that above the tumult may be heard the solemn, uninterrupted whisperings

---

[7]After that, the end of the film is a disaster, with music and imagery from earlier in the opera interpolated into the final moments.

of man and his destiny'.[8] To understand how he does this, we need to see each scene in *Pelléas et Mélisande* as an unfolding *process of encounter* with a symbolic object. Karl Jung, who devoted much thought to symbols, expressed the point perfectly: '[symbols are] not a disguised indication of something that is generally known, but … an effort to elucidate by analogy what is as yet completely unknown *and only in the process of formation'*.[9] We should speak not so much of symbolic objects as of symbolic processes or experiences, which give insight into truths that are impossible to express by any other means.

Except of course in music! Debussy's description in 1889 of his ideal opera text is an almost exact prefiguration of *Pelléas et Mélisande*, which he first read in 1893:

> I want to create a work in which music would take over at the point where words become powerless. For this I need a text by a poet who, by only half saying things, will allow me to graft my dream upon his dream … plain human beings, no specific country, no period. No compulsion on the composer, who must complete and give body to the work of the poet … I dream of a short text, and flexible scenes. Scenes which are diverse both in location and in style; characters who do not argue, but are submissive to their lives and to fate.[10]

To understand Debussy's musical illumination of *Pelléas et Mélisande* Act I scene 3, which is the first time we see Pelléas and Mélisande together, and to examine how a production can in its turn illuminate the text and music, we need to chart the process of the encounter in Maeterlinck's text between Geneviève, Pelléas and Mélisande and the ship which is leaving the harbour for an uncertain fate.

🖉 6 3 Pelléas et Mélisande

I.3 *In front of the castle.*

[1] *Enter GENEVIÈVE and MÉLISANDE*

6.3.1

MÉLISANDE

Il fait sombre dans les jardins. Et quelles forêts tout autour des palais!	It is dark in the gardens. And such forests all around the castle!

GENEVIÈVE

---

[8] Maeterlinck 1911, 108 and 98. His symbolist plays all date from the early 1890s; *The Intruder*, 1890; *The Blind*, 1891; *Pelléas et Mélisande*, 1892; *Interior*, 1894. *Pelléas* is the only full-length play; the others are in one Act.

[9] Jung, quoted at Brockett and Findlay 1973: 266. Italics mine.

[10] Quoted in Hoérrée 1942; translation by Lockspeiser 1962: I.205.

Oui; cela m'étonnait aussi quand je suis
arrivée ici, et cela étonne tout le monde.
Il y a des endroits où l'on ne voit jamais le soleil.

Yes; I too was struck by that when
I first came here, and it strikes everyone.
There are some places where you never see
the sun.

6.3.2 Mais l'on s'y fait si vite ...
Il y a longtemps ...
Il y a longtemps ...
Il y a presque quarante ans que je vis ici ...
6.3.3 Regardez de l'autre côté, vous aurez
la clarté de la mer.

But you get used to it so quickly ...
It is a long time ...
It is a long time ...
It is nearly forty years that I have lived here ...
Look on the other side, you will get
the light from the sea.

MÉLISANDE

J'entends du bruit au-dessous de nous ...

I hear a noise somewhere below us ...

GENEVIÈVE

Oui; c'est quelqu'un qui monte vers nous ...
Ah! C'est Pelléas ... Il semble encore fatigué
de vous avoir attendue si longtemps ...

Yes, that is someone coming up towards us ...
Ah! It's Pelléas ... He seems tired after
waiting for you for so long ...

MÉLISANDE

Il ne nous a pas vues.

He hasn't seen us.

GENEVIÈVE

Je crois qu'il nous a vues, mais il ne sait
ce qu'il doit faire ... Pelléas, Pelléas, est-ce toi?

I think that he's seen us, but he doesn't know
what to do ... Pelléas, Pelléas, is that you?

PELLÉAS

Oui! Je venais du côté de la mer ...

Yes! I was going towards the sea ...

GENEVIÈVE

Nous aussi; nous cherchions la clarté.
Ici, il fait un peu plus clair qu'ailleurs;
6.3.4 & 5 et cependant la mer est sombre.

Us too; we searched for the light.
Here, it is a bit brighter than elsewhere;
and yet the sea is dark.

PELLÉAS

[2] Nous aurons une tempête cette nuit. Il y en a
toutes les nuis depuis quelque temps ...
et cependant elle est si calme maintenant ...
On s'embarquerait sans le savoir et l'on
ne reviendrait plus.

We shall have a storm tonight. There has
been one every night for some time ...
and yet the sea is very calm right now ...
One could put out to sea without knowing it
and never return.

VOICES BACKSTAGE

[3] Hoé! ... hisse hoé!

MÉLISANDE

Quelque chose sort du port ...

Something's leaving the harbour ...

PELLÉAS

Il faut que ce soit un grand navire ...
Les lumières sont très hautes,

It must be a large ship ...
the lights are very high,

VOICES

Hoé! ... hisse hoé!

PELLÉAS

nous le verrons tout à l'heure
quand il entrera dans la bande de clarté ...

we will see her very soon
when she sails into the patch of light ...

GENEVIÈVE

[4] Je ne sais si nous pourrons la voir …   I don't know if we will be able to see her …
il y a encore une brume sur la mer.   there is still a mist on the sea.

VOICES

Hoé! …

PELLÉAS

On dirait que la brume s'élève lentement …   One could say that the mist is clearing slowly …

MÉLISANDE

(6.3.5) Oui; j'aperçois là-bas une petite lumière   Yes; I can see down there a small light
que je n'avais pas vue …   which I hadn't seen before …

PELLÉAS

C'est un phare; il y en a d'autres que nous   It's a beacon; there are several others which
ne voyons pas encore.   we still can't see.

MÉLISANDE

Le navire est dans la lumière …   The ship is in the light …
Il est déjà bien loin …   she's already quite distant …

PELLÉAS

Il s'éloigne à toutes voiles …   She's going away in full sail …

MÉLISANDE

[5] (6.3.1/6.3.5) C'est le navire qui m'a menée ici. That is the ship which brought me here.

VOICES

Hisse hoé! Hoé! … hisse hoé!

MÉLISANDE

Il a de grands voiles …   She has big sails …
Je le reconnais à ses voiles …   I recognize her by her sails …

VOICES *(at a great distance)*

Hisse hoé!

PELLÉAS

Il aura mauvaise mer cette nuit …   She will have rough seas tonight …

VOICES

Hisse hoé!

MÉLISANDE

Pourquoi s'en va-t-il cette nuit? …   Why is she going tonight? …
On ne le voit presque plus …   We can hardly see her now …
Il fera peut-être naufrage …   Perhaps there'll be a shipwreck …

PELLÉAS

La nuit tombe très vite …   The night is falling very fast …

VOICES *(distant sound with mouths closed)*

GENEVIÈVE

Il est temps de rentrer. (6.3.5) Pelléas,   It is time to go back. Pelléas,
monte la route a Mélisande.   show Mélisande the way.
Il faut que j'aille voir, un instant, le petit Yniold.   I must go and see little Yniold for a moment.
(She goes out.)

PELLÉAS

[6] On ne voit plus rien sur la mer …   Nothing more can be seen on the sea …

MÉLISANDE

Je vois d'autres lumières.   I see some other lights.

PELLÉAS

Ce sont les autres phares ...   They are the other beacons ...

Entendez-vous la mer? ...   Do you hear the sea? ...

C'est le vent qui s'élève ... Descendons par ici.   The wind is rising ... Let's go down this way.

Voulez-vous me donner la main?   Do you want to give me your hand?

MÉLISANDE

Voyez, voyez, j'ai les mains pleines de fleurs.   Look, look, my hands are full of flowers.

PELLÉAS.

Je vous soutiendrai par le bras,   I'll support you by the arm,

le chemin est escarpé   the path is steep

et il y fait très sombre ... (6.3.1)   and it's very dark there ...

Je pars peut-être demain ...   I'm leaving tomorrow maybe ...

MÉLISANDE

6.3.6 Oh! ... pourquoi partez-vous?   Oh! ... why are you leaving?

(They go out.)

First, [1] Geneviève contrasts the gloom of the encircling forests with the clarity of the sea, which she and Mélisande have sought out. Pelléas joins the two women, also in search of the sea and its light; but then Geneviève sees that the sea is in fact dark, and Pelléas foresees a gathering storm [2]. He concludes by saying 'One could put out to sea without knowing it and never return'. Immediately, [3] Mélisande sees that something is actually putting out to sea; and Debussy adds to the play text the evocative cries of the crew, 'Hoé! Hisse Hoé!' heard from an offstage chorus. [4] The characters now describe an interaction between the light and the mist, with beacons also visible; when the ship eventually comes into the light, it is already far out to sea. [5] Mélisande recognizes the ship as the one which brought her to Allemonde,[11] Pelléas foresees that it will have rough weather, and Mélisande fears that it will be shipwrecked. [6] After Geneviève makes an excuse and leaves, Pelléas can see nothing more, but Mélisande can still see some beacons. The wind is getting up, and Pelléas offers to hold her hand. She refuses – 'my hands are full of flowers'. He takes her by the arm, and helps her down the steep path. 'I'm probably leaving tomorrow ...' 'Oh ... why are you leaving?'.

The development through these six sections, and especially the encounter with the departing ship, parallels and illuminates the psychological development of the two principal characters. They have sought out the light as an escape from the gloom that encircles their lives; but the scene moves from momentary glimpses of brightness to uncertainty, the prospect of a storm, and possible shipwreck. When Geneviève has gone, Mélisande can

---

[11] The name of Arkel's kingdom is a German/French pun (from a Belgian, born in the country which divides those two nations); Alle (German 'all') and monde (French 'world') signify the universal implications of the drama.

still see some beacons, but Pelléas cannot. Why? Pelléas has already hinted
that he is falling in love with his brother's wife in section [2], with 'one
could put out to sea … and never return', and he reaffirms it more clearly
in his last line of the scene. This shocks Mélisande into a sudden intake of
breath ('Oh!'), and the curtain falls as her question is met with silence.

✽

The design by Karl-Ernst Herrmann for Peter Stein's production (Welsh
National Opera/Châtelet Théâtre Musical de Paris, 1992) does not show
either the forests or the sea; they are imagined as being offstage left and
offstage right respectively. But the liminal area in which the action is set is
provided with different levels. A large flight of stairs descends from high up
on stage left down to a platform stage right, about two metres above the
ground; and in front of it another, smaller flight of stairs descends in the
opposite direction from the platform at stage right, to reach ground level
at about stage centre. This will represent the 'steep path' to which Pelléas
refers near the end of the scene.

Debussy focuses the scene from the outset on Mélisande; an extended
version of the main theme associated with her in Act I scene 1 is heard just
before the curtain rises (**6.3.1 a and b**).

6.3.1 (1.35.1)

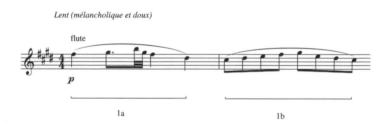

The music is quiet and resigned as Geneviève describes the gloom around
the castle, with a gentle pathos to express her resignation (**6.3.2**).

6.3.2 (1.36.7)

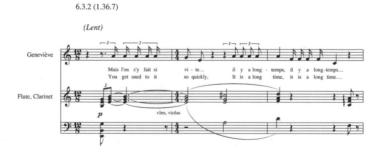

Her prophecy that Mélisande will see *'clarté'* (the French word conveys both literal light and insight)[12] evokes a glorious chord of F sharp major (**6.3.3**) – and, fascinatingly, another bright chord sounds only two bars later as Mélisande hears a noise below them – which turns out to be Pelléas. Will he bring light to her?

6.3.3 (1.37.2)

In Peter Stein's production Geneviève (Penelope Walker) and Mélisande (Alison Hagley) enter stage left, ground level late in the interlude after I.2, earlier than where their entry is marked in the score; they look upwards as if in search of light. But as the theme associated with her character sounds out in the flute (**6.3.1**) Hagley looks around her, sadly. They then cross right, and Geneviève starts to go up the smaller, steep flight of stairs at the tempo change to *un peu moins lent* just before Mélisande first sings. As Geneviève describes the gloom, Hagley looks around slowly, still at ground level; but Geneviève manages to entice her into coming up the stairs to the platform as she invites her to see the *clarté de la mer* – the light/clarity of

---

[12] At the end of the opera, after his futile interrogation of the dying Mélisande, Golaud sings 'I shall die here like a blind man'. His quest for *clarté*, which culminated in his using his son Yniold to spy on Pelléas and Mélisande from below their lighted room in a tower (III.4), finally fails. The imagery of light and darkness is fundamental to Maeterlinck's *Pelléas et Mélisande*, as also to his other great symbolist play *Interieur*. Debussy of course was highly aware of this and reflects it in many ways, especially by the use of tonalities, throughout the opera; see Langham Smith 1989, and cf. my examples **6.3.3** (a high chord of F sharp major for *clarté*) and **6.3.4** (a low chord of G minor for *obscurité*).

the sea – which is now shining on stage in a light from stage right which illuminates the two characters, as well as shining in the music of **6.3.3**.

The music remains light and positive as Pelléas arrives and (as Geneviève sings) 'here it is lighter than elsewhere; but the sea is gloomy'. Debussy now abandons *clarté*, and paints the gloom and the coming storm in the orchestra (a sudden low G minor chord, **6.3.4**). Pelléas broods on the storms, but then remarks 'and yet the sea is very calm this evening'.

At this point the motif which has already been associated with Golaud in Act I scene 1 sounds out in a muted solo horn (**6.3.5**; I.3.40.9); in Debussy's conception of the scene – adding greatly to the illumination which he has already bestowed on Maeterlinck's text – Mélisande's older, jealous husband is an unseen presence in the minds of both principal characters.[13]

---

[13] Nichols is wrong to suggest that the appearance here of the main theme associated with Golaud indicates that 'Golaud too is calm "at the moment"' (John [ed.] 1982a: 14). Elsewhere

This explains why Pelléas immediately thinks of sailing away and never returning;[14] he is attracted to his brother's wife, and he knows it. The voices from the departing ship are heard at once – 'Hoé! Hisse Hoé!' (I.3.41.2–3 + ff.) – and they, too, echo the Golaud theme; not because it is his ship but because in Debussy's vision his unseen presence in the thoughts of Pelléas and Mélisande is totally intertwined with their unfolding encounter with the ship. After this, when Pelléas optimistically hopes that they will see the ship properly when it enters 'that patch of light', the orchestra does not respond with a glorious chord like **6.3.3**; the music remains dark, and becomes agitated (I.3.42); indeed, when the mist lifts a little and Mélisande sees a small light that she had not seen before, once again Golaud's motif sounds in the orchestra (I.3.42.4–6). Does his sinister presence in her mind even corrupt this little piece of light?

Neil Archer as Pelléas joins Geneviève and Mélisande on the platform by ascending an invisible set of steps from upstage. When Geneviève sings 'here it is lighter than elsewhere', the light shines full on her; but as the gloom spreads (Pelléas: 'we shall have a storm tonight'), Mélisande sits on the steps. All three are now looking out to sea, i.e. stage right. After Golaud invades Pelléas's thoughts (**6.3.5**), and Pelléas imagines setting out to sea, in Stein's production his mother gently puts a hand on his shoulder, as if sensing that he needs reassurance.

As the ship leaves the port, Mélisande points towards it, and soon shades her eyes with her hand to see better. When Pelléas thinks the mist is lifting, he extends his hand; and when Mélisande sees a little light, her excitement grows; she points with her right hand extended, right throughout her line of text. Hagley leaves the Golaud-related motifs sounding in the orchestra to depict Mélisande's subconscious thoughts; on the surface, as Stein interprets the scene, she is oblivious.

Golaud is then absent from their thoughts for a few moments. When Pelléas and Mélisande see more lights and then the ship, delicate, animated figurations chart their growing excitement and warmth of emotion (I.3.42.6ff.), as, in the production, Mélisande looks at Pelléas for the first time in the scene, then turns sadly away on 'she's already quite distant'. Then the music reaches the climax: 'it is the ship which brought me here'. In some way which is hard to define this is a turning point, and Debussy marks

---

Nichols tries to tie the ship to Golaud: 'Golaud too, like the sailors, is heading blindly towards a storm' (1989: 67). This interpretation cannot be right; Golaud is not present during this scene, so the music (and the symbol of the ship) cannot convey his emotional state but only that of those who witness the ship's departure.

[14] On another level he might mean that one could embark on an adventure with Mélisande and never recover from it; equally, the departure of the ship that brought her might imply that Mélisande is now trapped in Allemonde, for good or ill. Maeterlinck's symbols are always multivalent, and become elusive when you try to tie them down to a specific 'meaning', a 1–1 correspondence between object and words.

it with uncharacteristically complex music. Mélisande's full motif floats over the lower textures in a flute/oboe solo; but those lower textures include, as well as unsettled *tremolo* triplets in the lower strings, another clear articulation of Golaud's motif in the horns and the Golaud-related cries of 'Hoé! Hisse Hoé!' from the ship (I.3.43). Hagley, as Mélisande, rises to her feet, very concerned, as Pelléas sings that the ship will have a bad night.

The ship now disappears into darkness (lights dim onstage in Stein's production); Mélisande fears that it will be wrecked – as will her life, torn between Golaud and Pelléas – and her vocal line droops a minor second on the last two syllables of *naufrage* ('shipwreck') (I.3.44.4–5).

Golaud is still a dominant presence in the thoughts of all three; when the ship finally disappears and the almost ethereal chorus falls silent, Geneviève's decision to leave is motivated by the summons of Golaud's motif in the horns (1 before I.3.45).[15] And then it is Pelléas's moment. He asks Mélisande to give him her hand – tentatively, and accompanied by absolute silence in the orchestra (I.3.46.6–7). In Debussy's world of understatement, this is almost a declaration of love.[16] And so in Stein's production Archer holds out both his hands to Hagley.

Hagley responds by smiling as Mélisande tells Pelléas that her hands are full of flowers. Then, as he takes her arm instead, the music changes both key and time signature (to F sharp major and 12/8; I.3.47), as it starts to slow towards the end of the Act. Mélisande's theme is heard again in its full glory, *very expressive*, high in a flute solo as Pelléas leads her down the steps, followed by a lower but no less expressive oboe solo – and the impact on Pelléas of her close physical presence is heard in the descending triplets of the rest of the orchestra, leading to his almost literally monotonous tonic 'Tomorrow perhaps I will leave'.

The last seven bars need to be quoted in full (**6.3.6**), and studied in close relation to Stein's production.

Hagley has been moving down the path, but she stops suddenly to sing 'Oh!' – an accented and *tenuto* G natural (in F sharp major G should of course be sharp, and the flattening emphasizes the shock of the moment); Mélisande is wounded by Pelléas's intention to leave. Recovering, she asks 'Why are you leaving?' – the last word in the French is *vous*, 'you', and on it Debussy returns her from another G natural to the key's normal G sharp supertonic. The gentle curve of *pourquoi partez-*, the semitone rise to *vous*, and the warmth of the string chord which underlies Mélisande's G sharp, are almost seductive; they show that she is attracted to him. In Stein's production, Pelléas and Mélisande look intently into each other's eyes as she sings this line. The orchestral music now offers, in a solo flute *pp espressivo*,

---

[15] Stein wrongly has Yniold appear at the top of the steps – not in accordance with the stage directions – just as the orchestra is articulating his father's motif.

[16] The orchestra will be silent again in Act IV, when the two declare 'I love you', 'I love you too'; IV.4.42.8–9.

6.3.6 (1.47.5)

a shortened version of the pattern of the second part of Mélisande's theme
(bar 2, cf. **6.3.1b**), then Neil Archer, as Pelléas, drops his hold on her arm,
and turns away. After that, the music becomes even quieter. Golaud is still
in Mélisande's thoughts (fragment of **6.3.5** in the horn in bar 3) – and so
Hagley moves on, away from her Pelléas. In bar 4, as her question ebbs
away in the solo flute, Hagley stops to look back at Archer – but then, as the
music dissolves still further (bars 5–6), Mélisande turns and goes. Pelléas is
left alone, looking after her and then following very slowly, in the emptiness
as the music dies away completely (bars 6–7) before the curtain falls. Totally
matching the dramatic situation, the harmony is unresolved in the final notes.

In this scene, the interaction between the principal characters and the
offstage ship, which is heard although it is not seen, symbolizes the development of the relationship between Pelléas and Mélisande from initial
darkness and a desire for *clarté* to a brief burst of actual *clarté* – and from
that to a new insight which neither of them is as yet ready to accept. For
from section two onwards Golaud is never very far from their thoughts,
and the departure of the ship parallels and illuminates a process of almost
unacknowledged growing mutual attraction. Stein's production reflects
closely all the stages of this development of the emotional situation.

Discussion question

Discuss the reactions of Alison Hagley as Mélisande and Neil Archer as
Pelléas to the encounter with the ship. Is Peter Stein's staging effective in

bringing out the two characters' interactions with the alternations of light and darkness during the departure of the ship?

6.4 Treasure, garden and domain (Bartók/ Balázs, *Duke Bluebeard's Castle*, doors 3, 4 and 5)

These three doors form the relatively light centre of Balázs' dark and brooding 'mystery play', which Bartók forged into a compelling one-Act opera. *Duke Bluebeard's Castle* is a profound (if pessimistic) dramatization of irreconcilable differences between males and females, which can separate even a man and woman who love each other deeply.

Balázs' scenario begins and ends in darkness (Bartók responds by beginning and ending the opera very darkly in low instruments in F sharp, and the opening of the climactic fifth door is greeted by a blazing sequence of triads in C).[17] As the first five of the seven doors are opened, each brightens the scene – a huge round gothic hall – with an influx of its associated colour; blood-red shines from the torture chamber, yellowish red from the armoury, gold from the treasure chamber, bluish green from the garden, and a gleaming torrent of white light from the fifth door, behind which Bluebeard's kingdom is revealed.

After this accumulation of colours, the stage begins to darken, when Judit opens the sixth door to reveal the lake of tears; and then, when the seventh door is opened, the fifth and sixth doors close, leaving the garish lights from the first four doors as the sole illumination of the hall. Then silver moonlight shines in from the seventh door as the three former wives appear. When the third wife has gone back inside the seventh door, the fourth and third doors close in succession, leaving the two reddish lights and the silver beam along which Judit follows the other three wives. Then the seventh door shuts behind her, and only the bloody light from the first two doors is left. It rapidly diminishes to extinction during Bluebeard's last words: 'Now all shall be darkness ... darkness ... darkness', so that he disappears into that blackness.[18]

The Minstrel who speaks the prologue challenges the audience: 'where is the stage? Within us or without? Here where I stand? In me? In you?'. For many lovers of this opera the question has been decisively answered as 'within us' – the opera has been recorded first on LP and then on CD with outstanding conductors (e.g. Dorati, Kertész and Boulez), and has probably

---

[17] For an analysis of the key structure of the opera, and the symbolic use that Bartók made of these two keys, see Leafstedt 1999: 55–61.

[18] For a table of Balázs' sequence of colours and their relationship to the spectrum of light, cf. Leafstedt 1999: 61.

been a far more enjoyable experience for solitary listeners imagining what lies behind the doors than for those watching the action (of which there is not very much) in an opera house, looking at a traditional set which represents the hall, with seven large doors and a smaller entrance-door. On the other hand, avant-garde productions which abandon the original set concept have often done little but obscure the meaning of a mystery play which is itself already more than a little obscure, due to Balázs' symbolic, enigmatic language and his use of archaic Hungarian words.

Bartók's music is in two separate styles, matching the changes of situation as the opera unfolds. Much of the pre- and between-door dialogue is scored for only a few instruments out of his very large orchestra, and is solemn and dark. For each door, by contrast, Bartók makes use of an extended sound-palette. In 1907, a few years before Bartók decided to compose this opera, Kodály had brought back from France some of the latest scores by Debussy, and Bartók had responded to this stimulus with an impression-istic, pictorial style of his own, in a short orchestral work, *Two Pictures* (1910). Now in the opera (composed in 1911) this new idiom was used on a larger scale. Impressionist music accompanies each of Judit's six journeys of discovery through to the inevitable moment when she sees blood, at which point the music of what lies behind the door is interrupted and undermined by Bartók's simple but highly effective blood *leitmotif* of dissonant minor seconds. In this opera the entire orchestra represents the 'noises off' (with additional brass backstage for door five).

*

There is of course a medium in which this opera can be fully realized, and visual images can be used to illuminate the meaning of Balázs' text and Bartók's music: film. Liberated from the confines of the opera house, a film director can create separate sets for the hall and for the interior of each of the seven doors, and stage Judit's exploration inside each of them. As Bartók's colourful orchestral palette portrays the contents of the door, we hear through her words and the orchestral illumination *what Judit sees*; so the film director can and must respond to the music with images which represent *how Judit imagines that area of Bluebeard's psyche*.

There are two available DVDs of *Duke Bluebeard's Castle*. The earlier (1981) is musically very good; Georg Solti conducted the London Philharmonic, and the action was subsequently filmed in Hungary under the direction of Miklós Szinetár. Silvia Sass is an impressive Judit (although sometimes rather abrasive; at all costs Judit must not appear to be an unsympathetic nag!). However Kolos Kováts, although he sings well, is a wooden actor in the role of Bluebeard. Bluebeard's castle is a rock-hewn cavern with sandy floors and the costumes are medieval, although modernist scenic elements are to be seen once we get inside the doors.

Szinetár's production provides less insight than Leslie Megahey's (to be discussed below), primarily because the sets are not as stimulating as a complement to the music. The contents of the third door are semi-abstract (also, silver, rather than the gold which they should be), and both this and the fourth door are less effective in their evocation of the riches of the treasury and garden than are those in the BBC production. Finally, Szinetár sees the fifth door not through Judit's eyes and music but through Bluebeard's rhetoric; as he shows off his domain, we view Bluebeard silhouetted against film of the sky, then of forests over which the sun sets. But the blood that Judit finds behind every door is not to be confused with the natural red of the setting sun. Sass performs well every stage of Judit's journey through these three doors, but without offering any profound insight. In a more understated performance under Megahey's direction, Elizabeth Laurence does. And this director's radical interpretation of the fifth door is highly original and very convincing.

Bluebeard cannot be played woodenly; he needs to be feeling the pain caused by Judit's insistence on exploring the castle, and, this, Robert Lloyd does superbly in Leslie Megahey's production, originally broadcast on BBC television in 1989, but released on DVD only in 2009. Laurence is a very strong Judit, and there is real chemistry between the couple in the emotionally crucial scene after the sixth door. The setting is high gothic, verging on Transylvanian; the costumes suggest the mid- to late-nineteenth century, and the castle has furnishings and props which are also appropriate to that period. Bluebeard wears a dark three-piece suit, Judit a flowing white bridal dress. This mirrors the fact that she has left her intended bridegroom to be with Bluebeard, and also makes an obvious but still telling symbolic contrast; she is here to bring light into his darkness.

✒ 6 4 Treasure, garden and domain

(JUDIT turns the key. The door opens with a deep, warm, metallic sound. A
  golden beam of light shines next to the other two on the floor.)
JUDIT[19]

Oh, be sok kincs!	Oh, how much treasure!
Oh, be sok kincs!	Oh, how much treasure!

(She kneels and digs into the treasure, placing jewels, a crown and a mantle on
  the doorstep.)

Aranypénz és drága gyémánt,	Golden coins and costly diamonds,
Bélagyöngygyel fényes ékser,	Lustrous jewelry encased in pearls,
Koronák és dús palástok!	Crowns and splendid cloaks!

BLUEBEARD

---

[19] Unpublished translation by Carl Leafstedt (2000). Reproduced with permission.

Ez a váram kincsesháza.	This is my castle's treasury.

JUDIT

Mily gazdag vagy Kékszakállú!	How rich you are, Bluebeard!

BLUEBEARD

Tied most már mind ez a kincs,	All this treasure is now yours,
Tied arany, gyöngy és gyémánt.	Gold, pearls and diamonds are yours.

JUDIT *(suddenly stands up)*

Vérfolt van az ékszereken!	There are bloodstains on the jewels!

(Puzzled, she turns to Bluebeard.)

Legszebbik koronád véres!	Your loveliest crown is bloody!

BLUEBEARD

Nyisd ki a negyedik ajjtót.	Open the fourth door.
Legyen napfény, nyissad, nyissad!	Let there be sunlight, open, open!

*(She becomes more restless and impatient. She turns to the fourth door and
quickly opens it. From the doorway flowery branches push inward, and the
opening in the wall is a square of blue-green. The new beam of light shines
next to the others on the floor.)* **6.4.1**

JUDIT

Oh! virágok! Oh! illatos kert!	Oh! Flowers! Oh! A fragrant garden!
Kemény sziklák alatt rejtve.	Hidden beneath hard rocks.

BLUEBEARD

Ez a váram rejtett kertje.	This is my castle's hidden garden.

JUDIT

6.4.2 Oh! virágok!	Oh! Flowers!
Embernyi nagy liljomok,	Lilies tall as a man,
Hüs-fehér patyolat rózsák,	Cool snow-white roses,
Piros szefük szórják a fényt.	Red carnations scatter the light.
Sohse láttam ilyen kertet.	Never have I seen such a garden.

BLUEBEARD

Minden virág neked bókol,	Every flower bows to you,
Minden virág neked bókol.	Every flower bows to you.
Te fakasztod, te hervasztod,	You make them bloom, wither,
Szebben úrja te sarjasztod.	And sprout anew more beautifully.

JUDIT *(suddenly bends down)*

Fehér rózssad töve véres,	Your white roses have bloody stems,
Virágaid földje véres!	Soil beneath your flowers is bloody!

BLUEBEARD

Szemed nyitja kelyheiket,	Your eyes open the flowers' calyxes,
S neked csengetyüznek reggel.	They ring bells for you by morning.

JUDIT *(stands up and turns towards Bluebeard)*

Ki öntözte kerted földjét?	Who watered your garden's soil?

BLUEBEARD

Judit szeress, sohse kérdezz.	Judit love me, never question.
Nézd, hogy derül már a váram.	See how my castle brightens.
Nyisd ki az ötödik ajtót!	Open the fifth door!

(With a quick movement Judit runs to the fifth door and flings it open. A high balcony and a far landscape are seen; light pours in in a brilliant flood.)

JUDIT

Ah!   Ah!

(Blinded, she holds up her hands to shield her eyes.)

BLUEBEARD

Lásd, ez az én birodalmam,	Behold, this is my domain,
Messze nézö szép könyöklöm.	My lovely parapet looking afar.
Ugye, hogy szép nagy, nagy ország?	Is it not a beautiful, great, great land?

JUDIT *(She is looking out, rigid and with her wits scattered.)*

6.4.3 Szép és nagy a te országod.   Your land is beautiful and grand.

BLUEBEARD

Selyemrétek, bársonyerdök,	Silken meadows, velvet forests,
Hosszú ezüst foljók folynak,	Long, silver rivers flow,
És kék hegyek nagyon messze.	And blue mountains far away.

JUDIT

Szép és nagy a te országod.   Beautiful and great is your domain.

BLUEBEARD

Most már Judit mind a tied,	Judit, now all is yours,
Itt lakik a hajnal, alkony,	Here live dawn and dusk,
Itt lakik nap, hold és csillag,	Here live the sun, moon and stars,
S lessen jeked játszótársad.	And they will be your playmates.

JUDIT

Véres árnyat ver a felhö!	The cloud casts a bloody shadow!
Milyen felhök szállnak ottan?	What sort of clouds drift over there?

BLUEBEARD

Nézd, tündököl az én váram,	Look, my castle glistens,
Áldott kezed ezt müvelte,	Your blessed hands did this,
Àldott a te kezed, áldott.	Blessed are your hands, blessed.

In Megahey's production, the treasure chamber is packed with a very great variety of golden objects, from chandeliers to statues, as well as jewels and of course a crown. Once she has gone in, Laurence first picks up a gold goblet, then a large gold pot and then a gold necklace. As she sings of Bluebeard's pearls and diamonds, Lloyd as Bluebeard comes in, picks up another gold necklace, richly ornamented with rubies, and gives it to her; a pair of solo violins decorate their initial melody enticingly as he does so (57.8) – and then the blood motif sounds out in the orchestra, while in the film blood seeps from around the jewels of the necklace.

After Bluebeard's unaccompanied encouragement to Judit to open the fourth door, and as a harp glissando leads to a sustained E flat major chord in *tremolo* strings, the scene cuts to a very lush garden, brimming with bushes, trees, stone garden ornaments and an abundance of (predominantly white) flowers. We see Judit open the door and come into the garden from inside it, and, as solo horn and clarinet compete to portray its beauty, the camera pans round the flowers. When the whole orchestra enters *molto espressivo* (4 before 63), she walks further in – and during the oboe decorations, just before the flute solo begins 2 after 64, she kneels to touch some of the flowers.

A white dove is perched in the branches of a tree as Judit comes into the garden. The flute breaks into decorations of this figure, which, in 1999, Leafstedt was to describe as 'bird calls to complete the image of nature at rest',[20] But Megahey had anticipated this insight in 1989: two doves take wing and fly round the garden (**6.4.1**).

6.4.1 (64.2)

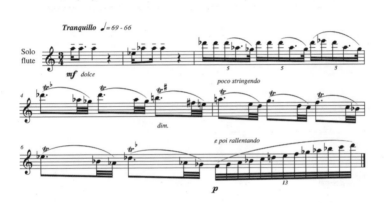

Judit finally sings, paying tribute to the flowers and the garden, and in this production she caresses a red flower as she does so. Later, she touches white lilies while Bluebeard watches her – proud of his garden, hands tucked confidently into his waistcoat pockets. Judit wanders around happily, as the music continues to seduce her by its yearning and its beckoning charm (**6.4.2**).

As she praises the garden, enthralled (*espressivo* at 68.7), she begins to pick white roses; while Bluebeard sings that she has the power to make them bloom and wither, she stands with her posy; but then the orchestral music turns into an *agitato tutti* (70). The film rightly interprets this as the castle's response to what Judit is now doing; she trims a rose and puts it into a vase – and precisely as the minor seconds appear at 71, blood oozes out into the water in the vase. Then she exclaims: 'Your white roses have bloody stems, / Soil beneath your flowers is bloody!' – and the camera pans down to illustrate the second line; the hem of her dress is now stained with blood.

Declining to answer when Judit asks who has bled on his garden, Lloyd as Bluebeard rushes her towards the fifth door, and now, while the whole

---

[20] Leafstedt 1999: 105.

6.4.2 (67.2)

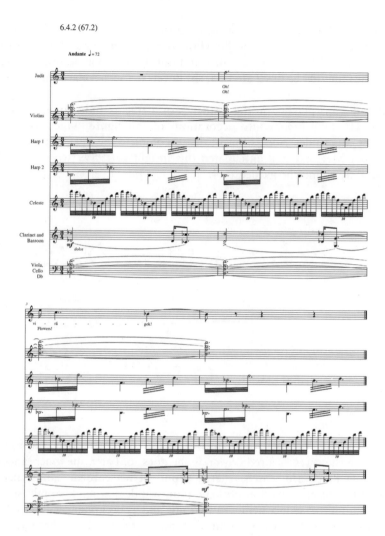

orchestra races towards the moment when the extreme dissonance of the last few minutes will be resolved, in Megahey's production the very walls of the castle part in front of Judit to reveal the landscape. The music achieves resolution in a *fff tutti* triad of C major; and, for the majestic series of triads which this one initiates, Bartók's large orchestra is augmented by an organ with all its stops out. There are also four trumpets and four trombones backstage, presumably to give added depth to the sound and a link between the outer world and the interior of this door – in the original *mise-en-scène*, the only interior into which the audience could see.[21] Blinded by the light,

---

[21] The audience saw, according to Balázs' stage directions, a high balcony, and past it a far landscape. Bartók required a stereo effect from the offstage brass; the four trumpeters should

Judit cries out on a sustained top C; and in Megahey's production there is a great disjunction between what Bluebeard sees, as he proudly describes the riches of his domain (forests, meadows, rivers and mountains), and what *we* see through Judit's eyes – a barren, lunar landscape covered in mist. This is brilliant expressionist directing, showing us in a visual image that all Judit hears in the succession of *tutti fff* triads is a suffocating male dominance undermined by an essential barrenness. This production fully explains why, when she responds, she *is looking out, rigid and with her wits scattered*, and sings her words *p senza espressione*, unaccompanied and in F sharp (notated as G flat).

6.4.3 (75.10)

F sharp is the key of the opera's opening and closing darkness. The overwhelming light of Bluebeard's domain momentarily blinded Judit at first sight, but now she has partially recovered she sees only darkness. And in this film, the second time she sings this text, we do not see her lips move; Judit has shut her complex feelings inside her psyche.

Now, Bluebeard is standing in the landscape, with a baleful sun shining behind him; and when, as they inevitably must, the minor seconds return to the orchestra (1 before 78), instead of just the clouds turning bloody as Judit sings, the blood-red colour shines on the whole landscape and on Judit's dress. The aspect of Bluebeard's psyche of which he is most proud has proved to be an empty grandeur; so in this production the blood infects both the landscape and his bride. And Bluebeard knows this – there is hollowness in the ensuing *vivace* music, when he tries to tell Judit that the castle is shining because of the achievement of her 'blessed hands'. His failure to impress her with this door is the beginning of the end of their relationship.

Discussion question

Analyse Elizabeth Laurence's reactions, as Judit, to the contents of each of these three doors.

---

be near the fifth door, and the four trombonists on the other side of the stage, near one of the other doors. See Leafstedt 1999: 213 n. 27.

6.5 'Peter Grimes!' (Britten/Slater *Peter Grimes* Act III scene 2)

This scene represents a remarkable and possibly unique use of 'noises off'. The orchestra is completely silent (save for an offstage tuba which provides the sound of a foghorn), and the demented Peter listens to the offstage voices of the villagers and responds to them. Normally, in a modernist 'mad-scene', the orchestra joins an agitated vocal line in representing the rapidly changing feelings and moods of the demented person – as in *Kát'a Kabanová* III.2 (see 7.3), or Wozzeck's two scenes of hallucination, one of which (I.2) is studied in this book as 7.4 (the second is of course the final monologue before he drowns, III.4). But in Britten's opera, with the orchestra silent, the voices of the chorus calling Peter's name do not portray the mood and feelings of the searchers (as they did when the villagers were heard approaching Grimes' hut in II.2). Instead they chart the evolution of Peter into complete dementia, and he responds with his sung voice to feelings inside him which the chorus articulates first. So the chorus now hardly portrays the searching citizens of the Borough at all; its voices replace the orchestra as instruments by which Britten charts Peter's descent into madness.[22] The scene is totally expressionistic, breaking through the bonds of realistic presentation which have been largely maintained in the earlier scenes of this opera.

🖜 6 5 Peter Grimes! Vickers

🖜 6 5 Peter Grimes! Langridge

Scene 2
(The stage is quite empty – a thick fog. Foghorn and the cries of the searchers can be heard distantly.)
CHORUS *(off)(SA)* 7.5.1 Grimes! Grimes!
(Peter comes in, weary and demented.)
PETER
[1] Steady! There you are! Nearly home!
What is home? Calm as deep water.[23] Where's my home? Deep in calm water.

---

[22] For reasons which will soon become evident, I mark in the following text the gender of the singers (SA or TB) whenever Britten does not deploy the whole four-part chorus.
[23] Vickers changed this sentence to 'Deep in calm water', which is then repeated identically at the end of the line. This removes the play with words which to me shows Peter trying to cling to language in a vain effort to retain his sanity.

Water will drink my[24] sorrows dry, and the tide will turn...
CHORUS
(SA) Grimes!
PETER
Steady! There you are!
Nearly home! The first one died, just died. The other slipped, and
    died...and the third will... "Accidental circumstances."
Water will drink his sorrows...my sorrows dry,
and the tide will turn.
CHORUS
(SA) Grimes! Grimes!
[2] **6.5.2** *(TB)* Peter Grimes!
PETER
Peter Grimes!
CHORUS
(TB) Peter Grimes!
PETER
Here you are! Here I am! Hurry, hurry, hurry, hurry, hurry!
Now is gossip put on trial. Bring the branding iron and knife for
    what's done now is done for life! Come on! Land me! "Turn the
    skies back and begin again!"
CHORUS
(TB) Peter Grimes!
PETER
"Old Joe has gone fishing and Young Joe has gone fishing and you'll
    know who's gone fishing when you land the next shoal!"
CHORUS
(B) (quasi niente) Peter Grimes!
[3] *(S)* Grimes!
PETER
Ellen! Ellen!
Give me your hand, your hand. There now ... my hope is held by you
    ... if you leave me alone, if you ...
Take away your hand! The argument's finished, friendship lost, gossip
    is shouting, ev'rything's said ...
CHORUS
[4] *(SA)* Peter Grimes!
PETER
To hell with all your mercy!
CHORUS

---

[24] Vickers sings 'his', for no discernible reason (unless it was a simple mistake on the day of
recording). Both Peter's own and his apprentice's sorrows are present when Peter repeats this
line four lines later, and it is natural for him to begin with his own.

(SA) Peter Grimes! Peter Grimes!
PETER
To hell with your revenge! And God have mercy upon you!
CHORUS
[5] *(B alternating with T)* Peter Grimes! Peter Grimes! Peter Grimes! Peter Grimes! Peter Grimes! Peter Grimes! Peter Grimes! Peter Grimes!
PETER
Do you hear them all shouting my name? D'you hear them? D'you hear them?
CHORUS *(The voices are now close at hand and very distinct.)*
Peter Grimes!
Peter Grimes! Peter Grimes! Peter Grimes! Peter Grimes! Peter Grimes! Peter Grimes! Peter Grimes!
PETER
Old Davy Jones shall answer:
Come home! Come home! Come home! Come home!
CHORUS Peter Grimes!
PETER *(roars back at the shouters)*
Peter Grimes! Peter Grimes! Peter Grimes! Peter Grimes! Peter Grimes! Peter Grimes! Grimes! Grimes! Grimes! Peter Grimes! Peter Grimes! Peter Grimes!
(ELLEN and BALSTRODE come in, and stand waiting till PETER has calmed.)
Grimes! .... Peter Grimes!
CHORUS
[6] *(SA)* Grimes!
ELLEN
Peter, *(ELLEN goes up to PETER.)* we've come to take you home. O come home out of this dreadful night! See, here's Balstrode! Peter, don't you hear me?
(PETER does not notice her. The voices are now very distant.)
CHORUS
Peter Grimes! Grimes! Peter! Grimes! Peter! Grimes! Peter! Peter! Grimes!
PETER
What harbour shelters peace,
CHORUS
Peter! Peter! Grimes! Peter! Peter! Grimes!
PETER
away from tidal waves, away from storms!
CHORUS
Peter! Grimes! Peter! Peter! Grimes! Peter! Peter! Grimes ...
PETER
What harbour can embrace

terrors and tragedies.
Her breast[25] is harbour too
Where night is turned to day, to … day …
CHORUS
Peter! Grimes! Peter! Peter! Grimes! Peter! Peter! Grimes … Peter!
    Peter! Grimes … Peter! Peter! Grimes … Peter! Peter! Peter! Peter!
BALSTRODE *(crossing to lift PETER up)*
(spoken) Come on, I'll help you with the boat.
ELLEN No!
BALSTRODE Sail out till you lose sight of land.[26] Then sink the boat.
    D'you hear? Sink her. Good-bye, Peter.
*(There is a crunch of shingle as BALSTRODE leads PETER down to
    his boat, and helps him put it out. After a short pause he returns,
    takes ELLEN by the arm, and leads her away.)*

*

[1] Peter appears on stage after the female voices take over a gentle, eerily
beckoning dominant seventh chord from the dying horns at the end of the
interlude (**6.5.1**).

6.5.1 (III.2.47.1)

This represents Peter's psyche trying to find steadiness and rest, and when he
becomes mournful and introspective over the next few lines it reappears to
help him to steady himself. Langridge, under Albery's direction, interprets
this section in precisely this way – he leans on an invisible support behind
the wall which is the main feature of the set down to 'and the tide will turn
…', then turns to hold onto the wall, facing the audience, for the second
'Steady! There you are!'. Vickers, by contrast, in Moshinsky's production,
playing on a virtually bare stage, uses expressive gestures up to this same
point, and then suddenly kneels down. This is not motivated by the text

---

[25] Vickers changed this to 'heart'. This coy piece of censorship disregards the fact that the
female quartet 'From the gutter', which is placed, crucially, just before the midpoint of the
opera, brings before the audience (in very eloquent text and music) the ways in which women's
bodies can provide troubled men with solace.

[26] In the scores, 'lose sight of the Moot Hall'. But both the productions under discussion change
this to 'lose sight of land', avoiding the original text's very local reference to the Moot Hall in
Aldeburgh, where Britten lived.

and music, and is fairly futile as he gets up again very soon, on 'the other slipped, and died'. Langridge makes much more of this sequence, as he stands with head bowed and forehead creased for 'the first one died, just died', and then on 'the other slipped, and died ...' compulsively holds out a hand downwards, exactly as he did to try to save the apprentice John from his fall at the end of Act II.

[2] Now the male voices are heard for the first time. Unlike the gentle chord of the females, they give an urgent cry which portrays Peter's paranoia – as you can hear from his instant vocal response on the same notes.

6.5.2 (III.2.48.3)

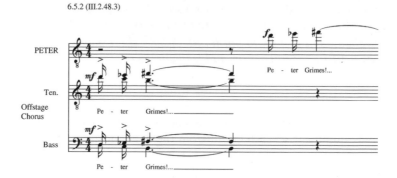

The aggressive call is immediately repeated, louder – and Peter responds with equal aggression *(vivace),* challenging the voices. He now sings three lines from the words which he heard the villagers singing as they approached his hut in II.2 – but not to their original music, as he is much more agitated than they were (every note accentuated, and rising to a high F sharp). Langridge makes a good physical response to this, running frantically to and fro behind the wall. Vickers does not move.

Then after singing 'Come on! Land me!' Peter recalls his deep desire to turn back time to before the deaths of the two apprentices; he quotes directly from the end of his Great Bear aria (see **2.6**): 'Turn the skies back and begin again'. The musical setting now is a similarly descending line, but beginning at a higher pitch (top A) and with ornamentation on the word 'skies' which was not present in the original. Much needs to be made of this heartfelt desire for a peace which is now unobtainable, and both singers achieve this, with highly expressive gestures and movements. Langridge rather literally whirls an arm backwards, while Vickers holds his arms wide up and out, as if appealing to some deity to turn back time.

The male voices now sing **6.5.2** again, showing that Peter is still under attack from within. And his mind is still on the scene in the pub, as he launches into a mad parody of the round which the villagers sang to restore peace after Boles' attack on him. This is rhythmic and *staccato*, and demands a corresponding response; Vickers looks quite crazed as he delivers

'Old Joe has gone fishing and young Joe has gone fishing', while Langridge opts for a hideously ironic smile, almost a grimace when he begins – but suddenly both singers rightly turn serious as Peter sings about death ('you'll know who's gone fishing when you land the next shoal'). Then the male call sounds once more, but now in basses only and *quasi niente*. Peter's mind is turning away from his feelings of persecution.

[3] A very serene triad of B flat major in the soprano voices, marked *ppp dolce*, shows that Peter's thoughts have turned to Ellen, and he immediately utters her name. This is a moment of peace,[27] and both Vickers and Langridge look visionary, Langridge even smiling broadly at the memory. When Peter sings 'There now ... my hope is held by you',[28] both interpreters extend a hand – ready for the violent contrast as Peter recalls refusing physical contact to Ellen in II.1 ('Take away your hand!', set here to almost the same notes as there), and the rush of emotion that follows it *(con forza)* is matched by great intensity in the performances of both Vickers and Langridge.

[4] Immediately Peter hears voices again – but now, with his recall of the rejection of Ellen in II.1, the *female* voices sing **6.5.2**, three times for greater insistence. Feeling persecuted by women for the first time, Peter roars his defiance and repeats his terrible demand on God (**4.4.3**). But now, remarkably, he pleads for mercy not for himself but for his persecutors. Here Langridge recalls the challenging hand which he held up to God in that scene, while Vickers holds his hands up more as in prayer.

[5] This does not, however, free Peter from his inner persecutors; he now encounters more torment. A new paranoia assails him; the men are pursing him in rapidly alternating cries of his name, tossed octaves apart (on E flat) between tenors and basses and culminating in another onset of **6.5.2**. Langridge peers intently, as if trying to see where the voices are coming from, but Vickers first buries his head in his hands and then, as Peter responds, raises his head with both hands around it. Moshinsky is right to accentuate by this that the accusing voices are inside Peter's brain. Then both singers make a strong response as they sing over continued choral persecution, which is now intensified, as it is delivered for the first time by female and male voices in alternation. Peter responds 'Old Davy Jones shall answer ...', Langridge puts his hands to his mouth as he calls out, while Vickers is kneeling, and both singers rightly have their hands wide out (challenging the persecuting voices to 'come and get me'!) as they utter the last *ff largamente call* of 'Come home!'. Death is calling, and Peter is welcoming it, in the image of Davy Jones' locker (which is here remembered, of course, from his dislocation of the round in the pub, I.2).

---

[27] The foghorn's sustained E flat, previously dissonant, is now in harmony with this chord.

[28] Slater deliberately has Peter misquote what he sang in II.1. Under the stress of his dementia, Peter lacks perfect recall even of the moments that are burnt into his memory.

This is the climax of the persecution; the voices are instructed to be at this point *close at hand and very distinct*. And now the entire chorus, very near and singing *ff*, cries out his name in octaves.

This precipitates Peter's final paroxysm. He repeats his name twelve times, in total madness, but gradually calming down. Vickers sings all this on his knees, with an agonized expression, and ending with his hands extended, low, in futility; Langridge, by contrast, in Albery's more modern and more physical production rushes around, staggering about, until as the madness fades he simply collapses and leans over the wall, exhausted.

[6] As Grimes reaches the slow *arpeggio* of his penultimate spasm, Ellen and Balstrode *come in, and stand waiting till Peter has calmed.*[29] The moment when Ellen is about to sing is heralded by a sustained 'Grimes' on one chord from the female voices; but it is no longer her comforting triad, as at the start of the scene and when he first thought of her – just a bare perfect fourth. Peter does not now recognize Ellen in person, although he saw her vividly in his imagination earlier. She sings gently, but the stage direction is that *Peter does not notice her*, and Langridge makes this fearfully apparent by simply staring forward, mouth open, registering nothing, almost catatonic. The dramatic irony is hideous that Peter sings of Ellen as his saviour using the same words as when he sang about her at the end of I.1, oblivious to the fact that she is now physically with him.[30]

The stage direction is *Ellen goes up to Peter*. Moshinsky obeys this: Harper first kneels and holds the shoulder of Vickers (who is still kneeling), on 'Peter, don't you hear me?', then begins to cry after 'What harbour shelters peace', and sinks her head on Peter's shoulder just before 'What harbour can embrace ...'. All this is in preparation for the moment where, after she rises and rests her hands on his shoulders, Vickers' Peter seems to realize that she is there; he finds and clasps her hand ('Where night is turned to day ...').

This is sentimental staging. Albery by contrast disobeys the stage direction that Ellen should *go up to Peter*, in obedience to the far more important direction: *Peter does not notice her*; Langridge remains catatonic, doing nothing whatever except blinking and closing his mouth as Cairns sings 'Peter, don't you hear me?' Then he sings facing straight out until the voices fade out of his psyche forever and the music is still – at which point he starts moving robotically towards his boat. This is much better staging; the last

---

[29] Moshinsky is very wrong to bring them on earlier, as soon as Peter starts *roaring back at the shouters* (51.1). This pulls focus from Peter, although, given that Vickers is static during all twelve repeats of his name, it is less damaging to the production concept than if Albery had pulled focus from Langridge's physical portrayal of Peter's agony.

[30] The stanza 'What harbour shelters peace...' is sung here with two lines missing from his original vision at the end of I.1, and with a new and gentle setting of the last two lines, in contrast to the vocal line which was distorted by the coming of the storm at the end of the original setting.

recurrence of the voices, underlying Peter's final words, his vision of Ellen, is a *molto tranquillo* setting for a beautifully harmonized, gently flowing alternation between the offstage voices (which are *now very distant*); Peter is finally at peace – but also totally within himself, beyond human contact.

So that he should have the minimum interaction with Balstrode, in Albery's production, Langridge – after stepping down and moving towards the boat as the music ends – stops for a moment, giving a silent stare to nowhere. This motivates Balstrode's speech, as he goes to hold the front of the boat. Peter stays motionless until Balstrode concludes his order with 'Sink her'. Then he and Balstrode push the boat out after 'Goodbye, Peter.'

Moshinsky, however, milks the final moments. Balstrode, in this production, does have to lift Peter up, in accordance with the stage directions in the score. However, Harper as Ellen does not interject 'No!' until after 'Then sink the boat.' After 'Sink her', Vickers' Peter stops moving towards the boat, and turns back to face them with his hands extended in supplication. Only after Balstrode's 'Goodbye Peter' does Peter bow his head and go. This is unduly melodramatic, and Langridge's portrayal of a Peter who is now totally withdrawn from the world, and can only respond mechanically to Balstrode's insistent command, is far more responsive to the way in which the music of section [6] has portrayed Peter's state of mind.[31]

Discussion questions

- Vickers and Langridge both give impressive performances of Peter's mad scene. Which do you think is more effective, and why?

- Albery disobeys one of the stage directions after Ellen and Balstrode enter, so that Langridge can play Peter as catatonic and unresponsive to them. Is this a better staging than Vickers' more traditional – and, I think, more melodramatic or sentimental – performance of Peter's last moments? Give reasons for your answer.

---

[31] 'By now the musical dream-world into which he has withdrawn has no connexion with reality, but Balstrode's spoken words penetrate into it with grim disenchantment' (Evans 1979: 115–16.).

It is interesting to note that neither production obeys the stage direction that Ellen should wait while Balstrode helps Peter to push out the boat, and then *returns, takes Ellen by the arm, and leads her away*. Both Ellens are visibly far too upset by the events to want to depend on any man for support, and they both go abruptly offstage left, leaving Balstrode alone on stage until just before the music of the new dawn begins.

6.6 Conclusion

These five examples show diverse ways of using 'noises off', and different ways of fusing offstage music with that from the pit and the onstage singers. They result from each composer's desire to create his own particular relationship between the onstage characters and the offstage events.

In the Berlioz, the offstage event – the procession (with its accompanying band of saxhorns) – actually comes onstage during the scene. Before, during and after this there is an intense relationship between the music of the procession – which, apart from one brief moment of doubt, proceeds uninterrupted on its course – and the reactions which Cassandre exhibits; her agony at seeing the Horse brought into Troy is conveyed both in her vocal lines and in the interjections of the main orchestra, which then focuses totally on her in the last moments of Act I, after the procession and the Horse have gone inside the walls. So there is a straight dialogue between the 'noises off' – a chorus and accompanying offstage instruments, some of which come onstage at the climax – and the orchestra, which supports Cassandre's dissenting voice. The director has to use Cassandre's costume, position on the stage (occupying and moving in the front half of the stage) and her reactions in gesture and movement to make a contrast between the lone prophetess and the mass of Trojans (represented by a double choir) who are heading to their destruction because of their ignorance. Kokkos achieves this extremely effectively.

In the final scene of *Carmen*, the offstage cries of the crowd and the fanfares from the offstage trumpets and trombones interject four times and add fuel to the flames of the interaction between Don José, who is progressively infuriated by the crowd's proclamation of Escamillo's success, and Carmen, who defies him and virtually invites her fate. This is a very simple use of 'noises off'; but it is devastatingly effective. However, it does demand that the director direct his two principals in ways which show the progressive escalation of their reactions during and after each of the four choral acclamations from inside the bullring. Zambello's version of this scene achieves this better than any other yet recorded on DVD.

In the ever-shifting world of *Pelléas et Mélisande*, the encounter with the ship stands out as one of the most effective uses of a symbol in the whole opera. Debussy makes the ship a sonic event, which it was not in Maeterlinck's original play; the cries of 'Hoé! Hisse Hoé!' which he added as it makes its way out of the harbour and onto the perilous open sea are suggestively set in parallel with the situation of the protagonists. Their feeling of love for each other exists, but neither Pelléas nor Mélisande is prepared to acknowledge it at this early stage in the drama. And Debussy uses the choral sounds as well as orchestral instruments to echo the music associated with Golaud, showing that he is often in the subconscious thoughts of Pelléas and Mélisande as the scene evolves to the moment when

Pelléas declares that he will leave the next day. All of this needs great sensitivity from the director, and in my view Peter Stein's production responds extremely well to this extraordinary text and music.

Bartók's use of noises off is wholly original. Unlike the other examples studied in this chapter, the music in *Duke Bluebeard's Castle* does not strictly include any instrumental or choral 'noises off' at all, except the brass instruments backstage, which simply reinforce the *tutti* (with full organ) at the fifth door. This is because when each door opens *the whole orchestra* represents the castle's contents. It is on Bluebeard's side in the sex-combat, and Judit is left alone and isolated; she is forced, while viewing most of the doors, to integrate her voice with the impressionistic music depicting a particular section of Bluebeard's castle, and at the fifth door, the turning point of the opera, she finds herself virtually silenced by the grandeur that is at Bluebeard's command, and can only comment on the deluge of *tutti fff* C major triads cowed, unaccompanied and in a remote key. The director must however bear in mind that the audience is seeing the castle through Judit's eyes; it is she who finds the blood disfiguring the contents of the first five doors, and this must be emphasized. This is especially necessary at the fifth door, where Megahey brilliantly opts to show us the inner barrenness of the landscape which Bluebeard has disclosed rather than the fertile territory which his words evoke, and which the orchestra supports extremely powerfully until, inevitably, Judit finds blood here too.

As argued just above, the penultimate scene of *Peter Grimes* is an extraordinary one. A chorus which nominally represents the villagers searching for Grimes in fact becomes, in the absence of orchestral sound, an expressionistic representation of the passions and paranoia inside the demented tragic hero, whose expressed feelings in reaction to them are portrayed by a mercurial and often highly agitated vocal line. This scene not only requires great singing, but also a convincing physical realization of Grimes' descent through paranoia into total dementia. Although both the recorded versions discussed are fine interpretations of a very demanding scene, in my view Langridge in Albery's production communicates Grimes' emotional journey better than does Vickers in Moshinsky's, because of his greater physicalization of the role and the absence of sentimentality at the end of the scene.

7

Interactions with the Numinous

This chapter will not delve into the many manifestations of gods, ghosts, monsters, Furies and magicians in seventeenth- and (especially) eighteenth-century opera. The supernatural existed in these works simply as an exotic element in an already exotic medium. As the Enlightenment demystified music in the eighteenth century some composers:

> developed procedures to distinguish the divine from the mortal, the supernatural from the natural, the magic from the rational ... magical and supernatural events in a libretto could become the stimulus and the source of inspiration for the artistic imagination to represent the transcendental element with special musical techniques...[and] by taking on this role, by creating music that represented metaphysical beings and events, composers assumed the creative force associated with the divine. This assumption is an essential basis of the sublime in music.[1]

However, there is the fundamental question of belief. When creating the music for magic and marvels, most eighteenth-century composers were setting to music scenes and characters from fables, stories and mythologies (such as those of classical Greece and of the 'exotic' ancient Orient) which their Christian and Enlightenment audiences did not believe in as realities outside the theatre. And they were not using their new musical vocabularies to do anything more than to stimulate emotions (including a great deal of awe and terror) in the theatre audience.[2] My concern in this chapter is by

---

[1] Buch 2009: 359.
[2] Cf. Buch 2009: 174ff. on the development after about 1750 of a new style (and instrumentation) for the musical evocation of terror in opera.

The situation is no different in the nineteenth century. No serious belief in ghosts was required from the audience when Berlioz wrote awe-inspiring music as he summoned the ghost of Hector to appear to Énée (*Les Troyens* II.12). Similarly, in the Wolf's Glen scene of Weber's *Der Freischütz*, terrifying harmonic effects occur – together with some remarkable orchestration – when Kaspar conjures up Samiel and forges the magic bullets. But the audience does not have to believe in Black Magic or in demons.

contrast to study work by some of the few composers who have set libretti
with supernatural elements in order to give their audiences genuine insight
into an interaction between human beings and the divine or numinous – a real
spiritual or metaphysical dimension which extends, in the composer's vision,
out from the world portrayed in the opera into the real life of the spectators.[3]

The majority of the nineteenth- and twentieth-century operas which
are regularly performed today set realistic libretti; they lack any sense of
the presence of the numinous, and moments of interaction between the
characters and divine or supernatural forces are rare.[4] But when such
presences and interactions occur, the use of music to link the human world
with the otherworldly can be a mystical experience. And, arguably, the
ability to illuminate such moments is one of the greatest achievements
possible for the opera composer. Michael Tippett argued correctly that in
opera, in contrast with the straight play:

> the greater percentage of the marvellous will allow the opera composer
> to present the collective spiritual experience more nakedly and immedi-
> ately – the music helping to suspend the critical and analytical judgment,
> without which happening no experience of the numinous can be
> immediate at all. For example, as soon as we begin to have critical
> doubts of the propriety, say, of the pseudo-Christian ritual of *Parsifal*,
> we are provoked, not enriched.[5]

Three of the five operas that are studied in this chapter move towards a
climactic scene which is a moment of *transcendence*, when select principal
characters are enlightened – initiated into a profound, higher level of
insight which the majority of human beings cannot experience. The crucial
common element is a search for self-knowledge, which unites the quests

---

[3]Cf. Ecklelmeyer 1991: 52–3. In *Die Zauberflöte* (8.1) the libretto includes stage miracles of
a kind familiar from tradition and from Schikaneder's earlier fairy-tale operas (for these see
Buch 2009: 293–308 and 335–7; for surveys of the sources of the *Zauberflöte* libretto see
Branscombe 1991: 4–34 and Buch: 333ff.). On the other hand the libretto contains strong
elements of Enlightenment philosophy (from a wide range of sources, including the fundamental Masonic imagery demonstrated by Chailley 1972; cf. Ecklemeyer 1991 *passim*);
and Mozart created a music which transforms the stage wonders into far more than simple
spectacle. Hence the frequent revival of this remarkable *Singspiel*, while the other eighteenth-
century magic operas have long since left the repertory.

[4]I exclude scenes of prayer, like the Ave Marias of Desdemona in Verdi's *Otello* and of Jenůfa
in Janáček's Act II. There is in such scenes no interaction with the divine, simply a prayer
which is sent heavenwards with no audible or visible response. (Indeed if there is a God in the
world of either of these two operas – I don't think there is – he disregards the prayers of both
of these unfortunate women.) And as the stage directions make clear, the vision of the Virgin
at the end of Puccini's *Suor Angelica* is just that; a subjective vision, not a real epiphany.

[5]Tippett 1974: 58 (=1995: 204). Tippett's two essays 'The Birth of an Opera' (from which this
quotation comes) and 'Drum Flute and Zither' are fundamental to understanding the special
sub-genre of opera to which *Die Zauberflöte*, *Parsifal* and *The Midsummer Marriage* belong.

through trials of Mozart's Tamino and Pamina, Wagner's Parsifal and Tippett's Mark and Jenifer. In all three operas their success is presented as a generational change and renewal.

Kát'a Kabanová and *Wozzeck* belong to a different genre. They are tragedies, and the special closeness to nature and the numinous, which the heroine and hero attain, leads them not to enlightenment but through madness to suicide.

We will discuss five scenes in which music represents the numinous, and takes the spectators inside the minds and emotions of characters who are experiencing contact with it. And of course such scenes present major problems for directors. How are they to be staged? Is the numinous to be made visible as well as audible? And how can this be done?

7.1 The trial by fire and water (Mozart/ Schikaneder *Die Zauberflöte* II.28, no. 21)

Surviving these ordeals confirms the worthiness of Tamino and Pamina to be initiated into the mysteries of Isis and Osiris, as they are when the temple opens to them at the moment when they emerge from the trial by water.

Tamino and Pamina become enlightened through having the strength to overcome the fear of death; in this way they transcend the level of existence of most normal human beings (as represented – delightfully – in this opera by Papageno and Papagena). The inscription which the Men in Armour read to them makes this clear:

Der, welcher wande dies Straßen voll Beschwerden,	He who travels these paths full of hardships,
Wird rein durch Feuer, Wasser, Luft und Erden;	Will become pure through Fire, Water, Air and Earth;
Wenn er des Tode Schrecken überwinden kann,	If he can overcome the fear of death,
Schwingt er sich aus der Erde himmelan!	He will soar up from Earth to Heaven!
Erleuchtet wird er dann im Stande sein,	Then he will be able to be enlightened,
Sich den Mysterien der Isis ganz zu wiehn.	To consecrate himself completely to the mysteries of Isis.

Mozart's music for the trials consists of the tranquil solo voice of the magic flute which Tamino plays, accompanied by solemn, low brass chords which mark the flute's pauses, and timpani which sound on the off-beat like an after-echo. The form is the march, the genre which was regularly used in eighteenth-century opera to accompany supernatural and magical moments; and 'the power of music, through the particular pattern of trombone chords and irregular drumbeats accompanying the serene but highly charged melody of the flute, achieves in a few bars a sense of far-reaching human development, of prolonged strain endured and turned to good, that is unmistakable but also indescribable'.[6]

*

The passage of the two young lovers through first fire and then water is a challenge which designers accept with enthusiasm. For example, both David Hockney, designing for John Cox at the Met in 1991, and Jürgen Rose, for August Everding in the Munich recording from 1988, evoke the fire and water very effectively – greatly aided by their lighting designers.

However, most modern directors make two fundamental and serious mistakes, which limit the transcendent effect of this climactic scene. One concerns the *mise-en-scène*; the other concerns the relationship between Pamina and Tamino.

The original stage directions ask for the presentation of two high mountains, from one of which the roaring of a waterfall can be seen, while the other spits out fire. Two grills, one in each mountain, enable the spectators to see the fire (*where it burns, the horizon should be as red as hell*) and the water, on which a thick mist lies. When Pamina and Tamino enter the doors to undergo their trials, *the spitting of fire and howling of wind can be heard; at times also the muffled sound of thunder and the rushing of water.*

These sounds are however almost never heard in production. As director Anthony Besch remarks, 'Many conductors have refused to permit these sound effects during the march played on the flute and drums. But conductors such as Sir Charles Mackerras have recognized how greatly the effect of the march is actually augmented when the appropriate sounds have been included.'[7]

Mackerras was absolutely right. It is pointless if the flute music is heard alone, without being surrounded by the sounds of fire, wind, thunder and rushing water. We are to hear the magic flute as the voice of the calmness and fearlessness with which Pamina and Tamino undergo the ordeals, and the sound effects make the aural image complete. We need not only to see but, even more importantly, to hear that the gentle poise with which the flute leads Tamino and Pamina is *surrounded by* the perils of the fire and the water. But this does not happen in Cox's, Everding's or Julie Taynor's recorded stage productions. However, in Ingmar Bergman's outstanding film we do at least hear the roaring of the flames – but not the rushing of the water.

The second problem with modern productions concerns Pamina. Many are content to follow a traditional direction that she should walk with her

---

[6]Cairns 1973: 36.
[7]Besch 1991: 189.

hand on Tamino's shoulder,[8] and this is interpreted as meaning that she should walk behind him through the fire and water. But she should in fact be the leader. As two scholars have rightly remarked,[9] Pamina has been seen during her trials earlier in the opera to suffer far more torments and emotional distress than Tamino; and, as the moment for the final trials by fire and water nears, she sings:

Ich werde aller Orten	I will in all places
An deiner Seite sein.	Be at your side.
Ich selbsten führe dich;	I myself will lead you;
Die Liebe leitet mich.	Love guides me.
(takes his hand)[10]	

After this Pamina reveals that the magic flute was created by her father,[11] and it is she who leads off the short but profound quartet in F major, in which the Men in Armour join Pamina and Tamino to celebrate the power of music which will enable the couple to face 'the dark night of death'.[12]

Pamina's fidelity and bravery are crucial to Tamino's success; so, when they undergo the trials, she should, as these lines imply, be leading him. Schikaneder and Mozart, although both were Masons, dissent in *The Magic Flute* from the general contemporary Masonic view that only men can achieve enlightenment.[13] There are, it is true, earlier in the opera some quite misogynistic utterances from members of Sarastro's temple, which are only partly justified by the behaviour of the Queen of the Night and her three Ladies; but in Sarastro's correct (albeit revolutionary) view Pamina, after successfully undergoing the trials, is as enlightened as Tamino, and therefore worthy to be admitted to the temple despite her gender; she appears in the finale dressed in the robes of a priestess.[14] Pamina and Tamino will lead the temple *together* after Sarastro has resigned his high office.

✒ 7 1 Trials by fire and water

Accordingly, Cox is wrong to have Pamina following behind Tamino with her hand on his shoulder as they undergo the trials; and in Everding's

---

[8]This inauthentic stage direction is in several vocal scores, but rightly does not appear in the *Neue Ausgabe Sämtlicher Werke.*
[9]Branscombe 1991: 108–9; Eckelmeyer 1991: 22–3. Cf. Chailley 1972: 147 and 151–3.
[10]II.28.21.293–302. Cf. Eckelmeyer 1991: 116: 'she declares her willingness to die to protect her love for Tamino. It is she, with this heart-knowledge, who leads Tamino through the final trials, because Love leads her.'
[11]On the symbolism of the flute's origins see Eckelmeyer 1991: 50–1.
[12]II.28.21.324ff.
[13]Cf. Chailley 1972: 74ff.
[14]Chailley 1972: 151–3 and 264–5.

production, also, she has her hand on his shoulder, although at least she walks beside him. We need to turn to Ingmar Bergman's classic 1975 film. He rightly shows Pamina leading Tamino through the gates into first the torment of fire and then that of water; she does hide behind Tamino, cowering a little, during the ordeal of fire, but she subsequently leads him through the ordeal of water. And this decision, to have her lead Tamino into the ordeals and through the water but not through the fire, may be deeply right; as Chailley has shown, in the Masonic symbolism which underlies *The Magic Flute*, Tamino, as a male, is aligned with fire and Pamina, as a female, with water.[15] It is fascinating to speculate whether Bergman had read Chailley's book, independently knew some of the fundamentals of Masonic belief, or intuitively reached a correct production decision which has eluded almost all other directors.[16]

At the end of the trials, *a door opens, through which a brilliantly lit temple may be seen. Solemn silence. This vision must be of the utmost splendour. The chorus, accompanied by trumpets and drums, begins to sing.* Although this section is brief, it is the crux of the opera. This is the moment of initiation: the fact that Pamina and Tamino have survived the trials shows that they have proved worthy and achieved the highest insight. This is symbolized by their vision of the light of the *brilliantly lit* temple, which the designer must (but does not always) show as an image *of the utmost splendour.* As Pamina and Tamino now sing:

> Ihr Götter! Welch ein Augenblick!   Oh you Gods! What a moment!
> Gewähret ist uns Isis' Glück.   Isis' happiness is granted to us.[17]

The last section of this scene is difficult to realize. While Pamina and Tamino continue to gaze in astonishment and delight at the revelation of the temple, a mixed chorus backstage bursts into song, hailing their triumph and their initiation in what should be a blaze of C major glory. The problem with this is that in the theatre the chorus often sounds rather muffled and distant. In an otherwise undistinguished production for Opera Australia, Göran Järvefelt solved this problem by actually bringing the chorus on; they entered upstage and rushed down to greet the successful couple. This has strong musical merits, but would need to be done in such a way that the designer and lighting designer were still able to highlight the splendour of the temple. Unfortunately, Järvefelt and his designers did not achieve this. By contrast, in Bergman's film Pamina and Tamino run away

---

[15] Chailley 1972: 98–9.
[16] Julie Taynor has the couple undergo the ordeals side by side. This is obviously better than Cox, but inferior to Bergman; and the cutting of the 'Triumph' chorus as part of her abridgment means that spectators are deprived of the moment at which Pamina and Tamino are initiated (!).
[17] II.28.387–9.

together from the grim location of the ordeals to a hall glowing with light in which crowns of flowers are placed on their heads. The chorus is unseen, but is mixed in, aurally, at a high level. In this way the film achieves the required effect; but there is no good reason why an opera director in the theatre could not achieve a solution which presents both the visual spectacle of the splendid, brilliantly lit temple and the aural effect of the music with which the chorus greet the new initiates.

Discussion question

How do you think the trials by fire and water should be staged? Can you suggest ideas which would improve on the images in Bergman's film?

7.2 Parsifal and the Grail (Wagner, *Parsifal*, Act III finale)

As an evocation of transcendence and an interaction with the divine, using the full resources of late Romantic harmony and orchestration, the last few minutes of *Parsifal* are extraordinary. Wagner simply – but most effectively – reuses fundamental melodic elements from the Prelude to the whole 'sacred stage festival play', and takes them to an ultimate level which could not have been imagined previously. What in the Prelude was yearning and aspiration now becomes fulfilment. And Wagner stages a sacred experience in which the numinous is present, both visually and aurally. A beam of light shines down from above and illuminates the Grail; unseen soprano and alto voices are heard from high in the dome, confirming with the voice of God the miracle and the redemption which the knights of the Grail are hailing from below; and (in the stage directions but, for obvious reasons, rarely in production) a white dove descends from the heights to hover above Parsifal, as he raises the Grail and *waves it in benediction over the knights who are gazing upwards.*[18]

There is already an intimation of ecstasy in the music, when Parsifal enters, heals Amfortas with the touch of the sacred spear and hails the supreme joy of this miracle. He commands that the shrine of the Grail should be opened, and then falls silent. The music modulates to A flat major, and remains in that sweet-sounding key (in which the drama also began) right to the end. The performing direction is *Sehr langsam und*

---

[18] The dove could simply be taken to represent the Holy Spirit; or Wagner could have included it because of the dove which came every Good Friday, in Wolfram von Eschenbach's *Parzival* (1980: 240), to refresh the Grail. But it is unlikely that many audience members would be aware of the allusion to Wolfram.

feierlich – 'very slow and solemn', and the music rises to peaceful heights, as it does again when the Grail starts to be illuminated from within and from above:

7.2.1 (III.2.579-83)

(Sehr langsam un feierlich)

As this music gently dies down again, (see continuation of the example on p. 237) Wagner moves on to deploy his spatial sonic effect – choirs of Knights and Squires on the ground, with altos *in the middle height* and sopranos *at the furthest height* of the dome celebrating together with them.[19] These voices in their turn fade away, as Parsifal raises the Grail, now illuminated to full brightness; the white dove appears, Kundry dies, and Parsifal blesses the company with the Grail. Then, as the curtain falls slowly on this tableau, the music reaches a final, even more tender and exquisite peace (**7.2.2**).

But can it still work its miracle today? Tippett commented that 'as soon as we begin to have critical doubts of the propriety, say, of the pseudo-Christian ritual of *Parsifal*, we are provoked, not enriched'.[20] This can be extended. He was arguing that operas can achieve transcendence in ways

---

[19] Wagner was surely inspired here by Goethe's *Faust*, in which a solo voice of redemption is heard from on high at the end of Part I, and in the final scene of Part II voices are deployed at different levels from the depths up to the heights of heaven.

[20] Tippett 1974: 58 (=1995: 204). See the Introduction to this chapter, above.

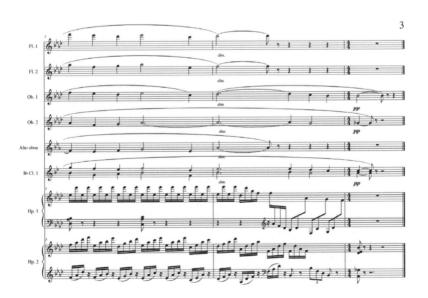

7.2.2 (III.2.591-2)

(Sehr langsam und feierlich)

in which plays cannot, because music '[helps] to suspend the critical and analytical judgment';[21] and there is no doubt that the music at the end of *Parsifal* is visionary and transcendent, in such a way that such a suspension of judgement could well be made during a performance. But there might be elements in the dramatic scheme of an opera which are very difficult to accept, and which undermine its ability to put its spectators in touch with the numinous; at that point the 'critical doubts' to which Tippett alludes will occur. Such, I believe, is the condition of Wagner's *Parsifal* today.

The problem centres upon the role of women in Wagner's operas and music dramas. If you are a woman who is confident in and proud of her sexuality, or a man who welcomes and celebrates the sensuality and seductive power of women, then Wagner should probably not be your favourite opera composer, since his works exhibit a deep ambivalence in regard to female sexuality and its ability to entrance men.

On the one hand Wagner portrayed, with deep understanding and emotional power, the growth and fulfilment of love between Siegmund and Sieglinde in *Die Walküre,* between Tristan and Isolde, and between Siegfried and Brünnhilde in the final scene of *Siegfried* and the first scene of *Götterdämmerung.* (However, all three of these grand passions are doomed, two of them because they are adulterous – and one because it is incestuous as well). And in his comedy, *Die Meistersinger von Nürnberg,* boy eventually wins girl – although it cannot be said that the love of Eva and Walther is particularly sensuous, either in the text or in the music.

But then there are the other operas: Senta is denied any earthly union with the man of her dreams, and must kill herself to ascend to heaven with her Dutchman; Tannhäuser abandons the delights of the Venusberg when his thoughts turn to the Virgin Mary, and he attempts without success later in the opera to suppress his sensuality and gain the favour of the chaste Elizabeth; Elsa loses her knight in shining armour because she, reasonably, wants to know her husband's name.[22]

That brings us to *Parsifal,* in which female sexuality is unremittingly treated as an evil temptation.[23] The women portrayed in it are, first, the fatuous bimbos of Klingsor's magic garden (whom Parsifal has no trouble in resisting) and secondly Kundry, who appears in Act II *in skimpy, fantastic clothing approximating Arabian style* as the first in a line of

---

[21] Ibid.

[22] Borchmeyer (1991: 372–3) rightly traces this 'negation of the erotic element in man' back to the character of Friedrich, governor of Palermo, in Wagner's second opera, *Das Liebesverbot.* Even Wagner's new title for this adaptation of Shakespeare's *Measure for Measure – The Ban on Love –* is significant!

[23] At the end of Act I, Gurnemanz throws Parsifal out of the temple for apparently failing to understand the Grail ritual, telling him that he is a gander – and ought to seek out a goose. Evidently, for Gurnemanz, lack of spiritual insight makes you fit only for marriage.

German and Austrian *femmes fatales* stretching into the twentieth century, and including Salome and Lulu.[24] She can only achieve grace in Act III by becoming a penitent, being baptized – and dying; so that at the end the world of *Parsifal* is totally male. Meanwhile Wagner defines the Christian concept of purity so narrowly that few would accept his vision; his 'purity' has no spiritual dimension, and only one criterion – successful resistance to female sexuality.[25] Amfortas has failed as the guardian of the Grail because he allowed himself to be seduced, and Klingsor has failed to become a member of the chaste Knights of the Grail because he could not resist his sensual desire for women, and attempted to attain 'purity' by the drastic – and unsuccessful – means of self-castration. Parsifal, the *reine Tor* ('pure fool') passes the test, and gains the power to redeem the Knights from the blight which Amfortas's sin has imposed on them, simply because he is able to resist Kundry's seductive power, and so is able to destroy Klingsor's magic castle.[26] It is true that there are some elements in Judaeo-Christian orthodoxy that foreshadow such a hostile vision of female sexuality – starting with the foundation myth of Adam, Eve, the serpent and the apple;[27] and the development of monasteries in medieval Christianity shows that in many men's view supreme devotion to Christ demands complete abstinence from the pleasures of the flesh; but few modern Christians (one hopes!) would adopt the extreme position which Wagner wholeheartedly embraces in *Parsifal*.

It is easy for a scholar, in his or her study, to mount a critique of *Parsifal*, such as I have briefly offered here. But the director has to stage the opera; and in a modern production of *Parsifal* there are only two ways to do this. One is to adopt a 'crash through or crash' approach, presenting the work pretty much as Wagner envisaged it, responding to its many felicities, its beautiful changes of mood, and the contrasting scenic demands of the settings for each scene – and hope that the audience will be sufficiently impressed by such a presentation, and by the sheer power of the music, to reach in the Finale the state of transcendence which Wagner attempts to give to them, disregarding the problematic aspects of the work's ideology.

---

[24] Wagner told his costume designer that 'ideally [Kundry] should be lying there naked, like a Titian Venus' (!) (C. Wagner 1980: 590 [4/1/1881]). On these three *femmes fatales* see Wurz 2000.

[25] As Beckett correctly notes (1981: 140–1) this is one of Wagner's own contributions to the legend. In the main source, Wolfram von Eschenbach's *Parzival*, the hero is happily married to Condwiramurs.

[26] Millington (1984: 267) claims that he also learns during his subsequent wanderings to channel his spontaneous feeling of sympathy for Amfortas and that his self-denial 'is not a question of chastity but acceptance of moral responsibility'.

[27] Christ himself is shown, in several incidents recorded in the Gospels, to have valued women more highly and sympathetically than was customary in his contemporary culture. The same cannot be said about St. Paul, or about several subsequent Church Fathers, including the reformed libertine St. Augustine.

The other, and much more difficult, task is for the director to express his or her dissent from the problematic aspects of Wagner's vision – to mount a critique of the work *from within, during an actual performance.* This is a formidable undertaking, and not to be attempted lightly. Indeed, can it be done at all, without wrecking the musico-dramatic totality of the piece?

We will consider one example of each of these approaches: for the first, Otto Schenk's 1993 Metropolitan Opera production, with Siegfried Jerusalem in the title role; for the second, Nikolaus Lehnhoff's production for ENO, recorded in 2004 at the Baden-Baden Festspielhaus, starring Christopher Ventris.[28] Fascinatingly, both productions feature the outstanding Waltraud Meier as Kundry. She presents – as you might expect – two extremely different interpretations, since Lehnhoff clearly sees a new concept of Kundry as being fundamental to his approach to the work as a whole.

Schenk basically follows the stage directions in the final scene, adding very little of his own. In a nice invention, after Parsifal has hailed the spear, and before *O! Welchen Wunders höchsten Gluck!* ('Oh, supreme joy of this miracle!'), he gives the spear to Gurnemanz, who circulates around all the Knights, allowing them to touch it. Then, when the Grail has been revealed, and at the moment when the music modulates to A flat major for the solemn close of the work, a white stream of light shining through a gentle mist descends upon Parsifal from the open dome of the temple. As the choirs finish singing, Parsifal lifts up the Grail, which is shining from within with a reddish glow, and walks slowly round the dais on which he is standing; as he exhibits it to each group of Knights, they kneel. And, when he turns it towards Kundry, she raises her arms towards it, then collapses and dies. In the final bars, Parsifal turns the Grail towards Amfortas, who advances towards him and kneels; then Parsifal goes back behind the altar on the dais, and holds the Grail up towards heaven as the curtain falls.

This is all effective *Personenregie*, and, if you are in the right mood, then it may give you an intimation of transcendence when you watch it; but it depends absolutely on the power of the music to carry the audience into accepting Wagner's problematic vision of humanity in *Parsifal*.

Nikolaus Lehnhoff started in 2004 from the premise that the world of the Knights, as portrayed in the opening scene of Act I, is sinking into decay; in his interpretation, the Knights and Amfortas represent all those secret societies which have had initial good intentions to help people but have lost sight of their original goals and are now celebrating meaningless rituals.[29] He notes that the Squires are asleep as the curtain rises, and that

---

[28] This production was also staged in San Francisco and Chicago.
[29] This approach was foreshadowed by Wolfgang Wagner's 1975 production; he blamed Titurel's 'inhuman insistence upon asceticism' for the Grail knights' having lost their original ideal of compassion (Bauer 1983: 291).

Gawan has left without leave – two breaches of the Rule.[30] The decay of Montsalvat is especially evident in Act III scene 2, where the Knights are truly desperate after months, maybe even years, without sustenance from the Grail. They surround Amfortas menacingly and demand that he uncover the Grail; in Denni Sayers' choreography, they are an unruly and dangerous mob.[31] Raimund Bauer's set designs for the first scenes of Acts I and III deliberately depart very far from Wagner's imagined forest clearing; they are bleak and confronting, and the walls of the temple have been both attacked by enemies and smashed by a large meteorite.

Lehnhoff's interpretation and critique do not become fully revealed until Act III, and Kundry is central to it because here Lehnhoff confronts head on the narrow masculine bias of Wagner's last drama. Kundry sings only two words in the final Act – *Dienen ... Dienen!* ('Let me serve ... serve!', in response to Gurnemanz after he has revived her); but she is onstage throughout, and in this production a new intimacy grows between the penitent Kundry and Parsifal. Already, when she is anointing Parsifal's feet, and passes the phial to him so that he may give it to Gurnemanz to anoint his head, she gazes at him with admiration; and she is profoundly moved when he baptizes her, bowing deeply and humbly before him when he has done this. Then she raises her eyes to him, and they stare at each other. The moment is broken only when the music of the beautiful meadows steals in. But, in Lehnhoff's reinterpretation, this is the moment when Kundry and Parsifal begin to find compassion and love for each other, and *that* is what makes possible the rebirth of nature in this decaying world, which now follows.[32]

🖉 7 2A Parsifal and Kundry

Gurnemanz now expands at length on the magic of Good Friday and the rejoicing of all creatures in the renewal and redemption by Christ's sacrifice. During this monologue, in Lehnhoff's production, Parsifal and Kundry first stare at each other across the width of the stage; then he crosses to her, she kneels, he too half-kneels very close to her and she collapses, resting her head on his knee; he holds her, gently touching her head and her back. (This goes a bit further than Wagner's direction that she *has slowly raised her*

---

[30] Cf. the interview with Lehnhoff in *Parsifal's Progress*, a film by Reiner Moritz which is included in the Opus Arte DVDs of Lehnhoff's production. He might have added the very unChristian way in which two of the Knights torment Kundry.

[31] Beckett (1981: 56) anticipated this interpretation: 'This scene, in which Amfortas is tormented by his own knights like a sick animal rounded on by the pack, has a chilling horror ...'.

[32] Borchmeyer (1991: 393) had already rightly argued that '[Kundry's] redemption through baptism ... is associated, symbolically, with the redemption of extrahuman nature in the Good Friday scene ...'.

head again and looks up at Parsifal with tearful eyes in calm and earnest entreaty.) As Parsifal responds to her tears,[33] he cups her chin in his hand, lifts it, and *kisses her gently on the forehead*, as Wagner instructs. But it is what follows that is all-important. Kundry and Parsifal stare into each other's eyes for one last time, then she falls onto his chest and they embrace tightly, each with both arms clasped around the other. When the sound of the bells leads Gurnemanz to declare that they must go to the temple, Kundry and Parsifal disentangle slowly and gently.[34]

All this is in preparation for Lehnhoff's dissent from Wagner's final scene. It is not Kundry who dies at the end of this production, but Amfortas, who feels that since the new king has come he can now have the death for which he has longed. He places his crown on Parsifal's head, and then dies in his arms.

✇ 7 2B The end of 'Parsifal'

Kundry has entered after Parsifal, but stands aside while he interacts with Amfortas and the Knights. As in Schenk's production, Parsifal gives the spear to Gurnemanz – but for a deeper reason. Lehnhoff rightly views Gurnemanz as the keeper of tradition, who still feels that the rituals of Montsalvat have meaning, has suffered while the world of the Grail has been in decay, and wants it to be restored. So Parsifal gives the spear to him, and as the drama draws to a close Gurnemanz holds the spear up with pride and the Knights gather round him in awe of it. They have their sacred relic once again, and will presumably now renew their rituals.

But Parsifal, led by Kundry, rejects Montsalvat. He gently lays the crown which Amfortas has placed on his head on the skeletal corpse of Titurel, and looks up at Kundry. She beckons to Parsifal, and he follows her slowly out of the temple. The Grail is unseen, not even represented, as it was at the end of Act I, by a beam of light; on the contrary, a bright light now comes from outside the temple, and it invites Kundry and Parsifal to leave for a new and different life. Seven individual Knights detach themselves, one by one, during the final bars from the adoring group surrounding the spear, and follow them. Lehnhoff's suggestion is that these Knights see that 'there

---

[33] 'Is it not her tears of remorse which conferred on Nature its present radiance? ... Parsifal himself recognizes the secret correspondence between Kundry's redemption and Nature'. (Borchmeyer 1991: 395). If I read Lehnhoff's staging of this scene rightly, it can be viewed as a development of the implications of Borchmeyer's insight.

[34] In Schenk's production, as you might expect, there is by contrast no interaction between Parsifal and Kundry in any part of Gurnemanz's monologue. Parsifal looks at Gurnemanz throughout, and only turns to Kundry – who spent half the monologue collapsed on the ground, and only rose to a kneeling position as it neared its end – when he likens her tears to a dew of blessing. At that point he puts an arm gently around her back, and gives her an extremely chaste kiss on the forehead. This staging entirely misses the close tie between Kundry's baptism and the blooming of nature.

might be another way, without the religious ideology which has led to many of the greatest crimes committed in the name of God'.[35]

Where are Kundry and Parsifal going? In her interview in Moritz's film, Meier rightly suggests that they are simply going to somewhere in the light, to a literal enlightenment which can be interpreted metaphorically by each member of the audience in accordance with his or her religious and/or other beliefs. Compare Moritz's own commentary:[36]

> In Lehnhoff's interpretation ... [Kundry] revokes the unnatural separation between men and women and leads Parsifal and other Grail knights back into the tunnel of mankind at whose end a faint glimmer of hope can just be discerned. With this image Lehnhoff connects Wagner's concept of redemption with the magnificent idea from Goethe's *Faust*: 'Woman eternal draws us on high'. It remains uncertain where Kundry will lead Parsifal and the other knights who have decided to make a fresh start, but we can be sure that they will choose a path beyond all religious ideologies. Undoubtedly, everybody who is searching for spiritual renewal in our time will feel that this idea is highly relevant.

Gurnemanz and the remaining Grail Knights may have had *their* ideology saved by the return of the spear, but Parsifal, led, as Moritz notes, by 'woman eternal' (Goethe's *Ewigweibliche*),[37] will have none of their all-male world and seeks his transcendence outside it. In the penitent and redeemed Kundry, who has inspired the creatures of nature to seek redemption in their turn,[38] Lehnhoff gives Wagner's enlightened Tamino the Pamina, whom in the composer's original conception he conspicuously lacks.

So ends a truly remarkable production. It presents an account of *Parsifal* which gladly accepts Wagner's underlying concept of redemption through compassion and love, but opposes and critiques his vision of how it can best be achieved. Lucy Beckett wrote in 1981:[39]

> To the extent that the spiritual certainty to which it refers is thought to belong to the past, [*Parsifal*] will seem nostalgic, embarrassing,

---

[35] Quoted from his interview in *Parsifal's Progress*. In Harry Kupfer's 1978 production in Copenhagen, Amfortas also died, and Parsifal left the temple; but, puzzlingly, he took with him the grail and the spear, as well as Kundry and a handful of knights (Bauer 1983, 292). Taking the ritual objects makes that a very different interpretation from Lehnhoff's; but, not having seen the production, I cannot tell if it anticipated Lehnhoff's most important innovation, the growth of affection between Parsifal and the repentant Kundry. Kundry also lived on in Wolfgang Wagner's 1975 production at Bayreuth (Millington 2012: 292).

[36] 'By pity lightened', Opus Arte booklet accompanying the DVDs, p. 11.

[37] Lehnhoff echoes this concept from the final scene of *Faust II*, whose sonic patterns of singers in heights and depths Wagner had adopted for his own final scene.

[38] Borchmeyer 1991: 394–5.

[39] 1981: 147.

unhealthy, quaint, boring ... But to the extent that the spiritual certainty to which it refers is still thought, whether from within or without, to have an incontrovertible experiential force, it will seem at once humbler, braver and more worthy of respect for the encouraging light it sheds on the tormenting questions of real, human life.

It is perhaps not surprising that she did not envisage, as far back as 1981, the third, new way that Lehnhoff pioneered in 2004: to confront the aspects of *Parsifal* which presuppose a kind of 'certainty' which modern civilization has rejected, and by dissenting from some central aspects of Wagner's text to restore to the work the 'incontrovertible experiential force' which in a straight production it no longer holds, chiefly because of its male-dominated view of the role of women in human society. Lehnhoff has given the 'sacred stage festival play' back to the twenty-first century, as a work which we can accept and live by.

Discussion question

Does Lehnhoff go too far in his re-conception of the end of *Parsifal* and centralization of Kundry?

7.3 Kát'a and the river voices (Janáček after Ostrovsky *Kát'a Kabanová* III.2)

In the final scene of *Kát'a Kabanová*, Kát'a, after confessing to adultery, is wandering alone, crazed, on the banks of the river Volga. In the source text, Ostrovsky's 1859 play *The Storm*, Kát'a claims to have heard voices in the past. And later, just before she leaps to her death in the river, she says that she is actually hearing them.[40] But the play's audience does not hear the voices, and so they simply perceive her from outside as 'mad'. In Janáček's opera, by contrast, the audience *does* hear the voices 'from the distance', just before and after Kát'a first sings that she hears them; they sing wordlessly and quietly the same melody as that of the powerful storm which in the previous scene spurred Kát'a to confess (7.3.1).[41] Since the music links interior and exterior and breaks down the barrier between the two zones, the voices are perceived both as subjective – sounds in Kát'a's mind, heard by her alone because of her altered state – and as the real voice of a force of nature; they are both inside her mind, and (mystically) objective and outside her.

---

[40] Ostrovsky 1972: 386 and 390.
[41] Janáček instructs that the sound should be *without text, sung between u and o.*

7.3.1 (III.2.21.9 -10)

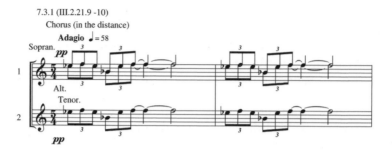

The voices are heard three times in Janáček's scene. First they sound quietly and evocatively in the distance – significantly, when they register in her mind, Kát'a likens the sound to that of a funeral procession (III.2.21.9–12); then, the second time, they summon Kát'a *like a sigh of the Volga* (Janáček's stage direction) to the edge of the river bank, after which she commits suicide (III.2.33.9ff.); finally, at the end of the opera, they comment stridently on her fate (III.2.40). The funeral has become Kát'a's own.

Nikolaus Lehnhoff made history, when his production premièred at Glyndebourne in 1986, by using costume and acting to express Kát'a's anguish in this final scene. Most previous productions had left this task to the music, whose overwhelming power was in total contradiction to the conservative dress and restrained demeanour which the lead singer usually presented on stage.[42] Under Lehnhoff's direction, Nancy Gustafson in the title role wears in this final scene nothing but a white shift, symbolizing that Kát'a's soul is now stripped bare; and this is complemented by a great volatility in Gustafson's posture and gestures, which physicalizes Kát'a's agitation. This image was, then, without precedent in any previous production of this opera; but it matches perfectly Kát'a's half-crazed state, as portrayed in the orchestral music and in her vocal line, especially during the section where she tries desperately to communicate her confused feelings to her lover, Boris (III.2.29–32). Here Gustafson's long and lustrous hair, flowing freely after being bound up tightly earlier in the opera, is symbolic of the spiritual freedom which text and music suggest she has now attained.[43]

---

[42] Cf. my comments above at **2.5** on David Pountney's views on directing this opera.

[43] For another fine example of the unbinding of a young woman's hair in the final scene after earlier constriction cf. Götz Friederich's film of *Salome*, **8.2** below. Note also that Kundry's hair flows spectacularly far down her back in the last Act of Lehnhoff's *Parsifal* (**7.2**), matching the fact that in his production there is such sexual chemistry between her and Parsifal that he lets her lead him out, away from the Grail kingdom.

♪ 7 3 Kát'a and the voices

After that, the singer enacts Kát'a's increasingly calm acceptance, as the wordless choral voices, together with a powerful summons in the orchestra (**7.3.2**), call Kát'a to the river; Gustafson shows Kát'a responding to the 'other world' represented by the voices, as the supernatural beckons her to join it.[44]

7.3.2 (III.2.33.10)

horns, vla, fl

At the very end of the opera, after Kát'a's dead body had been brought onstage, Lehnhoff overrode the stage directions. Janáček, following the original playwright's *mise-en-scène*, envisaged that Kát'a's domineering mother-in-law Kabanicha and the townspeople should remain on stage to the end; the closing tableau was to be (and is in most productions) that of Kabanicha standing in triumph over Kát'a's body, while the people look on in horror. But this leaves unexplored the most powerful aspect of the music: the reappearance in the closing bars of the river voices, now *fortissimo* and sounded together with the baleful eight timpani blows (**4.2.2**) which have punctuated several crucial moments earlier in the opera. Why *are* the voices, previously always heard *pp* when they called out to Kát'a, now so strident?

I believe that Lehnhoff thought about this, and changed the staging to give a better dramatic and visual interpretation of the meaning of the music. He correctly interpreted the wordless offstage voices as a power of nature which at the end of the opera reclaims Kát'a as its own; so he eliminated all the living characters one by one from the stage, leaving Kát'a's corpse alone after Kabanicha's closing remarks and exit. The body's posture is a twisted shape, almost blending into the green landscape like the roots of a tree, symbolizing in the final tableau that Kát'a has returned to nature.[45] In Lehnhoff's visual interpretation of what the music says, Kát'a has finally

---

[44] Adding to the sense of the supernatural was the extraordinary, non-naturalistic colour of the river in Hoheisel's set for this scene – an oscillating, beckoning web of purple and black.

[45] Bear in mind that as he composed the closing scenes of *Kát'a Kabanová* Janáček was already at work, at times on the reverse side of the same manuscript paper, on *Adventures of the Vixen Bystrouška*.

achieved in death the peaceful harmony with nature which she craved, expressed in her last words:

Ptáčci přiletí na mohylu,	Little birds will flutter to my grave,
vyvedou mládăta,	bringing their young ones,
a kvítka vykvetou, červeňoučká,	and flowers will blossom, red,
modroučka, žlut'oučka.	blue, yellow.
Tak ticho, tak krásně! Tak krasně!	What peace, what beauty! What beauty!
A třeba umřít!	And I must die!

In the final moments of the opera, nature protests in the orchestra, and in the chorus which is now *fortissimo* for the first time, against the world that has driven such a beautiful human being to her death.[46]

Discussion question

Discuss how Nancy Gustaffson's performance as Kát'a in III.2 emphasizes the character's affinity with nature, in particular (but not entirely) through her reactions to the voices of the river. Pay particular attention to the physicalization of the role in this scene.

7.4 Wozzeck in the open field (Berg/Büchner *Wozzeck*, Act I scene 2)

In this scene, where Wozzeck is tormented by the apocalyptic power of nature, the orchestra illuminates and makes real for the audience the terrors which Wozzeck undergoes, but which in Büchner's original play they can only imagine. This means that, in the opera, the audience is forced to hear the living reality of Nature, and experience the visions *from inside, from the point of view of Wozzeck*. When watching a performance of Büchner's original play, audiences have the option to remain outside, viewing Woyzeck's desperate state objectively; but in the opera they have no choice but to hear with him the horrific visions which he is experiencing. The one orchestra simultaneously communicates both the power – and the reality – of what Wozzeck hears and sees *and* his emotional reaction to it, showing *why* he is so agitated. Berg's orchestral music validates Wozzeck's visions, and gives an animate power to the visions in Büchner's text of an apocalyptic Nature.[47] In

---

[46] Lehnhoff's staging has made me rethink the more nihilistic reading of the last few moments of the opera which I published in the 1970s (M. Ewans 1977: 134–6).

[47] For a discussion of the apocalypse music of I.2, and its subsequent reuses later in the opera, cf. Treitler 1976.

7.4.1, the upper voice *Haupstimme* in the trombones (a), later joined by the horns (c), depicts Wozzeck's rising panic, while the steady *crescendo* of the *Nebenstimme* ostinato in the timpani, double basses and harp (b) communicates the gathering intensity of the sounds which he hears. At the climax, the frantic figurations in bar 278 (d) convey *both* the intensity of the sounds of Nature which Wozzeck hears *and* his consequent panic.

7.4.1 (I.2.271-8)

Similarly, a few bars later, in **7.4.2**, the strange rising thirds in harp and trombones, then harp and violins – (a), bars 286–7 – portray Wozzeck's growing alertness to the fire which he sees as he stares into the distance;[48] then the sweeping figurations which begin by rising in (b) in bar 291 (responding to the text, 'it rises from earth into heaven'), start from bar 293 to fall decisively, growing ever louder as the pattern of four chords – the

---

[48] Berg added to Büchner's text a detailed stage direction for bars 285–300, so that the fire in Wozzeck's vision is (or should be) paralleled by the setting of the sun on stage. His meticulous instructions for this effect are, however, usually disregarded in production.

first three a triplet – (c), *forte/fortissimo* and with emphasis, is tossed from
the woodwind down to the trumpets, then the first three trombones and
finally the fourth trombone and bass tuba. The panic is complete in bar
295, where Wozzeck's words 'wie Posaunen' ('like trombones') inspire a
rush of *fortissimo* semiquaver semitone oscillations in the trombones (d),
which is then taken up by two pairs of timpani (e) as the other percussion
crescendo from *ppp to fff* over three bars, when Wozzeck shouts out in his
final agony (*Wie's heranklirrt*, 'What a noise is rising up!'). Once again, the
same orchestral music both depicts the actual sounds which Wozzeck hears
and portrays his reaction to those sounds.

7.4.2 (I.284-289)

Unfortunately the quivering nervous intensity of Berg's intricate music is not always fully matched fully in production. This is due largely to a physical problem; many of the baritones who can sing this extremely difficult and demanding part are of solid build, and are not really capable of matching the music with the physicality which the music ideally demands (there are a lot of frown-creased foreheads instead!). *Wozzeck* has (inevitably) suffered from the excesses of 'concept' directors, who seem to think that the insanity into which Berg's and Büchner's hero declines is a licence to unleash almost anything they want on stage;[49] but it has also suffered from over-conservative direction.

In Franz Grundheber's performance under the direction of Adolf Dreisen (Vienna State Opera 1987), there is quite a good amount of physicality. For example, when Wozzeck stamps on the ground, and declaims in *Sprechstimme* 'Hollow! All hollow! A chasm! It's cracking!' (266ff.), Grundheber pulls away from his Andres and collapses on the ground; then

---

[49] Cf. e.g. the Frankfurt Opera production with Dale Duesing in the title role.

as **7.4.1** commences, he crawls along and lays the side of his head on the
earth to listen, then suddenly rises up on bar 277 and drags Andres away
from the sound of the thing which he has heard following them down below.
During **7.4.2**, as a red sunset appears on the cyclorama behind him, he raises
his head when Wozzeck sees the vision of a fire (287), accompanies 'it's rising
from earth to heaven' with the obvious gesture of a hand gradually raised,
then puts his hands over his ears and leans forward intensely on 'What a
noise is rising up!'. He only relaxes, gradually, after the terror is over.

Grundheber returned to the title role, under the direction of Patrice
Chéreau, in a production filmed in 1994 at the Deutsche Staatsoper Unter
den Linden in Berlin but only released on DVD in 2013. Chéreau used
a bare stage for this scene, and, in his production, rather than cutting
sticks Wozzeck and Andres are sweeping the ground with large brooms.[50]
Grundheber's performance shows how the same singer's interpretation can
be transformed when he is working with a superior director.

✐ 7 4 Wozzeck Open Field

Right from the beginning of the scene, this Wozzeck begins to interact with
the earth beneath him, circling around edgily and staring down intently
before his opening words ('You, this place is accursed!). Then **7.4.1** begins.
Wozzeck in this production is already seriously demented. In the powerful
crescendo bar before this excerpt begins, he has been waving his arms in
a wild and disturbing fashion, and as that music reached its climax he has
his hands clasped on his head. Next there is a short *fermata* before **7.4.1**
begins, during which he relaxes out of that position. Then Grundheber and
Chéreau brilliantly illuminate the sounds in the first four bars by having
Wozzeck move edgily to follow the dreadful reality which he can see and
hear moving beneath them, pointing at it as he seeks to locate it exactly.
Then just before he begins to declaim 'Listen...', he has found it, and lies
on the ground to hear the gathering intensity of **7.4.1b** and **c**, then abruptly
rises in terror (at 277, as in Dresen's production) and tries to run away
(Berg's direction is *in the utmost anguish*).

For **7.4.2**, the stage darkens abruptly during the general pause. When
Wozzeck sings 'A fire!', Chéreau makes the fire a real point of reference for
the character's actions; Grundheber sees it as offstage right, crosses towards
it, pointing in that direction – then stops in fear. He makes big gestures,
first upwards at 'to heaven' and then down again during the catastrophic
descent of **7.4.2c** in the woodwind and brass. The trombone-like sound
is imagined as coming from the same source as the fire; Wozzeck retreats
left away from it, and as the noise becomes overwhelming (timpani and

---

[50] At the point where in the original stage directions Wozzeck twice stamps on the ground,
265–6, in this production he stabs downward with the end of the broom handle.

percussion, **7.4.2e**), he bends forward in anguish, his hands once again clasping his head.

In these ways Chéreau brought out the close interaction between Wozzeck and the terrifying aspects of Nature which he sees and hears, and which the orchestra chronicles so vividly. In both the extracts under consideration the power of the scene is greatly enhanced by making us see Wozzeck first realizing the exact place from which Nature is crying out to him – and in **7.4.1** we actually see him searching for it and finding it – and then interacting with that point, which is of course invisible to Andres and to the opera's spectators.

This staging, which illuminates the way in which the music works, totally undermines the nihilistic interpretation of the opera which Perle and Jarman advanced in the 1980s.[51] Far from being mechanistic and indifferent to Wozzeck's sufferings, Nature is animate in this opera, and interacts with him, both in this scene and in III.4, where Wozzeck, now totally crazed, drowns in a pond, lured into it by the rising of a red moon. There are obvious parallels between that scene and the death scene which Janáček composed at about the same time for Kát'a Kabanová (**7.3**).

Discussion question

Analyse how Franz Grunheber's acting in Chéreau's production portrays Wozzeck's interactions with the sounds that the character hears and the visions which he sees surrounding him in *Wozzeck* I.2.

7.5 'Fire! Fire! St John's Fire.' (Tippett, *The Midsummer Marriage*, III.8)

Partly by design and partly by accident, *The Midsummer Marriage*, when it was premièred in 1955, was a new *Die Zauberflöte* for an England which was deeply wearied by World War II and by post-war austerity. Like Mozart's *Singspiel*, Tippett's opera shows the trials and eventual union of two pairs of lovers, one lofty and one earthbound, with the female member of the 'higher' couple needing to reject an angry, demanding parent;[52] and

---

[51] Perle 1980, 36–7. Cf. 93, 123 and Jarman 1989: 3, 65, 68. Some Büchner scholars used to claim that he too was a fatalist and pessimist: but this view has rightly been rejected in more recent work; cf. Reddick 1995, xvi.

[52] King Fisher plays the role in *The Midsummer Marriage* corresponding to the Queen of the Night, and his symbolic death is necessary for the renewal by the new generation to take place, just as the casting of the Queen into the depths of darkness must precede the final celebrations in the temple of Isis and Osiris.

in consequence Tippett's score like Mozart's had to encompass a very wide range of musical styles, from a comic *buffa* for the new Papageno and Papagena, Jack and Bella, all the way up to exaltation and ecstasy in the revelations of the penultimate scene.

As with *Die Zauberflöte*, the text of *The Midsummer Marriage* is initially puzzling. It invited ridicule from some early commentators, who were not prepared to adjust to its high level of symbolism and its need to express the almost inexpressible in words, as the foundation for a music which *can* express aspects of the numinous which are beyond words.[53] But like Mozart's, Tippett's music for his mystical opera is of exemplary clarity, luminous in its depth and indeed its sheer beauty. And as Cairns remarks:

> The score that the words generated incarnates the drama, and through it the drama is manifested and understood ... If the music is strong enough – if it impresses itself sufficiently on our imaginations – it imposes its own dramatic world within which everything is clear; but the significance may well transcend words. Music fills out the hints of the text and gives vibrant life to its bald statements, setting them resonating so that they strike answering chords in us. It endows the concepts of the text with reality and form, suggests the deeper, often contradictory meaning that lies below the surface, telescopes time, compresses experience. In short, it makes explicit. But it may do so in a way that cannot be, and does not need to be, exactly accounted for.[54]

Tippett contrasted his task with that of Mozart and Schikaneder, writing of *Die Zauberflöte*: 'Clearly no one now can match the innocence, tenderness and simplicity with which that mythological experience was presented.'[55] Writing an opera which conveys universal spiritual truths through a predominantly Masonic imagery was in fact a far from simple achievement

---

[53] Dent noted (1960: 218) that the libretto of *Die Zauberflöte* 'has generally been considered to be one of the most absurd specimens of that form of literature in which absurdity is regarded as a matter of course'. For initial hostility to the *Midsummer Marriage* libretto, similarly owing to failure to understand its symbolism, cf. e.g. Martin Cooper and Cecil Smith ('one of the worst [libretti] in the 350-year history of opera'); Schott 1977: 75–6. However, if any reader today thinks that *The Midsummer Marriage* is too peripheral a work to be included together with the acknowledged masterpieces studied elsewhere in this book, he or she should read David Cairns' outstanding essay on the opera (1973).

Lloyd Davies (1985) annotates the libretto with no fewer than 66 footnotes, some of which are quite extensive. But no one can read a footnote while watching an opera in performance! This exercise is valuable to scholars, but it goes against Tippett's Jungian belief that symbols can be understood intuitively, as welling up from the collective unconscious of mankind. As Cairns notes, 'though the ideas behind [*The Midsummer Marriage*] may be many-layered, the imagery through which they are conveyed is for the most part directly comprehensible by a Western audience' (1973: 36).

[54] Cairns 1973: 36.

[55] Tippett 1974: 56 = 1995, 202.

during the post-Josephine repression of the Order which was taking place while Mozart and Schikaneder created *Die Zauberflöte*; but Tippett was clearly right in that the development of psychology in the twentieth century has profoundly changed the parameters of our understanding, and has made the creation of this kind of opera a much more complex task than it was in 1790–1. Tippett's solution was to confront the challenge directly and take psychology on board; he uses the Jungian concepts of the *animus* and *anima* to generate the most important aspect of his plot. And like Schikaneder and Mozart he drew on symbols and images from non-Christian religions to express the deepest truths embodied in the opera; in Act I we encounter Jenifer transfigured towards Athena, and Mark towards Dionysus, and at the climax of Act III they appear united as the Hindu divine couple Shiva-Shakti.

'I would know my shadow and my light, / So shall I at last be whole'. Over twenty years after the première of *The Midsummer Marriage*, Tippett declared that these lines from his wartime oratorio *A Child of Our Time* make up 'the only truth I shall ever say'.[56] As the opera begins, Mark and Jenifer do not know enough about themselves to unite successfully in marriage. And their quest becomes in Act I literally a search for the light and the shadow. Jenifer mounts a broken spiral staircase and disappears into heaven; Mark enters a pair of gates that look *like the entrance to a cave* and goes down to Hades. Each comes back with partial truth; Jenifer has been exalted by the purity, peace and calm of the spiritual world above, and Mark is exasperated by the dullness of life on earth after the heady Dionysian experiences which he has undergone in the underworld. Echoing the Orphic tablet which provides the motto of the opera, they sing against each other: 'I am a child of the starry heaven / of the fruitful earth',[57] and their instrumental textures are vividly contrasted; a solo girl trumpeter interacts with Jenifer's coloratura as she describes heavenly peace, while cymbal clashes animate Mark's violent description of Bacchic dances and the ritual *sparagmos*, the rending apart of the sacrificial ewe and crushing of a child in Dionysian excess.

Each attempts to conquer the other. For the moment, Mark apparently wins, and they go off in the opposite directions; as the Act draws to a close Jenifer enters the cave to discover her inner beast, and Mark begins to climb the staircase. When they return to the stage in Act III, each will have confronted both their shadow and their light.[58]

---

[56] Quoted in Driver 1985: 20. Jenifer echoes these words from the oratorio at *The Midsummer Marriage* I.4.33a.9ff.: 'For me, the light! For you, the shadow!'.

[57] I.7.80.15–23.

[58] The verticality of a descent into darkness and an ascent into light makes another parallel with *Die Zauberflöte*. Pamina and Tamino descend into the depths under mountains to undergo the trials of fire and water, and then, after their victory and return, *the whole stage represents the sun.*

These upward and downward journeys are the opera's first encounter with the numinous. The second Act uses a different symbolism; that of the seasonal cycle and of the four elements of earth, water, air and (in Act III) fire. Although much of Act II is devoted to the more ordinary and earth-bound couple, Jack and Bella, the main focus is on the three Ritual Dances of 'The Earth in Autumn', 'The Waters in Winter' and 'The Air in Spring', which draw on a Welsh myth of the cycles of life and death.[59]

> The point of the dances is to show the logical male world of the mind being caught up and assimilated by the instinctive world of the subconscious emotions ... the dances clearly apply to both Mark and Jenifer, since the male being caught by the female is also the mind being caught by the body; the resolution of both dualities is necessary for wholeness.[60]

In Act III, wholeness can be attained, but only after the symbolic death of King Fisher; this makes possible generational change, such as we have already seen when Sarastro transferred his power to Pamina and Tamino, and when Amfortas resigned his role as the leader of the Grail Knights to Parsifal. Mark and Jenifer have attained transcendent power by undergoing their trials, as a result of which they now reappear, disclosed from within a lotus bud and completely united; they are clothed in red (fire) and gold (their names are from Cornish royalty) and posed in mutual contemplation as Shiva-Shakti.[61] King Fisher threatens Mark with his revolver, but is struck dead when *Mark and Jenifer turn their faces towards him in a gesture of power.*

So now the fourth and final culminating ritual dance, 'The Fire in Summer' uses fire as the metaphor for their complete rebirth.[62] However, problems arise in Tippett's attempt to portray the ecstasy of this renewal. The music of the first three ritual dances, in Act II, was purely instrumental; but now, to lead up to the climax of his opera, Tippett composes a large ensemble for Mark and Jenifer, the Ancients and mixed chorus, all singing different texts simultaneously. Since the orchestral writing is fast and quite busy, and Mark and Jenifer use glossolalia to express their ecstasy, not much text can be heard until the final moments when the couple has retreated into the incandescent lotus bud inside which they were first

---

[59] For Tippett's sources see Kemp 1984: 230–1 or Lloyd Davies 1985: 58.

[60] Lloyd Davies 1985: 58. Cf. also Kemp 1984: 222.

[61] Lloyd Davies (1985: 61; cf. Kemp 1984: 223) argues that the dominant religion of 1950s Britain, Christianity, has a horror of sexuality which made it necessary for Tippett to search as far east as Indian Hinduism to find a viable image of divine sexual unity.

[62] The fact that after the four ritual dances Mark and Jenifer have undergone trials involving the four elements, culminating in fire, is one last parallel with *Die Zauberflöte*; Chailley 1972: 137–53 has shown that Pamina and Tamino have already succeeded in trials by air and earth before they formally undergo the final trials by fire and water.

disclosed, and *the veiled mass glows from within and breaks into flame.*[63] At that point however, accompanied by powerful orchestral chords, the chorus once again sings in harmony, as it did when the dance began:

Fire! Fire! St John's Fire.
In the desert in the night.
Fire! Fire! Fire, fire, fire in summer.

And then, at the actual climax (478–80), Tippett expresses through music a height of ecstasy for which no words would be adequate. The orchestra is left alone, in a passage of solemn beauty and serene healing power, to set the seal on the transformation which has now been completed, and initiate the audience into the transcendence which Mark and Jenifer have attained. The iridescent semi- and demi-semiquavers of the woodwind and harp dance above two different, calmly flowing but ecstatic melodies, which surge in parallel in the brass and strings to a moment of supreme power (7.5.1).

After that, the members of the chorus find themselves left alone, anxiously waiting in the moonlight; but as dawn begins to break Mark and Jenifer appear from opposite sides of the stage, now dressed for their wedding. And they remake the moment of their quarrel at the start of Act I. Mark sings 'Jenifer, Jenifer my darling...' to the same music as in Act I scene 4;[64] but now, instead of being disappointed that she is not prepared to marry him, he can continue – and we at last hear how that music would have proceeded in Act I, but for the characters' lack of self-knowledge at that point:

... After the visionary night,
The senses purified,
My heart's at rest.[65]

He receives a warm and loving reply. Then, after he has placed the ring on Jenifer's finger, all go down the hill back to the world of ordinary 'reality', celebrating the renewal that has taken place with lines quoted from Yeats's poem *Lapis Lazuli*:

---

[63] It is probably just as well that the Ancients' commentary is inaudible, since it is obscure even by the standards of this often mystical and allusive libretto. But the chorus celebrates the transformation of 'carnal love through which the race / of men is everlastingly renewed' into 'divine consuming love whose fires shine / From God's perpetually revealed face', while Mark and Jenifer simultaneously sing how 'the world's splendor, yes even its pain' are transfigured 'in the bright / Furious incandescent light / Of love's perpetually renewed fire'. Both of these perspectives are important, but in performance only a few words of either can be heard and understood.
[64] III.9.506 1–2 cf. I.4.30.1–2.
[65] III.9.506.3–507.1.

7.5.1 (III.8.479)

'All things fall and are built again
And those that build them again are gay.'[66]

Now the sun has risen on midsummer's day; it is the culminating symbol of renewal here, as in the finale of *Die Zauberflöte*.

*

No one stage production has created a coherent set of stage pictures that wholly matches Tippett's exultant vision of transcendence, although Ande Anderson's production at Covent Garden in 1968 had many merits, despite struggling with a difficult and visually disappointing set. It made a whole new generation (including myself) aware of the splendour of a work which had attracted very mixed reviews at its world première in 1955; and then

---

[66] III.9.510.7ff.

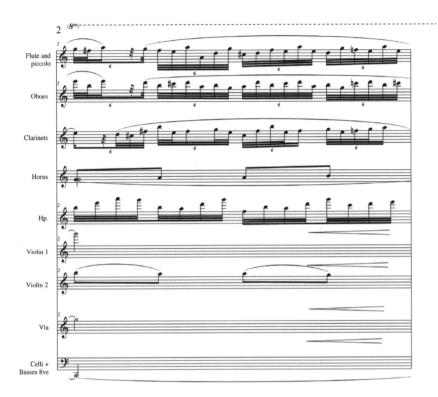

the 1976 Welsh National Opera production directed by Ian Watt-Smith was in general very effective – although with another poor set, and unfortunate costumes for the Ancients.[67] There has been only one performance in a video medium; it was transmitted by TV Channel 4 in the UK in the 1980s, but has not been issued commercially as a DVD. This is a pity, since Philip Langridge, as Mark, and Lucy Shelton, as Jenifer, headed a very strong cast under the baton of David Atherton, and Elijah Moshinsky's television production surpasses most stagings to date.

Moshinsky made two basic production decisions: that he would use all the resources of television, in particular cross-cutting and montage, to evoke the opera's numinous dimensions; and that he would treat *The Midsummer Marriage* as a period piece, setting it realistically in and around an English country house, and costuming the characters exactly in the clothes of the early 1950s. The Ancients, who have always caused problems in other productions, are now portrayed as an eccentric but insightful old couple, who live in an old house near the temple, filled with knick-knacks. King

---

[67] Successful productions of *The Midsummer Marriage* have also been mounted in Stockholm, San Francisco, Adelaide and elsewhere.

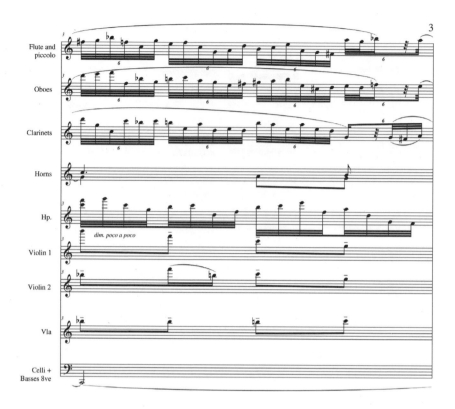

Fisher arrives in a luxury white, leather-seated convertible with a radio-telephone and the prestige number plate KF 2; and Jack drives a battered pick-up truck with the names JACK and BELLA prominently displayed on the windshield. The universal dimensions of the story are established during the instrumental introduction by gradually panning in from a view of Earth from space through clouds, first to a vista of rolling English countryside, then closing in on a flowing river, and only finally viewing the scene of the action. During the closing bars of the opera this sequence is reversed, so that we withdraw further and further away from the temple, ultimately with a view of the world from space during the luminous final chords.

Moshinsky's approach to the scene in Act I where Mark and Jenifer sing of their transcendent experiences is to set their return to earth inside the Ancients' study. Here the estranged couple confront each other over the length of a table, at which the Ancients also sit. There is on hand a book of Blake paintings,[68] which are viewed by the television spectator, and are used to illustrate first Jenifer's portrait of heavenly peace and then Mark's visions

---

[68] Presumably portraying the contest between Nadir and Zenith in *The Marriage of Heaven and Hell.*

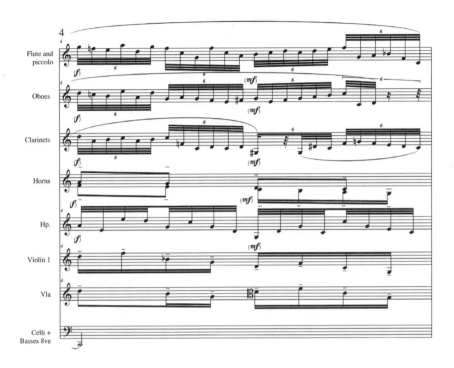

of Hades. This remarkable decision illuminates the transcendent nature of
the two principals' experiences, while also containing even these moments,
in which the text and music explore supranormal experience, within the
realistic parameters of the production concept. Here, and also earlier, when
Jenifer ascends the broken staircase (with the camera cutting across several
times to a little girl's legs ascending the same stairs, illustrating that Jenifer
has known the magic staircase 'In dreams since childhood at my mother's
knee'),[69] Moshinsky manages to combine realism, which is far more suited
to television than abstraction, with effective illumination of the transcendent experiences of Jenifer and Mark.

Anthony van Laast's choreography for the Ritual Dances in Act II is
competent, but the important differences between the three dances are
not brought out by changes in lighting, set or choreography. All three are
performed on an earthen floor in a bare setting. This is a serious flaw in an
otherwise excellent production.

In Act III Scene 8 Moshinsky spares no effect to convey to the spectator
the transcendent and ecstatic sexual union, which is the climax of this
opera. After the elegy and funeral music for King Fisher, the fourth and
final Ritual Dance begins in the realistic setting that has served so far for
Act III – the dining room of the Ancients' residence. Strephon, played by a
near-naked black male dancer, kindles a torch from the blazing hearth, and
dances with it.

✎ 7 5 Midsummer Marriage Climax (Fire! Fire!)

Then, as the chorus sing 'Fire! Fire! St John's Fire' for the first time,[70] images
of rising fire start to leap on the screen, and the realistic setting becomes
invisible. Soon a montage lets us see amid the flames the bare heads and
shoulders of Mark and Jenifer, kissing passionately.

In the second part of the fire dance, beginning at 462 after the intro-
ductory section for the voices of Mark and Jenifer alone, the fire becomes
brighter and sweeps across the screen. We see images of destruction –
footage of firefighters attempting to douse fires in the ruins caused by
bombing in World War II; then a flower bud opening (the image of an
opening lotus was of course central at this point in Tippett's original *mise-
en-scène*), and more lovemaking against a background of fire, as the voices
of Mark and Jenifer rise again into the intricate coloratura which conveys
their ecstasy in the music (469). Finally, when the chorus ends the ensemble
with the reprise of 'Fire! Fire! ...',[71] we see two naked bodies entwined,

---

[69] I.4.34.3.
[70] III.8.449.4ff.
[71] III.8.474.

tumbling through space in the midst of the flames. Mark and Jenifer have been transfigured in, and reborn by, their union.

Then comes the orchestral coda,[72] described and partially quoted above. In Moshinsky's production, this sublime music is accompanied at first by images of a pulsating womb, and then at the climactic second cymbal clash (479.1: **7.5.1**) it is as if fireworks are shooting out to dazzle our eyes. After that the music becomes peaceful, and as it calms we see first the throbbing pulse of a fetus and then shots of the entire fetus nestled in the womb. With these images, a child has been conceived and generational renewal has truly taken place.

This television interpretation of the climax of *The Midsummer Marriage* is an outstanding attempt to match Tippett's textual and musical vision of the blazing ecstasy of physical love between true partners with visual images that make explicit what is being portrayed, during a section of the opera where at times the complexity of the vocal ensemble makes it difficult for the spectator to receive the full meaning of the scene without strong visual aids. Arguably it is almost impossible to provide in the theatre adequate visual images for this climactic sequence, whether or not the stage directions in the libretto are followed closely. Tippett was subsequently closely involved with electronic mass media, and this interest culminated in *The Mask of Time*, an oratorio inspired by a TV series, and in his last opera *New Year*, which was conceived and written for television. It is therefore fascinating to see that his first opera has found in a television production a natural medium for true visual representation of its most numinous moments.

Discussion question

How effective do you think Moshinsky's cinematic montage is in complementing the feeling of supreme ecstasy that Tippett expresses in his music for the climactic union between Mark and Jenifer?

7.6 Conclusion

Audience interaction with the numinous cannot normally be achieved in a spoken play.[73] But it is within the power of an opera composer to use the transcendent 'language' of music to achieve this – provided that the stage images in production are a potent complement to the music.

---

[72] III.8.476.
[73] Cf. T. S. Eliot's acknowledgement of failure, when he showed the Aeschylean *Eumenides* (Furies) menacing his hero from a window embrasure during *The Family Reunion*, which was set in a contemporary country house in 1939; 1951: 30–1.

In these five operas, select principal characters achieve an enlightened vision, a heightened awareness which less insightful human beings cannot experience.

In the two scenes from tragic operas studied here, Kát'a Kabanová and Wozzeck interact with a numinous Nature whose presence cannot be seen (or heard) by the other characters present – Kát'a's lover Boris and Wozzeck's fellow-soldier Andres. But in both cases the deeper vision of these two hypersensitive people leads them ultimately to death. Lehnhoff's production uses highly effective visual images, and also violates the closing stage directions in the greater interest of illuminating Janáček's musical commentary; his staging successfully conveys Kát'a's relationship with the river and its voices. Similarly, in *Wozzeck* I.2, Chéreau has succeeded in conveying through physical action Wozzeck's highly emotional response to the terrifying sounds which he hears, and the apocalyptic visions which he sees – both of which are portrayed in Berg's score.

In *Die Zauberflöte*, *Parsifal* and *The Midsummer Marriage* the theme is a quest for enlightened insight; in all three operas this quest leads to a triumphant finale in which, it is hoped, the music and the visual experience will elevate the audience to share for a few moments the ecstasy which some special human beings achieve through, and as a result of, their earlier trials and sufferings. In *Die Zauberflöte*, Mozart achieves this very effectively – although many directors (Ingmar Bergman excepted) have been insensitive to important aspects of how to present the trials by fire and water, and in particular have failed to appreciate the leading role played by Pamina.

Wagner presents in *Parsifal* an ideology with a fear and rejection of the power of female sexuality, which is much more problematic than the visions of Mozart and Tippett; in their operas woman is given an equal place with man, when they are united in the closing scene. Wagner's viewpoint in this work was already one that was being challenged as the nineteenth century drew to a close, and it makes a straight presentation of *Parsifal* difficult for many members of a twenty-first century audience to accept. Lehnhoff's challenging staging makes a bold – and in my view almost wholly successful – attempt to retain what is valuable in Wagner's vision while critiquing its most contentious aspects, in particular by departing radically from the stage directions for the final scene.

In *The Midsummer Marriage* Tippett presents some difficulties to theatre directors, but triumphs by the splendour and insight of his music – which can, however, perhaps at the moment of transcendence be given an appropriate visual complement only in the medium of film.

PART THREE

Shaping the Opera

8

Characterization

In the last two chapters of this book we shall consider features of the interaction between words, music and stage action which are seen only in the unfolding of an entire opera in performance – characterization of an individual role (Chapter 8), and the creation of a sense of inevitability about the outcome of a tragic opera (Chapter 9). In this chapter we shall study the performances of singers in three title roles from three different periods, genres and styles of opera: Véronique Gens in Pierre Audi's production of Gluck's *Iphigénie en Aulide*, Rodney Gilfrey in Jürgen Flimm's production of Mozart's *Don Giovanni* (cf. **2.1**) and Teresa Stratas in Götz Friedrich's production of Strauss's *Salome* (cf. **1.1**).

No singer can truly inhabit a role on stage unless his or her costume and make-up are not only appropriate but also significant. Accordingly, this essential aspect of the *mise-en-scène* will be an important concern. But the main feature requiring analysis is the singer's performance itself. This must show:

(1) A dynamic, energetic concept of the character being portrayed.

(2) Integration – by which I mean that the director and the singer must have agreed upon a journey for the character which makes sense of the text and the music, and which harmonizes with the overall framework of the production. It must of course also harmonize with those concepts of *their* characters embodied in the performances of the other singers.

(3) A detailed and illuminating response to the text and the music in the singer's postures, gestures and expressions.

8.1 Véronique Gens as Iphigénie, directed by Pierre Audi

Pierre Audi's powerful productions in 2011 of the two Iphigénie operas, directed together on the same stage for De Neerlandse Opera and released on DVD in 2013, established new standards for the presentation to twenty-first century audiences of Gluck's masterpieces. Marc Minkowski conducted the music, working from the Urtext editions. His own ensemble, Les Musiciens du Louvre Grenoble, played on period instruments and performed at classical pitch, well below the modern A = 440. And Audi worked with exceptionally strong casts; in *Iphigénie en Aulide*, Véronique Gens in the title role was joined by Anne Sofie van Otter as Clytemnestre, Nicolas Testé as Agamemnon and Frédéric Antoun as Achille.

A perceptive contemporary critic had already realized at the second performance in 1774 that, in Gluck's revolutionary new style of dramatic opera, 'in contrast to some other operas in the same vein, it is the dances and divertissements which have become the wearisome part, because they are quite insignificant, they do not relate to the plot, and they express nothing'.[1] Audi rightly cut all but one of the dances and *divertissements* from *Iphigénie en Aulide*, kept the chorus behind the playing space until the final scene, and of course also omitted the dances and closing chorus which Gluck wrote to be performed after the end of the opera, and which are printed only as an appendix in the Bärenreiter Urtext edition. By taking away the scenes of spectacle which the eighteenth century expected, he was able to concentrate on bringing out in production for modern audiences the distinctive excellence of Gluck's two *Iphigénie* operas, which is the composer's powerful realization through music of the four principal characters' emotions.

Audi presented both tragedies in modern dress, immediately establishing that these episodes from ancient Greek myth dramatize situations and feelings to which audiences can relate today. And he set them both on a stark modern set. The playing space was a square arena, with entrances on each side down a steep set of steps from two platforms, built on scaffolding, which were used as additional playing areas. There was also a third entrance over a raised walkway running through the middle of the orchestra – which was placed behind and just below the playing area, partially visible to the audience; the chorus was located behind the instrumentalists.

Iphigénie endures some of the greatest emotional challenges of any operatic heroine. She comes to Aulis expecting to marry the man she loves, learns that Achille has apparently found a new object for his affections, is

---

[1] Trans. Howard 1995: 115. Gluck privately agreed with the critic; see his letter to Franz Kruthoffer, 31 July 1775.

gradually persuaded by him that his love for her is sincere, and is then told that the whole promise of marriage was a ruse by her father Agamemnon to lure her to the Greek camp. She has to be sacrificed so that the goddess Diane will allow his expedition to sail to Troy. After initial revulsion she accepts her fate – but Achille leads a frantic rescue attempt when she is in front of the altar. Iphigénie's life hangs in the balance; but, suddenly, Diane appears, pronounces that Iphigénie deserves to live, and blesses the happy couple. Not surprisingly, Iphigénie is emotionally bruised by all that has happened to her, and she sings with characteristic understatement:

Ah! Qu'il est doux,	Ah! It is sweet,
Mais qu'il est difficile	But it is difficult
De passer si subitement	To pass so suddenly
Du plus cruel torment	From the most cruel torment
A la félicité suprême!	To supreme happiness! (III.9. 82–9)

Performing the role of Gluck's Iphigénie requires an understanding of the imperatives which guided the conduct of a princess in seventeenth- and eighteenth-century France. In III.3 Achille, frustrated by his lover's determination to sacrifice herself, threatens to take her away from Aulis by force. Iphigénie stops him with these words:

Arrêtez!	Stop!
Quel est votre espoir?	What are you hoping for?
Avez-vu cru qu'Iphigénie	Do you think that Iphigénie
Pût oublier et sa gloire et sa devoir?	Could forget her honour and her duty?
Ils lui sont plus chers que la vie.	They are dearer to her than her life.

(III.3. 91–7)

Honour and duty are the primary values which motivate the heroine (and note the regal third person). Diane recognizes Iphigénie's superior qualities when she gives her reasons for no longer demanding the sacrifice:

Votre zèle des Dieux	Your sense of duty has turned aside
A fléchi la colère.	The anger of the gods.
Les vertus de la fille	The virtues of the daughter
Et les pleurs de la mère	And the tears of the mother
Ont trouvé grâce devant eux.	Have found favour with them. (III.9. 30ff.)

Véronique Gens based her characterization of Iphigénie both on this ethical foundation and on Gluck's music for the princess, which is intense but almost always restrained. Except for a few minutes when she is reacting to Arcas's news that she has been brought to Aulis to be killed, Gens'

Iphigénie is always dignified. She is far more than the 'virtuous and lovable' heroine[2] of the 1674 play by Racine, from which some scenes and words were adapted for the opera; she is a spirited young woman who is capable of great self-knowledge, as well as tender feeling.

The natural and easy option in costuming Iphigénie would be to clothe her in a simple white dress; this would emphasize her virgin purity, and contrast her feminine beauty strongly with the all-male military atmosphere of the Greek camp, in which Iphigénie, Clytemnestre and their female servants are the only women. And indeed this option has been pursued in many modern productions of Racine's play at the Comédie Francaise. Audi opposed it completely; both Clytemnestre's full-length, flowing dress with short train and Iphigénie's coat and dress, extending to just below her knees, are in patterns and colours – greens, browns, and touches of yellow – which are closely akin to camouflage. This suggests that the two women have already been assimilated into the military world where we find them; and they are isolated – for in this production they have no maidservants.[3]

Act I

A sinister dumb show in I.4 precedes Iphigénie's arrival. Immediately after the chorus has heralded the arrival of Clytemnestre and Iphigénie, a girl in dark clothes, with her head totally covered by a black hood, is brought in, hurled to the ground and surrounded by balaclava-wearing soldiers. The soldiers then torture this girl during Calchas's *air*, in which he warns Agamemnon of the need for even kings to bow down before the gods. This reference to the atrocities of Abu Ghraib (revealed in 2003) is the production's first evocation of the kinds of violence which are to be seen in our world today. It will not be the last.[4]

As the next chorus begins (I.5), both Clytemnestre and Iphigénie were, in librettist François Du Roullet's original scenario, supposed to arrive on a chariot surrounded by throngs of admirers; but in this production, to emphasize their isolation in this male encampment, Clytemnestre appears alone. She is reading the letter that Arcas has just given her, in which Agamemnon has written of Achille's supposed infidelity and advised her to take Iphigénie back to Mycenae. Iphigénie appears much later in the chorus (I.5.78) – also alone. She holds a large bouquet of white flowers, and radiates happiness as Clytemnestre embraces her affectionately. But

---

[2]Racine's own description; Preface to *Iphigénie*, trans. Cairncross 1963: 50.
[3]Their costumes are very similar in their colours to the greatcoat which Agamemnon wore for his first appearance in the opera (later he will change to the ceremonial blue uniform of a naval commander-in-chief).
[4]See on II.7 below.

Diane is hovering nearby, and Gens' Iphigénie changes her expression to look thoughtful even before Clytemnestre has sung a word.

Audi and Minkowski now omit one more reprise of the chorus, and then cut the remainder of scene 5, in which first Clytemnestre acknowledges the tributes and then leaves, and next Iphigénie accepts extended homage (but worries that she has not yet seen Achille). So in this production Iphigénie learns that her hope of marriage has apparently been dashed almost immediately after her arrival at Aulis.

Naturally, Iphigénie is unhappy when Clytemnestre tells her that she must leave without seeing Achille – but, in keeping with her character's royal status, Gens simply shakes her head to express her suffering. Clytemnestre explains the reason, and then launches into an *air* in which she tells Iphigénie to be courageous, 'stifle sighs / which are too unworthy of you' (I.6. 35–7), and to be righteously angry with Achille. Gens now shows how she sees the character of Iphigénie; she is still sufficiently in love with him to be unhappy with this second idea, and on the repeat she breaks away from her mother, rejecting her advice.

Iphigénie next sings an *air* of her own. The recitative begins with a passionate expression of disbelief, but in the *air* itself she expresses her betrayed feelings in a predominantly calm and self-reflexive way, which, however, gives way in the second, contrasting section to high passion:

Parjure! Tu m'oses trahir:	Perjurer! You dared to betray me:
Un autre objet a su te plaire:	Another has known how to please you:
Je te dois tout ma colère,	I must inflict all my anger on you,
Je forcerai mon coeur à te haïr.	I shall force my heart to hate you. (I.7 31–9)

When the opening music returns (40), now gentle, as she describes the feelings of her 'tender and sensitive heart' (I.7.10ff.), it is clear both from the music and from the singer's expression that Iphigénie has been deeply hurt.

Audi now has the brilliant idea of having Achille enter early for the next scene, during the reprise of Iphigénie's angry words (quoted above) which concludes this *air*. He does not of course know why she feels like this, but he receives the full brunt of her wrath; Gens points at Achille, grabs him by the lapels of his coat, then turns violently and decisively away from him and thrusts her hands in her pockets, ignoring him. He defends himself passionately, and seizes her from behind, on 'Oh, it is too much' (I.8. 36). Now, Gens makes us realize that they have a real bond between them. The text of Iphigénie's next *air* uses the aloof third person ('Iphigénie has let you know too much / For her honour [*gloire*] and for her happiness…' [44–9]); but in this production she turns slowly and gently to face Achille close up; and during the repeat she holds out her hands, inviting him to embrace her – which he does. But Gens conveys that Iphigénie is still angry with him; when he tries to kiss her at the end of the *air*, she breaks away, and she avoids facing him during his recitative, rejecting the tentative hand that he puts on hers just before his *air* in reply begins. This *air* is a passionate appeal to her, and when he accuses her of cruelty and of having a heart without feelings (82–5) she closes her eyes, showing that he has moved her.

And now Gens shows how Achille successfully wins back his beloved. As he sings of how his constant passion for her has turned to dreadful torment because of her suspicions (repeated twice for emphasis, 105–15), she turns anxiously to look at him; and on the repeat of 'if you loved me as much as I love you' (123–6) she approaches him from behind, and leans her head gently on his shoulder. So, naturally, he turns and holds her for the last two lines of the *air*. But Gens anticipates in her reactions what comes next, Iphigénie's admission of her *faiblesse* (weakness); she shakes her head and walks away from him.

✒ 8 1A Iphigénie and Achille I

All this finely studied interplay establishes their relationship as real before the duo, which closes the Act. It is notable for its *calm* intensity; Gluck rejects the excessive ornamentation which depicted passion in the *opera seria* before him, and he does not anticipate the equally excessive but different musical means used in love duets by some of the Romantics after him. In Audi's production the two characters are initially apart from each other, because of Iphigénie's feeling of unworthiness at the end of Achille's *air*. But after Achille's first line of text in the duo, 'Never doubt my passion' (154–6), Iphigénie's words, the music and Gens' expression show that she is starting to be convinced. Then the *allegro* begins at 188 with the couple singing the same text in harmony – and continues with that musical symbol of their complete unity sounding out over an ever more excited orchestral accompaniment.

In Audi's production, the change of tempo and mood at 188 is marked by the couple's standing close together, facing each other as they sing in harmony. However, the exultant fast music stops twice, and both times the lovers sing the word *Hymen!* slowly and gravely (197–200 and 226–9). On stage, Iphigénie and Achille exchange rings during these solemn, tender moments. Then the final words of the duo express their anticipation of marriage in ecstatic music (230ff.), and the couple clasp hands passionately. The production works together with the text and music to show the depth of the union between these lovers, which will make it a hard task for anyone, goddess or human, to separate them.

Act II

The first half of this Act continues the focus on the relationship between Iphigénie and Achille. In the opening scene, a female chorus reassures

Iphigénie that she will marry her beloved – but Véronique Gens, with Achille now absent, shows that her character has returned to a pensive mood, by looking first at her engagement ring and then at Clytemnestre. Her recitative tells us why she is disturbed: Achille is angry that Agamemnon has alleged that he scorned her love and broke his word. Iphigénie fears (rightly) that he will confront Agamemnon, and in the following *air* she tells her mother how her heart is tormented by the violence of its conflicting moods – hope and fear. Naturally, Gens shows the heroine to be agitated in this passage, as both text and music demand; she walks around, goes away from Clytemnestre, and, from the rear of the stage, sings her prayer for Love to soften the pride of Agamemnon and the anger of Achille, fingering her ring as the symbol of the marriage which the emotions of these two men now threaten.

Clytemnestre reassures her daughter, and Achille returns, presenting to Iphigénie his closest friend, Patrocle. After that, his Thessalians sing in celebration of her as their new Queen. But during all of this Gens depicts Iphigénie as serious and unable to get rid of her worries. She looks anxious, rather than pleased with this celebration of her impending marriage; she fidgets nervously with her bouquet of flowers, and only smiles at the very end of the chorus, at Achille – and then at Agamemnon as he approaches.

For, here, Audi makes an innovation. Both Euripides and Racine, in their treatments of the myth, included a meeting between Iphigénie and Agamemnon – a scene in which she greets him joyfully, and he replies hesitantly and with words of double meaning, a reaction which the audience refers to the imminent sacrifice but which the innocent Iphigénie does not understand. Du Roullet did not include such a scene in his libretto. Audi cut almost all the *divertissements* celebrating the impending marriage; but he retained the music of one of the dances, a *chaconne*. And he used this music to stage an expressive dumb show, in which Agamemnon encounters his daughter for the only time in the opera before the finale. The king makes a solemn entrance, and Achille and Iphigénie greet him together. Agamemnon confronts Achille coldly, then receives a low bow from Clytemnestre, embraces Iphigénie, and leaves solemnly. Gens' Iphigénie remains worried, even when her father embraces her; and she exchanges a long look with Agamemnon when he looks back, on his way out through the long, narrow platform that leads to the rear of the theatre.[5] Her voice then joins those of Clytemnestre, Achille and Patrocle in a quartet, with chorus invoking Hymenée to celebrate the marriage of 'the most happy spouses, the most tender lovers' (II.3. 760–7), but Iphigénie remains physically aloof throughout the number, at least two metres apart from her

---

[5]Iphigénie had entered with a bouquet of flowers. Agamemnon takes them from her hands before leaving, and exits holding them upside down – a potent symbol that he does not intend the wedding to happen.

fiancé, until he finally goes to her and takes her hands for his recitative, in which he proposes to take her at once to the altar.

All this is designed to show that Iphigénie has presentiments, which are now fulfilled in the most shocking way; Arcas joins them, sings that he can keep silent no more, and reveals why Agamemnon has brought his daughter to Aulis. Gens and Audi are aware that Iphigénie must receive even this horrific revelation in a way that is appropriate to her character. When Arcas reveals the truth, she breaks away from Achille, shakes her head in disbelief, and collapses on the stairs, her head in her arms. She cries, and Achille caresses her from behind as Clytemnestre begins a passionate *air* in which she calls on Achille to defend her daughter. During this *air* Iphigénie gradually sits up, looking anguished, and then goes to her mother for support, dropping her head on Clytemnestre's shoulder. Subsequently she breaks away and collapses again, hiding her face by leaning her head down close to one of the stair-rails. But then comes an extraordinary action, which demonstrates the strength of Iphigénie's character, as Gens and Audi perceive it. She realizes that her mother, who is now kneeling on the floor, needs support even more than she herself does; so she goes to Clytemnestre, and at the return of the heart-rending oboe solo of the *air* she and Achille raise Clytemnestre to her feet, one from each side, so that she can recover her dignity; the mother leans on her daughter's shoulder for support as the *air* ends.

Achille promises to confront Agamemnon, but the trio that follows creates a gulf between Iphigénie and her mother and fiancé. She reminds them that Agamemnon is still a father whom she loves, while Clytemnestre calls him a cruel monster and Achille a perfidious assassin. On stage, Gens' Iphigénie shows great sincerity and concern as she tries to dissuade them; but when the trio becomes a prayer to the gods, with the sentiments of the three principals still divided, Iphigénie is at first isolated in a spotlight, while the other two circle round her; then she appeals to each of them in turn, but they remain facing away from her. All of this motivates what Iphigénie does at the end of the scene. Achille approaches his fiancée from behind (she is now kneeling in a corner for her final prayer), and puts his arms round her; but she fights off this attempt at a caress, and leaves.

That is, in the original scenario, the end of Iphigénie's part in Act II; but right from the outset Audi has introduced on the two raised platforms either side of the stage, in dumb show, the people who are invoked by the characters singing below. This is dramatically effective, as it gives the singer a person above, to whom to play his or her invocation. The first instance was Diane's silent and cruelly indifferent presence during I.1, where Agamemnon defied the goddess in his opening *air*; and in the last scene of Act II Audi reprises this tactic to startling effect. In a tortured monologue, Agamemnon is torn between moments in which he determines to obey the gods and longer sections in which he imagines the full horror of slaughtering his own daughter. The extremely dramatic recitative finally blossoms into an *air*, in which he decides to attempt to save Iphigénie, and addresses her directly ('Oh you, most loveable of beings / cherished for so many virtues / pardon your guilty father...' [II.7. 99ff.]). At this point in Audi's production, Iphigénie appears above him in a gleaming silvery-gold dress, veiled and with a black cross on her forehead – and with wired plastic explosives encircling her waist. This powerful image is a hideous parody of the royal bride she thought she was going to be; it tells us that she has been prepared for sacrifice.[6] The apparition remains calm and emotionless throughout Agamemnon's appeal to her, and Iphigénie remains there, on the platform at the top of the stairs, ready to begin her dialogue with Arcas at the start of Act III.[7]

Act III

Iphigénie discards the veil and descends almost ritualistically, with her hands out and up, to signal that she opposes Arcas's attempt to stop her resolve to yield to the demands of the chorus of Greek soldiers – who are now heard calling for her death (III.1. 14–17). She sends Arcas (in the original scenario, her serving women) to help Clytemnestre, prevent her mother from seeing her last moments, to 'and allow me to assuage / the anger of the gods'. Gens delivers this, and the closing line 'I shall die, I obey' (royal 'we' in the original French), with great firmness (III.2. 5–8).

Achille arrives, intent on taking her away with him. Gens' Iphigénie resists him physically several times – pushing him away with her hands, shaking her head when he urges her to 'come safely, guarded by Achille' (III.3. 5–7), and after that holding up her hands in refusal and pushing him away again – twice. She then delivers a beautiful *air*.

✐ 8 1B Iphigénie and Achille II

Gens begins this *air* by turning gradually away from a posture with a hand gently extended to reject Achille, to face the audience in a position with arms down, a little away from her body and with the lower arms extended forwards (but with hands almost vertical, not palm out). This posture finely expresses her submission to 'the supreme law of my destiny' (III.3. 26–30). Later, as she sings that she will love Achille until the moment of her death, he goes to her and she takes his hands in hers. This *air* and the following

---

[6]Some have misconstrued it; Pierre Audi had to reject the suggestion from the interviewer that she is a terrorist, at six minutes into the Special Feature on the DVD. Iphigénie is not a suicide bomber (they *conceal* their explosives beneath their outer clothes), but a victim destined to die; and we will discover in the next scene that this is now by her own choice. That is why she wears the explosives.

[7]There are no intervals between Acts in Audi's productions of the two Iphigénie operas.

one, in which she bids farewell to him, are central to the understanding of Iphigénie's character; and Gens' use of gesture is outstanding throughout the scene. In particular, her movements as she slowly disentangles from her embrace with Achille on the final 'Adieu' of the second *air*, and gently pushes him away, are very movingly executed.

The remainder of this scene, in which Achille expresses his determination to try to save Iphigénie at the altar, naturally evokes from Gens first anguish and then angry rejection of his attitude; and the scene with Clytemnestre that follows is played closely and intimately. Iphigénie begs her mother to be calm, and even *not* (in French not just *pas* but *point*) to be angry with Agamemnon – a request which Clytemnestre will reject absolutely, as all who know the myth will be aware. And at the end of the scene, Iphigénie delivers an Enlightenment protest against the cruelty of the gods:

Il est temps d'obéir aux Dieux:	It is time to obey the gods:
Ah! Faisons les du moins	Let us at least make them
Rougir de leur ouvrage...	Blush for what they are doing... (III.5. 75–9)

Gens clasps von Otter's hands passionately in hers as she delivers these lines.

Iphigénie is supposed to leave the stage before Clytemnestre's great *air* of rage. And then, as that *air* ends, the original scenario envisaged its first and only change of scene – to the altar by the shore, where Iphigénie kneels ready to be sacrificed. But Audi did not want to make a scene change, and he used the modern theatrical convention that simultaneous events can be dramatized in different parts of the same playing area. Iphigénie does not leave, and while Clytemnestre sings her *air* on the stairs, envisaging the sacrifice of her daughter in gory detail, armed soldiers surround Iphigénie in the main playing area, blindfold her and then kneel in a circle around her. We see this tableau throughout the furious second part of the *air*, in which Clytemnestre invokes Jupiter to send his thunderbolts and the sun to go back in his course. And Audi segues straight from this into the final scenes. The crisis is finely staged: a bloodstained Achille fights his way to Iphigénie and tears off her blindfold, Clytemnestre embraces her daughter, Achille defends the two women fiercely – and suddenly Calchas restrains him with the words 'the goddess herself is coming / to tell us her desires' (III.9. 2–24).

✎ 8 1C Aulide Finale

Iphigénie kneels as Diane approaches her, and is joined by Achille; as the goddess blesses their marriage, Iphigénie looks at him, shocked; and after Diane has left, Iphigénie is far away from Agamemnon as they sing 'Oh my daughter!' / 'Oh my father!' (III.9. 73–4). During the key passage quoted near the start of this analysis, in which Iphigénie expresses her mixed emotions after the goddess has saved her, Gens endows the words with passionate intensity; and this prepares (although no one in the audience could guess it yet) for the ending that is to come. For indeed Iphigénie's heart cannot cope with the sudden transition from imminent death to total felicity. Gens' Iphigénie is flanked by her fiancé and her mother, but does not look at them. She takes off the bomb-dress, and now wears only a white knee-length shift – which expresses visually the vulnerability that she is now feeling. Achille picks up the bomb-dress, stays kneeling, and holds it closely as if it were Iphigénie while Iphigénie herself slowly retreats backwards, away from them all towards the rear of the stage. As the voices of Iphigénie and Achille lead off the music for the other soloists in the second stanza of the final ensemble, 'The Gods have taken pity on our sighs...' (135ff.), Iphigénie raises her hands high in a ritual acknowledgement of the supreme powers (Diane remains visible in the background, watching the scene from above), and then starts to leave upstage on the narrow walkway dividing the orchestra. Iphigénie does this as the chorus invades the main playing space, and the other principals exeunt (Clytemnestre and Agamemnon slowly ascending opposite sets of stairs, Achille invisibly); and while the final chorus whips up a storm of celebration of the marriage in a glorious C major, our last sight in the production is of Iphigénie walking along a gallery far from them – slowly, alone, and with a completely blank expression. The lights fade on the chorus first, leaving her alone in a spotlight, which dims only when the music ends.

In this way, Audi deliberately undermines the 'happy ending' with which the music and text of the opera conclude, in accordance with eighteenth-century expectations. It is literally too good to be true – for the newlywed Achille and Iphigénie would have had at most one night's enjoyment of each other before the Greeks set sail for Troy, and Achille was to die there in the ninth year of the war without ever seeing his wife again.[8] More importantly – for many in the audience will not think about the future as the performance ends – it assumes that Iphigénie has survived the action of the opera with her heart and mind unscathed. That conclusion is at odds with the emotional suffering which in Gens' performance the character has visibly undergone, through this traumatic sequence of events. Pierre Audi and Véronique Gens suggest that it is not merely 'difficult' but actually impossible for Iphigénie to move 'From the most cruel torment / To supreme happiness' (84–90).

---

[8]This marriage between Achille and Iphigénie, which is also foreshadowed at the end of Racine's play, diverges completely from the original Greek myth, in which Artemis (Diane) saved Iphigenia at the last moment and whisked her away to Tauria, leaving a hind for the Greeks to sacrifice instead. In Euripides' original play, although Achilles admires Iphigenia's heroism when she offers herself willingly to be sacrificed for the glory of Greece, he is not in love with her.

Discussion questions

- Discuss the interaction between stylized and realistic gestures in Véronique Gens' performance as Iphigénie.
- Discuss Audi's rejection of the original *lieto fine*. To what extent are Iphigénie's actions in the final scene in this production a logical development from Gens' interpretation of the part earlier in the opera?

8.2 Rodney Gilfrey as Don Giovanni, directed by Jürgen Flimm.

Don Giovanni is an enigma, and accordingly one of the most difficult title roles in the standard repertory. He does not develop as a character; and he presents to every other character except Leporello the image which he wants them to see and the words which he wants them to hear – always as if sincere. His solo performances are purely action-pieces (numbers 12, 17 and 18) – unlike the arias of the *seria* characters (Donna Anna, Donna Elvira and Don Ottavio), who have somehow found themselves enmeshed in this *dramma giocoso*; their solo numbers explore their characters' feelings in depth. Bernard Williams raises the questions posed by the title figure:

> What are we to make of Giovanni? The opera is named after him, it is about him, and it is he who holds together a set of scenes in other ways rather disconnected. He is in a deep way the life of the opera, yet the peculiarity is that such character as he has is not really as grand as that implies: he expresses more than he is. He seems to have no depth adequate to the work in which he plays the central role. He has, in a sense, a character – to a considerable extent a bad one. But we are not given any deep insight into what he really is, or what drives him on. We could not have been: it is not that there is something hidden in his soul. It is notable that he has no self-reflective aria – he never sings about himself, as Mozart's other central characters do. We have no sense of what he is like when he is by himself. He is presented always in action – the action, notoriously, of a seducer.[9]

In the same vein, Julian Rushton has authoritatively claimed that Mozart's music for Giovanni makes his reality, in comparison with the other

---

[9] Williams 1981: 82.

characters, 'doubtful' with its 'high-spirited heartlessness and *buffo* style'.[10]

It is not altogether true that we are given no 'deep insight' into what drives Giovanni. He does not have a Jago-like *Credo* (**2.3**) – it is hard to imagine either Da Ponte writing, or Mozart composing, such a piece in this opera[11] – but there is an illuminating exchange with Leporello at the start of Act II:

DON GIOVANNI

Lasciar le donne? Pazzo!	I give up women? Madman!
Lasciar le donne? Sai ch'elle per me	I give up women? You know that for me
Son necessarie piu del pan che mangio	They are more necessary than the bread that I eat
Piu dell'air che spiro!	And the air that I breathe!

LEPORELLO

E avete core	And you have the heart
D'ingannarle poi tutte?	To be unfaithful to them all?

DON GIOVANNI

È tutto amore:	It's all love:
Chi a una sola è fedele	He who is faithful to one alone
Verso l'altre è crudele.	Is cruel to the others.
Io, che in me sento	I, who feel in myself
Si esteso sentimento,	Such wide-ranging feelings,
Vo bene a tutte quante.	Wish all of them well.
Le donne, poi che calcolar non sanno,	Women, because they can't understand this,
Il mio buon natural chiamano inganno.	Call my good nature cheating.

(II.1, recit. after no.14, 12–25)

In the same spirit, later in the Act he celebrates women and good wine as 'the glories of humanity' (II.14, no. 24, 303–47). All of this is fully congruent with Leporello's statement at the end of the Catalogue Aria that Don Giovanni will go after any female: 'If she's wearing a skirt, you know what he will do' (I.5, no. 4, 143–70).

Don Giovanni suffers many setbacks during the action – for Da Ponte's libretto shows the great seducer in decline, harassed by those whom he has wronged, and thwarted by Elvira, before he consummates the one seduction which he manages successfully, that of Zerlina (**3.1**); but there is no journey over the course of the opera, since he remains virtually unchanged despite his misfortunes. Only at the final climax, when Giovanni unravels in the presence

---

[10]Rushton 1981: 104. Similarly Kerman (1956: 121) criticized what he called the 'blankness' of Giovanni's characterization, which he claimed is due to the character's alleged 'lack of involvement'.

[11]'The grand aria sought by Bassi would have marred all, rendering the character more solid, but less demonic, more conventional …', Rushton 1981: 109.

of the 'stone guest', is his defiant stance towards both his human and his supernatural pursuers undermined. And in Gilfrey's performance there is a quite shocking, sudden change in Giovanni's demeanour from heroic defiance to extreme terror at the moment, after his last refusal to repent, when the statue pronounces that his time has come (II. 15 no. 24, 549).

Gilfrey and Flimm find enough depth in Don Giovanni's character to create a convincing stage interpretation. In an interview, Rodney Gilfrey has traced Giovanni's obsession back to his boyhood. Gilfrey imagines his character as 'a bad boy not raised well', on whom his parents set no limits, and to whom they gave too many privileges. For Gilfrey, Giovanni is a sex addict, engaged in a constant quest for the ultimate high – hence his defiance of the Commendatore's statue at the climax of the opera, which the singer sees as manifesting a death wish (or at least the thrill of coming close to death, analogous to that sought out by sky-divers). Because of his pride, Giovanni refuses to repent.[12] Camus understood this aspect of the character well:

> Don Juan would find it natural that he should be punished. It is the rule of the game. And it is exactly a mark of his generosity, to have entirely accepted the rule of the game. But he knows that he is right, and that there can be no question of punishment. An inevitable end is not the same thing as a penalty.[13]

(1) This singer and his director start from the concept of Giovanni as over-privileged. Florence von Gerkan's expensive costumes – especially the full-length leather coat and feathered hat which Giovanni wears in many scenes – and Gilfrey's long hair tied up in a pigtail both signal that he lives to the full the life of an aristocrat. (His hair remains this way until the last scene, where he lets his hair down, both literally and metaphorically, as he feasts and drinks; the unbound hair also goes well with his terror just before he is dragged into hell). Don Giovanni's appearance contrasts sharply with the only other noble male in the cast; Roberto Saccà as Don Ottavio is much more plainly costumed. And Gilfrey inhabits these costumes in a truly aristocratic manner, which is manifested in many details of the performance – as for example when the Commendatore challenges him to a duel, and Gilfrey makes a disdainful gesture of refusal. This Don is also handsome – and he knows it; he therefore possesses a very winning smile, which he can turn on at once to begin his seduction of any woman.[14] He also makes sure

---

[12] These comments by Gilfrey are sourced from the interview with him in the Special Feature on disc 2 of the DVD set.

[13] Quoted from *Le Mythe de Sisyphe* at Williams 1981: 88.

[14] While Leporello sings the Catalogue aria in this production, Don Giovanni is seen upstage, happily accosting several young women who pass by – in most cases putting an arm round their waists and receiving warm smiles in response.

that he is always well turned out; for example, towards the end of Elvira's entry-aria (I.5 no. 3, 80ff.), he gets Leporello to adjust his clothes ready for his attempt to make up to her.

(2a) Gilfrey's characterization contains a strong element of cruelty; the singer uses the pulled-back hair, his makeup and his expressions to make his Giovanni's face look far more severe and cruel than his own appearance in real life. And the cruelty is manifested many times in the performance. For example, when he has stabbed the Commendatore, he callously lets go of the dying man, who then falls to the ground. There is also a fundamental petulance (the spoilt child again), which often becomes a threat of violence against Leporello. This is called for by the text, but emphasized by this production. Gilfrey plays these moments as if they have always been an everyday occurrence; whenever Leporello disagrees with him, or demurs from doing something which Giovanni has ordered, Gilfrey makes his threats quite unperturbed, with a calm menace which is much more sinister than if his character showed agitation when opposed by his servant.

(2b) But there is also physical violence. In the opening scene we actually see him blindfold Anna from behind so that she cannot identify him, pin her down and then mount her (she is wearing a nightdress) – a violent and almost successful attempted rape. When Leporello calls him a scoundrel for trying to rape a daughter, and then killing her father, Gilfrey's Giovanni strikes him – but when Leporello immediately agrees to be silent, this Giovanni (almost schizophrenically) kisses him on the cheek, delighted to have got his servant onside again (I.2, 6–13). Then in II.2 he forces Leporello at gunpoint to impersonate him and make up to Donna Elvira on his behalf – and later in the Act (II.11, no. 22, 28–31), when he threatens to kill Leporello if he does not invite the statue to dinner, Gilfrey pulls out a knife to reinforce the threat. These sudden oscillations of mood and outbreaks of violence add to the characterization of Giovanni as a dangerous man, which is essential as a follow-up to his impulsive murder of the Commendatore.

(3) The key element of Gilfrey's Giovanni, when interacting with characters apart from Leporello, is that he appears to be absolutely sincere in everything that he sings, even though most of Giovanni's words – especially (but not only) to women – are utterly false. Gilfrey can show this feigned sincerity even when silent; a fine example comes just after he has driven off Masetto and has Zerlina to himself, immediately before the start of the recitative which precedes no. 7.[15] In Flimm's production, Zerlina at this point is holding one end of the long tablecloth which she is about to fold up – and Giovanni is holding the other end, with the clear intention of bringing it towards her. For a few long moments, however, he simply stands, at a distance, but linked to her by the tablecloth, and looks into her

---

[15] See the beginning of ✏ 4 1 Don G seduces Zerlina.

eyes – with such longing that the eyes of Liliana Nikiteanu's Zerlina can do nothing but return the gaze; she is like a deer caught in headlights. Only then does he move towards her and begin the process of seduction, which was analysed at 3.1.

(4) When caught in tight corners – as he often is during the course of this opera – Gilfrey's Giovanni retains his cool. The best example of this is the quartet, no. 9 in I.8, in which he endeavours to persuade the increasingly skeptical Donna Anna and Don Ottavio that Donna Elvira is demented and that her accusations against him are false. He is in a tight spot, and he is aware of that, but at no point does he show agitation – even though Anna and Ottavio sing that the colour of Giovanni's face has changed (I.8, no. 9, 76–8). This Don Giovanni shows no fear even in the Act I Finale, where the disguised Don Ottavio has drawn a pistol on him, and then removes his mask simultaneously with Donna Anna and Elvira. When they denounce him, Giovanni sings that he does not know what to do – 'though I do not lack courage' (I.20; no. 13, 615–17). Gilfrey puts his hands to his head under the pressure, then collapses onto a step. But in the closing bars, as his victims threaten him with the wrath of heaven, he defies them, before escaping while the curtain falls. He has fully recovered his composure when we next see him, at the start of Act II, and his bravado is so great that at the end of the scene in the graveyard he salutes the statue defiantly before leaving. Then, when the statue comes to dinner, this Giovanni's defiance remains heroic right up until his last moments. His trembling, then, as he feels that devils are assaulting him, is, indeed, as he sings, an 'insolito' feeling – one that he has not previously experienced.

This is a commanding performance. Gilfrey fleshes out and develops the character of Don Giovanni in the four ways listed, and exemplified, above. Sparks fly in his interactions both with Lasló Polgar's excellent Leporello and with the three principal women (Nikiteanu is joined in the cast by Isabel Rey as Donna Anna and Cecilia Bartoli as Donna Elvira, all three of them highly expressive actresses as well as fine singers); and Gilfrey's performance under Flimm's direction shows how the character of Don Giovanni, which at first sight is problematic, can be developed in perfor-mance into a convincing onstage personality.

Discussion question

Does Rodney Gilfrey under Flimm's direction make Don Giovanni into a consistent and convincing character?

8.3 Teresa Stratas as Salome, directed by Götz Friedrich.

First Salome is transformed from an innocent virgin girl into a young woman whose sexuality has been totally aroused; then she becomes a coldly intense seeker of revenge; finally, when she has forced Herodes to grant her the head of Jochanaan, she plumbs previously unimaginable depths as a terrifying embodiment of unrestrained female desire. The opera accordingly divides, from the point of view of the title character's journey, into three parts: the first from her entrance to the orchestral *tutti* after Jochanaan's descent into the cistern; then through the first part of scene 4 to the moment, after the Dance of the Seven Veils, when Herodes yields to her demand for the head of Jochanaan; finally, from Salome's fearful tension while she waits for the executioner to bring her the head, through to the glorious triumph of her final bars, 'I have kissed your mouth, Jochanaan', before Herodes in horror and disgust cries out 'Kill that woman',[16] and his soldiers execute Salome by crushing her under their shields.

It is essential that the costume designer should provide the singer with a visual impact which illuminates the course of Salome's journey. And the costumes by Jan Skalický for Götz Friedrich's production are exemplary. He takes his initial inspiration from the point where Wilde and Strauss begin – with the interweaving between Salome, the moon and death, in the opening exchanges between Narraboth and the Page:

NARRABOTH
Wie schön ist die Prinzessin Salome
heute Nacht!

How beautiful is the Princess
Salome tonight!

PAGE
Sieh' die Mondscheibe, wie sie seltsam
aussieht. Wie ein Frau, die aufsteigt aus
dem Grab.

See the disc of the moon, how strangely
she rises. Like a woman, who rises from
the grave.

NARRABOTH
Sie ist sehr seltsam. Wie eine kleine Prinzessin,
deren Füsse weisse Tauben sind.
Man könnte meinen, sie tanzt.

She is very strange. Like a little Princess,
whose feet are white doves.
You could think she is dancing.

PAGE
Wie eine Frau die tot ist.
Sie gleitet langsam dahin.

Like a woman who is dead.
She glides slowly up there. (0–3)

---

[16] 'Man töte dieses Weib!' This was badly mistranslated by Tom Hammond for ENO as 'Go, crush that girl to death!' (John 1988: 54). The whole point of Wilde's last line ('Tuez cette femme!') is that Salome is no longer a girl but a woman. (If you are a connoisseur of old translations, Alfred Kalisch's contribution to the vocal score is priceless: 'Go, kill at once that wench!')

Strauss underlays these lines with a tapestry of intricate, delicately orchestrated chromatics (chromaticism will be characteristic of Salome's accompaniment later in the opera); and he binds the moon to Salome even more securely than does Wilde's text, by introducing to depict it a seductive motif which will become one of her major themes:

8.3.1 (0.1-3)

So both text and music align Salome with the moon. In this production, so does her costume. Until Salome leaves the stage to prepare for the Dance of the Seven Veils, Stratas wears a jewelled silver headpiece under which all her hair is concealed; and her full-length dress is also silver. She looks both virginal and moonlike – but the dress indicates her as yet unawakened sexuality. Her shoulders are entirely bare, and the dress is secured only by two bejewelled silver shoulder-straps. It is cut low over her cleavage, and the bejewelled fastening at the front of her silver belt dips low over her womb, so as to invite the male gaze down towards her pubic region. This costume achieves three things: it establishes that Salome is indeed a teenage virgin; at the same time it hints clearly at her potential sexual power, and so explains why both Narraboth and Herodes are besotted by her beauty this evening; its colour also augments the text and music by aligning her with the pale, silver moon, and with death.[17]

Salome changes out of this costume to perform the Dance of the Seven Veils, which in this production (although not in all others!) is indeed danced with seven veils, which Salome successively discards. After the first two veils have been removed, viewers can see through the diaphanous veils that are still shielding Stratas's face that she has lustrous black hair, which has been pinned up in preparation for the dance; and later on in the dance, after she has discarded the veils which had covered her face and head, she removes the two large pins, so she can kneel down in front of Herodes and gyrate, swishing her hair erotically to excite his lust. Then, after the brief moment of nudity which concludes the dance, Salome's maidservants throw a grey

---

[17] When Narraboth looks into the banqueting hall to stare at Salome, he comments on how pale she is (9.1–5), and her deathlike aspect is observed later by Herodes ('your daughter is sick to death. Never have I seen her so pale', 170.3–171.2). Stratas's makeup supports this.

robe round her. This, with nothing underneath it, will be her costume for the remainder of the opera.

With her long black hair finally let down, and clad only in a robe, Stratas's Salome is then visually ready to become the *femme fatale* of the closing monologue. Her appearance now shows that the dance has fully released her sexuality, and this greatly assists Stratas in playing both the scene in which she forces Herodes to give her the head of the prophet, and the extraordinary monologue of frustrated love which forms the last stage of her character's journey.

(1) Scenes 2 and 3

When Strauss played the score of *Salome* to his father, the latter commented: 'Oh God, what nervous music. It is exactly as if one had one's trousers full of Maybugs'. Strauss, when recording this comment in *Recollections and Reflections*, remarked that 'he was not entirely wrong'.[18] The score does indeed contain very many passages of highly-strung, nervous music; these begin with Salome's entry, which is instructed to be *excited*, and continue throughout the next two scenes, in which a fluid orchestral and vocal chromaticism is almost constantly associated with her part – and opposed to the large-scale, foursquare diatonic phrases associated with Jochanaan. Stratas is therefore right to be physically active, changing her moods and postures vibrantly and rapidly from the moment of her first entrance; she runs out of the hall, trailing behind her a light silver off-the-shoulder wrap (which she later discards). Then she shows Salome's budding sensuality by caressing herself as she enjoys the sweetness of the air outside, and raises her hands up towards the moon (which looks just like her headpiece) as she enjoys its beauty and describes it as 'a virgin, who is forever pure'. In these ways the very first minutes after her appearance establish both her energy and her soon-to-be-unleashed sensuality.

Salome is also an imperious Princess. So, when she learns that Herodes has forbidden any contact with the prophet, Stratas rises to her full height, angry and obstinate, and when directed to become *still more passionate* she rushes towards the unfortunate Soldier who is trying to resist her, and brushes him aside. She does not simply *look down* into the cistern as the orchestral music descends to the depths, but rushes over to it and collapses right onto the bars of the lid, peering into the blackness below. Then she rises suddenly and pushes past the Soldiers, who are refusing to disobey their orders, as her eyes look for, and light on, Wiesław Ochman's Narraboth. He is of course no match for Salome when she turns the full force of her seductiveness onto him; Stratas does this first by fully obeying

---

[18] 1974: 152.

the stage direction by *going up to Narraboth and speaking softly and excitedly*, then by kneeling beside him and looking up into his eyes as she keeps asking him to look at her. She circles round Narraboth, who is trying to avert his gaze, but is finally defeated when she stands facing him and looks him straight in the eyes.

When she has achieved her success, Salome cries out in triumph, and Stratas goes for a few moments to lean against one of the walls of the courtyard, trembling with anticipation. But once the cistern is opened, Stratas crawls towards it on the ground, and kneels looking down over the edge, breathing heavily – an intense physicalization of her excited anticipation, of a kind which not many singers in the role attempt; it is premonitory of much more to come in Stratas's interpretation. And when Jochanaan appears, she does not just *step slowly back* but runs away in horror to take refuge beside the courtyard wall. As played by Bernd Weikl, Jochanaan is her polar opposite; a large-framed, shaggy-haired, fully bearded male who stands before her barefooted and in a ragged garment made of animal skins, and declaims to extremely powerful diatonic music. Salome recovers from her initial fear of him only after several minutes, but then she starts to explore in words the wonder of the first man to whom she has ever been attracted ('How thin he looks! He is like a statue carved out of ivory ...' [79]); then she suddenly goes nearer to Jochanaan.

Salome proudly tells him her name, and he denounces her mother. At first Stratas shows that Salome is furious, but then, in a turning point of the opera, Salome changes her mood completely, ignores Jochanaan's denunciation and begs him: 'Say more ... your voice is like music in my ears' (85.2–8). At this point Stratas looks right up into her Jochanaan's face, very close to him. When he tells her fiercely to leave him she looks genuinely puzzled. She approaches him, he rebuffs her again and she runs away; but then she turns, and stretches her arms straight out as she calls out his name, long and languorously (91).

This outburst initiates the three mini-arias directed to parts of Jochanaan: his body, his hair and his mouth. In this production, Stratas's Salome actually touches his skin and his hair, at the end of each of the first two mini-arias respectively. Each of them concludes when Jochanaan draws angrily away, and Salome furiously rejects that which had previously attracted her. Stratas plays both of these sections with physicalized anger; after Jochanaan's first rejection of her she falls to the floor, then rises gradually to her feet again, runs around bent forward, hands quivering, then clenches and shakes her hands in rage before turning to praise his hair. But as she describes his hair, she kneels again and extends a hand to him in entreaty. This of course has no effect, so, when Jochanaan once more rejects her, Stratas's Salome bends forward, shakes her fists again and clenches her teeth, before singing *with the utmost passion* her hymn to his mouth – in which, for virtually the first time since her appearance, Stratas conveys Salome's intense emotions primarily with her voice. The decision not to use the body here is a deliberate *recul pour mieux sauter* before the final outburst, which she will make when he rejects this last appeal. She ends in tears, pitiful, as she entreats 'Let me kiss your mouth' (121.6–122.5). At this point she brings her lips very close to his, but does not kiss them, since Jochanaan – for the first time quietly – sings to her the word 'Never!'

Salome ignores the suicide of Narraboth, repeating her last demand ('Let me kiss your mouth, Jochanaan!') again and again (122.10ff.). Stratas first extends her outstretched hands in an appeal to Jochanaan, then kneels and crawls across the stone flags towards him, and she is thrashing around on the floor at his feet in abject misery when Jochanaan denounces her as the daughter of a harlot. Stratas enacts more of Salome's acute suffering as Jochanaan counsels her to seek out Jesus; she is now sobbing, full length on the ground, then rolls over onto her back, and finally lies at his feet, clasping his calf with her right hand as she repeats *desperately*: 'Let me kiss your mouth, Jochanaan' (130). Now he retreats from her as far as he can go, until he comes up against the wall. She crawls in pursuit, extending both her hands up towards him. At the end Weikl's Jochanaan, as he sings 'I will not look at you' (139.1–2), suits the action to the word and hides his face behind his hands; Stratas climbs up his body, grasping his clothes with her hands to raise herself, and wrestles with him for a kiss. He hurls her away and, after his last 'You are accursed' (140.6–9), goes back down into the cistern. Stratas crawls towards it as the cover crashes down behind him.

All this physicalization of Salome's newly unleashed erotic emotions is in preparation for the extraordinary performance which Stratas gives after Jochanaan has descended into the cistern. There, under Friedrich's direction, Stratas takes her physical depiction of Salome's passion and frustration to an electrifying level – as we studied in detail in **1.1** – before her mood changes, and she rises to her feet, both literally and metaphorically, as Salome reaches her resolve. At that point the intense and sometimes chaotic music of her declarations of passion is all gone, burnt out by the *stretto* orchestral *tutti*; and gone, too, after her emotional journey in this sub-section where the character is silent, are the corresponding very fluid and dynamic, sometimes violent postures and gestures, which Stratas had deployed to convey Salome's intense and fluctuating emotions ever since she determined that she would make the soldiers let her see the Prophet. By the end of the scene, Stratas's Salome is standing fully erect – resolved and calm. Some more 'Maybug' music will be heard in the next scene; but it will be associated with Herodes, not Salome.

(2) Scene 4, to the moment when Herodes yields

As Herodes (Hans Beirer), Herodias (Astrid Varnay) and the court come out from the banqueting hall, the film cameras turn to them. Skalický marks the affinity between mother and daughter by giving to Herodias a headpiece completely concealing her hair, like Salome's – but hers is a regal gold, and she wears a golden cloak over a red dress, which matches her almost perpetually angry character. When we see Salome again, Stratas is frozen in a peculiar posture – sitting on a rock and leaning up against a wall, with her right hand raised and half concealing her face. Salome is biding her time, and will do nothing until she has her opportunity. So when Herodes invites her to drink wine with him, and then to take fruit, Stratas is still sitting there – now with two hands on the stone wall, absolutely frozen and indifferent. She moves nothing except her lips when she declines Herodes' offers. There is a tremble of emotion when the voice of Jochanaan is heard again from the cistern (184.4). However, she is more agitated by his vision of the coming of the Lord (207), and for the first time since Herodes' entrance she moves – around the wall, away from the cistern. (I am not sure that this move is really necessary.) When Jochanaan prophesies the end of the world (219.6ff.), Stratas breathes deeply, with eyes open and lips half parted – but still leaning against the wall.[19] She only leaves her seat by the wall when the Tetrarch offers to give her whatever she desires if she dances for him. Then she turns suddenly, looking first at Herodes and then at the cistern, before she approaches him and questions him intensely to make sure that the bargain is secure.

This section does more than just to provide an almost essential rest for the singer, between the intensity of the confrontation with Jochanaan and the even greater intensity of the closing phases of the opera. Salome attained an absolute equanimity after the turmoil of the orchestral *stretto* which followed Jochanaan's descent into the cistern. The enunciation then of 1.1.8, which will now before too long be attached to the words 'I want the head of Jochanaan', gave us a completely new Salome – focused on her revenge, calm, and indifferent to all else in her surroundings. That is what Stratas's posture and her almost total immobility, extending from her moment of resolve until Herodes offers her whatever she desires, conveys.

During the dance, which is well choreographed by Robert Cohan in this production, Stratas's expression, when it can be seen through the veils, is calm but also enigmatic. Where the music quotes a motif associated with her praise of Jochanaan's flesh and hair (letter S), Stratas, who has gone over to the cistern during the course of the dance and rolled around on the stones which surround it, now faces straight down into it. This temporary diversion from focusing her attention on pleasing Herodes means nothing to him, but it means a great deal to Salome and to the audience. Especially when she subsequently drops the seventh and last veil into the cistern!

After the dance, Salome's body is fully covered; but Stratas's long and lustrous black hair is loose, and she now looks completely different – a new,

---

[19] We do not see whether she reacts to Jochanaan's prophecy of her death crushed by shields (216), as the camera is not on her at that point.

grim-faced woman. While she repeatedly demands the head of Jochanaan, this Salome faces her Herodes with a look of unremitting intensity. As he fails again and again with the alternatives that he offers her, Herodias laughs in his face ('and you, you are ridiculous with your peacocks!'), while Salome remains calm and utterly indifferent, even when he kneels to supplicate her. And then she once again demands the head of Jochanaan, singing close to Herodes' face. At that moment the Tetrarch *flares up*. In this production he runs away from Salome, but she does not move. She simply looks at him with calm intensity, and a touch of contempt. He has no choice but to return to her, and he sings: 'Oh! You won't listen to me. Be calm, Salome. Look, I am calm' (284.6–285.7). Of course the reverse is true; she is calm and he is not.

Herodes' last, desperate attempt is to offer her the curtain shielding the Holy of Holies. The Jews cry out in horror, and in Friedrich's production Herodes collapses at Salome's feet. Stratas bends to sing once again straight into his face, and demands one last time, *ferociously* – Stratas almost spits out the last word – 'Give me the head of Jochanaan!' (297.11–13). Herodes crawls back to his seat and yields to her demand, as he climbs up onto it with difficulty.

And so Friedrich has created an uncanny symmetry between the first and second parts of Salome's role. In her opening scenes, Stratas's Salome was tense, agitated and constantly shifting her mood; by contrast Jochanaan stood rock-solid, at least until near the end of their confrontation. In this first part of scene 4, the tension and agitation have been transferred to Beirer's Herodes, while Salome is rock-solid in her determination – almost literally so in the opening few minutes, when she appears immobile in a pose which, given the colour of her costume, makes her seem almost to be carved out of the grey rock against which she is leaning. This is true to Wilde, who sets up a parallel between the streams of imagery with which Salome praised aspects of Jochanaan and the catalogues of glorious objects with which Herodes tries to persuade her to take something else, other than the head. And it is also true to Strauss, who bestows a constantly shifting chromaticism on the passionately agitated Salome when she has fallen in love with Jochanaan, and then in the next scene transfers it to the neurotic, superstitious and almost hysterical Tetrarch.

(3) The dénouement

After the executioner has descended into the cistern, Salome waits in an agony of impatience. Stratas leans forward, with her hands extended behind her back, looking like a menacing bird of prey while the notorious double bass B flat, in the centre of the treble clef, sounds out to express, as Strauss himself insisted, 'signs of anguish from the heart of an impatiently expectant Salome'.[20] As the music becomes more agitated, Stratas again physicalizes Salome's emotions; when she hears a noise, but nothing happens and she thinks the executioner has lost courage, Stratas rolls on her back and writhes around. Then she turns on the Page, shakes him fiercely, and then goes straight to *scream* in Herodes' face.

Wilde now deploys one of the most obvious phallic symbols in all drama. *A huge black arm of the Executioner stretches up from the cistern, bearing on a silver shield the head of Jochanaan.* The music then explodes orgasmically (one bar before 314) to express Salome's overwhelming sexual satisfaction. Stratas walks towards the head, breathing deeply, lips slightly parted and body quivering, and takes the silver dish at 'Well, now I am going to kiss it!', when the main motif of her passion, 1.1.2, explodes in the orchestra (315.2). With intense effort, as if it weighs far more than it actually does, Stratas lifts the head on the dish up above her shoulders, staggering a little, before lowering it to the ground as the music gradually calms. Then she addresses the head, leaning extremely close over it, very near to Jochanaan's face, her hair actually falling down over his head, and with visible tears.

Stratas maintains this posture as long as the mood is lamentation. But as she becomes angry with him ('that scarlet viper, which spat its venom against me', 326.4–327.1), she rises to her feet to proclaim herself, 'Salome, the daughter of Herodias, Princess of Judaea'. As she exults in her mastery of Jochanaan's head, she kneels down again beside it, but, rightly, without the intimacy which characterized her recent lament. Next she praises his beauty – and now Friedrich deploys for the first time in the monologue the movements and posture which will also accompany the penultimate moments of the opera; Stratas does not address the head intimately. Instead she kneels up, raises her head and addresses her words upwards with a visionary look; then, as soon as she ends with 'and when I looked at you I heard mysterious music' she slowly inclines her head further back still, until it is almost horizontal, and closes her eyes.

In the next section, Salome becomes more passionate, confessing that she lusts after Jochanaan's beauty. Stratas leans down again, becoming ever more anguished, extends her arms and leans over on her side, then rolls on her back, holding her head in her hands and rocking from side to side to express Salome's desolation after 'What shall I do now, Jochanaan?'. Then suddenly she is above the head, demanding 'Why did you not look at me? If you had looked at me, you would have loved me.' During the second of these lines she is kneeling up and gradually once more leans her own head back. Then of course, after the closing line 'and the secret of love is greater

---

[20] 1974: 151. In the orchestral score, after advising how the note is to be fingered, Strauss demands *a short, sharp attack with the bow, so a sound is produced, which resembles a woman's suppressed groaning.*

than the secret of death', which is sung looking forward with a half-smile, she lowers her head right down, and, finally, kisses Jochanaan's lips.[21]

After Herodes' outburst, the focus returns to Salome. Strauss deploys a magnificent piece of tone-painting, the mysterious low chord which symbolizes the clouds covering the moon, as Salome resumes her monologue. Stratas begins the final section leaning right over the head of Jochanaan in near-total darkness, but, after she sings 'it may be the taste of love', there is a rising motion in the orchestra, using a theme which had been associated earlier with her desire for Jochanaan:

8.3.2 (357.3-5)

Like the orchestral motif itself, Stratas rises a little at this point, and then as the music becomes more and more triumphant (358–9) she rises to her full height, gazing out and upwards, and reprises her earlier movement; as she completes her last line – 'I have kissed your mouth, Jochanaan. I have kissed it, your mouth' – and the orchestra surges towards the devastating dissonance in the last bar of 360, she leans her head fully back in ecstasy. Finally, when she is crushed under the soldiers' shields, our last image is of her hand outstretched, quivering, trying to touch Jochanaan's head but just falling short.

Stratas's performance is worthy of close study. Strauss turned a decadent French play into an expressionist German music drama. In doing so he never imagined that his shimmering, volatile and extremely powerful score could be complemented by an acting style which provides a full physical response to it: 'Generally speaking, the acting of the singers should, of course, in contrast with the excessive turmoil of the music, be limited to the utmost simplicity...Turmoil on and in front of the stage simultaneously – that would be too much'.[22] But it is now well over a hundred years since Strauss unleashed this score on ears which were then totally unused to so much chromaticism and dissonance played by an extremely large orchestra. As the music has become more accepted, its strong clues to action demand far more from a modern director than 'the simplest and most restrained of gestures'.[23] Acting styles, and also the ability of singers to act convincingly with their bodies, advanced very considerably between the première

---

[21] This should *never* be done earlier in the scene than here.

[22] Strauss 1974: 151–2.

[23] Strauss 1974: 151.

of *Salome* in 1905 and the Böhm/Friedrich/Stratas film of 1976. And in my view what can now be done should be done, to achieve a performance on stage which is comparable in intensity to the accompanying music, and which responds to its many, often sudden, changes of mood. Under Friedrich's direction, Stratas achieves a performance of Salome's journey which is totally convincing, and no other Salome recorded since on DVD has so far equalled it.

Discussion question

Do you agree with this favourable assessment of Teresa Stratas's highly physical performance as Salome. If so, why? If not, why not?

8.4 Conclusion

Successful performance of a role needs a clear overall concept of the character, expressed through the overall style of movement adopted by the performer, and augmented by costume and makeup; it also needs the development in rehearsal of detailed postures, expressions and gestures which physicalize the feelings latent in the text and music at each moment when he or she is onstage. All three of these performers are physically vigorous and dynamic, giving life to their respective characters by being highly responsive to the moods implied by the text and expressed by the music. In the Gluck, Gens creates a fine embodiment of Iphigénie's strength, as she suffers great changes of emotion; her relationships with her fiancé and her mother are studied with close attention to detail. And she, together with the director, also shows how despite her strength Iphigénie is numbed at the end by what has happened to her during the opera. In the Mozart, Gilfrey successfully develops a coherent and full character where some critics have felt that Don Giovanni is without adequate depth in either Da Ponte's text or Mozart's music. And, in the Strauss, Stratas physicalizes to an unparalleled extent the 'clues to action' which Strauss's rich and intricate score provides for a performer in the title role, marking off clearly the three very different stages of the character's development. All three performances are fine examples of great operatic acting.

9

The Sense of Inevitability

Introduction

The distinguished translator and classical scholar Richmond Lattimore published in 1964 a short book, *Story Patterns in Greek Tragedy*. In this he argues that in all tragic drama there comes a climactic moment at which all the details of the story cohere, and 'we feel a sense of necessity, of must-be-so; one could almost call it fate'.[1]

I would agree absolutely with his view that there is (or should be) a sense of inevitability about the climactic deed of a tragedy, but I would hesitate to call it 'fate'. This is because the old view still lingers on that the characters of Greek tragedy are controlled by an inexorable fate – which in my view would reduce them to mere puppets, of no dramatic interest.[2] Men and women make their tragic outcomes for themselves, and this is as true of Romantic and Early Modernist opera as it is of Greek tragedy.

In interpreting both Greek tragedy and modern tragic opera, I have found the Homeric concept of a person's *moira* (and its synonym *aisa*) helpful. This concept is the nearest that the ancient Greek language has to 'destiny' or 'fate', and it is often mistranslated by one or the other of these two English words; in fact *aisa* and *moira* mean a person's lot in life – including, most importantly, his or her death. In the *Iliad*, Hector soothes Andromache's anxiety before he returns to battle with these words:

---

[1] Lattimore 1964: 7.
[2] M. Ewans 1995: xxix–xxx (on the *Oresteia* of Aeschylus). Cf. my comments on the contrast between the heroes and heroines of Greek epic and tragedy and those of Tippett's pessimistic Cold War opera *King Priam*, in which the characters are indeed, as Priam himself sings, 'toys, dupes, decoys of fate'. M. Ewans 2007: 136–45.

Strange one, do not grieve overmuch for me;
For no one will hurl me to Hades beyond my *aisa*;
But I say that no one has escaped from his *moira*,
Coward or brave man, once it has first taken shape.[3]

There is no predetermined Fate in Hector's vision; rather a person's inevitable lot in life gradually *takes shape* as the action of an epic poem, a tragic drama or a tragic opera unfolds through time, until the tragic outcome takes place and is seen, then – but only then, *at the moment when it occurs,* as inevitable. At the climax the tragic outcome is surprising only on the surface; on a deeper level the action of the drama, through the free choices of the characters, has made it thoroughly expected. Indeed, the audience would feel frustrated and disappointed, if any other outcome were to eventuate.[4]

In romantic and modern opera, the music is frequently the main vehicle for communicating this growing sense of inevitability; but the text and a good production are also important. The director needs to bring out visually the connections between events which the music expresses in sound. To convey the growing sense of inevitability, several composers have used either one or a few select recurrent motifs, and many commentators have seized on these and wrongly called them 'Fate themes'. In fact these themes are not all-encompassing themes representing an inexorable fate, but refer in each opera to a specific aspect of the dramatic situation which recurs, often with increasing intensity, as the opera unfolds, and constricts the outcomes available to the characters. Examples would include the theme in *Carmen* which is associated with Don José's destructive passion for the heroine (**6.2.1** and below **9.1**), the eight timpani blows in *Kát'a Kabanová* (**4.2.2**) and the *Hauptrhythmus* in *Lulu* (**4.3.2b**). Composers show by their music how they hear the action developing to an outcome at the climax which by then – but only by then – is inevitable, and directors must respond with a production which complements the music and itself assists in conveying the sense of the increasing inevitability of only one, usually fatal, outcome to the sequence of events seen earlier on the stage.

---

[3]Homer, *Iliad* VI. 486–9. For a full discussion, see M. Ewans 1996: 438–45. That chapter discusses the application of this world-view in tragedies by Sophocles and Shakespeare.

[4]Cf. Aristotle, *Poetics* 1453a: 36–9: '[it is comic, not tragic if] those who in the myth are the greatest enemies, like Aegisthus and Orestes, become friends and leave together at the end, and no one dies at anyone else's hand'.

9.1 *Carmen* (Meilhac and Halévy/Bizet/Zambello)[5]

Carmen is an *opéra comique*, and as such is a much more discursive theatre work than, for example, German operas in the Wagnerian tradition (cf. e.g. *Elektra*, **9.2** below). The principal subject is of course the destructive relationship between Carmen and Don José, from its intense beginning to its tragic ending; but the opera contains many numbers which are incidental to this central narrative, starting with the opening promenade scene; their main role is to set the atmosphere of Bizet's deft evocation of Spanish life and manners, and they either do not advance the plot or contribute very little to its advancement.

There is only one recurrent musical theme concerned with the relationship between Don José and Carmen:

9.1.1 (Prelude 121 ff)

This has often been called the 'fate' theme; for example, it is labelled 'Carmen's fate' in the ENO Opera guide.[6] It is nothing of the kind; it is an aural representation of Don José's intense passion for Carmen, as is plain from its use both earlier in the opera and, especially, in the final scene (see **6.2**). Some commentators clearly do not recognize this, but it has been perfectly evident to the directors of two strong recent productions. Francesca Zambello lifted the curtain early, as this theme sounds out near the end of the prelude to Act I (121ff.), and showed in flashforward a handcuffed Don José caressing the flower, his keepsake of Carmen, just before the executioner leads him off to his death. Similarly, Adrian Noble makes sure that when this music first sounds in Act I (I. 6. 13ff., just after Carmen's famous *habañera* aria), his Don José looks piercingly at Carmen

---

[5]In this section scene numbers are omitted; reference is by Act, Number and bar.
[6]John (ed.) 1982b: 51.

across the full width of the stage, and in response she gives him a sultry look, and crosses sexily over towards him.

In Act II, Don José interrupts Carmen's seductive dance for him when he hears the bugle sound the retreat; they argue intensely, and **9.1.1** recurs in solo cor anglais as he insists 'you will listen to me' before launching into the flower aria in which he shows just how much he is bound to her (II.17.166). It returns in the last moments of Act III when Don José sings to Carmen: 'I'm going – but we'll meet again', while Micaëla drags him off (III. 24.142–3.). Then in the Finale of Act IV (see **6.2**) it becomes central to the music, bursting out in the orchestra after the second choral stanza heard from inside the bullring. It shows the new and dangerous intensity of Don José's frustrated desire, and it erupts again in the full orchestra just after he has killed Carmen, generating the final words in which he sings of his love for her.

No other motif in this opera has similar power. Bizet meets the normal expectation of *opéra comique*, and provides fresh music for each new number; almost the only other themes which recur (at appropriate moments) are the Prelude's opening *allegro*, which becomes associated at the opening of Act IV with the fiesta and the bullfight, and the theme of Escamillo's Toreador aria. But these two themes are not directly related to the love affair between Don José and Carmen – although of course, as shown in **6.2**, the offstage chorus's singing of the Toreador song to hail Escamillo's victory plays a dominant part in the final scene: it spurs Don José on to murder Carmen. Accordingly, **9.1.1** carries the full burden of conveying through music the gradually increasing inevitability of a tragic outcome to their relationship.

The text therefore plays an important part in providing the feeling of growing inevitability. There are two related elements in the libretto which do this; Carmen is a gypsy, and as such is highly superstitious; she has already told Don José that the outcome of their relationship will be death (II.2, quoted below), before the card-reading (**5.3**) confirms for her the inevitability of her death. And several times she either dares Don José to kill her or predicts that he will. Indeed, she mentions the relationship between love and death as early as the scene in Act I where she has been arrested and refuses to answer Zuniga; there she sings (with, in Zambello's production, a meaningful cross to deliver the line closely to Don José) 'I love another, and die while saying I love him' (I.9.18–21). This textual theme culminates in the final scene of the opera, where she defies Don José and insists that she would rather die free than return to him. 'Carmen was born free, and free she will die' (III.27. 108–10).

Because the music uses only one recurring theme to chronicle the stages of Don José's obsession, and the text provides only scattered references to support it, *Carmen* requires a director who can not only provide the spectacle which this opera demands, a detailed and expansive evocation of Spanish city and gypsy life, but who can also bring out the main narrative of the affair between Carmen and Don José in such a way as to make the tragic outcome seem inevitable.

As we have already seen in our analysis of the final scene (**6.2**), the most powerful performance on DVD is that directed by Francesca Zambello at Covent Garden, with Anna Caterina Antonacci as Carmen and Jonas Kaufmann as Don José. It is preferable to any other *Carmen* available on DVD, not merely because it does very effectively – and obviously at considerable expense – evoke the milieu in which the action takes place, but because of the extraordinary sexual chemistry between the two lead singers, which is not equalled in any other recorded production.

The action of each of the four Acts takes place within high ochre-coloured walls, giving a sense that the characters are confined, despite the availability of entrances and exits; and, as already noted, Zambello seizes upon **9.1.1** the moment it first sounds; the curtain rises before the Prelude ends, and we see Don José in a narrow pool of light, caressing the flower which Carmen will give him in Act I, before an executioner comes to lead him away to his death.

Jonas Kaufmann as Don José is indifferent to Carmen during the *habañera* – he is sitting at a table, studying some papers; and he remains so when, after the aria, she first takes notice of him and circles round him. He only responds when she makes an obvious and striking attempt to arouse his attention – she poses in front of him with her skirt pulled up to expose one leg, holds the rose between her teeth and then throws it at him. (His response comes, correctly, at the climax of the first occurrence in Act I of **9.1.1**, I. no.6, 21.[7])

Kaufmann gets up and stares at his Carmen – and she stares right back, which illuminates an eloquent string melody (I.6.35ff.). He then picks up the rose after Carmen and the other women have gone back into the factory. In the spoken monologue which follows, he admits that she has struck him with the flower 'like a bullet between the eyes…if there are witches, this girl is certainly one of them'. And in this production he is so besotted with the flower that he is still holding it in his hand throughout the next scene, even when Micaëla is kissing him warmly on the lips on behalf of his mother![8] In this way, following up the final vision of the condemned José which Zambello has given us in the Prelude, she enforces on the audience the central role of the rose, which thus becomes a visual *leitmotif* of Don José's fatal passion.

In scene 10, Zambello's Don José is holding captive a half-undressed and beautiful woman with her hands tied behind her back and the rope wound

---

[7]Zambello and conductor Adriano Pappano here omit a short and trivial spoken dialogue between Carmen and Don José, which is present in the *Urtext* but is not usually performed. Gardiner and Noble do include it in their recording; and its effect is to weaken the impact of the first encounter between the two principals.

[8]There is a good contrast here with Adrian Noble's production, in which Don José stuffs the flower hastily inside his jacket as Micaëla greets him.

several times around her waist – a posture of forced erotic submission. The rope is very long, and the scene between them begins with Carmen at the far end of its full extent, which crosses the wide Covent Garden stage. Carmen rapidly comes close to José, however, when she begs him to have pity on her; and although he dismisses it as nonsense, she will turn out to be right, when she says 'you will do anything you want because you love me'. Then in the *seguidilla*, as she sings: 'who will love me? I will love him!' (I.10, 66–8), Antonacci comes very close to Kaufmann's José, pushes his papers out of his hands to force him to look at her, and then circles round him several times so that *he* is bound by the rope as she dances the *seguidilla* (very sexily!). She follows that up by sitting on the table opposite him and running a bare foot up his body, exposing her legs to him, while singing that she could love him (119–23). After this he has to admit that he is 'like a drunken man' in his love for her (141ff.), and he is very soon nuzzling her bare shoulder as they fondle each other.

It is vital that the seduction of Don José should be performed with total conviction and erotic intensity, and Zambello achieves this brilliantly by the symbolic use of the long rope, which at first seems to hold Carmen captive but which she effortlessly transforms into a bond which encircles Don José and holds him as her prisoner of love. In this way the crucial action which begins José's downfall – his letting her escape at the end of the Act – is shown to have become inevitable.

In Act II we see the beginning of the deterioration of their relationship. When Carmen and Don José are left alone, she calls for sherry, oranges and sweets, and then sets about seducing him with a dance which in Zambello's production is intensely erotic and physical; indeed, at the moment when Don José hears the bugles sounding the retreat, Carmen, who is dancing on the table above the chair in which he is sitting, has placed her skirts over his head. As Don José tries to obey the summons and leave, Carmen mocks him, tells him that she no longer believes in his love (II.17.150ff.), and in this production, when he replies angrily: 'you will listen to me' (155ff.), he throws her to the ground. At that point 9.1.1 sounds again, soft in the cor anglais, to remind the audience of Don José's obsession with Carmen, as he produces the flower and launches into his aria. Zambello makes the theme mark the moment at which he commits physical violence against Carmen for the first time – and the text and music of the subsequent aria shows that he has done so because he is totally obsessed with her, and so cannot bear her mockery.

At the end of the aria Kaufmann's José breaks into tears, overcome with emotion. The relationship is now very fragile; crawling towards him, Antonacci's Carmen sings repeatedly that if he really loved her he would follow her far away (222–46), and she snuggles up very close to him. He is reduced to begging her, unsuccessfully, to be silent (297–8); but she is soon straddling him, and his hand is up her skirt, so, when Don José finally breaks out and tells her that he must go (*allegro*, 337ff.), Kaufmann has to throw his Carmen off him brutally. It would appear that all is over between them, as she sings that she does not love him any more, and they bid each other 'farewell for ever' (346ff.).

The return of Zuniga forces the couple together again, and makes José's return to the army impossible; so at the end of the Act they make up and pledge their love – in this production, Le Dancaïre cuts their wrists so that they can mingle their blood, and José snaps his necklace, and puts the ring which he has carried on it onto Carmen's wedding finger. But in this Act Don José has been trapped between love and duty, and has not given the unconditional response that Carmen demands. Although he is welcomed into the band of smugglers at the end, his acceptance that he must do this ('I'll have to', III.18.87–8) is – as Carmen notes – not exactly *galant*, and he sings nothing more before the curtain falls. In this way the librettists have laid the groundwork for the breakup of the relationship in Act III. And Carmen, although at first indifferent, became very interested in Escamillo[9] when she sang 'L'amour!', while looking at him, and he singled her out in his reply (II.14, stage directions at 119). Antonacci, needless to say, made much of this moment.

As a result, in Zambello's production Carmen and Don José are seen quarrelling (silently) during the opening chorus of Act III. Then in the spoken Scene 2 they quarrel violently. She tells him that she is loving him less and less than she did before, and might in the end not love him at all. 'I don't want to be tormented and above all not to be ordered about. What I want is to be free and to do what I want'. This introduces the idea that will return to cause her death in Act IV – Carmen's insistence on her freedom – and it is developed further to close the spoken dialogue:

DON JOSÉ
… if you talk to me again about us breaking up and if you don't
    behave with me as I want you to …
CARMEN
You will kill me, perhaps? *(JOSÉ does not reply.)* Whatever…I have
    seen many times in the cards that we are going to end our lives
    together *(clacks her castanets)*. Bah! Come what may…
DON JOSÉ
You are the devil, Carmen.
CARMEN
Yes, I've told you that already.

Don José goes away from her, and the card trio (**6.3**) follows immediately. Carmen reads death – for her first, and then for him; and her belief that the

---

[9]In this production Escamillo arrives and departs on horseback, which, added to his elegant costume and Ildebrano D'Arcangelo's fine physique, made him a very impressive and desirable specimen of manhood for the women gathered at Lillas Pastia's.

cards tell no lies, and that everyone's fate, happy or sad, is written in 'the book of heaven', greatly increases the audience's foreboding for her.

Carmen rescues Escamillo from the duel as Don José is about to stab him – and, as the toreador takes his leave, in Zambello's production he does not merely *look at Carmen* but takes from her his knife, which she has retrieved from where he dropped it, and kisses her hand, further inflaming Don José.

In the Finale to this Act, once again the text reinforces the fatal nature of their bond. Carmen tells Don José to go with Micaëla to his mother, and Don José sings that he will not leave her, even if it costs him his life, and that 'the chain which binds us together / will bind us until death' (III.24.97–105). At this point in Zambello's production, Don José clasps Carmen's chin, half affectionately and half violently, then pushes her to the ground, as Micaëla and the chorus of Gypsies burst into song, imploring him to break the chain that binds him to Carmen (*allegro*, 109ff.) He tells Micaëla that he is damned, and then addresses Carmen:

Ah, Je te tiens, fille damnée,	Ah, I've got you, daughter of Hell,
Et je te forcerai bien	And I will make you
À subir la destiné	Submit to the destiny
Qui rive ton sort au mien.	Which welds your fate to mine.
Dût-il m'en couter la vie,	Even if it costs me my life,
Non, Carmen, je ne partirai plus.	No, Carmen, I will never go. (116–28)

Throughout this passage Kaufmann holds his Carmen (who is now sitting on the ground) from behind, and manhandles her. As he finishes she kicks him away; yet again she rejects absolutely his demand that she submit to him.

But 'destiny' does not quite work out the way that Don José intends. Micaëla only has to tell him that his mother is dying and he agrees to go with her. His last words to Carmen in Act III are: 'Be happy, I'm going – but we will meet again'. At this point Bizet has the orchestra sound out **9.1.1** loud and clear, with the timpani punctuating the phrases as in the overture, to reinforce this. José is indeed bound to Carmen by a chain which cannot be broken. But he has lost her love; as José and Micaëla leave, Escamillo is heard singing the Toreador song in the distance, and in the stage direction Carmen *leans, listening, on the rocks*. Zambello rightly goes further than this; once Micaëla and Don José have gone off, Antonacci as Carmen declines to respond to Le Dancaïre, who invites her by a gesture to follow him and the other gypsies. Instead, as the curtain falls she runs off, smiling happily, in the direction of Escamillo's voice. This anticipates the beginning of Act IV, where we see her completely in love with the toreador.

The closing scene of Act IV, where Don José confronts Carmen outside the bullring, develops from the total breakdown of the relationship between them which we have seen in words, music and stage action by the end of Act III. He tries to make her submit to his will; she defies him even in the face of death. I have traced in **6.2** how their final confrontation is developed by the librettists and the composer with the use of the offstage music of the chorus watching the *corrida*, which progressively increases the gulf between the characters, leading Carmen to greater defiance and Don José to greater desperation. There, too, I have described how Zambello physicalizes the mental and emotional struggle leading to the death of Carmen, which by the time that it occurs has become so inevitable that **9.1.1** – which has already erupted as Don José declares that she has condemned his soul to perdition (IV.27.166–75) – sounds out in the full orchestra at the moment when she dies (IV.27.201–5). It is the last thematic material to be heard in the opera, because it has recurred at every crucial moment in the development of their passionate affair, from their first meeting to its disastrous and tragic end. But the development of that passionate affair needs to be shown in production in physical terms, with an intense relationship between Carmen and Don José at every stage of the drama, and Zambello achieves this with great success.

Discussion question

Do you agree that as Zambello's production unfolds she progressively demonstrates the inevitability of Don José's killing Carmen?

9.2 *Elektra* (Hofmannsthal/Strauss/Friedrich)

Hofmannsthal's *Elektra* does not in itself develop to an outcome which is seen, when it occurs, as inevitable. But the play does have a central idea which generates the outcome; unlike any of the previous dramatists, ancient or post-Renaissance, who have treated this myth, Hofmannsthal creates an ending in which Elektra can no longer live after her desire for revenge is fulfilled by the deaths of Klytämnestra and Ägisth, and she dances herself to death.[10] This outcome is supported by a concept which lies at the foundation of the play.

In the moments where Elektra refuses to allow her brother to embrace her (155a ff.), Hofmannsthal's heroine describes how she had been totally, sexually possessed by the spirit of her dead father, who cried out to her for vengeance – as a result of which she lost her virgin beauty and her womanly shame and modesty, and became:

a prophetess for evermore,
and I have given nothing out from myself

---

[10] Full discussion at M. Ewans 2007: 92–6.

and from my body
but curses and despair! (170aff.)

The fundamental concept of Hofmannsthal's *Elektra* is that the heroine is destroyed from within by the dominance over her of her murdered father, Agamemnon. But words alone could not convey that her death becomes inevitable as a result of this domination.

In order to create the growing sense of the inevitability of Elektra's death after her sole purpose in living has been fulfilled, Strauss had to give the play the coherent theatrical structure which it lacked. In Hofmannsthal, the murdered king is a background presence, so ominous that his name is spoken only once.[11] Hofmannsthal, who was, when he wrote his *Elektra*, an acclaimed poet but a novice playwright, failed to see that this device, which might have been effective in a written poem, would be coy and unsatisfying in the theatre. Strauss therefore introduced Agamemnon's name into the text at several different points, unified by its common musical setting. By its presence as a ritual refrain in Elektra's first monologue, it is established as a dominant feature of the opera. Then, while composing the closing sequence, Strauss abandoned his first idea, which was to end with mysterious, muted sounds, unrelated to any previous musical material.[12] He decided to end the opera as he began it, with a violent, *fortissimo* declamation of the musical motif that has become totally associated with Agamemnon's name by its use as a principal *Leitmotif* throughout the opera, starting with the first bars.

9.2.1 (0.1)

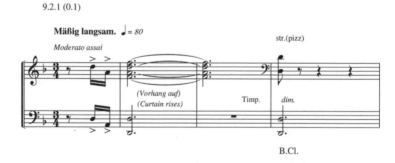

The resultant circularity, the strong feeling of a return at the end to the beginning, is central to Strauss's final vision of the story. His Elektra has her end implicit in her beginning.

---

[11] Elektra to Ägisth, as he is being murdered: 'Agamemnon hears you' (126a).
[12] See Gilliam 1991: 231–3 for a transcription and discussion of Strauss's original sketch for the ending.

Strauss framed his opera, and gave it an overall shape, by returning in the final minutes to 9.2.1, and to two more motifs, which were introduced during Elektra's monologue after the maids have left. Here Elektra invokes Agamemnon, as she has each day at this, the hour of his death. We are watching a ritual, in which a witch conjures up her familiar, and he retakes possession of her soul.

🔊 9 2 Elektra's monologue

ELEKTRA

Allein! Weh, ganz allein. Der Vater fort
hinabgescheucht in seine kalten Klüfte ...
(towards the ground)
4.1.8>9.2.1 Agamemnon! Agamemnon!
Wo bist du, Vater? Hast du nicht die Kraft,

dein Angesicht herauf zu mir zu schleppen?
(softly) Es ist die Stunde, unsre Stunde ist's,
die Stunde, wo sie dich geschlachtet haben,
dein Weib, und der mit ihr in einem Bette,
in deinem königlichen Bette schlaft.
A 1[13] Sie schlugen dich im Bade tot, dein Blut
rann über deine Augen, und das Bad
dampfte von deinem Blut. Da nahm er dich,
der Feige, bei den Schultern, zerrte dich
hinaus aus dem Gemach, den Kopf voraus,
die Beine schleifend hinterher: 9.2.2 A2
dein Auge,
das starre, offne, sah herein ins Haus.
So kommst du wieder, setzest Fuß vor Fuß,

Und stehst auf einmal da, die beiden Augen
weit offnen, und ein königlicher Reif
von Purpur ist um deine Stirn, der speist sich

9.2.2 aus des Hauptes offner Wunde.
A 3 Agamemnon! Vater!
Ich will dich sehn, laß mich heute nicht allein!
Nur so wie gestern, wie ein Schatten dort
Im Mauerwinkel zeig dich deinem Kind!

Alone! Ah, all alone. My father gone,
shoveled away into his cold grave ...

Agamemnon! Agamemnon!
Where are you, father? Have you not the
strength
to drag your face up here into my sight?
It is the hour, it is our hour,
the hour when they slaughtered you,
your wife, and he who slept with her in bed,
in your royal bed.
They butchered you in the bath, your blood
ran over your eyes, and the bath
steamed with your blood. Then he took you,
the coward, by the shoulders, dragged you
back out of the room, your head in front,
the legs dragging behind:
your eyes
stared, wide open, back into the house.
So do you come back, set foot in front of
foot,
and stand there all at once, the two eyes
wide open, and a royal crown
of purple is around your forehead, which
feeds itself
from your head's open wound.
Agamemnon! Father!
I must see you, do not leave me alone today!
Only, just as yesterday, like a shadow there
in the corner of the walls, show yourself
to your child!

---

[13] The A + number markers indicate the appearances of Agamemnon's spirit in Friedrich's film, which are discussed below.

9.2.3

A4 Vater! Agamemnon! Dein Tag wird kommen.
Von den Sternen
stürzt alle Zeit herab, so wird das Blut

aus hundert Kehlen stürzen auf dein Grab!

So wie aus umgeworfnen Krügen wird's
aus den gebunden Mördern fließen,
und in einem Schwall, in einem
geschwollnen Bach wird ihres Lebes Leben
aus ihnen stürzen.
(with solemn pathos)
A 5 Und wir schlachten dir
die Rosse, die im Hause sind, wir treiben sie
vor dem Grab zusammen, und sie ahnen

den Tod und wiehern in die Todesluft
und sterben. **A 6** Und wir schlachten dir die Hunde,
die dir die Fuße leckten,
die mit dir gejagt, denen du
die Bissen hinwarfst, darum muß ihr Blut
hinab, um ihr zu Dienst zu sein, **A 7** und wir, wir,
den Blut, dein Sohn Orest und deine Töchter,

wir drei, wenn alles dies vollbracht und
Purpurgezelte aufgerichten sind, **A 8** vom Dunst
des Blutes, den die Sonne nach sich zieht,
dann tanzen wir, dein Blut, rings um dein Grab: **A 9**

(in ecstatic pathos)
und über Leichen hin werd' ich da Knie

hochheben Schritt für Schritt, **9.2.4** und die
mich werden
so tanzen sehn, ja, die meinen Schatten
von weitem nur so werden tanzen sehn,
die werden sagen: **A 10** einem großen König **9.2.3**
wird hier ein großes Prunkfest angestellt
von seinem Fleisch und Blut, **A 11**
und glücklich ist,
wer Kinder hat, die um sein hohes Grab
so königliche **A 12** Siegestänze tanzen!
Agamemnon! Agamemnon!
9.2.3 9.2.4 9.2.2

Father! Agamemnon! Your day will come!
From the stars
all Time rains down, and just so will
　the blood
from a hundred throats pour onto
　your grave!

As if from overturned pitchers it will
flow from the fettered murderers,
and in a wave, in a
swollen stream their life-blood will
pour from them.

And we kill for you
the horses that are in the palace, we drive
them together in front of the grave, and
　they scent
death and whinny in the death-laden breeze
and die. And we kill for you the dogs,
that licked your feet,
which hunted with you, to whom you
threw tit-bits – their blood must flow
to do service to you, and we, we,
your blood, your son Orest and your
　daughters,
we three, when all this is accomplished and
the fumes of blood, drawn up by the sun,
hang in the air like purple pavilions,
then we shall dance, your blood,
　around your grave:

and over the corpses there will I raise
　my knees
high step by step, and those
who see me
dance like this, yes, they who just see
my shadow from afar dancing like this,
they will say: for a great king
has a magnificent feast been set out here
by his flesh and blood, and he is a
happy man,
who has children who round his high tomb
dance such royal dances of victory!
Agamemnon! Agamemnon!

4.1.8 is Elektra's solemn invocation, summoning Agamemnon's spirit to rise. As she sings her father's name to the earth the audience realizes in retrospect that the gigantic gesture (**9.2.1**), which opened the opera in ominous, tragic D minor, represented the presence of Agamemnon. Elektra summons Agamemnon's spirit by painting a vivid picture of the moments of his death. Then she imagines him returning, and the fanfares of **9.2.2** start to rise in the orchestra; they are played *ff*, spanning six octaves, as she completes her word-picture. Like Götz Friedrich (see below), I believe that these rising fanfares portray the success of her invocation; Agamemnon's spirit rises from below the earth, and advances towards her.

Elektra is not aware of his presence, so she tenderly invokes her father, pleading to him with a rapturous A flat string theme (**9.2.3**), which depicts the depth of her love. Later, it will return and be developed when she recognizes Orest. This melody expresses all the longing for Agamemnon which she will then project onto her brother; Orest in the music is a shadowy figure, whose role is primarily to be what Elektra wants him to be – Agamemnon returned.[14]

After a vivid evocation of the carnage which will take place when Agamemnon's day of vengeance comes, Elektra concludes the monologue with the image of herself, Orest and Chrysothemis dancing round the

---

[14] Strauss cast Orest as a baritone, against the normal operatic convention that young men should be tenors, and introduced him by a solemn, almost spectral sequence of chords in the lower brass (*langsam und fierlich*, 123a).

funeral pyre of the usurpers, their supporters, and Agamemnon's dogs and horses (53ff.).

9.2.4 (57.5)

Here, **9.2.4** is heard, gradually swelling throughout the full orchestra to convey the power and intensity of Elektra's vision of the dance. It plays on after her last cry of 'Agamemnon', becoming almost perilously prolonged, until the fanfares of **9.2.2** rise again. This final sequence is highly ominous, since the return of the fanfares shows that, when Elektra dances herself into a state of ecstasy, the spirit of Agamemnon wells up inside her. That is precisely how Elektra will be destroyed at the end of the opera (260a4 ff.); but at this point the entry of Chrysothemis halts the momentum before Elektra's dance, and her psyche, get out of her control.

In Hofmannsthal's original conception, Elektra destroys herself during the maenadic final dance because 'the individual is dissolved in an empirical way, in which even the content of her life is burst asunder from inside, like water which has turned to ice in an earthen jug. Elektra is no longer Elektra precisely because she has consecrated herself to being wholly and completely Elektra...'.[15]

Strauss replaced this rather mystical and untheatrical vision of self-dissolution with a different vision, in which Agamemnon's dominance over her psyche destroys Elektra's life. In the Finale, the four principal motifs from Elektra's monologue return to illuminate what has happened to her as a result of the action of the opera. A dance-like version of the theme of Elektra's love for Agamemnon (**9.2.3**) and the rhythms of Elektra's earlier triumphant dance (**9.2.4**) begin to reappear even before Chrysothemis leaves; they enter the orchestra as soon as Elektra has claimed as her own the music with which an offstage chorus of followers is celebrating Orest's

---

[15] Hofmannsthal 1959: 201.

triumph; 'It [their music] comes from me' (230a). And now, no one can stop Elektra as Chrysothemis had stopped her at the end of her opening monologue. Strauss's massive orchestra depicts the driving force of the dance welling up out of Elektra's psyche. The dance music develops as a gigantic waltz, with a combination of tragic exultation and banality that perfectly expresses the condition, at once both super- and sub-human, of those in a state of *enthousiasmos* – possession by a god or by a hero's spirit.

The final bars of the orchestral score communicate the exact nature of the catastrophe. The dance reaches a climax of uncontrolled, reckless and unprecedented intensity (259a–260a); then, suddenly, the triple rhythms are halted, and the fanfares of **9.2.2** rise up again in the brass (260a 4), *fortissimo*, and now accompanied by an appalling sound effect, which is intensified to an unbearable intensity just before Elektra falls – the tam tam scraped with a triangle stick (260a 4–12). The meaning is clear; Agamemnon's spirit rises up again, inside his daughter's psyche – and destroys her. After Elektra lies still (261a 1), Strauss's response to the final moments is on the largest scale. To end the opera, the motif of Agamemnon's name (**9.2.1**) is declaimed by the full orchestra, at first alternating with a sombre lament in the form of sustained *piano* chords for the low brass, in the remote and sinister key of E flat minor. But first these chords, and then Chrysothemis's plaintive cries of 'Orest!', are swept away by monumental C major repetitions of the Agamemnon motif. However, the opera does not conclude in an unalloyed triumph of Agamemnon's desire for vengeance. Strauss felt that the triumphant revenge of the matricides should leave a nasty taste in the mouths of the audience. The horrible lurch of the *fff* brass and string *tutti* away from a glowing, triumphant C major back for a moment to distant E flat minor, in the penultimate semiquaver, achieves just that.[16]

This music creates a real feeling that the ending is inevitable, which Hofmannsthal's text alone could not convey. Agamemnon's cataclysmic motif returns, its full symphonic implications now revealed, to conclude the opera as it began it, enforcing through music the central idea of Hofmannsthal's play, that her dead father's possession of her has first turned Elektra into a hideous, outcast prophetess of doom, and has now destroyed her utterly.[17]

*

Josef Svoboda's set for Götz Friedrich's film of *Elektra* is extraordinary. Outside the palace it consists of a large grey brick and stone courtyard, which looks like a war zone, with outcrops of rock and ruined brick walls;

---

[16] Cf. Whittall 1989: 72–3.
[17] The above analysis of the music appeared in a similar but different form in M. Ewans 2007: 96–102.

on a pedestal stand two feet, which are all that is left of Agamemnon's statue
– except the head, which Elektra has hidden away and preserved. Stone
staircases go down to hidden rooms, many of whose roofs have fallen in;
the slaves' quarters are however intact – low grey huts on the periphery. The
façade of the palace, which dominates the courtyard, lies in total contrast; it
is made of a gleaming metal, and is multi-storey with a very large number
of windows on every level. This set serves two vital dramatic purposes: first,
the condition of the courtyard conveys the *miasma*, the psychic pollution
which has fallen on the House of Atreus since the death of Agamemnon,
and gives a fit environment for Leonie Rysanek's half-demented Elektra to
inhabit; second, the threshold of the tyrants' gleaming palace becomes a
point of liminal transition. Elektra never enters the palace, but she succeeds
in luring Klytämnestra to come down from the first floor and out into the
decaying ruins for their confrontation (4.1) – against the advice of her
Trainbearer and her Confidante; this illuminates Elektra's power over her
mother. Conversely, later on, she successfully persuades Ägisth to cross the
threshold into the palace to meet his murderers. Finally, at the end of the
opera, Orest and the Tutor have all the windows and doors of the palace
closed to leave the dead Elektra and the distraught Chrysothemis outside,
cut off from the celebrations within.

Friedrich begins the opera by placing on screen just before the music
starts a quotation from the first scene of Maeterlinck's *Pelléas et Mélisande*
– the scene outside the castle door which Debussy omitted from his
setting: 'Pour out the water, pour out all the water of the Flood; you'll
never finish'. Maeterlinck (characteristically) never makes clear what the
servants in his play need to wash away, but Hofmannsthal is utterly direct
later on in the first scene of *Elektra*, when the First Maidservant reports
that Elektra said:

> 'There is no dog that can be degraded to the state
> We have been trained to; that we must wash away with water
> And with always fresh water
> The eternal blood of murder from the floor'. (25.1–27.3)

The opening image of the film is therefore a close-up of the maids' hands
pushing and pulling scrubbing brushes, trying and failing to remove
blood from the cobbles of the courtyard. They should be helped, but are
not, by the heavy rain which is falling as they work. This rain, which
cannot cleanse the pollution of the House of Atreus, returns at the end of
the opera in Friedrich's production; it is falling heavily again as Elektra
dances herself to death, while the entire façade of the palace is polluted
by streams of blood which pour down the smooth metallic walls, seeping
out from under the metallic shutters which Orest has ordered to be closed.
In this way, Friedrich matches Strauss's ring-composition with his own.
The indelible blood is there, and cannot be washed away by water, at the

end as at the beginning – and indeed we even see flickers of its redness illuminating Elektra's swirling feet as she dances herself to death. The final images are of Chrysothemis appealing in vain to Orest, facing a blank façade of bloodstained walls, and of Elektra's corpse reflected by the bloody wall.

Friedrich's handling of Agamemnon and Orest is the principal way in which he makes real Hofmannsthal's vision of a woman destroyed by the calls for vengeance of her murdered father's spirit, and so complements and illuminates Strauss's music. This being a film and not a stage production (although it was all shot on the large, but sole, claustrophobic set), Friedrich is able to use superimposition. When Elektra, in her opening monologue, describes Agamemnon's death, we see her blood-hued vision of her father being murdered in the bath by Klytämnestra, with Ägisth looking on (A 1), and then we see the bloodstained head and staring eyes of Agamemnon (A 2). Then, when she invokes him by name and begs him to come to her, he appears (A 3), first as a shadow on the walls and then in full black armour with a black face mask.

As the rapturous theme of Elektra's love for Agamemnon (9.2.3) unfolds in the strings, she repeatedly and passionately kisses the lips of the head of his statue; the spirit of Agamemnon takes off his mask and watches her as she invokes him again (A 4). Then, when she sings *with solemn pathos* of slaughtering for him his horses and his dogs, the spirit appears twice, looking at her in a sad, slightly pitying way; we now see that he has an open wound in his forehead where the axe struck him (A 5, A 6). Then, as she becomes more obsessive in her ritual and moves into her final dance (where she places the statue on the ground and dances with her skirt over it, with obvious sexual overtones), he watches her, still sad (A 7–12). Each time he appears, until the last time, there is a clean cut back from his image to Elektra; but at A 12 the spirit fades away, leaving a blank wall where it had been, as she sings her last words of the monologue; perhaps it shuns the imminent arrival of Chrysothemis. By these appearances, Friedrich thoroughly establishes in visual terms a complement to the music in which Strauss shows Elektra summoning up the spirit of her father.

The spirit of Agamemnon makes one appearance, as a shadow cast on a rock, during the confrontation between Elektra and Klytämnestra, when the Queen has described the nameless Something that oppresses her at night; but Friedrich then holds the spirit in reserve, and uses it to go to the heart of the opera in the scene between Elektra and Orest. Orest, too, appears in all-black armour – even with the same black mask as his father's spirit, making him a most sinister figure; and we first see him as a shadow cast on the wall, just like Agamemnon. Friedrich does not follow Hofmannsthal's stage direction that *Orest is standing by the courtyard gate, a silhouette against the last rays of sunlight*, but he does replicate the effect of this; Orest is seen in silhouette back-lit by torches.[18] The black armour and the shadow and silhouette effects fully complement and illuminate Strauss's vision of Orest as Agamemnon returned, which is soon clinched in the music by the rapturous return of **9.2.3**, repeated several times as the theme developed in Elektra's recognition-aria. Then at the core of the opera, when Elektra sings to Orest of how Agamemnon's calls for vengeance forced her to lose her womanly modesty and shame, in Friedrich's film Agamemnon looks on again, enigmatically; but his final appearance is when Elektra sings to Orest that the deed (of revenge-murder) is:

… wie ein Bett von Balsam,	… like a bed of balsam,
drauf die Seele rufen kann,	on which the soul can rest,
die eine wunde ist, ein Brand,	when it is like a wound, a firebrand,
ein Eiter, eine Flamme!	an ulcer, a flame! (175a)

Indeed it is; and both these black-armoured warriors bring death, not just to the murderers who deserve it but also to Elektra herself – who had sung to Orest during the recognition:

Es sei den, daß ich jetzt gleich	It may be that I now
sterben muß und du dich anzeigst	must die, and you have revealed yourself
und mich holen kommst: dann sterbe ich	and come to fetch me: then I will die
seliger, als ich gelebt!	more blessed than I have lived! (151a 4ff.)

So Friedrich complements Strauss in two vitally important ways, through his vivid evocation of the motif of *miasma*, of psychic pollution caused by the literal pollution of indelible blood, and by allowing us to see Agamemnon's spirit, who came to Elektra at night and destroyed her young womanhood with his cries and groans (167a–8a):

Eifersüchtig sind die Toten:	Jealous are the dead:
Und er schichte mir den Haß,	and he sent me Hate,
Den hohläugigen Haß als Bräutigam.	hollow-eyed Hate as bridegroom. (168a–169a)

The appearances of the spirit of Agamemnon in the film, and the parallels between his visual appearance and that of Orest, ensure that the production reinforces Strauss's vision of Elektra's death as ultimately inevitable, which the music shows by the return of motifs from Elektra's opening monologue in the final dance of death. And to echo the parallelism which Strauss created, Friedrich makes sure that the final posture of each of the two

---

[18] In this production it is now already dark – as, *pace* Hofmannsthal, it logically should be, since Klytämnestra had called for torches much earlier in the opera when given the news: 'Orest is dead'.

dances is the same; Elektra twirls round rapidly on tiptoe, with her arms extended horizontally, both in the last moments of the monologue before Chrysothemis interrupts her and at the end of the final dance, just before she suddenly stiffens, and falls lifeless to the ground.

Discussion question

Does Friedrich's film complement Strauss's use of *leitmotive* to give a feeling of inevitability to the triumph and death of Elektra?

9.3 Conclusion

Directors have many other things that they must do, in order to make an opera's text and score come alive on stage, but in a tragic opera reinforcing the growing sense of the inevitability of the climactic moment – which is very often the death of a principal character, as in the two operas studied in this chapter – is one of the director's most important tasks. He or she must respond to those passages in both text and music, which are staging posts on the way to the climactic moment where the tragic outcome is shown to have been inevitable. The production must illuminate each of these moments visually.

We have studied two very different operas from very different national traditions. Bizet illuminates the developing affair between Don José and Carmen with only one theme, that of José's destructive passion for her. By contrast, Strauss composes a full symphonic development of (among other *leitmotifs*) four separate principal themes devoted to illuminating why Elektra destroys herself. One of them raises the curtain (there is no prelude), and the other three are introduced to complement the first during Elektra's opening monologue. They appear at various points throughout the opera, and they return at the end, to enforce the vision that Elektra's dance of death is the inevitable result of her obsession with Agamemnon.

Zambello and Friedrich, aided by outstanding singer-actors who are ideally cast for their roles, devise action which enhances the development of a feeling of inevitability through the unfolding of the text and the music. This is not the only reason why their productions of *Carmen* and *Elektra* are the best that have been recorded and issued on DVD; but the fact that they reinforce the growing sense of inevitability through action and visual images at every staging post of the opera is a major contribution to the great dramatic intensity of their interpretations.

10

Conclusion

We have studied how operas make their effect on the spectator, by examining the interaction between text, music and stage action in video recordings of thirty scenes, or sub-scenes, from a selection of twenty-three operas by thirteen composers from Mozart to Britten and Tippett, and by examining in the last two chapters issues which affect the whole opera, using as examples five complete operas, including one by Gluck which was not featured elsewhere in the study.

During the last few decades, directors have required the singers whom they cast to be excellent actors and actresses, who look credible in their roles and are as flexible in their bodies and facial expressions as they are with their voices. The directors whose work has been praised in this book have all clearly studied the text and especially the music in minute detail, before developing in rehearsal patterns of expression, movement, posture and gesture which illuminate both the libretto and the score. Their singing actors and actresses physicalize the changing moods and feelings of the characters as the drama and the music unfold, and I have analysed how they do this and to what effect.

The diverse range of features in the productions which have been discussed in this book shows that we are very far from being able to lay down any systematic theoretical basis on which to map the responses of directors and singers to operatic music and words, and their effects on spectators. Nevertheless, I hope that, by reading this book in conjunction with clips of the thirty scenes studied in chapters 1 to 7 and DVD recordings of the five complete productions discussed in chapters 8 and 9, you will have gained increased insight into the ways in which you as singers and directors can create the kinds of interactions between words, music and stage action which make opera, at its best, an overwhelming experience for your audiences.

BIBLIOGRAPHY

Ashbrook, W. and Powers, H. (1991) *Puccini's Turandot: The End of the Great Tradition*. Princeton: Princeton University Press.

Bauer, O. G. (1983) *Richard Wagner: The Stage Designs and Productions from the Premières to the Present*. New York: Rizzoli.

Beaumarchais, C. de (1964) *'The Barber of Seville' and 'The Marriage of Figaro'*, (trans.) J. Wood. Harmondsworth: Penguin.

Beckett, L. (1981) *Richard Wagner: Parsifal*. Cambridge: Cambridge University Press.

Besch, A. (1991) 'A Director's Approach' in Branscombe 1991, 178–204.

Borchmeyer, D. (1991) *Richard Wagner: Theory and Theatre*. Oxford: Clarendon Press.

Branscombe, P. (1991) *W. A. Mozart: Die Zauberflöte*. Cambridge: Cambridge University Press.

Brett, P. (ed.) (1983) *Benjamin Britten: Peter Grimes*. Cambridge: Cambridge University Press.

Brockett, O. and Findlay, R. (1973) *Century of Innovation: a History of European and American Theatre since 1870*. Englewood Cliffs, NJ: Prentice Hall.

Brown, B. A. (1995) *W. A. Mozart: Così fan tutte*. Cambridge: Cambridge University Press.

Buch, D. (2009) *Magic Flutes and Enchanted Forests: the Supernatural in Eighteenth Century Musical Theater*. Chicago: Chicago University Press.

Budden, J. (1973) *The Operas of Verdi: vol. 1 From Oberto to Rigoletto*. London: Cassell.

Budden, J. (1981) *The Operas of Verdi: vol. 3 From Don Carlos to Falstaff*. London: Cassell.

Cairncross, J. (trans.) (1963) *Racine, Iphigenia/Phaedra/Athaliah*. Harmondsworth: Penguin.

Cairns, D. (1973) *Responses*. London: Secker and Warburg.

Cairns, D. (1980) 'A Vision of Reconciliation' in N. John. (ed.) *The Magic Flute*, 17–40. Opera Guide 3. London: John Calder.

Carpenter, T. (1989) 'Tonal and Dramatic Structure' in Puffett (ed.) 1989, 88–108.

Carter, T. (1987) *W. A. Mozart; 'Le Nozze di Figaro'*. Cambridge: Cambridge University Press.

Chailley, J. (1972) *The Magic Flute: Masonic Opera*. London: Gollancz.

Clément, C. (1988) *Opera, or the Undoing of Women*. Minneapolis: University of Minnesota Press.

Da Ponte, Lorenzo di (1967) *Memoirs*, (trans.) E. Abbott. New York: Dover.

Dent, E. J. (1960) *Mozart's Operas: A Critical Study* (2nd edn). London: Oxford University Press.

Donington, R. (1963) *Wagner's 'Ring' and its Symbols: The Music and the Myth*. Faber and Faber: London.

Donington, R. (1990) *Opera and its Symbols: the Unity of Words, Music and Staging*. New Haven: Yale University Press.

Driver, P. (1985) 'A Ritual of Renewal' in John (ed.) 1985, 19–24.

Ecklemeyer, J. (1991) *The Cultural Context of Mozart's Magic Flute*. Lewiston, NY: Edwin Mellen Press.

Eliot, T. S. (1951) *Poetry and Drama*. London: Faber and Faber.

Engstrom, J. (1981) 'Chéreau's *Ring*, 1976–1983'. *Theater* 12.3, 86–90.

Eschenbach, W. von (1980) *Parzival*, (trans. A. Hatto) Harmondsworth: Penguin.

Evans, P. (1979) *The Music of Benjamin Britten*. London: Dent.

Ewans, J. (1980) *The Relationship between Les Troyens and the Aeneid*. PhD thesis, University of Newcastle, Australia.

Ewans, M. (1977) *Janáček's Tragic Operas*. London: Faber and Faber.

Ewans, M. (1982) *Wagner and Aeschylus: The Ring and the Oresteia*. London: Faber and Faber.

Ewans, M. (1985a) 'Music and Stagecraft in Wagner's *Ring*'. *Miscellanea Musicologica* 14, 83–98.

Ewans, M. (1985b) 'The Bayreuth Centenary *Ring* by Patrice Chéreau and Pierre Boulez'. *Miscellanea Musicologica* 14, 167–73.

Ewans, M. (1989) *Georg Büchner's Woyzeck: Translation and Theatrical Commentary*. New York and Bern: Peter Lang.

Ewans, M. (ed.) (1995) *Aeschylus: Oresteia*. London. J. M. Dent.

Ewans, M. (1996) 'Patterns of Tragedy in Sophocles and Shakespeare' in *Tragedy and the Tragic*, ed. M. Silk. Oxford: Clarendon Press.

Ewans, M. (2007) *Opera from the Greek: Studies in the Poetics of Appropriation*. Aldershot: Ashgate.

Ewans, M. (2015) 'Two Landmarks in Wagner Production: Patrice Chéreau's Centenary *Ring* (1976) and Nikolaus Lehnhoff's *Parsifal* (2004).' *Context*

Ewans, M. (forthcoming 2016) '*The Tempest* by Thomas Adès and Meredith Oakes'. *Studies in Musical Theatre*.

Gilliam, B. (1991) *Richard Strauss' Elektra*. Oxford: Oxford University Press.

Godefroy, V. (1975) *The Dramatic Genius of Verdi: Studies of Selected Operas* vol. 1. London: Gollancz.

Hawes, J. (1994) *An Examination of Verdi's* Otello *and its Faithfulness to Shakespeare*. Lewiston, NY: Edwin Mullen Press.

Hepokoski, J. A. (1987) *Guiseppe Verdi: Otello*. Cambridge. Cambridge University Press

Hoérré, A. (ed.) (1942) *Inédits sur Debusssy*. Paris: Les Publications Techniques.

Hofmannsthal, H. von (1959) *Aufzeichnungen*. Frankfurt: Fischer.

Hornby, R. (1977) *Script into Performance: A Structuralist View of Play Production*. Austin: University of Texas Press.

Howard, P. (1995) *Gluck: An Eighteenth-Century Portrait*. Oxford: Oxford University Press.

Jarman, D. (1989) *Alban Berg: Wozzeck*. Cambridge: Cambridge University Press.

John, N. (ed.) (1982a) *Pelléas & Mélisande*. Opera Guide 9. London: John Calder.

John, N. (1982b) *Carmen*. Opera Guide 13. London: John Calder.

John, N. (1982c) *Rigoletto*. Opera Guide 15. London: John Calder.

John, N. (ed.) (1985) *The Operas of Michael Tippett*. Opera Guide 29. London: John Calder.

John, N. (ed.) (1988) *Salome/Elektra*. Opera Guide 37. London: John Calder.

Keller, H. (1983) '*Peter Grimes*: The Story, The Music not Excluded' in Brett 1983, 105–20.

Kemp, I. (1984) *Tippett: The Composer and his Music*. London: Eulenberg Books.

Kemp, I. (ed.) (1988) *Berlioz: Les Troyens*. Cambridge: Cambridge University Press.

Kerman, J. (1956) *Opera as Drama*. New York. Vintage.

Langer, S. (1953) *Feeling and Form: A Theory of Art Developed from Philosophy in a New Key*. London: Routledge Kegan Paul.

Langham Smith, R. (1989) 'Tonalities of Darkness and Light' in Nichols and Langham Smith (eds.) 1989.

Lattimore, R. (1964) *Story Patterns in Greek Tragedy*. London: Athlone Press.

Leafsteadt, C. (1999) *Inside Bluebeard's Castle: Music and Drama in Béla Bartók's Opera*. New York: Oxford University Press.

Levin, D. J. (2007) *Unsettling Opera*. Chicago: Chicago University Press.

Littlejohn, D. (1990) 'Reflections on Peter Sellars' Mozart'. *Opera Quarterly* 7.2, 6–36.

Lloyd Davies, J. (1985) 'A Visionary Night' in John, N. (ed.) 1985.

Lockspeiser, E. (1962) *Debussy: His Life and Mind* (2 vols). London: Dent.

Macdonald, H. (1988) 'Composition' in Kemp (1988), 45–66.

MacDonald, H. (2007) 'A New Source for Berlioz's *Les Troyens*' in *Berlioz and Debussy: Sources, Contexts and Legacies*, eds. B. Kelly and K. Murphy. Aldershot: Ashgate.

Matthews, D. (1983) 'Act II scene 1: an examination of the music' in Brett (ed.) 1983, 121–47.

McClary, S. (1992) *Bizet: Carmen*. Cambridge: Cambridge University Press.

Maeterlinck, M. (1911) *The Treasure of the Humble*, (trans.) A. Sutro. London: Allen.

Millington, B. (1984) *The Master Musicians: Wagner*. London: J. M. Dent.

Millington, B. (2012) *The Sorcerer of Bayreuth*. Oxford: Oxford University Press.

Moberly, R. B. (1968) *Three Mozart Operas*. New York: Dodd, Mead.

Muller, D. (1934) *Janáček*. Paris: Éditions Rieder.

Nattiez, J.-P. (1983) *Tétralogies: Wagner, Boulez, Chéreau – Essai sur l'infidelité*. Paris: C. Bourgois.

Nichols, R. (1982) 'A Musical Synopsis' in N. John, (ed.) 1982a.

Nichols, R. (1989) 'Synopsis' in R. Nichols and R. Langham Smith (eds) *Claude Debussy: Pelléas et Mélisande*. Cambridge: Cambridge University Press.

Noske, F. (1977) *The Signifier and The Signified*. The Hague: Nijhoff.

Osborne, C. (1969) *The Complete Operas of Verdi*. New York: Da Capo Press.

Ostrovsky, A. (1972) 'Thunder' [The Storm] in J. Cooper (ed.), *Four Russian Plays*. Harmondsworth: Penguin.

Parker, R. (1982) 'The Music of *Rigoletto*' in John (ed.) 1982c, 15–24.

Perle, G. (1980) *The Operas of Alban Berg volume 1: Wozzeck*. Berkeley: University of California Press.

Perle, G. (1985) *The Operas of Alban Berg volume 2: Lulu*. Berkeley: University of California Press.

Porges, H. (1983) *Wagner rehearsing the 'Ring'*, (trans.) R. L. Jacobs. Cambridge. Cambridge University Press.

Pountney, D. (1982) 'Producing 'Kát'a Kabanová' in Tyrrell (ed.) 1982, 184–98.
Puffett, D. (ed.) (1989) *Richard Strauss: Salome*. Cambridge: Cambridge University Press.
Reddick, J. (ed.) (1995) *Georg Büchner: Complete Plays, Lenz and Other Writings*. Harmondsworth: Penguin Books.
Redlich, H. (1957) *Alban Berg: The Man and his Music*. London: John Calder.
Rushton, J. (n.d) *Don Giovanni*. Entry in Grove Music Online.
Rushton, J. (1981) *W. A. Mozart: Don Giovanni*. Cambridge: Cambridge University Press.
Rushton, J. (1988) 'The Musical Structure' in Kemp 1988, 119–49.
Schmidgall, G. (1977) *Literature as Opera*. New York: Oxford University Press.
Schott (1977) *A Man of Our Time* (exhibition catalogue, no credited compiler). London: Schott.
Seymour, C. (2004) *The Operas of Benjamin Britten*. Woodbridge: Boydell Press.
Shaw, G. B. (1923:1967) *The Perfect Wagnerite: A Commentary on the Niblung's Ring*. New York. Dover.
Strauss, R. (1974) *Recollections and Reflections*. Westport: CT, Greenwood.
Tippett, M. (1974) *Moving into Aquarius*. St. Albans: Paladin.
Tippett, M. (1995) *Tippett on Music*, ed. M. Bowen. Oxford: Oxford University Press.
Treitler, L. (1976) '*Wozzeck* and the Apocalypse: An Essay in Historical Criticism'. *Critical Inquiry* 3.2, 260ff.
Trilling, L. (1951) *The Liberal Imagination*. London: Secker and Warburg.
Tyrrell, J. (ed.) (1982) *Leoš Janáček: Kát'a Kabanová*. Cambridge: Cambridge University Press.
Tyrrell, J. (1992) *Janáček's Operas: A Documentary Account*. London: Faber and Faber.
Wagner, C. (1978) *Cosima Wagner's Diaries* vol. 1, 1869–1877, (trans.) G. Skelton, London: Collins.
Wagner, C. (1980) *Cosima Wagner's Diaries* vol. 2, 1878–1883, (trans.) G. Skelton, London: Collins.
Wagner, R. (1907) 'Music applied to the Drama' (Über die Umwendung der Musik aus das Drama) in *Gesammelte Schriften und Dichtungen* (4th edn) vol. 10. Leipzig: Siegel.
Wagner, R. (1892–9) *Richard Wagner's Prose Works*, (trans.) W. Ashton Ellis (8 vols), repr. New York: Broude Brothers, 1966.
Warren, R. (1995) *Opera Workshop: Studies in Understanding and Interpretation*. Aldershot: Scolar Press.
Whittall, A. (1989) 'Dramatic Structure and Tonal Organization' in D. Puffett, (ed.) *Richard Strauss: Elektra*. Cambridge: Cambridge University Press.
Williams, B. (1981) 'Don Giovanni as an Idea' in Rushton 1981, 81–91.
Wurz, S. (c. 2000) *Kundry, Salome, Lulu: femmes fatales im Musikdrama*. Frankfurt: Peter Lang.

SELECT DISCOGRAPHY

c = conductor d = director

Bartók *Duke Bluebeard's Castle*
Lloyd, Laurence *c* Adam Fischer *d* Leslie Megahey
Kultur 2009 (recorded 1989)

Berg *Lulu*
Migenes, Mazura *c* James Levine *d* John Dexter
Metropolitan Opera 2010 (recorded 1980)
Schäfer, Schöne *c* Andrew Davis *d* Graham Vick
Kultur 2003
Petibon, Holland *c* Michael Boder *d* Olivier Py
DGG 2011

Wozzeck
Grundheber *c* Claudio Abbado *d* Adolf Dresen
Arthaus/Kultur 1987
Grundheber *c* Daniel Barenboim *d* Patrice Chéreau
EuroArts 2013 (recorded 1994)

Berlioz *Les Troyens*
Antonacci Graham Kunde *c* John Eliot Gardiner
d Yannis Kokkos
BBC 2009

Bizet *Carmen*
Antonacci Kaufmann Vizin Xanthoudakis, *c* Antonio Pappano
Francesca Zambello
Decca 2007
Antonacci Richards Pochon Gill *c* John Eliot Gardiner *d* Adrian Noble
FRA 2009

Britten *Peter Grimes*
Vickers, Harper, Bailey *c* Colin Davis *d* Elijah Moshinsky
Kultur 2003
Langridge, Cairns, Opie *c*. David Atherton *d* Tim Albery
Kultur 1994

Debussy *Pelléas et Mélisande*
    Hagley, Archer, Walker *c* Pierre Boulez *d* Peter Stein
    DGG 2002

Gluck *Iphigénie en Aulide*
    Gens, von Otter, Testé, Antoun *c* Marc Minkowski *d* Pierre Audi
    Opus Arte 2013

Janáček *Jenůfa*
    Roocroft, Dvorský, Polaski *c* Ivor Bolton *d* Stéphane Braunschweig
    Opus Arte 2009
    Suunnegårth, Frank, Sjöberg *c* Marko Ivanovic *d* Orpha Phelan
    Arthaus 2012

    Kát'a Kabanová
    Gustafson, Winter, Davies *c* Andrew Davis, *d* Nikolaus Lehnhoff
    Arthaus 1988

Mozart *Così fan tutte*
    Bartoli, Nikiteanu, Saccà, Widmer, Chausson *c* Nikolaus Harnoncourt
    d Jürgen Flimm
    Arthaus 2000

    Die Zaüberflöte
    Urrila, Köstlinger *c* Eric Erikson *d* Ingmar Bergman
    The Criterion Collection 2000

    Don Giovanni
    Gilfrey, Nikiteanu *c* Nikolaus Harnoncourt *d* Jürgen Flimm
    Arthaus 2001

    Le Nozze di Figaro
    Sylvan *c* Craig Smith *d* Peter Sellars
    Decca 1991
    Terfel *c* John Eliot Gardiner *d* Olivier Mille
    Archiv 1993

Puccini *La Bohème*
    Stratas, Carreras *c* James Levine *d* Franco Zeffirelli
    DGG 2002 (1985)
    Barker, Hobson *c* Julian Smith *d* Baz Luhrmann
    Kultur 2006 (1993)

    Madama Butterfly
    Barker, Silveus *c* Patrick Summers, *d* Moffatt Oxenbould
    ABC 2005

Strauss *Elektra*
Rysanek, Varnay, *c* Karl Böhm *d* Götz Friedrich
DGG/Unitel 2005

Salome
Stratas, Weikl, Varnay, Beirer *c* Karl Böhm *d* Götz Friedrich
DGG/Unitel 1988

Tippett *The Midsummer Marriage*
Langridge, Shelton *c* David Atherton *d* Elijah Moshinsky
Channel 4, UK. Not released on VHS or DVD.

Verdi *Otello*
Domingo, Te Kanawa, Leiferkus *c* Georg Solti *d* Elijah Moshinsky
Kultur 1992

Rigoletto
McLaughlin, Rigby; Rawnsley, Davies *c* Mark Elder *d* Jonathan Miller
Kultur 2007

Wagner *Die Walküre*
Jones, McIntyre, *c* Pierre Boulez, *d* Patrice Chéreau
DGG 2005 (1978)
Evans, Tomlinson *c* Daniel Barenboim *d* Harry Kupfer
Kultur 1992

Götterdämmerung
Jones, Hübner, Mazura *c* Pierre Boulez, *d* Patrice Chéreau
DGG 2005 (1978)
Evans, Kang, Brinkmann *c* Daniel Barenboim *d* Harry Kupfer
Kultur 1992

Parsifal
Jerusalem, Meier *c* James Levine *d* Otto Schenk
DGG 1993
Ventris, Meier *c* Kent Nagano *d* Nikolaus Lehnhoff
Opus Arte 2005

SCORES

The examples follow the musical text of the orchestral scores whose publishers are listed below.

IPHIGÉNIE EN AULIDE
Bärenreiter Urtext
LE NOZZE DI FIGARO
DON GIOVANNI
COSÌ FAN TUTTE
DIE ZAÜBERFLÖTE
Mozart, *Neue Ausgabe Sämtlicher Werke*, (Bärenreiter)
Bühnenwerke 4-6
LES TROYENS
Bärenreiter Urtext
RIGOLETTO
Dover reprint of 'Italian' 1914 score
DIE WALKÜRE
Eulenburg
CARMEN
Eulenburg Urtext
GÖTTERDÄMMERUNG
Eulenburg
PARSIFAL
Dover reprint of Peters of Leipzig full score
OTELLO
Dover reprint of Ricordi full score
LA BOHÈME
Dover reprint of Ricordi full score
PELLÉAS ET MÉLISANDE
Durand
MADAMA BUTTERFLY
Dover reprint of Ricordi full score 1907
JENŮFA
Universal Edition (ed. Mackerras/Tyrrell)
SALOME
Boosey and Hawkes
ELEKTRA
Boosey and Hawkes
DUKE BLUEBEARD'S CASTLE
Universal Edition

KÁT'A KABANOVÁ
  Universal Edition
WOZZECK
  Universal Edition
LULU
  Universal Edition
PETER GRIMES
  Boosey and Hawkes
THE MIDSUMMER MARRIAGE
  Schott (study score, now republished under the Eulenburg imprint)

INDEX

Bold type is used in part 1 to mark the entries for sections of the book where a particular opera, or the work of a particular librettist, composer, director or singer, is analysed in detail. Similarly bold type is used in part 2 where a character is studied in detail.

(1) People, Operas, Opera Houses and Texts

Adès, Thomas xiii
Aida 35
Albery, Tim x, **57–9**, 60, 129, **133–7**, **221–5**, 227
Allan, Thomas 62
Anderson, Andy 258
Antonacci, Anna Caterina 72, 179
    Carmen **152–61**, **197–9**, **297–301**
    Les Troyens **187–92**
Antoun, Frédéric **268–78**
Archer, Neil **206–10**
Atherton, David 259
Audi, Pierre 5 n.5, 267, **268–78**
Australian Opera, The *see* Opera Australia

Balázs, Béla 210–11, 216 n.21
Barker, Cheryl **44–7**, **80–4**
Bartók, Béla 2, 3, 140, **210–17**, 227
Bartoli, Cecilia **143 (n.4)–7**, 282
Bauer, Raymond 242
Bayreuth (Festspielhaus) 23
Beaumarchais, Pierre Caron de 15–16
Bechtler, Hildegard 57
Beckett, Lucy 242 n.31, 244
Beethoven, Ludwig van 2
Beirer, Hans 287, 289
Belasco, David 41
Bellini, Vincenzo 3 n.5

Berg, Alban 2 n.2, 3, 6 n.14, 23, 46, 55, 139
    Lulu **115–28**
    Wozzeck **248–53**
Bergman, Ingmar **232–5**, 264
Berlioz, Hector viii, 2, 10 n.18, **69–74**, 91, **183–92**, 226
Berner, Erna 62
Bernstein, Leonard 139
Besch, Anthony 232
Billy Budd 34, 140
Bizet, Georges **152–61**, 178, **192–9**, **295–301**, 311
Bjørnson, Maria 56
Black, Jeffrey 62
Blake, William 260
Bohème, La **74–84**
Böhm, Karl 7, 106 n.7, 292
Boito, Arrigo 33, 35, 39, 40
Bolton, Ivor 85, 175
Bondy, Luc 7 n.16
Boulez, Pierre 1 n.1, 23, 210
Braunschweig, Stéphane 85, 88, **175–8**, 180
Britten, Benjamin xiii, xviii, 34, 138, 140, 313
    Peter Grimes **56–9**, **128–37**, **217–25**
Brown, Paul 124
Büchner, Georg ix, 248

Budden, Julian 39
Butlin, Roger 56

Cairns, David 254
Cairns, Janice 129, **133–7**, 138,
  221–5
Camus, Albert 280
Candide 139
Carmen viii, xv, xvii, **152–61**, **192–9**,
  226, 294, **295–301**
Carreras, José **80–4**
Carter, Tim 16
Chailley, Jacques 234
Châtelet, Théâtre du 18, 72, 143, 204
Chausson, Carlos **144–7**
Chéreau, Patrice 1 n.1, 60, 179, 264
  Götterdämmerung **166–7**
  Walküre, Die **23–33**
  Wozzeck **252–3**
Cohan, Robert 288
Copley, John 80 n.15, 83 n.17, 176
  n.31
Così fan tutte **140–7**
Covent Garden (Royal Opera) xiii, xv,
  xvii, 39, 57, 129, 257, 298
Cox, John 232, 233
Crozier, Eric 34

Da Ponte, Lorenzo 15–16, 61, 62, 68,
  140, 143, 279, 292
Davies, Ryland xii, **108–14**
Debussy, Claude ix, 2, 3, 140,
  199–210, 211, 226, 308
Destiny (Osud) 140
Deutsche Staatsoper Unter den Linden
  252
Dexter, John 123
Dido and Aeneas xiv
Domingo, Placido 72, 199
Don Giovanni **61–9**, 143, 267,
  278–82
Donizetti, Gaetano 3 n.5
Dorati, Antal 210
Dreisen, Adolf 251
Du Roullet, François viii, 270, 273
Duke Bluebeard's Castle ix, xv, xviii,
  3, **210–17**, 227
Dürr, J. M. 85
Dvorský, Miroslav **88–9**, 180

Elektra 6 n.14, **93–108**, 137, 295,
  301–11
English National Opera (ENO) xii, xv,
  57, 129, 283 n.16
Euripides 273, 277 n.8
Evans, Anne 26, 27, **166–8**
Everding, August 232, 233
Excursions of Mr Brouček, The 140

Faust (Goethe) 244
Flimm, Jürgen, 90–1, 179, 267
  Così fan tutte **143–7**
  Don Giovanni **62–9**, **278–82**
Forster, Edward Morgan 34
Frank, Daniel 89
Freni, Mirella 46 n.52
Friedrich, Götz 137, 267
  Elektra **100–8**, **301–11**
  Salome **7–12**, **283–92**
From the House of the Dead 168
Furtwängler, Wilhelm 62

Gard, Robert 177 n.31
Gardiner, John Eliot 72, 143, 198
Gens, Véronique 267, **268–78**, 292
Gerkan, Florence van 280
Gezeichneten, Die 101 n.5
Giacosa, Guiseppe 41, 74
Gilfrey, Rodney **62–9**, 267, **278–82**,
  292
Gill, Annie **157**
Gluck, Christoph Willibald Ritter von
  xii, xiii, 2, 267, **268–78**, 292,
  313
Glyndebourne xii, 84, 108
Goethe, Johann Wolfgang von 244
Götterdämmerung 139, **161–8**, 178,
  239
Graf, Herbert 62
Graham, Susan **72–4**
Gran Teatre del Liceu (Barcelona) 85,
  125
Grundheber, Franz **251–3**
Gustafson, Nancy **47–56**, 60, **108–14**,
  245–8

Hagley, Alison **205–10**
Halévy, Fromental 152, 192, 295
Halmen, Pet 101

Hampe, Michael 143 n.5, 147 n.13
Harnoncourt, Nikolaus 143 n.4, 147
   n.14
Harper, Heather 129, **133–7**, 138,
   221–5
Hawes, Jane 33, 36
Hepokoski, James 36
Herrmann, Karl-Ernst 204
Hobson, David **80–4**
Hockney, David 232
Hofmannsthal, Hugo von 93, 94, 100,
   302–11
Hoheisel, Tobias 47 n.53, 84, 247
   n.44
Holland, Ashley xii, **125–6**
Homer **293–4**
Hong, Hei-Kyung 62
Hornby, Richard 4–5
Hume, Lindy 62
Hytner, Nicholas 145 n.10, 147 n.13

Ibsen, Henrik 55, 137
Illica, Luigi 41, 74
Iphigénie en Aulide 5 n.5, 267,
   268–78
Ivanovic, Marco 85

Janáček, Leoš 2, 3, 46, 91, 138, 140,
   180, 264
   Jenůfa **84–90**, **168–78**
   Kát'a Kabanová **47–56**, **108–14**,
      245–8
Janes, Fiona 62
Järvefelt, Göran 234
Jenůfa ix, 3, **84–90**, 91, 140, **168–78**,
   180
Jerusalem, Siegfried 241
Jones, Gwyneth **23–33**, 60
Jung, Karl 200, 255

Kát'a Kabanová ix, **47–56**, 84, 101
   n.5, **108–14**, 168 n.26, 218,
   231, **245–8**, 264, 294
Kaufmann, Jonas **197–9**, **297–301**
Keller, Hans 58
Kemp, Ian 72, 189
Kerman, Joseph 279 n.10
Kertész, István 210
Kodály, Zoltán 211

Kokkos, Yannis **72–4**, 91, **187–92**,
   226
Kovařovic, Karol 85
Kováts, Kolos 211
Kunde, Gregory **72–4**
Kupfer, Harry 23, 30, 32, 33, 179
   Götterdämmerung **166–8**
   Walküre, Die **26–8**

La Scala (Milan) 149 n.5
Laast, Anthony van 262
Lachmann, Hedwig 3
Langer, Suzanne 4
Langridge, Philip **57–9**, 60, 129,
   133–8, **218–25**, 227, 259
Large, Bryan 62
Lattimore, Richmond 293
Laurence, Elizabeth **212–17**
Lawless, Stephen 62
Leafsted, Carl xviii, 212 n.19, 215
Lehnhoff, Nikolaus 5 n.5, 60, 84, 88,
   101 n.5, 107 n.8, 264
   Kát'a Kabanová **47–56**, **108–14**
   Parsifal **241–5**
Leiferkus, Sergei xvii, **39–41**, 60
Lepage, Robert xiii
Levine, James 123
Liebesverbot, Das 239 n.22
Lind[t]ner, Anton 3 n.4
Lloyd, Robert **212–16**
Ludwig, Christa 46 n.52
Luhrmann, Baz **80–4**, 90
Lulu 2 n.2, 3, 5 n.5, **115–28**, 138,
   139, 140, 294

McClary, Susan 159
Macdonald, Hugh 189
McIntyre, Donald **23–33**, 60
Mackerras, Charles 232
Madama Butterfly 6 n.14, **41–7**
Madrid, Teatro Real 85
Maeterlinck, Maurice 3, **199–210**,
   226, 308
Mahler, Gustav 120, 121
Malfitano, Catherine 7 n.16
Malmö Opera 85, 89, 91
Martaler, Christoph 56 n.58
Mask of Time, The 263
Master Builder Solness (Ibsen) 137

Maurel, Victor 39, 40
Mazura, Fritz **123–4**
Medium, The xiv
Mefistofele 33
Megahey, Leslie **212–17**, 227
Meier, Waltraud 101 n.5, **241–5**
Meilhac, Henri 152, 198, 295
Meistersinger von Nürnberg, Die 239
Melville, Herman 34
Mentzer, Susanne 62
Merchant of Venice, The 71
Metropolitan Opera (New York) xiii, 123, 199, 232, 241
Midsummer Marriage, The xviii, 140, **253–63**, 264
Migenes (–Johnson), Julia **123–4**, 199
Mille, Olivier, **16–21**, 60
Miller, Jonathan 1 n.1, **151–2**, 179
Mills, Paul 199
Minkowski, Marc 268
Moberley, Robert 15
Monteverdi, Claudio 2
Moritz, Reiner 244
Moshinsky, Elijah xvii, 60, 129, 227
    Midsummer Marriage, The **259–63**
    Otello **39–41**
    Peter Grimes **57–9**, **133–8**, **221–5**
Mozart, Wolfgang Amadeus 2, 90, 178, 254, 264, 267, 292, 313
    Così fan tutte **140–7**
    Die Zauberflöte **231–5**
    Don Giovanni **61–9**, **278–82**
    Le Nozze di Figaro **15–21**
Muller, Daniel 111

Neederlandse Opera, De 268
New Year 263
Nibelung's Ring, The xvii, 1 n.1, 2, 22 n.14, 178
Nichols, Roger 206 n.13
Nikiteanu, Liliana **62–9**, **143 (n.4)–7**, 282
Noble, Adrian **153–61**, 179, 193, **198**, 295
Noske, Frits 16
Nozze di Figaro, Le **15–21** 60, 143

Obratsova, Elena 199
Ochman, Wiesław 285

Opera Australia 55 n.56, 62, 80
Ostrovsky, Alexandr ix, 47, 245
Otello xv, **33–41**
Otter, Anne Sofie van **268–78**, 276
Oxenbould, Moffatt 44–7

Parker, Roger 150–1
Parsifal 5 n.5, 101 n.5, 230, **235–45**, 264
Peduzzi, Richard 23, 60
Pelléas et Mélisande 2 n.2, 3, **199–210**, 226, 308
Peter Grimes xviii, **56–9**, **128–37**, 140, **217–25**, 227
Petibon, Patricia **125–8**
Phelan, Orpha 85, **89–90**, 91
Piave, Francesco 147
Pochon, Virginie **157**
Polgar, Lasló 282
Ponelle, Jean–Paul 46 n.52
Porges, Heinrich 22–3
Pountney, David 55–6
Preissová, Gabriela 3, 85, 89
Puccini, Giacomo 2, 6 n.6, 60
    Bohème, La **74–84**
    Madama Butterfly **41–7**
Py, Olivier 5, 115, **125–8**, 138

Racine, Jean 270, 273, 277 n.8
Rey, Isabel 282
Rheingold, Das 23, 24, 139
Richards, Andrew **198**
Riders to the Sea xiv
Rigoletto xvii, **147–52**, 178
Rodrigue et Chimène 2 n.2
Roocroft, Amanda xii, **88–9**, 180
Rose, Jürgen 232
Rosenkavalier, Der 140
Rossi, Francesco 199
Rossini, Gioachino 3 n.5
Rushton, Julian 67, 278, 279 n.11
Rysanek, Leonie **100–8**, 308

Saccà, Roberto **144 (n.7)–7**, 280
Salome 3, **6–12**, 140, 267, **283–92**
Salzburg Festival Opera 56, 62, 101 n.5
Sass, Sylvia 211
Sayers, Denni 242

Schäfer, Christine **124–5**, 127
Schenk, Otto **241**
Schikaneder, Emanuel 231, 233, 254
Schmidgall, Gary 33
Schneider, Peter 85
Schöne, Wolfgang 125
Schreker, Franz 101 n.5
Scottish National Opera 55 n.56
Sellars, Peter **16–21**, 60, 62 n.1, 143
Shakespeare, William 33, 71
Shaw, Bernard 139–40
Shelton, Lucy 259
Siegfried 139, 239
Siegfried's Death 139
Siepi, Cesare 62
Silveus, Ingrid **44–7**
Skalický, Jan 282, 287
Slater, Montagu xviii, 56, 128, 217
Solti, Georg 106 n.7, 211
Sophocles 93 n.1, 94
Stein, Peter **204–10**, 226
Stratas, Teresa 267
    Mimì **80–4**
    Salome **7–12**, **283–92**
Strauss, Richard 2, 3, 23, 48 n.54,
    140, 267
    Elektra **93–108**, **301–11**
    Salome **6–12**, **283–92**
Strehler, Giorgio 62, 65 n.5
Strindberg, August 126
Sunnegåardh, Erika 89
Svoboda, Josef 100, 107, 307
Sylvan, Sandford **19–21**
Symphonie Fantastique 10 n.18
Szinetár, Miklós 211–12

Tambosi, Olivier 85, 88
Taynor, Julie 232, 234 n.16
Tempest, The xiii
Terfel, Bryn **18–21**, 62
Testé, Nicolas **268–78**
Tippett, Michael xii, xiii, xviii, 140,
    230, 236, 239, 264, 313
    Midsummer Marriage, The
    253–63

Tomlinson, John 26, 27
Tristan und Isolde 2
Troyens, Les xv, **69–74**, **183–92**

Varnay, Astrid **100–8**, 287
Ventris, Christopher **241–5**
Verdi, Guiseppe 2, 60, 140, 178, 179
    Otello **33–41**
    Rigoletto **147–52**
Vick, Graham xii, 115, **124–5**, 127,
    128, 138
Vickers, Jon **57–9**, 60, 129, **133–8**,
    218–25, 227
Virgil 69, 71, 183

Wagner, Richard viii, 2, 3, 11, 46, 55,
    139–40, 178, 179, 264
    Götterdämmerung **161–8**
    Parsifal **235–45**
    Walküre, Die **21–33**
Walker, Penelope **205–8**
Walküre, Die **21–33**, 60, 139, 239
Watt-Smith, Ian 258
Wedekind, Frank 115, 119, 123, 126,
    127
Weikl, Bern 286–7
Weitz, Pierre–André 126
Welsh National Opera 55 n.56, 258
Widmer, Olivier **144 (n.7)–7**
Wiener Staatsoper (Vienna State
    Opera) 199, 251
Wilde, Oscar 3, 6, 283–4, 289, 290
Williams, Bernard 278
Winter, Louise 54
Wozzeck 2 n.2, 3, 6 n.14, 55, 231,
    248–53, 264

Yeats, William Butler 256

Zambello, Francesca xvii, 23 n.17,
    179, 311
    Carmen **153–61**, **196–9**, 226,
    295–301
Zauberflöte, Die **231–5**, 253–4, 264
Zeffirelli, Franco 62, **80–4**, 90, 199

(2) Characters

Achille 268–78
Agamemnon (in *Iphigénie en Aulide*) 268–78
Agamemnon (spirit of, in *Elektra*) 103 n.6, 105, **302–311**
Ägisth 102, 301, 308
Alberich 22, 25, 27, 29, 30, 31, 161–8, 178
Alwa 120, 123, 125
Amfortas 235, 240, 241, 242, 243, 256
Ancients, The (*The Midsummer Marriage*) 260
Andres 252–3, 264
Arcas 269, 274, 275

Balstrode **221–5**
Bella 253, 256, 260
Boris (*Kát'a Kabanová*) 246, 264
Brünnhilde **21–33**, 60, 139–40, **161–8**, 178, 179, 239

Calchas 270, 276
Carmen **152–61**, 179, **192–9**, 226, **295–301**, 311
Cassandre 72, **183–92**, 197, 226
Cassio 39
Chrysothemis 94 n.2, 102, **306–11**
Claggart 34
Clytemnestre **268–78**
Colline 76–7
Commendatore, The 280, 281

Dancaïre, Le 299, 300
Desdemona 33, 39 n.47
Diane **269–77**
Didon xv, **69–74**, 90
Don Alfonso **141–7**
Don Giovanni **61–9**, 90, 143, **278–82**, 292
Don José 152, 157, 161, 179, **192–9**, 226, 294, **295–301**, 311
Don Ottavio 278, 282
Donna Anna 278, 281, 282
Donna Elvira 68, 278, 279, 281, 282
Dorabella **141–7**, 179

Duke Bluebeard **210–17**, 227
Duke of Mantua, The **147–52**, 179

Elektra 6, **93–108**, 137, 138, **301–11**
Elizabeth (*Tannhäuser*) 239
Ellen Orford **129–38**, **218–25**
Elsa 239
Énée xv, **69–74**, 90
Erda 27
Escamillo 192, 195, 226, 296, 299, 300
Eva 239

Ferrando **141–7**, 179
Figaro **15–21**, 22
Fiordiligi **141–7**, 179
Flying Dutchman, The 239
Frascita **153–61**, 179
Fricka 21–2, 28–9

Geneviève **200–10**
Geschwitz, Countess 120
Gilda **147–52**, 179
Golaud 205–9, 226
Grandmother (*Jenůfa*) **168–78**
Guglielmo **141–7**, 179
Gunther **161–8**, 178
Gurnemanz 241–4
Gutrune **165–8**

Hagen 22, 31, 33, 60, 139, **161–8**, 178, 179
Herodes 11, **283–92**
Herodias 287, 289, 290

Iphigénie **268–78**, 292
Isolde 239

Jack 253, 256, 259–60
Jago xv, xvi, xvii, **33–41**, 279
Jano **173**, **176–7**, 178
Jenifer 231, **253–63**
Jenůfa **84–90**, 91, **168–78**, 179, 180
Jochanaan 6–11, 283, **286–92**
Judit **210–17**, 227

Kabanicha 114, 138, 247

Karolka 88, 89, **168–78**
Kát'a Kabanová **47–56**, **108–14**, 138, **245–8**, 264
King Fisher 256, 259, 262
Klingsor 239, 240
Klytämnestra **93–108**, 137, **301–11**
Kostelnička, The 84, 85, 87 n.20, 89, **168–78**
Kundry 236, **239–45**

Laca **84–90**, 91, **168–78**, 179, 180
Leporello **278–82**
Lulu **115–28**, 138, 240

Madama Butterfly **41–7**, 60
Maddalena **147–52**, 179
Marcello 76–7
Marie 6
Mark 231, **255–63**
Masetto 61, 65, 67, 281
Mayor (*Jenůfa*) **170–8**, 179
Mélisande **199–210**, 226
Mercédès **153–61**, 179
Mercure 69, 90
Micaëla 296, 297, 300
Mimì **74–84**, 90

Narraboth 3, 6, **283–7**
Norns 139

Orest 104, 105, **304–11**
Otello 33

Page (*Salome*) 6, 283
Pamina **231–5**, 244, 256, 264
Papagena 231, 253
Papageno 231, 253
Parsifal 231, **235–45**, 256
Patrocle 273

Pelléas **199–210**, 226
Peter Grimes **56–9**, 60, **128–38**, **218–25**, 227
Pinkerton 42–7, 60

Queen of the Night, The 233

Rigoletto **147–52**, 179
Rodolfo **74–84**, 90

Salome xvi, xvii, **6–12**, 240, **283–92**
Sarastro 233, 256
Schaunard 76–7
Schön, Dr **115–28**, 138
Senta 239
Siegfried 140, **161–8**, 239
Sieglinde 22, 24, 29, 239
Siegmund 22, 24, 28, 29, 30, 32, 239
Števa 87–90, **168–78**
Strephon 262
Susanna 17–18
Suzuki 42–7

Tamino **231–5**, 244, 256
Tannhäuser 239
Tichon 47, **108–14**, 138
Titurel 243
Tristan 239

Varvara **48–55**, 113
Vere, Captain 34

Walther von Stolzing 239
Waltraute 139
Wotan xvi, **21–33**, 60, 161–8, 178
Wozzeck 218, **248–53**, 264

Zerlina **61–9**, 90, 143, 279, 281
Zuniga 296, 299